The New European Financial Marketplace

ALFRED STEINHERR

THE NEW EUROPEAN
FINANCIAL
MARKETPLACE

NEW YORK UNIVERSITY PRESS
Washington Square, New York

First published in the U.S.A in 1992 by
NEW YORK UNIVERSITY PRESS
Washington Square, N.Y. 10003

Library of Congress Cataloging in Publication Data
The New European financial marketplace/ [compiled by] Alfred Steinherr.
   p.   cm.
   Includes bibliographical references and index.
   ISBN 0-8147-7970-0 (cloth)
   1. Banks and Banking – European Economic Community countries.
   2. Capital market – European Economic Community countries. 3. Banks and
   banking – Europe, Eastern. 4. Capital market – Europe, Eastern.
   I. Steinherr, Alfred.
   HG2980.5.A6N48   1992b
   332. 1'094–dc20
   92-19950
   CIP

Printed and Bound in Great Britain
at the Bath Press, Avon

Contents

CHAPTER ONE

Introduction and overview

Alfred Steinherr*

In this overview I shall attempt to achieve three objectives. First, in section 1, to lay the grounds for the reader's understanding of why financial markets have achieved such prominence in the 1980s and have become the policy-makers' favourite bet. Then, in section 2, to describe and evaluate the achievements at European level to provide a regulatory framework for a single financial market and, in sections 3 to 6, to summarise the contributions to the volume.

1. The acceleration of deregulation and of financial innovations during the 1980s

In most countries the business of banks did not change significantly from the late 1940s to the 1970s. The products offered, the management and sales techniques applied showed great constancy. While manufacturing became increasingly international and sold its products on world markets, banking remained constrained to national markets in most countries, and this is still the case in many countries. In 1958 the European Community started to set up a customs union and since then has steadily moved forward to the ultimate goal of a single market. Financial services did not follow this trend. Some of the most trade-intensive economies in Europe and elsewhere still had a virtually closed, domestically oriented financial sector. Innovation, the driving force of most industries, had not changed the financial landscape significantly until recently. Whilst an Italian car of the 1980s has little in common with its predecessor of the 1940s, fund collecting, lending and enterprise financing more generally are only marginally different in many countries now compared to forty years ago.

*The views expressed are strictly personal and in no way reflect those of the European Investment Bank.

I would like to thank Luit Bakker, Declan Costello, Stefan Dab, Ronald de Ridder, Ali Tourani Rad, and above all Yves Le Portz and Karel Lannoo for their helpful contributions.

Why? The most important explanation certainly relates to regulation. The interwar depression has left a big mark on financial institutions and their regulators. Regulatory systems were, therefore, set up to prevent a repeat of the banking crisis of the thirties. Even more damaging was the evidence produced proving that the financial sector is exposed to risks that ultimately put the whole economy in danger. This sector needs, therefore, to be supervised more closely than others. Added to this the obvious interest of governments to collect seigniorage and to assure priority access to privileged borrowing, and it becomes quite understandable that governments are eager to act as regulator, as protector from foreign influences and sometimes as owner of major banks. As a result, all the countries in the world have national banks which, more often than not, are protected from foreign competition. Thus, it is not just the regulatory aspect of preserving stability, avoiding negative spill-over effects and protecting savers, but also the key intermediary role of financial institutions in the economic system that has led governments to intervene and exercise tight control on this sector. Entry as well as exit is also controlled and protects this sector not only from foreign but often even from domestic competition. Product innovation is regulated and, in particular, the role played by banking in the monetary system of a country has rendered monetary authorities very prudent and reluctant to authorise innovations such as money market funds, free deposit rates, elimination of credit ceilings, and so on.

Controllability of monetary aggregates is only one macroeconomic issue directly linked with banking operations. Another, of equal importance, is controllability of external accounts. Capital controls have been seen as necessary for keeping savings at home and preventing speculative crises, i.e., the market's judgement of domestic policy management.

In this tightly regulated and circumscribed environment internationalisation and innovation had little scope and lacked strong incentives. To this may be added that strong competitive forces are quintessential for innovation in finance. Financial institutions need to be forced to innovate otherwise there is not enough incentive to do so. The major reason is limited appropriability, that is, any financial innovation can easily be copied as there is no way of keeping the process or product technology inaccessible to competitors for extended periods of time, nor is there scope for intellectual ownership protection.

Finally, it is economies of scale that make it acceptable to leave worldwide production of airplanes to a handful of companies. If the same were true in banking, it would have been very costly, and in the end impossible, not to internationalise. But economies of scale are too limited to justify giving up banking even in very small countries.[1]

Only recently has global reach become technologically, and hence economically, feasible. Developments in computer technology and telecommunications reduced the cost of information processing and transmission. Such cost reductions enlarged the markets in which financial institutions could provide services. Advanced computer technology and statistical information systems made possible the pricing of new instruments, including options and their derivative products. Twenty-four hour trading, linking exchanges in different time zones, is the visible result of globally linked financial markets through technological advances.

Thus, there are numerous reasons why the financial sector has been lagging behind industry in innovation and internationalisation for a very long time. But in the 1980s, particularly in the late 1980s, there has been a remarkable renaissance of finance.

1.1 WHY IN THE 1980s?

It is, of course, not correct to limit the financial renaissance to the 1980s. American and some European banks have been setting up foreign operations for most of this century, the Euromarkets started in the 1960s, Regulation Q was phased out gradually up to 1986, some countries achieved convertibility of their currency without capital controls in the 1950s, etc.[2] What happens now is both a quantitative and a qualitative jump with deregulation proceeding in many countries at a sharply accelerated pace, capital controls being reduced in many parts of the globe, innovation becoming a driving force and finance rapidly internationalising. It is the simultaneous occurrence of these factors, at a rapid pace and in many parts of the world, which is the new phenomenon. Nevertheless, 1980 is clearly a major watershed for financial innovations such as variable rate loans, money market accounts, options, futures and derivative products.

How can this be explained? I think there are two major forces at work mutually reinforcing each other. One is the increasing *internationalisation of the non-financial sector*. The other is that *existing regulations were largely set up for the needs of the past* and are therefore not well suited to present needs. Innovative ingenuity of bankers was, therefore, for a long time concentrated on the question of how to circumvent regulations. This search often drove them outside of national boundaries and contributed to internationalisation. Pressure was therefore put on regulators to rethink their approach and thereby repatriate financial business which had moved abroad or even to attract foreign business.

Increasingly it also becomes evident that some regulations, designed to avoid 1930s-type problems, may now be responsible for other, equally serious, difficulties. The whole regulatory approach has thus become exposed to increasing criticism. It is frequently argued that one major reason for high involvement of US money centre banks in Latin America is that growth in their traditional domestic markets was limited and regulation prevented them from moving into other domestic areas. Similarly, savings and loan associations (S&Ls) ran into major difficulties in the early 1980s when yield curves became inverted. Desperate to get out of this difficulty and to diversify their assets, they moved with the approval of regulators into non-traditional but *high-risk businesses* (oil, real estate, securities) and completely broke their necks. Regulations are seen as being doubly responsible: first, by quasi forcing S&Ls to finance long-term mortgages with deposits without adequate sectorial risk diversification and, second, by guaranteeing deposits with the effect of providing subsidised short-term funding.

One particular feature of the main product of banking, i.e., money, makes national regulation of the banking industry extremely difficult: unlike goods, money can be transported virtually without cost and, to some extent, invisibly. Hence, border controls are not very effective and low transport costs (in terms of time and freight) do not represent cost barriers. As long as all countries regulate tightly and control capital movements this potential mobility is not exploited. But as soon as a few countries open their financial markets or as soon as uncontrolled markets exist outside of sovereign control (Euromarkets), real international competition occurs and this eventually implies competition among regulators. Quite often innovations start in the Euromarkets where no regulatory constraints exist and then find their way into national markets through competitive pressure to deregulate. If German authorities do not allow their residents ecu holdings, they will have them in Luxembourg; if they cannot obtain money market funds, they will also obtain them in Luxembourg. Some regulators see the danger of losing a certain amount of business to outside financial centres and of not being able to bring these funds back home even when regulation catches up. Quick regulatory adaptation is therefore necessary.

Regulatory reaction was felt necessary not only on the national level. Internationalisation of financial transactions made it necessary to establish comprehensive prudential practices to ensure that banks' foreign operations do not escape supervision. The problems created by the failures of Bankhaus Herstatt and of Franklin National Bank in 1974 led to the formation of the Cooke Committee which in 1975 endorsed a concordat on international bank supervisory cooperation. The proposal that banks' capital adequacy should be monitored on a consolidated basis was endorsed in 1978 by BIS Governors. The problems of Banco Ambrosiano Holding, Luxembourg, in 1982 revealed that there were still gaps in the supervisory framework and that revision of the concordat was necessary.

By 1986 consolidated supervision for purposes of capital adequacy of foreign branches and majority-owned subsidiaries had been established among the G-5 and Switzerland. The ulterior approach to capital adequacy in an integrated financial market was greatly inspired and facilitated by the work of the Cooke Committee.

Parallel to the search for circumventing regulations and escaping national controls, was an increasing internationalisation of the world economy accompanied by deep structural changes.

The major features can be summarised as follows. For the last thirty years the growth of international trade has outpaced the growth of production. Over time most economies have therefore become more trade dependent. This evolution has stimulated trade finance, foreign currency hedging operations and management of foreign currency holdings. Over the years the US dollar has somewhat lost its dominating vehicle currency role so that foreign currency management has become more diversified and complex.

This complexity has been further enhanced by high volatility and, during the late 1970s and 1980s, extreme medium-term exchange-rate movements. These movements can be more significant for producers than variations in costs and prices. Unhedged positions generate large gains or large losses, at times pushing some otherwise healthy firms to the brink of bankruptcy. Direct and indirect hedging has thus become a standard for sophisticated trading firms.

A double impetus influenced the growth of international financial transactions. Current-account imbalances reached record dimensions in the 1980s, promoting Japan and Taiwan to the top of the world's net lenders and, inversely, turning the US from top lender to top borrower. Most of this financing was done by private capital. Unlike in the 1960s and 1970s when Europe lent short-term to the US and the US invested long-term in Europe with only limited net flows, the net flows are now huge. Because they are so large, investors are keen on diversification. Funding of the US current account occurs through securities purchases by all types of borrowers and not only treasury bills. These include investment funds, stocks, direct investments, real estate acquisitions and takeovers of companies.[3]

Not only industry is moving into a global role, investors are also turning global. They take advantage of differences in business cycles, hence differences in growth performance, interest-rate differentials and hedging possibilities. Until the 1970s individual investors focused mainly on domestic markets. Three developments have contributed to internationalisation. First, in order to take advantage of international differences in performance, freedom to exit and enter home and foreign currency markets is required. Reduced capital controls made this possible. Second, modern portfolio theory stresses the benefit of diversification and the fact that even a more volatile asset can reduce aggregate risk through less than perfect positive correlation. A foreign asset is always intrinsically riskier for returns measured in domestic currency but may still serve to reduce overall portfolio risk. This also shows up in the search for investment possibilities in LDCs with high expected returns, but also high risk. These risks can only be handled through diversification. Third, increasing shares of private wealth are managed by institutional investors (investment funds, pension funds, insurance companies) which have the sophistication to apply modern portfolio management techniques, use hedging products and have the resources to collect and treat information from the major markets. There is, therefore, not only net foreign investment to channel current-account surpluses but, more importantly, there is two-way trade as each institutional investor seeks international portfolio diversification.

Internationalisation of financial markets was clearly stimulated by macro-economic events. Initially the search for escaping regulations helped further. Successful escapes, in combination with more market-oriented macroeconomic policies, made reduced controls and regulation both necessary and acceptable. The efficiency gains for resource allocation provided these policy changes with a further rationality.

Once Euromarkets developed and national markets opened up, the possibilities for innovation lost their predominantly defensive character to escape regulations. Swaps are a typical example of exploiting comparative advantages across market segments and they contribute to reducing market (and not only regulatory) imperfections. Similarly, leveraged buy-outs represent a type of financial engineering that exploits fiscal distortions and completes the market's control over management.

Innovations directly affect regulations either by posing new problems or by providing escapes from existing regulations. They also feed back into internationalisation. A swap desk is like a telephone system: the more telephone owners there are, the more efficient and useful is the system. A profitable swap desk is therefore necessarily international and as close to global as possible. Mergers and acquisitions (M&A) require tremendous experience and skill which is clearly not usefully bottled up in one national market. Any citizen or institution of this world, eager to acquire liquid, high-value securities in a diversified portfolio, cannot neglect the securities markets of the handful of major currencies.

1.2 THE TREND TOWARDS GLOBAL BANKING

I hope to have shown the tight interrelationship and mutual reinforcement between deregulation, innovation and internationalisation, all made necessary by the evolution and structural changes in the world economy.

It would be amazing if the banking industry itself had not been profoundly affected by this turbulent evolution. Although in many countries adaptation has been slowed down by regulatory barriers, deep changes have occurred in all major markets. Not only have international operations augmented more than domestic business, but financial institutions have set up operations abroad at a very accelerated pace, particularly in the 1980s. Most larger European banks have subsidiaries or branches in London, New York and Asia. Their product range has been substantially enriched through innovation in their traditional product markets and through expansion into new product markets. One trend observable worldwide is for banks to 'despecialise'. In the United States, Japan and the United Kingdom this means that the legal or traditional separation of commercial banking from investment banking is increasingly considered as outlived. UK commercial banks have already expanded into investment banking, US banks have done so abroad and are pressing for legislative changes at home, as are Japanese banks. On the continent, where universal banking has been the norm in many countries, the model spreads and the Second Banking Directive accepts universal banking. It could hardly have done otherwise as creation of an integrated financial market is considerably easier through extending the freedom of choice of banking organisations rather than through the splitting up of existing banking structures. In countries where universal banking was legally ruled out, such as Italy, legislation is being adapted ('polyfunctional banking'). Existing universal banks even reinforce their reach by moving massively into insurance business, business consulting and, by stepping up investments, into investment banking.

There are several economic trends underlying this quest for 'Allfinanz'. First, as argued by Steinherr and Huveneers, a universal banking system slows down the development of securities markets. In countries where universal banking is dominant, securities markets are underdeveloped, the prime example being Germany. The single market will, however, emphasise 'Europeanisation' of non-financial firms, lead through M&A to larger firm size and thereby diminish exclusive firm–bank relationships. Such firms, with greater sophistication in financial management, will increasingly use the securities markets for their financial needs and their investments. In addition, with stock exchange liberalisation and increasing institutional wealth to be invested, securities markets will gain in cost-effectiveness and depth.

The effect of this trend (called disintermediation) on securities markets is reinforced by banks themselves through securitisation. Higher capital requirements and the greater need for risk management induce banks to increasingly securitise their assets. Competition on the funding side (deposits versus short-term securities) will also shift a larger share of funding into securities.

Both disintermediation and securitisation displace business opportunities from deposit taking/lending to advisory services and securities business. Advisory services include global financing and investment services and contribute to breaking up traditional lending activities into their components (loan initiation, financing, monitoring, insurance, etc.). This shift in activity takes place within the reach of the universal bank while the specialised commercial bank risks losing part of its traditional business.

The recent tendency to merge banking and insurance activities is motivated by the general quest for global finance. Banking and insurance products are either close substitutes or direct complements. Both products deal with risk and, in the case of life insurance, are placements for savings. Other insurance products are complements to banking products (e.g., real estate or car finance and insurance). Bank distribution systems also serve to market insurance products at low fixed costs to captive clients, whilst bank products can be marketed more aggressively to individuals through the insurance sales force.

To offer both types of products is therefore natural for both banks and insurance companies. Recently, the incentive for banks to move into insurance increased dramatically: on the continent, a rapidly ageing population requires insurance-based old-age provisions to alleviate an otherwise overburdened state social security system financed from current tax receipts. During recent years, in the major countries of the continent, the share of savings invested in insurance and pension fund products has been increasing to the detriment of the share in banking products.[4]

This general trend in favour of 'despecialisation' is not unchallenged. The major challenge is certainly going to be cost-effectiveness and not regulation. But, at least in the longer run, when regulatory generosity will have generated its own problems, there may be corrective regulatory constraint. On the way to the European integrated financial market there are several potential hurdles which will be discussed in the next section.

1.3 OUTLOOK FOR THE INTEGRATED EUROPEAN FINANCIAL MARKET

In the late 1980s Europe was in 'Aufbruchsstimmung' (break-free mood) and ready to move towards a single market. The basis of this fundamental breakthrough is a remarkable convergence of national views in the domain of economic policy. Protectionism, national economic policy choices, private ownership are all issues that no longer raise ideological debates. Since 1983, when France abandoned its policy course adopted in 1981, this basic convergence of economic policy has resulted in a more stable and better functioning EMS. It also made it possible to gradually eliminate capital controls in some member countries. The Community finally reached a macroeconomic balance and found general political readiness allowing it to embark on integration of its financial markets.

It has certainly not been easy to reach overall support for liberalising trade, capital flows and, more generally, a largely market-oriented economy. The latter, in turn, was a precondition for the wave of privatisation of publicly owned firms (including banks) in preparation for more open competition in the integrated market. Privatisation and other strategies preparing for the integrated market through M&A give securities markets a substantial boost and will reinforce the development of capital markets which only recently started to be deregulated and liberalised.

Stock exchanges around the world, in reaction to London's 'big bang' (which only occurred in 1987!) and in preparation for their more complex tasks, in terms of volumes, products, costs, and their international role, are completely revising their rules, procedures and technological support systems.

There is, of course, a long and difficult road from the general willingness and the macroeconomic preconditions to a practical legal, fiscal and regulatory framework. The Communities' approach has been pragmatic and therefore successful. It has not attempted to set up a fully harmonised regulatory and fiscal framework. Much is, therefore, left to regulatory and fiscal 'competition'. In order to accept and encompass the banking systems of all member countries, the approach is in no sense restrictive. And through the principle of 'home regulatory control' no national system or product can be prevented from being exported to other member countries. One can therefore witness a regulatory flexibility and permissiveness that is unique in this century.

The conditions that made this progress possible and the approach adopted both suggest that there is a considerable risk that the integrated financial market may still encounter delays and difficulties that are perhaps underestimated in the current euphoria.

Politics and economics tend to be cyclical. A shift to the political left, a prolonged recession, difficult adjustment to completely open frontiers in some countries, massive acquisition of national enterprises by foreigners, may all contribute to the slow down of market integration and to the reversion to what is now considered 'old-fashioned' nationalistic policy-making.

On the more technical level there are still many unresolved, important issues. Recent attempts to harmonise withholding taxes on capital income failed and are unlikely to be successful in the near future. Hence competition will remain tax biased. At any rate the only economically rational solution would be the elimination of withholding taxes. At any other level European tax-shy funds would find their way out of the Community rather than to Luxembourg. But, even if withholding taxes were eliminated in the Community, there would still be the problem of very different corporate and income tax structures. These distort competition because, in the integrated market, competition is not limited to domestic and foreign firms established in a national market.

Another serious difficulty for a European regulatory approach is that accounting systems are not uniform across member countries. This seriously limits and distorts regulations. For example, in the Second Banking Directive, the proposed restrictions on bank holdings of participations in non-financial sector firms depend crucially on how shareholdings are to be valued.

Community acceptance of the universal bank model also implies potential distortions and unresolved questions. In some countries proxy-voting is admitted, in others not. In Germany, for example, proxy-votes provide banks with more votes than owned shares. The risk of conflicts of interest, which is present in all banking systems, is certainly more acute for universal banks.[5] Again it is unlikely that much progress is going to be achieved in this domain.

Finally, there is the question of 'excessive' economic power of large diversified banks. The restrictions on their shareholdings are too easily circumvented to ease the critical observer's mind. If the largest European banks team up with large insurance companies and have effective control over industrial enterprises in their home markets, plus a market presence throughout Europe, all traditional concepts of anti-trust would be seriously boggled. What is lacking is a European anti-trust policy, one that gets away from concentrating on traditional market-share analysis restricted to the home market or to trade flows.[6] The difficulties in this field are such, however, that significant progress is unlikely to be seen. In the US, where preservation of competitive conditions is perhaps most fully supported politically, the only feasible, even if not in all instances optimal, approach was chosen: prohibition for commercial banks to hold investments in non-financial firms.

To conclude, it seems to me that the integration approach chosen was the only one feasible and that Europe seized a chance offered through political and economic convergence. It was not possible to reach for an integrated financial market earlier. The current euphoric fashion may, however, overlook a number of essential unresolved (unresolvable ?) issues and some quite serious implications. One can also foresee with confidence an explosion of innovations in European markets hitherto lagging behind. However, because this lag is due to regulations and restrictions on international competition, a substantial part of this innovatory bout represents a catching-up effect and not a new trend. Beyond 1993, when most of this catching-up will be realised, innovatory progress will return to a level that is unlikely to be in excess of the macroeconomic average.

It can also be expected that, while the 1980s were characterised by innovatory profit generation, the 1990s will rely on production and distribution efficiency. This could favour Japanese and continental European banks rather than more flexible American institutions.

2. The Community approach to financial market integration

The Commission's efforts to liberalise capital movements within the Community, to promote free trade in financial services and freedom of establishment for financial institutions date back to the early 1960s. The legitimacy of the Commission's actions springs mainly from Articles 52–58, 59–66 and 67–73 of the Treaty of Rome which respectively elect *freedom of establishment*, of *provision of services* and of *capital movements* as major goals in the process of economic and political integration of the Community. This section sketches the progress of the Community's actions in pursuit of a freer and unified European financial area.[7]

2.1 LIBERALISATION OF CAPITAL MOVEMENTS AND FREE PROVISION OF BANKING SERVICES

It was only in early 1983, after a series of partial initiatives and no doubt under the beneficial influence that a relatively well-functioning EMS was having on European currency stability and monetary convergence, that the Commission presented to the European Council of Ministers a wide-ranging communication [COM(83) 207] on the desirability of resuming actions in the sphere of European economic and financial integration. This line was further pursued, in June 1985, with the publication of the *White Paper* on the achievement of a large and unified European internal market, part of it dedicated to the *freeing of capital movements, the unification of internal markets for financial services and the setting up of a common regulatory structure for financial institutions.* Three main objectives were assigned to the process of liberalising capital flows. First of all, free movement of capital was deemed to be a necessary corollary to the achievement of an integrated internal market for goods and services. Secondly, open capital markets represent a strong incentive for member states to adopt sound economic policies conducive to price and exchange-rate stability, two major preconditions for achieving economic and monetary union in Europe. Finally, the opening up of the Community's capital markets was seen to enlarge the freedom of choice for European investors and to lead to a more efficient allocation of savings as well as to greater overall welfare.

A few very basic principles were laid out concerning the accompanying measures to be taken in connection with the freeing of European financial services and capital movements. First of all, the general principle that if a particular financial product is authorised in a member country it should not be possible to block it in the remaining eleven member states on the grounds that it does not satisfy certain domestic technical requirements. According to this principle, any duly authorised and properly supervised bank can make its services available in any member state even though they are designed according to the regulations prevailing in the bank's home country and do not meet the standards of the host state. The only requirement is that these services fall into an agreed list of banking activities. The adoption of this approach should gradually eliminate that 'eccentric difference in European thinking between the production of goods, where competition is deemed to be beneficial, and the production of financial services, where competition is deemed to be antisocial and regulation desirable' (H.G. Johnson, 1973, p. 320). Secondly, it was recognised that an indispensable component of a stable financial environment is represented by the *harmonisation* of the most basic rules governing *prudential supervision* of banking establishments (in areas such as: size and composition of own funds; solvency and liquidity coefficients; concentration of credit risks) and of the setting of *common standards of investor protection.*

It was, however, felt that following the principle of harmonisation to its extreme consequences would be too complex and lengthy a task and that, beyond a certain point, the goal of achieving a coherent and stable European regulatory banking environment would be better served by a process of *mutual recognition* of each member country's supervisory criteria. The principle of mutual recognition is a fundamental aspect of the Commission's liberalisation actions in the area of finance: it not only applies to banking, but also forms the core of the directive on the free selling of mutual fund shares across Europe and is at the basis of the proposal of a draft directive on investment services.

The White Paper also recommended the adoption of the principle of *paren-tal (or home-country) responsibility* in the supervision of foreign branches of financial institutions, with the host country's authorities taking a subsidiary (though not negligible) role. The Commission has subsequently qualified this choice in the SBD: 'responsibility for the financial soundness of a credit institution, and in particular for its solvency, will rest with the competent authorities of its home Member State . . . whereas the host country authorities retain responsibility for matters relating to liquidity and the implementation of monetary policy; . . . supervision of market risk should be the subject of close cooperation between the competent authorities of the home and host countries' [COM(87) 751 final].

In the Commission's view it is important that perfect harmonisation of prudential measures need not necessarily have to precede the complete liberalisation of capital movements and the freedom of the cross-border supply of financial services. It would be development somehow forced on member governments by the gradual movement towards an integrated market for financial services. The same thinking characterises other domains such as *tax issues*, where huge disparities in the fiscal treatment of financial transactions (e.g., levies on capital gains, withholding taxes on coupon and dividend income or stamp duties on securities transactions) represent a serious obstacle, complicated by *bank secrecy laws*, in the pursuit of a smooth passage to an integrated European financial market. Such fiscal and regulatory disparities in the treatment of savings and investments could also risk destabilising capital movements and threaten progress towards the complete freedom of international exchange of financial assets.

Further progress on the fiscal issue is therefore necessary and appears to have just started. Significant advances have, however, been accomplished for *regulatory treatment of financial establishments* in insurance, securities and banking markets. Key roles are played by the second directive on coordination of the rules governing the conduct of banking business (SBD), the directive on the harmonisation of the national approaches to the assessment of the capital adequacy of financial institutions (see paper by Richard Dale) and the directive under preparation on the evaluation of the interest rate and liquidity risk incurred by banks in their securities dealings. These directives, as well as others to come, should form the core of a European banking legislation designed to build a common background for the Community's regulatory environment, making it able to accommodate the trend towards free movement of capital and free cross-border provision of financial services.

In February 1986 member states signed the *Single Act*, establishing year-end 1992 as the limiting date for the achievement of an integrated European market in goods, services and capital and setting in motion a *two-phase programme* for complete and unconditional liberalisation of capital movements.

If all goes according to plan, by mid-1990 most of Europe will enjoy virtual freedom in cross-border capital transactions. The necessary background will thus be in place to permit further progress towards liberalisation of financial services and the freedom of establishment of banking units.

2.2 THE EUROPEAN BANKING DIRECTIVES

As far as the *liberalisation of the European banking market* is concerned, the Commission initiated its actions in June 1973 with a directive aiming at the termination of restrictions and the principle of freedom of establishment. The *first directive* on the coordination of national laws, regulation and administrative provisions pertaining to the setting up and pursuit of banking activities followed in December 1977. It also established the Banking Advisory Committee, a consultative body made up of representatives of bank supervisory authorities of member states and designed to assist the Commission in legislating matters concerning banking and finance.

Between 1983 and 1986, several more *specialised directives or recommendations* were proposed. They covered various subjects ranging from the presentation of banks' accounts and financial statements of the branches of banks from Third World countries to the control of large credit exposures, from the reorganisation and winding up of distressed financial establishments to the supervision of banks on a consolidated basis and, from the introduction of deposit guarantee schemes to the common definition of own funds and capital ratios. They are expected to be gradually adopted by year-end 1992 and are intended to facilitate the most basic harmonisation of the ground rules for the conduct of prudential supervision of banking establishments. The most fundamental step towards the achievement of a common market in financial services is represented by the proposed SBD. It establishes a list of bank activities with respect to which the principle of freedom of cross-border exercise through mutual recognition applies (this list also includes underwriting and trading, for customers or for own account, of practically any type of security, the participation in share issues, money brokering, leasing and issuing of credit cards); it introduces minimum requirements as to the size of own funds of credit institutions (ECU 5 million) and eliminates the need to maintain a separate endowment capital for foreign branches; it requires the disclosure of the identity of a bank's more important shareholders and of any taking, or changing, in the level of a qualified participation; it limits the banks' holding of shares in other financial and non-financial establishments; it regulates the exchange of information between home and host-country supervisory authorities and provides for the former to carry out on-the-spot verifications on the territory of the latter.

The SBD establishes the so-called *single banking licence* valid across the EEC, namely the principle that once a certain institution is authorised to pursue its activities in the home country according to the laws and regulations prevailing there and is properly supervised in its country of origin, it may conduct the same operations in any member country irrespective of whether or not these activities (which, however, must fall within those listed in this directive) are allowed in the host country and, above all, without the need to obtain any supplementary authorisation. The role of the host country's authorities will be to supervise the liquidity, the administrative and accounting procedures and the mechanisms for internal control applied by the foreign credit establishments operating in its territory.

The initial rules on *reciprocity* were particularly criticised by Japan and the United States given the separation their legislations impose between commercial and investment banking activities (see also the chapter by Key and Scott). It was feared that the expansion in Europe of credit institutions from these two countries could be blocked on the grounds that European banks are not allowed to exercise the full range of banking activities in their territories. This fear should have been tempered by the fact that, under Community law, subsidiaries (but not branches) of non-Community banks incorporated in the EEC are considered Community institutions. They can thus benefit from the planned single banking licence, giving them the right to expand throughout the EEC without additional authorisations.

In the latest version of the SBD, the rules on reciprocity are softened considerably. Each member state can authorise establishment of a non-Community bank, subject to notification of the Commission. The Commission can be authorised to negotiate access on similar terms with non-Community countries, but only with full respect to national restrictions on banking activities (Article 9).

From this brief overview of the actions undertaken by the Commission in the domain of freedom of movements of capital and free cross-border provision of financial services, it is apparent that significant progress has been made in the second half of the 1980s and that the goal of a unified European banking market has drawn considerably closer.

2.3 EVALUATION

The Community's approach to financial market integration is a reflection of recent trends in internationalisation and deregulation of financial markets. It consists in providing a minimum of regulatory harmonisation, leaving much to further harmonisation efforts and to national regulatory competition. The main features of the Community's approach are mutual recognition of national regulations, home country responsibility for banking supervision and host country responsibility for the purpose of monetary management and rules of conduct. Regulatory highlights are minimum standards for capital adequacy, limits on shares owned by the non-financial sector and deposit insurance.

Mutual recognition requires that none of the banking structures in any member country are put into question. Hence, one of the most prominent tools of regulation – segmentation of banking by activity or geographic extension – is no longer available. This raises several questions. First, about the optimality of unrestricted banking, particularly when banks can freely enter into non-banking financial services (see chapter by Steinherr and Huveneers). Second, as long as some countries still maintain some segmentation, restricted banks may suffer from a regulatory bias (see chapter by Van Cayseele). If strong enough, such institutions may be able to resist becoming universal for regulatory, rather than efficiency, reasons. Preferences of national regulators concerning regulatory priorities are severely restricted.

The Community approach is focused on greater efficiency and on levelling the playing field. It does not extensively deal with traditional concerns about systemic stability. National authorities therefore retain their responsibility in this area. They are free to set standards higher than the minima imposed by the Community directives, to impose restrictions on bank portfolios, to regulate interest rates, to restrict activities and instruments and to exercise their role of lender of last resort. However, they cannot discriminate between national and other financial intermediaries and their scope of freedom will be constrained by competition among financial systems.

It is unlikely that by 1993 a totally integrated financial market will exist. Uncertainty about the future regulatory framework in each member country, maintained implicit and hidden protectionism, the costs and risks of competing in foreign retail markets, all point to limits on financial integration. The major competitive pressure is likely to be provided by capital flows and trade in financial services. The main effect of the Second Banking Directive is therefore not to be seen in its contribution to market integration, but to the overall gain in efficiency by supplanting over time excessively restrictive and inefficient national regulations. On balance, this overall efficiency gain should materialise, but should not be taken for granted. The proposed framework still shows signs of potential inefficiencies. Much depends therefore on future complementary actions and on national implementation. In this evolution, progress in related areas, such as fiscal harmonisation, creation of a European company law and European anti-trust policy, will be of critical importance.

3. Generalisation of banking and its changing scope

Financial market integration within the wider goal of a single European market will offer opportunities to reach beyond national frontiers by exporting financial services and by acquiring or establishing service centres abroad in markets that were formerly inaccessible to foreign penetration. A key issue of this integration process will be the optimal scope and organisation of banks. This question is investigated by *Ugur Muldur* who analyses economies of scale in the banking sector. He demonstrates that economies of scale are rather limited in the financial sector.

As far as the Belgian market is concerned, reference is made to a specific study which comes to the conclusion that there seems to be an optimal scale for medium-sized banks. Larger financial institutions seem to be characterised by diseconomies of scale partly due to expense preferences linked to non-price competition. The empirical results suggest eonomies of scale at the branch level but global diseconomies of scale at the firm level.

Regarding the French financial sector, the author first points out that there is a tendency towards decreasing concentration as a result of the deregulation process that has taken place in France. Concerning economies of scale, the author concludes that, overall, there is no evidence of increasing returns in the French financial sector. In terms of operating costs, scale economies in banks and diseconomies in savings institutions seem to exist. However, these economies (diseconomies) of operating costs are compensated for by diseconomies (economies) of financial costs.

Since there is no evidence of important economies of scale, the policy recommendation is that a more stringent anti-trust policy should be adopted towards the financial sector.

Even if economies of scale are not substantial, there may be economies of scope justifying the multiproduct bank. With this conjecture as a starting point, *Alfred Steinherr and Christian Huveneers* look at the advantages and problems posed by universal banking.

As far as the economics of universal banks is concerned, a theoretical approach suggests that universal banks may benefit from information superiority and from economies of scope. By meeting all the financial needs of a company and being involved in advisory functions, a universal bank can minimise the cost of information. Several arguments suggest that economies of scope may be considerable. First, there is the fixed cost of managing a client relationship. Second, financial institutions produce highly substitutable goods and can cope more easily with demand shifts between products.

However, Steinherr and Huveneers point out that the empirical literature fails to support the hypothesis that economies of scope are important. Therefore, the evidence in favour of universal banking still needs to be delivered. Moreover, one should not neglect some drawbacks that may be linked to universal banking. First, there is a 'contagion risk' that relates to a possible loss of confidence; bank runs due to bankruptcies of affiliated companies may occur. Second, universal banking, with control over firms in the non-banking sector and the possible control of large banks by non-banking companies raises the issue of market power and uncompetitive strategies. However, this problem is somewhat irrelevant in a future competitive European integrated market.

Steinherr and Huveneers also focus on the banks' control over firms. They conclude that the importance of universal banks may lead to underdevelopment of the securities market because the shareholder's agency problems are not resolved. As a result, resource allocation may suffer from inefficiencies because managers of banks and non-banks have large free cash flows and are not subject to strict board and market controls. Outside financial resources may also be expensive in a system based on universal banking. On balance, they arrive at the conclusion that the alleged advantages of universal banking tend to be overemphasised.

In anticipation of the complete realisation of the single European market, waves of mergers and acquisitions are taking place within the financial sector. At the same time it is expected that there will be an increase in competition. However, it remains unclear whether or not there are significant economies of scale. This issue is of great importance because the welfare gains that are associated with the realisation of the European Internal Market are generally based on the assumption that economies of scale exist. In this context it is also appropriate to ask how the concentration process within the financial sector will affect the competitive structure of the financial market itself.

The Second Banking Coordination Directive adopted on 15 December 1989 will become effective on 1 January 1993. It is based on the Home Country Principle (HCC). It has often been argued that the HCC principle could induce banks to locate themselves in countries with the least stringent regulations, especially low solvency requirements. It has also been argued that countries could engage in a downward regulatory competition (in order to avoid a loss of banking activity).

Patrick van Cayseele challenges this view and the fact that banks compete according to strict minima regarding solvency. He argues that the *de facto* re-regulation taking place at the European level to avoid a downward regulatory spiral (imposition of minimal standards) might create room for the creation of entry barriers.

The downward regulatory spiral argument states that, in a world based on mutual recognition, banks operating from countries with high solvency ratios face a competitive disadvantage because they have higher capital costs. According to Van Cayseele, counteracting forces to the downward spiral exist mainly because the solvency of each individual bank remains an important aspect of competitive strategy. By imposing tough standards, that is, high solvency ratios, a country might give its banks a safe appeal abroad. Due to the higher capital adequacy requirements, banks of that country cannot offer competitive deposit interest rates but will offer safer deposits. Branches from the country with the highest solvency ratio have a safety advantage and could then attract clients. Therefore, a downward deregulatory spiral is not likely and for Van Cayseele it is appropriate to ask whether high minimal standards are a *sine qua non* for mutual recognition to yield a safe outcome.

He asserts that minimal standards might help to unify the market. But, on the other hand, if minimal standards are enforced at too high a level, it will imply that some banks will be unable to participate in the 1992 wave. Hence barriers to entry on the global market are imposed, which are inefficient; therefore, minimal standards have to be handled carefully.

Throughout Europe financial intermediaries are repositioning themselves in preparation for the increased opportunities offered and the tougher competition accompanying the single market. One of the means of strengthening an intermediary's position is by merging with a competitor or with a firm offering complementarities.

Jack Revell asserts that the present situation concerning bank mergers is more difficult because of increased competition. This is very different from earlier periods when a merger between two banks within the same group evoked other mergers, because the remaining banks sought ways to restore the balance within the group. Often the first merger was necessary because a smaller bank was in difficulties. Nowadays, the circumstances are different. Banks are pressed to merge through the need for a larger capital base and for cost reduction. To understand these developments it is necessary to take a closer look at the organisational structure and activities of banks. A useful tool in these matters is the so-called McKinsey scheme, which states that universal banks in the original sense are diversified banks at the heart of which is a deposit bank. All activities are under review by one board of directors and controlled firmly by this central authority. Diversification of activities creates the opportunity for cross subsidisation, which makes the organisation very vulnerable on those markets where costs are (too) high. As such, cross subsidisation might create inefficiencies.

An answer to this kind of problem might be found in the 'federal bank' (or polyfunctional) concept, which is meant to break down the universal bank into a number of specialised units. These units might achieve real competitive advantages for the bank concerned. The application of this scheme can be considered a natural consequence of recent developments. Through this concept, banking systems in various countries might begin to show substantial differences. Furthermore, it might lead to a smaller number of competitors, although this does not necessarily mean that there would be less competition. Although differences exist with respect to the structure of universal banks and with respect to the banking structure at large in different regions, this scheme can also be applied to savings banks, cooperative and mutual institutions.

One of the dominant features of repositioning and restructuring in European financial markets is the rapid interpenetration of banking and insurance. Such a globalisation is, however, not always a strategy that can be recommended and depends on a number of criteria.

Geoffrey Nicholson stresses that successful mergers or other forms of cooperation between banks and insurance companies depend on several factors, such as regional differences, the nature of the products sold to the public and the existence of distribution channels. At first sight it looks as if there are large differences between banks and insurance companies. Therefore, it can be questioned whether there is an economic rationale for a combination of these different types of financial institutions. Can any real economic advantages be expected from such combinations? And what about economies of scale and scope?

Concerning the prospect for growth in the medium term, the outlook for insurance seems to be better than for banking products. On the other hand, selling insurance products through banks has proved to be easier than the reverse, which might lead to a reduction of distribution costs. However, one should not forget that for special products banks may not be the right institutions.

The possibility of telescoping banking and insurance activities also depends on similarities between more specific characteristics of the institutions involved. In some countries, like for instance the UK, insurance companies have well-developed equity capabilities, contrary to merchant banks; but quite the opposite holds for investment capabilities. So there might be large differences from country to country when combining banking and insurance activities.

Moreover, the success of 'bank insurance' is heavily dependent on the quality of implementation and strategic insight. This means that one should have an eye for potential difficulties concerning the integration of banking and insurance systems, the training of staff and employees and projecting and controlling management targets. But, generally speaking, integration will continue in retail banking, retail and life insurance, although banks may benefit more from combinations of banking and insurance activities, due to their large distribution networks.

All the above papers taken together suggest that competition between financial institutions must be understood by investigating the influence of financial intermediaries on the market process and by the way this process is regulated. An important item in these matters is the discussion around the positive impact of European integration. Considering these aspects, the questions whether the financial system and its regulation are stable and how the benefits of integration are distributed need to be answered. For example, will European integration lead to large gains or to destabilisation by excessive competition?

The degree of competition plays an important role in the analysis of these questions. One can expect some kind of imperfection in present and future competition. This might be caused by entry barriers, which are difficult to prevent and will diminish the future benefits of integration. But this is not the only countervailing force. An absence of sufficient competition may stimulate the continuation of segmented markets. In this case European integration will not lead to a unified, perfectly competitive market, but to more or less separate markets with different degrees of competition. As a result, the benefits of integration will be distributed unequally between the market segments. On the other hand, it may be expected that integration, responding to harmonisation of legislation and deregulation, will stimulate competitive forces. But even then the opposite may be true as a result of some kind of overshooting, because financial institutions faced with more intense competition might try to reverse this development and opt for collusive behaviour.

It may be concluded that different forces work in different directions and at the moment it is not very clear what the result will be. What once were stable markets may tomorrow change by the entrance of new market participants into destabilised ones as a result of overcapacity. There are conflicts of interest that regulators must be aware of. Competition needs to be encouraged, but there is the risk of overshooting and this conflicts with another target of regulation, stability. This conflict of interest suggests the importance of creating a workable scheme of supervision.

4. Towards pan-European capital markets

Innovations require deregulation and free trade and this is what characterises the 1980s. *Christophe Belhomme, et al.* in their absolutely fundamental chapter discuss the financial innovations of the 1980s in four major European countries, their motivations and the regulatory contribution or response. The four countries are Britain, France, Germany and Italy. After a description of innovations in securities markets, in markets for derivative products and in markets of collectively managed instruments (UCITS or SICAVS), they evaluate the resulting changes in the overall market configuration. Then they proceed to assess the efforts of innovation on the borrowing and investment behaviour of households, enterprises, banks and governments. Their analysis quite naturally results in the question whether innovations ultimately produce a better allocation of resources and contribute to promotion of real economic growth. Their results suggest the following sober conclusions.

While innovation allowed a steady, robust growth throughout the 1980s, the process came up against its intrinsic limits by the end of the decade. Aggressive borrowing – an acceptable strategy in high growth periods – becomes dangerous when the economy slows.

The increase in financial market activity and the sizeable inflow of savings removed the domestic ceiling on financing volume. The expansion of market-raised finance is tangible proof of this. The build-up of outstanding debt thus represents the hidden side of the fast, innovation-driven growth of the 1980s.

Firms took advantage of easier credit to meet the increased financial needs entailed by their heavy investment programmes. First, debt accumulation was justified by the leverage effect, as their gross operating surpluses were rising faster than their interest expenses. However, indebtedness becomes critical as soon as the value-added growth rate begins to slow. To maintain self-financing ratios consistent with the share of profit in value-added, companies must either reduce their interest payments or cut their investments. As the first solution is not within firms' power, the debt stock obviously places a limit on growth. Until this problem is solved, the authors argue that all future growth seems compromised. The question of financial innovation and growth is pursued further in the chapters by Viñals *et al.* and Aglietta, summarised in section 5.

Households became indebted in order to keep their consumption growing despite stagnation of their disposable income. They were prompted to borrow by the relative fall in the cost of credit – as rival banks sparked a price war to win this captive market segment. The ratio of household debt to disposable income grew steadily over the period. In France, the ratio climbed from nearly 50 per cent at the start of the decade to 64 per cent in 1986 and 78 per cent in 1989.

Banks, for their part, took advantage of the financial momentum to increase their lending operations by gathering fresh funds on the financial markets. But their expansion undermined the soundness of their balance sheets. New loans often originated in high risk sectors, such as real estate, consumer credit and small- and medium-sized businesses. Meanwhile, the proportion of equity in the balance sheet total shrank as bonds and short-term securities swelled. By the end of the decade the banking system had become so fragile that its solvency ratios often fell short of the international Cooke ratio requirement.

Thus, overindebted economic agents and an undercapitalised banking system were the two prominent features of the financial landscape at the close of the 1980s. Compared with the United States, however, these problems are far less acute in Europe and their intensity differs from country to country – they are more pronounced in Britain and France, less so in Germany. But, by and large, they put a cap on the benefits of innovation.

Giovanni Majnoni et al. investigate the synergies between monetary and financial market integration. They maintain that monetary and financial integration generates public goods and because the two processes interact and produce externalities (e.g., reduction in bearing of risk and uncertainty by economic agents) close monitoring and corrective interventions by the authorities were assumed to be necessary. The need for monetary and financial coordination may, furthermore, increase in the coming years in response to a rise in the cross-border substitutability of financial assets. From the economic viewpoint, the task will be to counter some of the distortions in current-account imbalances, interest rates and competitive conditions, to which the integration achieved so far may have contributed. Furthermore, from the institutional point of view, the task will be to revise the coordination procedure adopted in the past and reduce the asymmetry in the definitions of objectives and methods that has so far been a feature of the monetary and financial aspects of integration.

The European monetary union process by itself would impose some fiscal discipline on certain countries. However, some generally accepted rules should be respected as well.

Full convergence of fiscal, monetary and other macroeconomic aspects appears necessary for an integrated market. The final objective of the EMU should be set up clearly so that market forces can find out where they are heading. At present, monetary union is far ahead of the other objectives required for the final results to be obtained.

The next two chapters deal more specifically, and more technically, with regulatory issues pertaining to securities markets. The first deals with integration of the Western European securities markets, the second with the quite distinct problem of developing securities markets in Eastern Europe.

Richard Dale reviews the current developments in the Community regulatory framework for securities business, which the second banking directive has ranked among the ordinary activities of banks, and focuses on the Commission proposals for the capital adequacy directive. He stresses the 'formidable policy problems' arising from three conflicting considerations.

1. Given the important risks involved in the securities business, a strong prudential regulation is needed.
2. With the heavy and growing direct and indirect involvement of European banks in the securities business, prudential regulation should apply to banks as well as to non-banks.
3. However, the traditional dual approach to the regulation of credit operations and securities business reflects important differences in the perception of risks. The risk of credit operations is mainly long term; banking regulation aims at ensuring solvency and focuses on equity. The main risks of securities business are short term; regulation aims at ensuring liquidity and may accept short-term subordinated debt as capital.

The conflict between the basic regulatory requirements and the traditional approach has, in Dale's view, led to dangerous compromises (like alternative definitions of capital for the securities activities of banks) and more stringent capital requirements for securities firms than parallel requirements in the US, impairing the competitive position of EEC firms.

Amendments were likely to be made to the Commission's proposals, following discussions in the G-10 banking supervisory committee and in the IOSCO technical committee. These discussions in broader forums should lead to a common approach to prudential requirements for the securities business of banks and non-banks, and to more convergence in the definition of capital.

With regard to the Investment Services Directive, Dale stresses two problems: an excessive role given to the 'host country' in matters of 'general interest' and the possibility of divergent regulatory requirements by the 'home country'.

It appears, however, that the discretionary powers of the 'host country' are now seriously limited by the recent addition of the conduct of business principles in the directive, and that harmonisation of regulatory requirements should result from the pressure of competition and from coordination at the Community level.

In my view, the possible integration of the currently fragmented securities markets of the Community raises a number of issues. The stakes are high: a truly integrated European securities market, pooling liquidity available on the different markets, would offer European issuers a broader and more effective primary market; it could also significantly increase the European share of the global securities market. But building up a successful market does not depend on the will of governments or regulators, it rests on the initiative of the market organisers and the way they respond to users' needs.

In fact, some projects to integrate the EC's stock markets have already been undertaken. There was the EUROQUOTE project for a common technical infra-structure, a project which in the meantime has been abandoned. The EUROLIST project, which has recently been adopted, will introduce a joint listing and trading system for the shares of larger European companies. The European Wholesale Market proposes to create a distinct market for large blocks of shares. The Euroquote project was set up to deseminate to market users a coherent stream of information, including prices, volumes, market events and other financial and economic data. Additional phases of the development of EUROQUOTE were also planned. Stage 2 would or-ganise a network providing interactive access to market systems operated by stock exchanges, third parties and the EUROQUOTE database. Stage 3 would create a point for order matching automated trade execution, trade confirmation and settle-ment message routing. In each phase EUROQUOTE would be the common vehicle for the two other integration projects, EUROLIST and the European Wholesale Mar-ket (EWM).

EUROLIST is a project initially promoted by the Société des Bourses Françaises (SBF). The ultimate objective of the EUROLIST project is to organise linkages between European exchanges on the American/Canadian/Australian model, so that market users will be able to make easy comparisons of quotes, prices and quantities for a list of European securities traded on all the EC exchanges, send their orders, and be assured of their quick and safe execution, irrespective of the exchange to which they had been routed. Technically, in its basic current first phase, EURO-LIST will consist of a joint listing of a few hundred, beginning perhaps with 150 'Eurolisted' shares on the stock exchanges in the Community. Eurolisting will carry the following consequences: trading on every participating exchange; pricing in the same currency on all exchanges; extensive dissemination of quotes, prices, traded quantities and company events and priority, as far as is technically feasible, in the organisation of quick and secure clearing, settlement and delivery procedures. At a later stage the EUROLIST system should be developed in parallel with Stages 2 and 3 of EUROQUOTE, in order to build an effective integrated market through interac-tive access to markets and/or automated order matching and trade execution.

The principles underlying the European Wholesale Market (EWM), a con-cept promoted by the International Stock Exchange in London (ISE), are simple. EWM would aim at meeting the needs of institutional trading. It would extend to the whole Community the success of SEAQ International, the international arm of ISE, by bringing back into a regulated exchange the bulk of the cross-border share trading currently going through OTC channels. Conceived on the model of SEAQ International, EWM would be open to institutional trading of large blocks of securities, including non-European securities, so as to attract the largest share possible of international securities trading in the European time zone. EWM should be as lightly regulated as possible, maintaining, nevertheless, a complete reporting system to market authorities.

The basic concepts underlying these projects are sound and should be made as complementary as possible. However, the coexistence of widely different systems of regulation for the trading of the same securities in the same geographical area would inevitably raise problems, especially as regards the visibility of the market. This problem is not unrelated to the current discussions on the Investment Services Directive in the EC Council of Ministers and one would hope that these problems will be resolved through reasonable compromises, acceptable to market users and regulators.

5. Financial intermediation and economic growth

The value-added provided by the financial sectors consists in channelling resources from savers to investors, in diversifying risks and in minimising the transaction costs of reallocating resources and of the payments system. Such functions are clearly essential for the efficiency of any economy and one should expect that, *ceteris paribus*, an economy with a well-developed, sophisticated and innovatory finance industry would do better than one without it. Prima facie, at least, such a positive correlation is not visible. Fast growing countries are not those with the most developed financial industries. Therefore, it seems necessary to look more closely into this complicated matter.

To verify the link between finance and growth, *José Viñals et al.* analyse the relationship between innovation in financial instruments and capital formation. The wave of financial innovation in Europe is, in general, credited with increasing the efficiency of financial markets and with facilitating the channelling of savings into the most profitable investment opportunities. However, in practice, the impact of new financial instruments on investment decisions seems not to have been very important. In the short and medium term, the role of new financial instruments has only a very limited impact on firms' investment. By reducing their external constraints, financial innovation is more important, but limited in market size. This implies that, for promoting investment, deregulation and freeing financial markets are not essential policy objectives. More could be done through appropriate supply and demand policies. However, investment may have been indirectly affected through the impact of financial innovation on the savings rate of the economy, supplying savers with a wider variety of products and firms with more effective cash management.

Michel Aglietta investigates household saving behaviour as a major source of imbalance in the investment–saving process. He emphasises the significance of the decline in deposits and the rise in non-deposit savings for inflation in stock and property values. Using an overlapping generations model, he shows that in the long term, even with perfect competition in the capital markets, channelling savings into speculative assets lowers the capital ratio, raises the real interest rate and generates potential instability in the growth process.

The unfavourable long-term effect on interest rates is aggravated by the development of consumer credit. In the short to medium term, with non-neutral monetary policy and imperfect capital markets, other problems have to be faced. They include the consequences of the deflation in asset markets for the solvency of financial institutions, the threat of a credit crunch engineered by undercapitalised banks, and the unknown impact of a possible world recession on securitised economies. Aglietta concludes that examination of the excesses of deregulation from the point of view of systemic risks and the uniqueness of banks in the credit process is long overdue.

The Community is entering into the 1990s with a practically liberalised capital market. The prospects for progress along the road to full monetary integration are very promising. *Jorgen Mortensen's* contribution to a prospective, quantitative analysis of the evolution of the European capital markets in the 1990s is based on a portfolio approach to model capital movements, formation of national wealth and its distribution in main financial and real components as a function of the return on assets. Mortensen observes that the degree of freedom of capital movements within the EC has increased significantly. There has been large-scale abolition of domestic barriers and the efficiency of capital markets has grown as well. He suggests that the future evolution of the saving/investment balance and the portfolio structure in the main non-EC countries are likely to affect the state of the EC's capital markets and be influenced in turn by the EC's approach to monetary integration in the 1990s.

For the allocation of savings in the European capital markets, Mortensen examines the inward and outward capital flows with respect to regional and sectoral savings/investment balances. The gradual narrowing of the interest-rate differentials within an EC monetary union would reduce the incentives for 'interest arbitrage' but increase the scope (and the need) for flows based on assessment of the creditworthiness of individual borrowers. On the whole, the author sees little ground for expecting a significant lowering of real interest rates over the coming years. If, in this manner, a climate of competition of claims upon limited financial resources were to prevail, countries and regions with a comparatively low rate of return on fixed capital would be likely to suffer even more than today. The capacity of peripheral and/or underdeveloped regions to attract capital from the rest of the Community or from the rest of the world would, therefore, be determined to an increasing extent by the level of local labour costs in relation to local productivity. The allocation of savings in the Community in the 1990s may thus prove to be a tough, highly competitive game rather than a smooth handout from the rich to the poor.

Growth of the real economy is closely related to efficient specialisation. Hence one of the main reasons for the long period of prosperity since the late 1940s has been the successful and steady progress in trade liberalisation. However, services have been largely excluded from the move towards freer trade and the difficulties witnessed in the Uruguay-round illustrate the political obstacles.

In their chapter *Sydney Key and Hal Scott* puts forward a conceptual framework for analysing international trade in banking services, focusing on regulatory problems. Despite the increasing internationalisation of financial services and markets, substantial differences still exist among national regulatory systems. In particular, countries have adopted varying regimes to support their banking system (safety net). The most generally accepted principle for international trade in banking services is national treatment, the aim of which is to ensure equality of competitive opportunity for domestic and foreign firms providing banking services in a host country.

Key and Scott proposes to step back from conventional terminology and use instead more basic terms that reflect the underlying concepts. National treatment, and each of the principles that go beyond it, can be understood in terms of three basic components: (1) host-country rules, (2) home-country rules and (3) harmonised rules that apply in both countries.

The public-policy question is then what basic principle, or combination of these three principles, should govern international trade in banking services? According to the chapter, this question can best be answered by focusing on the principal forms in which banking services are provided internationally – across borders or through entry and operation of a branch or subsidiary – and on the different, and sometimes conflicting, public-policy goals. To this end, the chapter proposes a 'Banking Matrix', which sets forth possible combinations of public-policy goals and forms of provision of banking services.

The matrix – with the principles of host, home or harmonised rules – enables one to go beyond conventional formulations, such as national treatment or effective market access, which often ignore underlying concerns and the complexities of the issues. While differences can exist over the details of the analysis and the solutions proposed for each cell of the matrix, the systematic approach of the matrix in relating policy goals to the method of providing services to countries remains useful. Indeed, a similar approach could be used for other financial services, such as the securities business and insurance.

6.   Banking and finance in Central and Eastern Europe

For the restructure and reconstruction of Eastern Europe, the financial sector is called upon to play a central role. In the past government agencies allocated resources and banks acted as integrated parts of this system. Privatisation and decentralisation will create opportunities close to those in market economies. Starting conditions will be particularly difficult, hampered by lack of experience, the evolutionary redesigning of property rights and the weight of old, non-recuperable debt.

Tad Rybczynski examines closely the role of finance in restructuring in Eastern Europe. For the transformation of command into market economies attention has so far focused on the re-establishment of property rights, liberalisation of prices and competition. However, the establishment of an efficient financial system is clearly equally important. An overview is therefore given of the basic functions of the financial system in the West. This is compared to the position of the financial system in the command economies in order to indicate in what way it should be altered to enable these economies to move to self-sustaining and non-inflationary growth.

According to Rybczynski, the restructuring of the financial system must be undertaken simultaneously with the restructuring of non-financial enterprises. This process requires contraction of the liabilities of non-financial firms, and there must be a corresponding contraction of assets of commercial and credit banks. Such an operation can best be undertaken by a special agency, which can bear the financial burden of non-viable industrial enterprise liabilities and replace their debt with its own obligations. This operation could be financed through receipts from the privatisation of the agency or from the budget. A similar approach must be adopted towards banks which would work on a two-tier system and within the regulatory framework of universal banking. This element of the transition should be placed at the head of the list of the various measures necessary. Otherwise the cost of the transition may be higher than planned.

Jacques Girard investigates the role of multilateral organisations in the transition to market economies in Eastern European countries.

The macroeconomic imbalances and heavy debt burden of these economies have only become apparent recently, since they were not seen as being in deep economic crisis before and the central challenge was that of structural reform. However, heavy foreign and domestic debts became apparent in the late 1980s, as a result of lax monetary policies, not corresponding with the countries' reduced real growth. The authorities responded with partial reforms, which only accentuated the imbalances. Inflation accelerated, there were massive shortages and a lack of positive supply responses.

The current question is how to implement a reform programme which will encourage efficient responses and limit output decline. Price liberalisation can lead to the chain effect of enterprise failures, without resulting in the survival of competitive enterprises. It should, therefore, be combined with macroeconomic stabilisation measures. The danger of monopolistic price-setting can be avoided through the opening-up of these countries to international trade. This requires convertibility of the currency and elimination of all trade barriers. Their economies should be liberalised through privatisation and the demonopolisation of large enterprises. Furthermore, their infrastructures should be modernised, their energy sectors restructured and their environment rehabilitated. Domestic capital will not be sufficient to finance investment needs so external capital will be essential.

Poland and Hungary have already embarked on this path. Poland introduced radical stabilisation measures: liberalisation of prices and trade, introduction of currency convertibility, a tough monetary policy and institutional changes. Before stabilisation Poland experienced high unemployment and hyperinflation; through the stabilisation package shortages have been eliminated, inflation has been greatly reduced and a trade surplus (net of oil) was achieved in 1990. Privatisation, however, has been delayed and unemployment remains high.

Hungary launched a gradual reform plan. The authorities referred to the economic reform under way for the past twenty years to justify their preference for a gradual approach over a shock therapy. However, recent events prove that the gradual approach is even more difficult to implement, due to social and structural impediments.

To this can be added severe external disturbances: the Gulf crisis and the Comecon price reform. Since 1991, trade between former Comecon countries is settled in convertible currencies. This, together with the rise in oil prices, has substantially increased import costs and further stressed the need for financial and structural support from multilateral organisations. Drastic changes will be needed in the energy sector, which should be redesigned taking real costs and dependency into account. More attention should also be given to the environment in this respect.

The IMF took the lead in assisting these countries. An agreement with the IMF on a stabilisation plan was made conditional for help from other institutions. Such a condition avoids external assistance being diverted from its original goal and assures efficient allocation of multilateral funding resources. It was also necessary to achieve some coordination without heavy procedures, taking into consideration the dimension of the problem and the availability of resources.

James Larkin gives a broad view of the events which were hallmarks for Europe in 1990.

A cohesive strategy for restructuring the economies of Eastern European countries is still missing, due to insufficient understanding of the general environment in the East and of its political diversity, the focus on the cost of German unification, the EC's internal market focus and the crisis among Western banks. It is certain that the moves towards European unification hold a powerful attraction for Eastern European countries, but resources currently dedicated to the internal market should not be reallocated to the East. Moreover, an immediate opening of the EC market to the East would jeopardise West European integration and political stability in the long run.

However, the danger of doing nothing is even greater: it could lead to the re-emergence of ethnic divisions, the split-up of Europe and a flood of West-bound immigrants. The West should therefore urgently help these countries in their return to market economies. By developing local capital markets, banks' balance sheets should be freed from the old bad loans and new capital should be injected. Western capital should be used to finance regional projects rather than local ones.

The initiatives taken so far are small compared to the problems. The funds tend to be given to individual governments and local projects rather than to regions as a whole. The Atlantic partners should therefore work out an Atlantic plan of aid to Eastern Europe as one unit. As Western banks are very cautious about the East, due to the debt crisis and the current unfavourable climate, they could play a major role in providing technical expertise and education. Once these preconditions are met, private capital can flow in.

Hartmut Amberger specifically discusses the strategy of the Dresdner Bank towards the former GDR. One year after the fall of the Berlin Wall, Dresdner Bank already has 107 offices in the former GDR, employing 4500 persons. However, this step was not easy to take as events developed rapidly and, at each stage, a lot of uncertainties remained. The decision to open offices was based upon economic, strategic and also historic reasons: Dresdner Bank having originally been founded in the East German city of Dresden. A systematic market preparation was conducted shortly after the Wall fell and, later, a collation of all statistical and quantifiable information on the former GDR. The result was rather depressing in the economic, structural, environmental and social fields. The country was in the grip of a monopolistic state distribution receipt mentality, with a massively inefficient administrative apparatus.

Of the different alternatives for the establishment of a distribution structure, Dresdner Bank chose to build up its own new offices on the one hand and take over parts of Deutsche Kreditbank's network, the former state-owned corporate bank, on the other. But Dresdner did not take the old commitments over from its acquisition.

A definitive target group strategy is at present not possible in the former GDR. In the field of personal banking, the full range of services has to be offered. In corporate banking the accent is laid on privatisation, reorganisation of state-owned companies and the setting up of new businesses. The same situation is applicable to product strategy. East Germany has some specific products which are not known in the West, but even more Western banking products are unknown in the East. What can be expected from market surveys is a clearer view of the demand for durable consumer goods and property financing.

In fact, the practical problems are perhaps the most difficult to overcome when implanting a strategy. The lack of skilled personnel, suitable technical equipment, housing and infrastructure pose enormous obstacles. Nevertheless, Amberger expects a break-even on investment in two to three years.

Notes

1.   See the contribution of Muldur. For a survey of the empirical literature, see Clark (1988); the difficulty of determining an optimal size for banks is discussed in Artus and Pollin (1990).

2.   However, the UK placed restrictions on the use of sterling for financing Third World trade in 1957, the US imposed the interest-rate equalisation tax in 1963 (discouraging foreign borrowers from issuing securities in the US) and a voluntary Foreign Credit Restraint Programme inhibited lending to foreign entities. Only by 1974 were these measures and administrative guidelines removed and the withholding tax levied on non-resident bondholders was abolished in 1984. In the UK exchange controls were removed only in 1979. In Germany restrictions on capital inflows, i.e., authorisation requirements, were gradually removed in the 1980s.

3.   For more details, see Steinherr (1990).

4.   Mutual penetration is also facilitated by the fact that regulatory restrictions of capital participations by banks only apply to the non-financial industry. Whether a concentration of banking and insurance is desirable from an anti-trust point of view remains an open question.

5.   For extensive discussion of these problems, see the chapter by Steinherr and Huveneers.

6.   In principle, Articles 85 and 86 of the Treaty of Rome could be applied to banking. However, market dominance, abuse of a dominant position and trade restrictive behaviour are concepts that are particularly difficult to apply empirically to banking.

7.   This section draws on Steinherr and Gilibert (1989).

References

Artus, P. and **Pollin. J. P.** (1990), 'Les effets de la règlementation et le comportement des banques', in D.E. Fair and C. de Boissieu, *Financial Institutions in Europe Under New Competitive Conditions,* Dordrecht: Kluwer Academic Press.

Black, F. (1975), 'Bank funds management in an efficient market', *Journal of Financial Economics,* No.2.

Clark, J. A. (1988), 'Economies of scale and scope at depository financial institutions: a review of the literature', *Economic Review Federal Reserve Bank of Kansas City,* September/October.

Johnson, H. G. (1973), 'Problems of European Monetary Union', reprinted as Chapter 12 in *Further Essays in Monetary Economics,* Cambridge, MA: Harvard University Press.

Steinherr, A. (1990), 'Financial innovation, internationalisation, deregulation and market integration in Europe: Why does it all happen now?', in Fair and de Boissieu, *Financial Institutions in Europe Under New Competitive Conditions,* Dordrecht: Kluwer Academic Press.

Steinherr, A. and **Gilibert, P. L.** (1989), 'The Impact of Financial Market Integration on the European Banking Industry', Centre for European Policy Studies (CEPS), Brussels, Research Report No.1.

PART ONE

THE CHANGING SCOPE FOR EUROPEAN BANKING

CHAPTER TWO

Economies of scale and scope in national and global banking markets[1]

Ugur Muldur

1. The fundamental problems of the literature

The international literature on returns to scale in banking has been dominated by American studies. There are several reasons for this, including the development of theories of industrial economics and of banking regulation and the establishment by the US Federal authorities of a database (FCA) for the study of banking costs, giving economists access to detailed information on the direct and indirect costs of each banking service. However, the most important reason is the preponderant role of competition policy in banking in the United States.

In Europe and Japan, public competition policy based on the 'structure–behaviour–performance' paradigm has never been fully applied to banking. European and Japanese regulatory bodies have always taken a softer line on concentration and diversification in banking than their American counterparts, on several grounds: the small size of their home markets, the need for banks big enough to mobilise huge amounts of capital for public and private financial needs and considerations of monetary policy.

In the United States, anti-trust policy was applied very early in the banking and financial sectors. A body of legislation on interbank competition was gradually built up and the general rules of competition were adapted to suit these sectors' special needs. Industrial organisation theory applied to banking was in part developed to provide arguments for or against the use of anti-trust policy in the financial service sector. The first American studies on scale returns in banking appeared at a time when this policy was being much more severely applied, through the bank holding company and bank merger laws of 1956 and 1960.

1.1 THE CHOICE OF BANKING MODEL IS NOT NEUTRAL

The first microeconomic studies of banking from this period use very simple models and resemble ratio-based analyses. However, each study adopts a different indicator of banking output.

Thus, from the outset, the problem arose of defining and measuring the input and output of the industry. This problem persisted as the banking literature developed over the next thirty years. Nor is it simply a specialist problem, because each definition of input and output carries with it a particular set of banking concepts. These fall into three main groups.[2]

The production approach, which dominated the literature until the beginning of the 1980s, was one in which a bank was defined as a producer of two types of services: collection of funds (current accounts, deposit accounts, bonds) and uses of funds (commercial loans, mortgage loans, shares). From the point of view of their cost, all these services are considered separate outputs.

The unit of measurement in models based on this approach can only be the number of accounts administered, as opposed to their value in monetary terms. The problem raised by the cumulation of bank accounts of widely differing sizes is considered minor, especially as one can partly cure it by introducing proper output homogeneity variables. The exclusion of interest charges from the analysis, however, is harder to justify, in view of their increasing importance in the cost-structure of American banks (Benston, Hanweck and Humphrey, 1982a). If one completely excludes banking charges, only operating costs are left in analyses based on the production approach, and these costs depend essentially on the two main factors of production: labour and capital.

The main problem with the production approach is that the management of a bank's assets is treated as independent of that of its liabilities. This assumption is undermined by the portfolio approach, which shows that, in view of the varying maturities and holding periods of bank capital, decisions about the management of assets and liabilities cannot be taken independently. On the other hand, the portfolio approach has contributed little to the theory of the banking industry because, as Sealey and Lindley have pointed out, 'the determination of scale size of the institution is virtually ignored, and asset and liability decisions are hypothesized to be made independently of scale operation'.

As a reaction to the two preceding approaches, the intermediation approach, which brings in the management of deposits as a production constraint, reappeared towards the end of the 1980s. Considering financial intermediation as an essential banking function, this approach includes a third input, namely deposits. As a result, not only operating costs are to be taken into account, but also the interest charges which make it possible to collect this third input. Output is then measured in value terms and no longer by the number of accounts managed by the bank.

As noted by Benston, Hanweck and Humphrey (1982a and b), 'since the intermediation approach takes account of operating costs and interest charges, it is preferable to the production approach in an analysis which includes competitiveness. A competitive firm will minimise its total costs whatever its output.' Nonetheless, this approach has a number of theoretical and empirical flaws. Not only are we back to the debate about whether deposits lead to credits or vice versa, but it is very hard to justify reducing a bank's financial input to its deposits or its borrowed funds.

Every financial institution is permanently involved in a choice between several kinds of financial resource (deposits, mandatory and interbank loans), depending on the going rates. It may also seek to increase its capital in order to

.

strengthen its own resources. Taking account of only one form of financial resource – deposits – is therefore a very reductive approach. On the other hand, a broader definition of the third input – liabilities – is likely to cause major problems. The necessary equalisation of total liabilities and total assets means that the volume of output is strictly related to that of financial input and so it is also necessary to calculate the cost of a bank's own funds.

A fourth approach, called the transactional cost approach, was suggested by Benston and Smith (1976). This approach, rarely used by specialists, also poses real problems for modelling and quantitative evolution in banking.

In short, the different models of banking behaviour pose problems of their own. Until these problems have been solved, the choice of approach should reflect the activity of each type of banking institution and its specific regulations.

1.2   THE CHOICE OF PRODUCTION FUNCTION

This question also runs through the literature on scale returns in banking. The Cobb–Douglas, CES and translog production functions have all enjoyed prominence. But here again, it is difficult to find a consensus in the research carried out in the US and Europe.

The problems with the use of the Cobb–Douglas function are well known. Recently, moreover, its use has begun to die out, for two reasons: the invariability of scale returns as a measure of output level, and the impossibility of taking account of the joint nature of some costs. The first shortcoming was partly remedied by the introduction of size-indicator variables; but the second led to the Cobb–Douglas function being abandoned in favour of a more flexible one because it inherently denies all possibility of joint costs.

The use of the translog production function has solved the problems of the Cobb–Douglas function, but these new models themselves have a number of shortcomings and the results are not always reliable. Kim (1985) mentions three: the translog function is undefined at point 0, and major problems arise both from the grouping together of different outputs in a composite output index and from the endogeneity of outputs likely to be increased by deregulation.

The lack of analytic accounting data on the different banking services are as widely separated as possible, and the rather small sample of financial institutions, especially in Europe, pose almost insuperable obstacles for econometric research. Moreover, one must avoid makeshift econometric adjustments tending to favour one outcome or another. As Benston, Hanweck and Humphrey point out (1982a or b), 'any result showing economies of scope can lead to the opposite conclusion if a sufficiently small μ is chosen'.[3]

Thus, both the Cobb–Douglas and translog specifications raise problems. Clark (1988) and Kilbride and Miller (1984) defined a particular version of the generalised functional form in which all the variables are transformed by a 'Box and Cox' procedure and came to the conclusion that the Cobb–Douglas specification of banking costs gave a better grasp of the data. More recently, Lawrence (1989) has shown that the rejection of the variables' supposedly flexible functional form is a necessary but not sufficient condition for the use of the Cobb–Douglas function in the banking industry.

In the face of this theoretical debate, researchers must be rigorous and test all the available specifications, and, finally, compare their results, before claiming to observe economies of scale or scope.

2. The main results of US research

The first American studies claimed to find substantial economies of scale (Schweiger and McGee, 1961), mainly arising from a more efficient use of labour (Horvitz, 1962; Gramley, 1962).

Two studies by Benston published in 1965 mark a turning-point in research into scale returns in banking. Going beyond the technical improvement of existing approaches,[4] Benston (1965a and b) introduces the time factor. This important factor was ignored by Benston's successors, until Humphrey's forceful reminder (1987) that regulatory changes significantly affect banks' cost structures.

Benston noted that the growth of demand deposits led to small economies of scale in 1959, but growing ones in 1960, 1961 and 1962, thus showing the possibility of rapid fluctuations from one year to another. In general, he argued, large banks derive a competitive advantage from deposits and from administering mortgages and securities activities (while the making of loans to industry, for example, is not a profitable activity in terms of cost). Benston therefore concluded that real, if minimal, economies of scale were present in the management of US banks' assets and liabilities alike. From this he deduced that the size variable alone cannot explain large banks' advantages over small ones. In fact, large banks gain by being able to employ specialised managers, but this is cancelled out by the high cost of coordinating the activities of the different branches and specialised services.

The theoretical and empirical contributions of Benston (1972), Bell and Murphy (1968) (the so-called BBM model) were the most valuable of their time. They opened up a new field of investigation – banks' cost-efficiency seen according to their organisational structure, whether they be branch banks, unit (i.e., single-agency) banks or banks affiliated with holding companies. Three conclusions emerge from these studies. First, the cost functions of the three types of banks are very different. Second, the number of branches does not significantly affect deposit services' production costs where the same output level is involved. Third, branch banks are more cost efficient than the single-agency variety, with the definition and the choice of banking output being the determining factors in the calculation of costs. Affiliation with holding companies, on the other hand, makes it possible to bring costs down (Longbrake and Johnson, 1974; Longbrake and Haslem, 1975; Mullineaux, 1975).

A last group of studies may be mentioned, which differs from its predecessors in terms of methodology rather than results (Greenbaum, 1967a and b; Powers,

1969; Schweitzer, 1972). These authors adopt a U-shaped average-cost function, which stipulates that the optimal position of constant returns will be preceded by increasing returns and succeeded by decreasing returns. Through its methodology, this group of authors foreshadowed the third, post-1975 stage of theoretical research, in which translogarithmic functions were introduced in order to reproduce a similar pattern of returns.

Greenbaum (1976a) occupies a special place in this group. He seems to have been the first to try to go beyond the dominant microeconomic framework and build bridges between banking and financial economics. He also went against the prevailing view that concentration of activity in banking was a brake on competitiveness. In this he was the precursor of a strain of thinking which has recently developed in the USA, which analyses concentration as a direct consequence of the high performance of efficient banks.

One general conclusion emerges from this research: economies of scale are present in the American banking industry, ranging from 3 per cent to 7 per cent and varying according to the bank's internal organisation. Benston, Hanweck and Humphrey arrived at the same conclusion in their synthesis of the Cobb–Douglas studies: 'A consensus emerges from retrospective research into banking costs that there are constant economies of scale irrespective of the size of bank.' On the eve of the great wave of deregulation, this conclusion was very significant, because according to the theories of the time it implied a potential monopoly. Only regulation prevented a level of concentration in banking which would prove damaging to customers' interests.

At the end of the 1970s this conclusion began to come under fire on both theoretical and methodological grounds and by the 1980s was seriously held in doubt. The first frontal attack came from Baumol (1977), who showed that economies of scale were neither a necessary nor a sufficient condition to prove the existence of a monopoly in a multiproduct industry. Banking was such an industry; so it was necessary to introduce new indicators in the analysis of banking costs. The main purpose of these indicators was to determine whether monopoly was a natural outcome of unregulated market forces. Since scale returns by themselves were an inadequate pointer, economies of scope or joint production were added, the source of the latter being the combined use of the same inputs to produce different goods or services. The analysis of these two indicators should suffice. However, it was subsequently shown that they did not in fact suffice to prove a potential monopoly; only the subadditivity of the cost function was a necessary and sufficient condition (Baumol, Panzar and Willig, 1988). Sub-additivity is an indicator of monopoly insofar as it allows one to see whether it is more expensive for two (or more) banks to provide a given volume of output than to do so via a single organisation. Bailey and Friedlander (1982) stress the complementary aspect of these indicators: 'The concepts of economies of scale, of scope, of sub-additivity and contestability together allow a better understanding of the structure and behaviour of multiproduct industries.'

The theory of contestable markets is not only an attempt to define a monopoly with the help of sub-additivity, but also a comment on monopoly in the case of a multiproduct industry. More precisely, if monopoly or oligopoly represents the most efficient way to organise an industry, is it possible to fight off their negative effects, such as the tendency to collusion? Is there such a thing as a 'good' monopoly?

The theory of contestable markets brings a theoretical solution to this problem. Briefly, it maintains that one must avoid collusion and price-manipulation by facilitating the entry of new competitors employing hit-and-run tactics into a market without entry barriers or sunk costs. The fear of new arrivals prevents the monopoly from using its price-fixing capacity to increase its gains at consumers' expense. Thus one can obtain results similar to those obtained under conditions of perfect competition even with a monopoly or oligopoly.

This revolutionary theoretical advance, of course, was bound to be of interest to the banking world, which (rightly or wrongly) had long been accused of taking advantage of its oligopolistic position. The recent evolution of banking, moreover, has also absorbed the lessons of theory. Competition in banking has intensified these past few years following the progressive abolition of regulatory or technological barriers.

The introduction of the translog model in empirical research in banking coincided with a reversal of previous results. In the great majority of recent studies adopting the output or intermediation approach and using the translog function, either the presence or the absence of economies of scale is observed for a very low level of output – always lower than $100m, and sometimes as low as $25m (Benston, Hanweck and Humphrey, 1982b; Benston, Berger, Hanweck and Humphrey, 1983; Gilligan, Smirlock and Marshall, 1984b; Berger, Hanweck and Humphrey, 1987; Humphrey, 1987). Studies of savings and loans and credit unions come to more or less the same conclusion (Murray and White, 1983; Le Compte and Smith, 1985; Mester, 1987b). The average cost function in these studies is U-shaped but the optimal size is very small. These results amount to an economic condemnation of large banks.

In order to explain the viability of large banks, some economists have sought economies of scope which would make up for diseconomies of scale. Others have found that economies of scale are sometimes balanced out by the disadvantages of diversification. Shaffer (1985), in his research on unit banks, notes:

> Larger banks tend to have lower average costs than smaller ones, all else equal, regardless of the size range. However, the patterns of observed specialisation have compensated for the cost handicap of smaller banks: unless the regression equation corrects for specialisation, constant returns to scale are found, as we should expect from the historical coexistence of banks of many sizes.
>
> (p. 468)

Recent studies, however, with a few exceptions (Gilligan, Smirlock and Marshall, 1984a and b), point either to a lack of evidence or to diseconomies of scope once a very small size is exceeded (Benston, Berger, Hanweck and Humphrey, 1983; Mester, 1987b; Lawrence and Shay, 1986; Berger, Hanweck and Humphrey, 1987).

The first studies dealing with the problem of sub-additivity date from the beginning of the 1980s (SEC, 1981; Gilligan, Smirlock and Marshall, 1984b). Though more numerous today, studies of this subject still suffer from two major defects. First, the authors do not check that the sufficient condition defined above is fulfilled. They replace transconvexity and concavity analysis, which are difficult to verify, by another cost indicator which is easier to calculate. The practice nevertheless leads to an endless quarrel between researchers who accuse each other of not respecting the sufficient condition determined by mathematicians. Some have attempted to camouflage their methods by introducing an intermediate indicator. The sufficient condition of sub-additivity is finally reduced to the checking of the traditional indicators of returns to scale and scope economies; but these indicators are neither a sufficient nor even a necessary condition of sub-additivity.

In any case, the checking of these properties requires knowledge of the origin and context of the cost function. Baumol (1977) insists on this crucial point: 'Proving sub-additivity requires knowledge of the form of the cost function from its origin to the level of output studied; this involves drawing on data which might be outside the information base.' However, with the translogarithmic model undefined at point 0, the problems mentioned above re-emerge. In short, the American literature does not provide us with evidence of economies of scale or scope, or indeed of sub-additivity in banking costs.

3. European studies of scale and scope

From the end of the 1960s to the beginning of the 1970s a wave of industrial and banking mergers engulfed European economies. Governments' policies of championing their own market leaders aided firms' internal and external growth and spurred on their internationalisation. The banking sector was caught up in this movement. The first deregulatory steps, which concerned the opening of new branches, exchange controls and the borderline between commercial and investment banks, were taken in a number of European countries. Banking mergers and acquisitions occurred in the great majority of national systems.

During the 1970s, the first studies of economies of scale began to appear (Maes, 1975; Lévy-Garboua and Lévy-Garboua, 1975; Lévy-Garboua and Renard, 1977). All the empirical studies of this period adopted the production approach, or a hybrid form of it, largely because of the absence of information on the number of accounts or cheques. In some instances comparison of size indicators led to a focus on the capital involved instead of the number of accounts, total assets or deposits (Lévy-Garboua and Renard, 1977). The most commonly-used specification was the log-linear form of the Cobb–Douglas function. The influence of the American BBM model was evident.

However, the first European studies attempted to adapt this approach to the particular conditions and structure of each banking market. For example, Lévy-Garboua and Renard, writing on the growing size and autonomy of interbank operations in France, divide their study into two parts: retail and corporate operations and treasury and interbank operations. This division is based on an estimate of the profitability of each of these activities. They conclude, moreover, that, by comparison with retail and corporate operations, 'effects of scale are less significant for the profitability of treasury operations, which largely depends on banks' employment and re-source structures' (p. 69). This point is taken up by Muldur and Sassenou (1990), who introduce the structure of banks' liabilities as a homogeneity variable in their model.

While all the French and Italian studies of this period observe substantial economies of scale, that by Lévy-Garboua and Lévy-Garboua (1975) is notable be-cause its analysis is time-series based (1950–71). The authors conclude, moreover, that 'over an extended period, operating unit costs for French banks decreased; con-siderable productivity gains were made by relative reductions in staff and a better distribution of responsibility; a certain critical mass must be attained before it becomes profitable to set up a branch' (p. 81).

These authors' analysis suggests that the more accounts held in the French banking system, the greater the average savings on the cost of each account. How-ever, during the 1970s the total number of cheques and bank accounts more than doubled while their average cost remained the same. During the 1980s, the French banking profession united in condemning this anomaly as a major source of the in-crease in their operating costs. This shows that over the long term the macroecon-omic relationship between size and costs was not at all borne out on the microeconomic level.

The fact is that the chronological basis of Lévy-Garboua and Lévy-Garboua's study did not allow a cross-section of banking customers to be examined, so that the traditional indicators of economies of scale in relation to banks' size could not be assessed. Moreover, as the authors acknowledge, 'the problem with this his-torical study is that it is unable to eliminate the differences in operating costs due to monetary policy or inflation'. Another study (Lévy-Garboua and Renard, 1977), this time firmly microeconomic and cross-sectional, complemented the preceding one. This study, testing the hypothesis of similar behaviour for all banks rather than the stability of their behaviour over time, confirmed the substantial economies of scale in French banking. In fact, the economies of scale observed in intermediation activities were about 30–50 per cent – ten times those observed in the American research of the time. This difference could be explained by the differences in structure in the two banking markets and by the characteristics of the Cobb–Douglas model used, al-though despite a considerable increase in banking activity French banks' average operating costs did not subsequently go down.

However, the fact that the findings of this research were not borne out by events does not rule out the possibility of economies of scale in French banking at this time, since many regulatory, monetary and salary rigidities still in existence may have prevented the banks from fully exploiting economies of scale. In Italy, for example, the strict regulations on opening new branches were justified with the argu-ment that research had revealed substantial economies of scale which could increase the concentration of the Italian banking market.

The only empirical study of this time which pointed to diseconomies of scale in large banking institutions was that on Belgium by Maes (1975). Maes' findings were later substantiated by studies using both the Cobb–Douglas and translog specifi-cation (Pacolet, 1986; Pacolet and Verheirstraeten, 1981). The large Belgian banks seem to have exhausted their domestic room for development very quickly, reaching a size far greater than the Belgian market allowed. As Pacolet (1986) remarks:

> In particular, banks and savings banks can be represented by a similar U-shaped charge curve, where the big banks and perhaps the biggest public credit institutions have grown too large, with the result that they lose their cost-efficiency, their development slows down, and their market share diminishes, in favour of medium-sized establishments which have attained their optimal size.
>
> (p. 497)

This situation also explains the early diversification and internationalisation of Belgian banks, relative to their European counterparts, as a means to improve their falling performances. Moreover, studies of these banks' profit functions confirm that diseconomies of operating costs do not have direct repercussions on banking profits (Pacolet, 1986). Specialists find economies of scale in the Belgian banking system of the 1970s, with the exception of a few large banks (Pacolet and Verheirstraeten, 1981).

The first Italian studies of the 1970s showed substantial economies of scale in the banking sector. These studies also adopted the production approach, often in a modified form because of the absence of sufficiently reliable statistics to establish a physical output indicator, and used total assets and number of branches as indicators of banks' size. In general, moreover, they noted that substantial economies of scale tended to disappear with an increase in branches. Such studies only strengthened the views of the national regulatory bodies, who maintained their barriers to entry to the domestic banking market.

Recent empirical research in Italy, finding somewhat smaller economies of scale than in the preceding decade, comes to very different conclusions (Lanciotti and Reganelli, 1988; Prometeia, 1989; Onado, 1989). Yet the dominant methodology remains much the same: the intermediation approach and the translog model are rarely used. The wide variations observed in the conditions for banks' cost efficiency makes it impossible for the authors to claim that one size of bank is superior to others. Focusing on the optimality of Italian banks' size, they assert that this factor cannot be analysed independently of the level of risk faced by each bank.

Small banks' higher vulnerability to risks leads certain authors (Prometeia, 1989; Onado, 1989) to ask whether the stability and efficiency of the banking system would not gain from a relaxation of competition policy, especially towards mergers and acquisitions, which would make it possible for less efficient and more risk prone banks to be weeded out. In addition, Onado's findings based on his Cobb–Douglas model lead him to the conclusion that cost and price efficiency are interlinked. The question arises from this whether the slight economies in operating costs (about 3 per cent) which Onado observes would not be balanced out, as in France, by diseconomies of financial costs. The latter are supposed to be identical for all Italian banks by virtue of the competition prevailing on the market. Nevertheless, Italian studies also lack empirical evidence to support the view that the larger and more diversified banks are the efficient ones. Onado wonders whether

> from this point of view, one can suppose that the effects of European competition, involving different regulatory frameworks, different economic

and financial situations of individual banks, can be even more complex
and not so close to the sort of promised land [which] the European
markets of the 1990s are supposed to be.

(p. 105)

In France, two series of studies reaching completely opposite conclusions appeared at the end of the 1980s. Dietsch (1990 a and b) carried out an analysis of a mixed sample of 243 local, national commercial and savings banks. Using the translog function and analysing both operating costs and total costs (including interest costs), Dietsch found an elasticity 'of bank costs with respect to total output' of 0.96 in the former case and 0.95 in the latter. He concluded that 'on the basis of these results, concerning economies of scale, the competitive viability of small banks is not guaranteed for the future'. After noting that the pairs of products (deposits/loans, loans/investments, loans/interbank activity and investment/interbank activity) have negative coefficients, he deduces the presence of economies of scope. He concludes: 'For the French banking industry, our results tend to demonstrate that universal banking gives an advantage compared to specialisation and that competition between banks in the future must be analysed on the ground of the imperfect competition theory' (Dietsch, 1990a, p. 26).

The econometric results of Dietsch's research, however, do not entirely support his conclusions. The main problem is that the author failed to carry out any tests on the parameters of scale and scope. The elasticities are very close to unity. A slightly higher standard deviation would be enough to draw a conclusion opposite to Dietsch's, namely that there are no economies of scale, as other recent studies have claimed (Muldur and Sassenou, 1990; Sassenou, 1990).

These studies are not without their critics either. Their attempts at achieving homogeneity reduce the initial sample from 129 to 59 commercial banks, which makes it essential to interpret the results with caution as far as size is concerned. Using Cobb–Douglas and translog specifications, the authors arrive at three conclusions. First, operating-cost economies exist for branch banks, but tend to diminish over time. Second, since economies of total costs are balanced out by diseconomies of financial costs, scale returns are constant in French banking. Third, complementarity exists only for certain pairs of products, suggesting reciprocal compensation for economies of scope in cases of highly developed diversification.

However, the diseconomies of financial costs noted by these authors do not derive from the fact that big banks remunerate deposits better than their smaller rivals. This is not a price effect, but the effect of banks' accounting structures. The proportion of a bank's low-cost resources diminishes as the bank increases in size. It is well known that large banks operate more intensively on the securities and interbank markets. Since the rates prevailing on the markets are generally higher than the return on deposits, the average cost of large banks' liabilities increases out of proportion to their size. Thus it is a structural effect.

It is interesting to note that recent Belgian studies (Pacolet, 1986) also insist on this possibility of reciprocal compensation for the different economies of costs. The large Belgian banks, in fact, seem to achieve diseconomies of operating costs which are partially offset by gains in terms of financial costs. The small Belgian market may explain the larger Belgian banks' proliferation of domestic branches. This loss of efficiency in operating costs appears to be partly offset by the large banks which, taking advantage of their widespread branches, offer rather lower deposit rates than their small and medium rivals. Pacolet also notes that the use of the Cobb–Douglas function does not make it possible to discern the diseconomies of scale shown up by the translog function for large Belgian banks.

4. Economies of scale and scope in Japan

In Japan studies of economies of scale and scope are a very recent phenomenon. The surveys by Kasuya (1986) and Nakajima and Yoshioka (1987) tend to refer to the American literature and adapt its model to the economic and regulatory conditions of Japanese banks. Tachibanaki, Mitsui and Kitagawa (1990) adopt the production approach and translog specification. In their two-output model (credit and other services), they stress Japanese banks' shareholdings in industrial firms, which amount to 40 per cent of the shares quoted on the Tokyo Stock Exchange. This feature is reminiscent of German 'universal banks', but unlike their German counterparts, Japanese banks are not able to engage directly in share dealings.

In their analysis of 1985, 1986 and 1987, Tachibanaki *et al.* perceive economies of scale of about 20 per cent. They note that economies of scale and scope grow in line with positive indications for the banks' shareholdings. This suggests that the efficiency of Japanese banks is closely linked to the state of the stockmarkets. Moreover, contrary to the situation in certain Western countries, Japanese economies of scale grew each year from 1985 to 1987; and complementarity between the two outputs, that is to say economies of scope, appears only in 1985. This suggests that the technical efficiency of the big Japanese banks has been increasing daily.

If interest-rate fluctuations are kept down, as Osano and Tsutsui (1965) suggest, thanks to implicit agreements between banks and their customers, there is no doubt that Japanese banks gain an extra advantage in cost and risk terms over their Western counterparts. In the next section, however, I shall show that, given different banking models, it is difficult to transfer the results of research into banking efficiency from one country to another.

5. The non-transferability of results

In Europe frequent reference is made to American empirical studies to justify the presence (rarely the opposite) of economies of scale and/or scope on national or EC-wide banking markets. This practice may be justifiable for industry, but is dubious for services, especially financial services, whose products are not subject to industry's physical constraints. Instantaneous production and distribution and non-durability make banking highly subject to demand and regulation. The cost and distribution of financial services are directly influenced by prices related to factors of production, but also by customers' behaviour and geographical dispersion, by regulation and prudential rules, by risks and by general macroeconomic conditions. This makes it impossible to transfer the results of studies of costs from one industry or country to another, as a few examples will show.

For the whole range of financial services offered to consumers and small and medium-sized firms, the extent and configuration of the banking network is first and foremost a function of the size of the markets and the customers' geographical dispersion. These factors vary enormously from one country to another. A bank established in Britain or Belgium will cover two-thirds of the domestic market by setting up its network in the capital and one or two other large towns. On the other hand, banks in bigger countries with greater demographic dispersion will find the management of their networks more expensive, with few economies of scale, because of the more irregular flow of banking activities per branch.

Setting interbank competition according to quality or proximity can lead to a needless proliferation of branches, where the volume and regularity of demand per branch will diminish because of the lower switching costs. Where different regulations govern the opening of branches, international comparisons of economies of scale demand, to say the least, a great deal of imagination.

Now, if there is one point on which European and American studies agree, it is that restrictions on opening branches have a considerable negative impact on economies of scale (Bruno and Eakin, 1990). Differences in regulatory conditions also in part explain why it is possible to find economies of scale in Italy, or their gradual disappearance from France after the hectic development of the mid-1970s, or economies of operating costs in Belgium and Luxembourg, both of which are saturated with banking branches. The effects of regulation and monetary policy, however, do not stop there. International divergences on prudential rules (risk and solvency ratios) or monetary policy (reserves, credit controls and interest-rate ceilings) or fiscal regimes, all modify banks' cost structures and make it impossible to compare national or local findings on economies of scale or scope.

Differences in savings rates or demography, and the evolution of interest rates and the needs of public and private financing observed in Western countries, also have differing effects on banking costs. The same applies to the different ways of managing banks' human resources. The variable element of salaries (i.e., premiums and commissions) paid to US bank employees is much bigger than in European banks. The latter also face greater constraints on reducing staff numbers when business conditions require it. Hence it is more difficult for European banks to tie their salary costs to performance. This leads them on occasion to seek greater flexibility in staff deployment through the internal and overseas expansion of their networks. But this cannot be achieved without extra costs, notably in staff training and mobility. These factors making for difficulty in comparing research findings are compounded by differences in accounting, consolidation and investment as practised by international banks.

Finding a neutral size indicator also becomes extremely difficult. Where total assets are chosen, the average costs of Japanese, German and French banks will be underestimated for different reasons. The scale of interbank activity in France, and the industrial shareholdings of those in Germany and Japan, can lead to overestimates of their size and consequent underestimates of the average costs of their factors of production. The choice of a physical indicator like the number of accounts held or cheques issued leads to equally serious distortions. Finally, international banks' sectoral diversification and their cross subsidisation of prices and costs, owing to their different national origins, also make it difficult to compare their efficiency. In a banking network distributing services connected with, for example, insurance or tourism, the spread of fixed costs and of information differs from that in a specialised distribution network, again affecting assessment of economies of scale or scope.

As a result of this non-transferability of results, one can perceive economies of scale or scope in one country and not in another. This is likely to create distortions for international banking competition. Foreign banks' entry into a system marked by substantial economies of scale is made more difficult by the need for a larger optimal size than on other domestic markets. In countries with an absence of substantial economies of scale, foreign banks may enter with very slight sunk costs, enabling them to cream off the profits of long-established banks.

It is also the case, of course, that national findings cannot be transferred to the international context, so that an absence of economies of scale and scope on the national or local level does not imply their absence from the international level. Adopting a global strategy, banks could easily gain from the economic, regulatory and fiscal differences between countries to improve their productive efficiency or their financial performance. This means that they could borrow where rates are lowest and develop branches and cash dispensers/automated tellers according to salary costs and customer behaviour, or tailor their loan strategies to local demand. They could also minimise their costs while increasing their size on the international level. (As yet, however, this is only a hypothesis which needs to be tested in practice.)

6. Conclusions

A survey of the specialised literature only confirms the view expressed by Gilbert (1984) and Clark (1988) that there is no incontestable evidence of potential economies of scale and scope in the financial-service industry. However, a shift in the literature does occur in the 1980s, towards the view that economies of scale scarcely exist, or indeed that there are diseconomies. In addition to the technical or theoretical approaches outlined earlier in this chapter, changes in general technological and economic circumstances seem to have played a role in the shift of opinion.

As early as 1965, Benston ascribed changes in economies of scale from one year to the next to technological progress, pointing out that banks' unit costs went down in proportion to increases in their size, and that the bigger banks were also the most advanced in the application of new technology. Bell and Murphy (1968) drew attention to changes in the organisation of work in banking and suggested that the use of information technology was making some explanatory models appear out of date. This led to further studies of the impact of technology on costs and deposit-taking, which concluded that the use of information technology was only economically worthwhile in big banks with their large volume of accounts. Hunter and Timme (1986) found that technological change had a positive influence for economies of operating costs in the period 1976–82.

In the middle of the 1970s, the spread of new technology, particularly microelectronics, began to bring about enormous changes. The decreasing cost and increasing flexibility of microelectronic equipment enabled small banks to overcome their technological lag and enjoy equal access to this powerful source of economies of scale and scope (Metzker, 1982). Shared cash dispenser/automated teller networks, multibank credit cards and user-friendly databases have helped to erode the comparative advantage of large financial institutions.

It would, however, be an illusion to think that small and medium banks' viability is permanently assured. The progressive abolition of geographical and functional regulatory barriers seems to serve the interests of large banks at the expense of smaller ones. In France, for example, if the deposit market is completely deregulated, the big commercial banks will be able to use their economies of operating costs to increase their competitiveness in deposit-taking and to transform the constant returns to scale observed above by including interest costs in total costs. Obviously, if this happens the larger savings banks and local and regional banks will be penalised.

Humphrey (1990) stresses the combined effects of deregulation and technological change. He shows that American deregulation at the beginning of the 1980s had a negative impact on banking costs and turned technological change itself into a negative phenomenon. Small and medium-sized banks, he claims, were those which suffered most. Given the special character of financial services, the big international banks' gains from the globalisation of markets have outweighed the gains which smaller banks made from their adaptation to technological change.

In the current context of global financial markets and institutions, therefore, the question of economies of scale and scope is of major importance. Since there is no single controlling authority on world markets, and no harmonised competition policy concerning banking, one must ask whether the current wave of mergers and acquisitions will not lead to a cartel controlled by financial mega-conglomerates, instead of more competitive and stable markets. Market integration on the geographical and functional levels, in Europe and the world as a whole, accentuates the need for fresh thinking on a banking competition policy adapted to the new conditions.

Notes

1.   Translated by Peter Lomas.

2.   Other models of banking behaviour exist, but here I deal only with those used in studies of scale returns. For a more complete survey, see Santomero (1984).

3.   The translogarithm being undefined at point 0, the latter is replaced by a negligible quantity, usually m = 0,001.

4.   The analysis of banking output involves the study of several products, and logarithmic equations make it possible to compare costs according to the quantity, quality or growth of each product.

References and bibliography

Bailey E.E. and **Friedlander, F.A.** (1982), 'Market structure and multiproduct industries', *Journal of Economic Literature*, 20, September.

Baumol W.J. (1977) 'On the proper cost tests for natural monopoly in a multiproduct industry', *American Economic Review*, 67, December.

Baumol W.J., Panzar J.C. and **Willig, R.D.** (1988), *Contestable Markets and the Theory of Industry Structure*, rev. edn, New York: Harcourt Brace Jovanovich.

Bell F.W. and **Murphy, N.B.** (1968), 'Costs in commercial banking: a quantitative analysis of bank behaviour and its relation to bank regulation', Research Report 41, Federal Reserve Bank of Boston.

Benston G.J. (1965a), 'Economies of scale and marginal costs in banking operations', *National Banking Review*, 2, June.

Benston G.J. (1965b), 'Branch banking and economies of scale', *Journal of Finance*, 20, May.

Benston G.J. (1972), 'Economies of scale of financial institutions', *Journal of Money, Credit and Banking*, 4, May.

Benston G.J., Berger, A., Hanweck, G. and **Humphrey, D.** (1983), 'Economics of scale and scope in banking', Proceedings of a Conference on Banking Structure and Competition, Federal Reserve Bank of Chicago, May.

Benston G.J., Hanweck, G.A. and **Humphrey, D.B.** (1982a) 'Operating costs in commercial banking", *Federal Reserve Bank of Atlanta Economic Review*, November.

Benston G.J., Hanweck, G.A. and **Humphrey, D.B.** (1982b), 'Scale economies in banking: a restructuring and reassessment', *Journal of Money, Credit and Banking*, 14, November.

Benston, G.J. and **Smith, C. W.** (1976), 'A transaction cost approach to the theory of financial intermediation', *Journal of Finance*, 31 (1), March.

Berger A. N., Hanweck, G.A. and **Humphrey D.B.** (1987), 'Competitive viability in banking, scale, scope and product-mix economies', *Journal of Monetary Economics*, 20, May.

Bruno, M.J. and **Eakin, B.K.** (1990) 'Branching restrictions and banking costs', *Journal of Banking and Finance*, 14.

Clark, J.A. (1988), 'Economies of scale and scope at depository financial institutions: a review of the literature', *Federal Reserve Bank of Kansas City Economic Review*, 73 (8), September/October.

Dietsch, M. (1990a), 'Returns to scale and returns to scope in the French banking industry', paper presented at 3rd Franco-American Seminar, National Bureau for Economic Research, July.

Dietsch, M. (1990b), 'Economies d'échelle, économies d'envergure et structure des coûts dans les banques de dépôt françaises', Conseil National de Crédit et Association des banques françaises.

Gilbert, R.A. (1984), 'Bank market structure and competition: a survey', *Journal of Money, Credit and Banking*, 16, November.

Gilbert, R.A. and **Kalish, L.** (1973), 'An analysis of efficiency of scale and organisational form in commercial banking', *Journal of Industrial Economics*, 21, July.

Gilligan, T., Smirlock, M. and **Marshall, W.** (1984a), 'Scale and scope economies in the multi-product banking firm', *Journal of Monetary Economics*, 13.

Gilligan, T., Smirlock, M. and **Marshall, W.** (1984b), 'An empirical study of joint production and scale economies in commercial banking', *Journal of Banking and Finance*, 8.

Gramley, L.E. (1962), *A Study of Scale Economies in Banking*, Federal Reserve Bank of Kansas City.

Greenbaum, S.I. (1967a), 'Competition and efficiency in the banking system: empirical research and its policy implications', *Journal of Political Economy*, 75.

Greenbaum, S.I. (1967b), 'A study of bank costs', *National Banking Review*, 4, June.

Horvitz, P.M. (1962), *Economies of Scale in Banking in Private Financial Institutions*, Englewood Cliffs, NJ: Prentice-Hall.

Humphrey, D.B. (1987), 'Cost dispersion and the measurement of economies in banking', *Federal Reserve Bank of Richmond Economic Review*, 73, May/June.

Humphrey, D.B. (1990), 'Cost and technical change: effects from bank deregulation', paper presented at 3rd Franco-American Economic Seminar, NBER, July.

Hunter, W.C. and **Timme, S.G.** (1986), 'Technical change, organisational form and the structure of bank production', *Journal of Money, Credit and Banking*, 18 (2), May.

Kasuya, M. (1986), 'The theory of economies of scope and its application to the banking sector', *Kinyu Kenkyu*, 5 (3).

Kilbride, D.B. and **Miller, R.** (1984), 'A re-examination of economies of scale in banking using a generalised functional form', *Journal of Money, Credit and Banking*, 18, November.

Kim, M. (1985), 'Scale economies in banking: a methodological note', *Journal of Money, Credit and Banking*, 17, February.

Lanciotti, G. and **Reganelli, T.** (1988), 'Funzioni di costo e obiettivi di efficienza nella produzione bancaria', in *Banca d'Italia, Temi di Discussione del Servizio Studi*.

Lawrence, C. (1989), 'Banking costs, generalised functional forms and estimation of economics of scale and scope', *Journal of Money, Credit and Banking*, 21 (3), August.

Lawrence, C. and **Shay, R.** (1986), 'Technology and financial intermediation in a multi-product banking firm: an econometric study of US banks, 1979–1982' in C. Lawrence and R. Shay (eds), *Technological Innovation, Regulation and the Monetary Economy*, Cambridge, MA: Ballinger.

Le Compte, R. and **Smith, S.** (1985), 'An empirical analysis of scale and scope economies in the savings and loan industry', Texas Christian University and University of Florida Working Paper, September.

Lévy-Garboua, L. and **Lévy-Garboua, V.** (1975), 'Les coûts opératoires des banques françaises: une étude statistique', *Revue d'Economie Politique*, 80.

Lévy-Garboua, V. and **Renard, F.** (1977), 'Une étude statistique de la rentabilité des banques en France en 1974', *Cahiers Economiques et Monétaires*, 5.

Longbrake, W.A. and **Haslem, J.A.** (1975), 'Productive efficiency in commercial banking', *Journal of Money, Credit and Banking*, 7.

Longbrake, W.A. and **Johnson, M.K.** (1974), 'Economies of scale in banking', *Magazine of Bank Administration*, July.

Maes, M. (1975), 'Les économies de dimension dans le secteur bancaire belge', *Tijdschrift voor het Bankwezen*, 4.

Mester, L.J. (1987a) 'A multiproduct cost study of savings and loans', *Journal of Finance*, June.

Mester, L.J. (1987b) 'Efficient production of financial services: scale and scope economies', *Federal Reserve Bank of Atlanta Business Review*, January/February.

Metzker, P.H. (1982), 'Future payments system technology: can small financial institutions compete?', *Federal Reserve Bank of Atlanta Economic Review*, November.

Muldur, U. (1990), 'Jalons pour une analyse microéconomique des restructurations bancaires', in M. Humbert (ed.), *Investissement International et Dynamique de L'Economie Mondiale*, Paris: Economica.

Muldur U. et **Sassenou M.** (1990), 'Economies of scale and scope in French banking and saving institutions', *Journal of Productivity*, July.

Mullineaux, D.J. (1975), 'Economies of scale of financial institutions', *Journal of Monetary Economics*, 1, April.

Murray J. and **White, R.** (1983), 'Economies of scale and economies of scope in multi-product financial institutions: a study of British Columbian Credit Unions', *Journal of Finance*, 38, June.

Nakajima, T. and **Yoshioka, K.** (1987), 'Economies of scale in the Japanese banking industry', *Kinyu Kenyu*, 6 (2).

Onado, M. (1989), 'Competition in banking services and its implications: the Italian case', in C. De Boissieu and D.E. Fair (eds), *Financial Institutions in Europe under New Competitive Conditions*, Dordrecht: Kluwer Academic Press.

Osano, H. and **Tsutsui, Y.** (1965), 'Implicit contracts in the Japanese bank-loan market', *Journal of Finance*, 20.

Pacolet, J. (1986), 'Analyse d'économie sectorielle du marché des banques d'épargne' in A. Van Put (ed.), *Les Banques d'Epargne Belges*, Tielt: Lannoo.

Pacolet, J. and **Verheirstraeten, A.** (1981) 'Concentration and economies of scale in the Belgian financial sector', in A. Verheirstraeten (ed.), *Competition and Regulation in Financial Markets*, London.

Powers, J.A. (1969), 'Branch versus unit banking: output and cost economies', *Southern Economic Journal*, 36.

Prometeia (1989), 'La dimensione e l'articulazione delle aziende di credito ordinario: gli effetti sulla produttività et sulla redditività', Milano: Assbank.

Pyle, D.H. (1971), 'On the theory of financial intermediation', *Journal of Finance*, 36, June.

Revell, J. (1989), 'The future of savings banks: a study of Spain and the rest of Europe', *Institute of European Finance Research Monographs in Banking and Finance*, 8, 1989.

Santomero, A. (1984), 'Modelling the banking firm – a survey', *Journal of Money, Credit and Banking*, 16, November.

Sassenou, M. (1990), 'Accroissement d'activité, diversification des produits', Document de Travail n° 1990- 09/T Caisse de Dépôts et Consignations.

Schweiger, I. and **McGee, J.** (1961), 'Chicago banking: the structure of banks and related financial institutions in Chicago and other areas', *Journal of Business*, 34, July.

Schweitzer, S.A. (1972), 'Economies of scale and holding – company affiliation in banking', *Southern Economic Journal*, 39.

SEC (1981), 'Multi-product economies of scale in the securities industry: an application of developing theory', *Capital Market Working Papers*, March.

Shaffer, S. (1985), 'Competition, economies of scale, and diversity of firm sizes', *Applied Economics*, 17.

Tachibanaki, T., Mitsui, K. and Kitagawa, H. (1990), 'Economies of scope and intercorporate share ownership in the Japanese banking industry', paper presented to the conference on Industrial Economics, Lisbon, September.

CHAPTER THREE

Universal banking in the integrated European marketplace

Alfred Steinherr and Christian Huveneers

1. Introduction

Regulators, bankers and consumers are preparing for the expected integration of financial markets within the wider goal of a Single European Market by 1992 or at some later date. Whether the 1992 deadline is met or not financial markets will change dramatically to the point of bearing little resemblance to what they used to be. In a previous study it has been argued that, while the overall economic benefits may not be all that overwhelming, the effect on financial institutions could well be just that (Steinherr and Gilibert, 1989). Hence, it is of paramount importance for financial institutions to understand the implications of financial market liberalisation and integration in order to be able to prepare and adapt.

Financial market integration will offer opportunities to reach beyond national frontiers by exporting financial services, by acquiring or establishing service centres abroad in markets hitherto inaccessible to foreign penetration. In this context, a key issue will be the optimal scope and organisation of banks. Unfortunately, our knowledge about competing organisational forms is far from what a scientist would call a conjecture; there are some partial theoretical arguments and there is some empirical evidence. Taken together it still does not add up to scientific knowledge. In the end, only experience will be able to tell and survival of the fittest will be the ultimate proof.

Bearing these provisos in mind, this chapter is a modest attempt to evaluate the advantages and the problems posed by a particular model of the bank referred to as universal banking. In most countries regulations have restricted banking activities by activity or geographically. In only a few countries, and notably German-speaking countries, have banks been allowed to carry out virtually all banking activities within a single firm and without geographical limitations. It is often felt that, if it were not for regulations, all large banks in Europe would become universal. Such trends can be observed even in countries traditionally committed to banking segmentation, such as Japan and the United States. One interpretation of this trend is that the universal model is the most efficient one. Another is to argue that it may not be the most efficient one, but that it serves to maximise size and market power and, ultimately, generate non-competitive rents. Both arguments would be consistent with the hypothesis of survival of the fittest, but the social implications would be different. Hence, there is a nut to be cracked by regulators.

Segmentation of banking activity was introduced in the United States with the Glass Steagall Act to separate commercial banking from investment banking and with the McFadden Act to limit branching to individual states. One main reason for segmentation was the concentration of power by some bankers, in particular J.P. Morgan, through their industrial holdings and the spillover of stockmarket risks to the deposit base.

In Europe the attitude of regulators was split into two opposing schools. The US experience significantly influenced countries such as Italy and Belgium; others saw in diversified banking a source of increased risk diversification and greater stability of bank revenues. In these countries (typically German-speaking countries) banks were also used to take over certain roles of industrial policy, both in the creation and the rescuing or restructuring of ailing firms.

Reduced segmentation is being increasingly accepted for several reasons. Indeed, countries with universal banking have experienced greater stability than others. Of course, instability in segmented banking systems may be due to reasons other than segmentation. Deregulation and the opening up of national markets to foreign competition have also had a deep effect on regulatory views. Dividing lines between different banking activities become increasingly unclear so that segmentation is both conceptually and pragmatically somewhat muddy. Moreover, rightly or wrongly, it is felt that restricted banking is at a competitive disadvantage in international competition with universal banks.

Foreign competition and deregulation tend to lower the value of the banking franchise. Enlarging the scope of banking can then be seen as a compensation for the decline of the franchise value of banking.

The phenomenon of disintermediation and securitisation poses a threat to commercial banks and creates an incentive to compensate for losses in traditional commercial banking business by entering into investment banking. The incentives for investment banks to enter into commercial banking also exist, but are less pronounced. Investment banks vie for the large capital resources of commercial banks, particularly needed during stockmarket downturns, the deposit base and the branch network which could serve as a retail distribution network for brokerage.

The definition of universal banking is not engraved in stone. In the United States the Bank Holding Act allows a regrouping of various financial and non-financial legally independent corporations within one holding group. This model of universal banking is close to the one now adopted in Italy.

In the United Kingdom large city banks have acquired investment banks and other financial enterprises without touching their legal independence.

The most widely defined concept of universality can be found in Germany where banks within one legal entity can carry out virtually all financial transactions and can hold any amount of industrial participations. Participations in non-banking firms are important, with direct voting rights reinforced by proxy-votes for shares held in custody for clients.

Section 2 of this chapter discusses the analytical issues involved concerning efficiency and market power. Section 3 investigates the actual and potential influence of universal banking on corporate control. Section 4 summarises the main conclusions in view of financial market integration in post-1992 Europe.

2. Economic efficiency of universal banking: a theoretic framework

Universal banking is generally thought to benefit from its wide-spread activities and the global banking services it can offer to customers. In economic terms, universal banking may benefit from economies of scope and from informational superiority. In addition, the multiple relationships with a corporate client, including shareholdings, may give the universal bank a special relationship and, at the limit, control over corporations, which could give rise to non-competitive behaviour. This section discusses these considerations in turn, reserving the wider issue of corporate control for section 3.

2.1 ACQUISITION OF INFORMATION

The theory of financial intermediation has extensively addressed the question: why do financial intermediaries exist? Answers to this question should provide assistance in evaluating the competitive advantages of universal banks as a particular type of financial intermediary. The main reason advanced for the existence of financial intermediaries is *asymmetric information*, that is, the borrower has information about the amount and risk of future cashflows which is superior to the information available to the lender (Diamond, 1984). Diversification by itself is a necessary, but not a sufficient, response by lenders because of adverse selection problems. What is needed is acquisition of information in order to narrow the information gap. In cases where, or to the extent that, information can be acquired by anyone at a certain cost, an independent agent (rating agency) would be socially efficient. The rating agency has an incentive not to cheat and make information available as a public commodity. The borrower has an incentive to bear these costs and benefit from market access. However, in many cases, the hypothesis that information can be acquired by an outsider is too strong.

When information is asymmetric it can often only *be acquired through a continuous relationship in credit evaluation and monitoring*. Banks gain from accumulating information which will be reflected in lending conditions. Nevertheless, once acquired, it is difficult to prevent revelation of this information to competitors. Every time a bank awards a loan or a back-up facility it provides a signal to the market. Indeed, the studies of James (1987) and Slovin, Sushka and Hudson (1988) confirm that share prices rise after a loan agreement and conditions for commercial paper issues improve.

How does the universal bank compare in this respect with a commercial bank? From the point of view of information collection, the universal bank seems to be better placed. By meeting all the financial needs of a company and being involved in advisory functions, the universal bank exploits economies of scope and minimises the cost of information and the cost of monitoring the relationship (Steinherr and Gilibert, 1989). Supplying an additional service does not involve information and monitoring costs. If, in addition, the *bank holds stock* of the company concerned and *is represented on its board*, the *information gap can be narrowed further* and monitoring of the company becomes easier and more efficient.

Doubts about universal banks' informational superiority are, however, raised by performance comparisons. *If the information superiority of universal banks, as compared to commercial banks, was really significant* then one should be able to observe at least one of the following differences in loan contracts: *loans granted by universal banks should exhibit greater differentiation in risk premiums, lower default ratios* or *credits with longer maturities*. But there is no empirical evidence that loan portfolios of universal banks differ significantly in these respects from those of traditional commercial banks.

Even if universal banks did enjoy informational superiority some problems would persist. One is that risk is less diversified for a given amount of resources if the bank is the lender, adviser, bondholder and shareholder. The empirical weight of this argument is, however, likely to be marginal. More concern is raised by another consideration: loan commitments by a commercial bank are useful signals to capital markets and improve the borrowing firm's access to it. When the lending bank acts as the underwriter of the firm's debentures or share issues, the informational value of loan signals is reduced: a bank may be motivated to underwrite debentures in situations where it would not be ready to extend more loans. In fact, the *adverse selection problem re-emerges*: if the firm is sound the universal bank has an incentive to increase its loans. If the firm faces difficulties the bank would prefer to refinance the firm through the market. And the firm cannot be sure of obtaining the best conditions. If captive to the universal bank, it may not be able to search for the best conditions in the market.

2.2 ECONOMIES OF SCOPE

The question whether *universal banking is more efficient than specialised banking depends on whether there are economies of scope or not*. Economies of scale are irrelevant as they measure the importance of the size of production on average cost given the product mix. Global economies of scope exist when the costs of joint production are lower than the sum of costs of separate production for a given scale for each product. Product-specific economies of scope arise when production efficiency can be enhanced by adding a particular product to a given product mix. Baumol, Panzar and Willig (1981) have suggested that economies of scope and cost complementarities in production arise from inputs that are shared or utilised jointly.

For universal banks, several arguments suggest that economies of scope may be sizeable. First, there is the *fixed cost of managing a client relationship*: it includes the branch network, the accumulation of human skills, computerised systems, etc., and such overhead costs can be spread by offering a whole array of financial services to clients. From the client's point of view, it is also convenient to concentrate all sources of funding (short-term borrowing, long-term financing and equity holding) within one bank: it reduces transaction costs and reduces the marginal costs for new services (see also Dermine, 1990). This argument has been extended to the case of diversified banks which engage in insurance, so that the same distribution network can be used.

Second, *financial institutions produce highly substitutable goods.* Specialised institutions are, therefore, exposed to the risk of demand shifts among products. Universal banks are believed to cope more easily with such substitutions due to their economies of diversification: resources can more easily be shifted in-house in line with changes in demand.

Third, in meeting all the financial requirements of a company, the universal bank *minimises the costs of information and of monitoring* the relationship, as argued above.

The empirical literature on the US, reviewed in Clark (1988) and in Kolari and Zardkoohi (1987), not only fails to support the hypothesis that economies of scale are important in banking, but also the one that economies of scope are important. The general conclusion is:

1. that economies of scale are significant only for small-sized depository institutions (less than US$100 million in total deposits);
2. that the empirical evidence does not support a conclusion of global economies of scope; and
3. that there appears to be some evidence of economies in joint production among some specific pairs of products.

None of the studies surveyed by Clark and Kolari–Zardkoohi uses European data. Studies on European banks, mainly by Muldur–Sassenou and Pacolet, refer to France and Belgium. They do not suggest strong economies of scope either. More specifically, it appears that the largest banks enjoy some economies of scope which compensate for the diseconomies of scale from which they suffer. More strikingly, when one includes the off-balance sheet operations of securitisation, economies of scope tend to vanish even for the largest banks (Pallage, 1990). This is consistent with Mester's work for the US (1990) that finds diseconomies of scope between the traditional lending activities and the activities of loan selling and buying. Similarly, estimates of cost functions in the insurance sector do not support the hypothesis of significant economies of scale and cost complementarities (Colenutt, 1977; Cummins, 1977; Doherty, 1981; Dubois, 1988). Of course, data for these empirical studies have their weaknesses. Furthermore, universal banks of the German mould are not admitted in France and Belgium. The Japanese case might be more suggestive as Japanese banks are permitted to some extent to hold shares in other corporations. In a recent empirical work, Tachibanaki, Mitsui and Kitagawa (1990) observe that economies of scope are evident only when the effect of current values in shares held by banks is taken into account. The degree of economies of scope seems to rise with the value of corporate holdings.

2.3   CONTAGION RISK (EXTERNALITIES)

Corporate control by diversified banks may generate not only information and monitoring advantages but also some drawbacks. The most obvious pitfalls are the risks of contagion and conflicts of interest. Conflicts of interest are discussed below.

Bankruptcies of affiliated industrial companies could endanger the bank's assets, with a possible loss of confidence and run on deposits; for this reason regulation in some countries assures that the risks and failures of industrial companies are not transmitted to the bank's deposits (corporate separateness).

Ownership of universal banks could also give rise to problems. When an industrial company gains control of a bank, it obtains not only a cheap and large source of funding (less so with competition from deregulated capital markets), but also important information about competitors: universal banks could therefore become a source of distortions in the non-banking sector. This would be all the more the case if markets were not competitive and if anti-trust laws did not exist or were not rigorously enforced.

Universal banking with control over firms in the non-banking sector and the possible control of universal banks by large non-banking concerns raises the issue of market power. We do not think that universal banks are equipped and willing to engage in the usual uncompetitive strategies within the industries in which they hold participations (price-fixing cartels, coordination of industrial firms whose products are complementary or substitutes, vertical concentration). Instead, the set-up of large universal banks (or even of financial conglomerates) could generate power beyond the confined boundaries of some industrial markets: one thinks of interlocking directorships, the ability of the banking sector to shape and coordinate the behaviour of affiliated companies. Again, these possibilities are particularly relevant warnings for economies that lack competitive structure. These warnings are less pertinent for the future integrated European market.

It is not immediately obvious why banks would benefit from holding major stakes in industrial companies as they are already exposed to the risk of failures of their corporate clients. A lesson may be gained from the experience of industrial conglomerates. Whilst in fashion in the 1960s and 1970s as a device to spread managerial capacity and diversify risk, the ultimate result has been failure. Lack of focus and managerial dilution has generated underperformance, forcing conglomerates into divestment and restructuring. Why should a conglomerate managed by a bank, itself perhaps controlled by a non-bank, achieve superior results? We see no convincing reasons from an efficiency point of view limited to returns from shareholdings. But this may be a too narrow approach.

The dual role of banks as lenders and shareholders of the firm is studied by Aoki (1984) in the context of the Japanese financial system. Two important conclusions emerge from this study which assumes that banks fix their strategy as lenders and shareholders so as to maximise net income. (This may not always correspond to reality, as argued in section 3.) First, the model generates a level of indebtedness of firms such that their equity value is maximum. However, *this is only an equilibrium solution when shares are held by individuals*. If banks are also shareholders, *the debt of the firm exceeds the level which maximises the firm's value*. This solution is preferable for banks because the losses incurred from lower share prices are more than compensated for by higher credit amounts at, in fact, higher effective interest rates. *This compensating feature also suggests that banks have no advantage in holding all shares of the firm* (as they lose on shareholdings) and would prefer instead to hold a stake small enough to minimise the loss on shareholdings under the constraint of effective control over the firm's borrowing decisions. Equity stakes as small as 5–20 per cent seem to be in the optimal range and this is precisely what can be observed in Japan, Germany and elsewhere. Second, banks as lenders and shareholders *share the industrial risks of the firm* and, as a result, *have an interest to influence not only the financial but also the industrial decisions* of affiliated non-financial corporations. What seems to be valid for Japan also appears consistent with observations in Europe.

2.4 CONFLICTS OF INTEREST

The major reason for the separation of commercial banking from investment banking in the United States was the alleged *risk of conflicts of interest*. This is the conflict between the promotional role of the investment banker and the obligations of the commercial banker to provide disinterested services to savers (Dermine, 1990).

The issue is difficult to evaluate because direct information is not available. But it is a curious fact that conflicts of interest, which should increase with reduced segmentation of banking activities, receive much less legal and supervisory attention on the European Continent than in Anglo-Saxon countries. In fact, there are no legal provisions dealing with issues such as 'inside information' in the German legal system.

At times, administrative 'provisions' to reduce the scope for conflicts of interest have been discussed in Europe (e.g., the Commission for Fundamental Problems of the Credit Sector appointed in 1974 by the West German Minister of Finance), but without tangible results. These 'provisions' would certainly be useful, but may be insufficient. Only intense competition and an extensive choice among suppliers within and outside of the universal banking system would provide a sufficient basis for ignoring conflicts of interest. In particular, competition in the non-banking sector needs to be high in order to force firms to minimise finance costs; they need access to specialised investment banks (and hence to securities markets) to be able to opt out of a universal bank relationship; and investors also need alternatives.

As stressed by Caves (1989), international differences among national institutions can provide insights concerning the determinants of market performance. In this respect, universal banks in Germany and their close relationships with industrial firms are an intriguing institution for control and ownership of enterprises.

3. Banks' control over firms

German banks, through voting shares that they own or hold in custody, account for 36 per cent of the votes in the top 100 companies. Because small investors deposit their shares with banks and tend to invest in large, well-known companies, proxy-votes exercised by banks tend to rise with the size of companies. For the ten largest companies the average proportion of votes controlled by banks exceeds 50 per cent. In 1988 the number of board seats held by private banks in the top 100 corporations amounted to 104 and that of all banks and insurance companies to 161 (Bundesverband Deutscher Banken, 1989).

Corporate control can be exerted directly by shareholders or, if this control is deficient, by the market through takeovers. The latter aspect is discussed below.

Shareholders' control is brilliantly analysed by Grossman and Hart (1988). Their main conclusion is that any voting structure restricting the principle of 'one share – one vote' is detrimental to value maximisation of the firm. It facilitates fending-off a value-enhancing takeover to dethrone an inefficient incumbent management and may also facilitate a value-reducing takeover. The most significant deviation from the principle of 'one share – one vote' is proxy-voting which gives banks more votes than the shares they own. Therefore, the structures of voting rights and of dividend streams are different. Exercise of proxy-voting creates another principal–agent problem. The shareholder (principal) has little monitoring capacity of the agent which, in turn, may have wider objectives than value maximisation.

An empirical analysis which sheds some light on the possible benefits of universal banks for the performance of their affiliate corporations is the study by Cable and Dirrheimer (1983) and Cable (1985). Their cross-section multiple-regression analysis of forty-eight of the top German companies concludes that those companies subject to internal control exercised by financial institutions (the three big universal banks) display – all other things being equal – a higher rate of return on capital than other companies in the sample (other companies are foreign or publicly owned). Cable and Dirrheimer suggest in their conclusion that, in the German environment, external control by universal banks maintains the tendency of large corporations to focus on profit goals, minimise costs and guide resources towards highest yield uses.

This interpretation calls for some reservations. It is true that larger companies, when no longer controlled by families, are subject to the danger of managerial control. The results of Cable and Dirrheimer suggest then that the presence of bank representatives on the companies' boards allows for better control. However, multiple-regression analysis may not be the best method for controlling the sample of forty large firms for other forms of ownership and management (e.g., multinational enterprises and their transfer pricing, public sector enterprises pursuing more widely defined goals than profit maximisation). Furthermore, Cable's data do not reject the hypothesis that the profit increments could be monopoly rents, although they are inconsistent with that as the sole explanation. Higher return on capital could also reflect a higher debt–equity ratio brought about by banks' control. The question of corporate control is further analysed below in the context of macroeconomic performance.

Managers of corporations controlled by banks have considerable leeway in allocating free cashflow (in the case of German companies, another name for free cashflow is hidden reserves, which are high on average, using as a yardstick the difference between accounting and market values). They are unhampered by the market for corporate control and by boards with interlocked directorships (and with directors appointed by employees in the case of Germany) whose objective cannot be value maximisation for shareholders. Agency costs tend, therefore, to be high, making investment in equity stocks less attractive to those shareholders who cannot participate in sharing the free cashflow. The underdevelopment of the stockmarket in a country like Germany has thus less to do with the allegedly peculiar psychology of German savers, as is often claimed, than with a major agent–principal problem that reduces returns to individual shareholders.

As argued before, the performance of a financial system needs to be appreciated in terms of its capacity to allocate resources efficiently and in terms of the cost of financing intertemporal resource allocation. The two aspects are separable: at any financial cost, static resource allocation can be efficient or not. Similarly, one can have an efficient static Walrasian equilibrium without corresponding intertemporal efficiency.

Investments are financed either through retained earnings, equity or debt. *Retained earnings* have already been discussed and, in the absence of strict monitoring of the agent (corporate management), as is the case in Germany, there is the risk of inefficient intertemporal resource allocation. German firms are highly indebted to banks and finance, in international comparison, a very high share of their investments through retained earnings. These data are consistent with the hypothesis of managerial discretion. *Equity financing* is best discussed on the basis of *Tobin's q-ratio*, that is, the ratio of the market value of firms to the replacement value of their assets. The hypothesis that investment is positively related to the q-ratio is supported by a plethora of empirical studies, although q-ratios explain only a small part of variation in investment. If q-values for Germany are downward biased because shareholders cannot appropriate the full return and because funds are not used for value maximisation, then investment will also be lower. Not only is this a macroeconomic effect, but, to the extent that the downward bias is not uniform, *firms with the largest undervaluation of their market value will experience the highest disincentive* (or highest foregone reduction in capital costs) *to invest*. Free cashflow comes back with a vengeance! An international comparison of Tobin's q-ratio in nine OECD countries displays a striking decline in the q-ratio for Germany related to a decline in pre-tax returns on capital (Chang-Lee, 1986).

There could, of course, be some circularity in the argument. The importance of the q-ratio for investment is formally derived from the assumption of value maximisation of the firm. With another objective function for the firm, the q-ratio might not be as relevant for investment.

Finally, there is the *cost of debt*. Because most firms are not able to securitise their debt they have to rely on bank lending. The question then is whether banks provide long-term funding with small intermediation margins.

TABLE 3.1 Spreads between prime and money-market rates*

	Germany			United Kingdom		
	Prime rate	Money-market (3 m-interbank)	Spread	Prime rate	Money-market (3 m-interbank)	Spread
December						
1990	8.65	8.88	-0.23	15.00	14.00	1.00
1989	8.15	8.11	0.04	16.00	15.12	0.88
1988	6.00	5.50	0.50	13.00	13.19	-0.19
1987	6.25	3.65	2.60	8.50	9.00	-0.50
1986	6.75	4.90	1.75	11.00	11.25	-0.25
1985	7.25	5.60	1.65	11.50	11.94	-0.44
1984	7.75	5.70	2.00	9.50	9.88	0.38
1983	7.75	6.30	1.45	9.00	9.31	-0.31
1982	8.75	6.20	2.55	10.00	10.50	-0.50
1981	13.00	10.50	2.50	14.50	15.69	-1.19
1980	11.50	10.20	1.30	15.00	14.75	0.25
1979	9.75	8.70	1.05	18.00	17.00	1.00
1978	5.50	3.70	1.80	13.50	12.50	1.00
1977	6.00	3.60	2.40	8.00	6.50	1.50
1976	6.50	4.80	1.70	15.50	14.38	1.12

Note: *These rates were chosen because they are less influenced by regulation than others. Spreads are not interpreted as margins which depend on a variety of funding sources and on commission structures. Spreads ought rather to indicate the degree of competition in these markets.
Source: Morgan-Guaranty, World Financial Markets

It is sometimes argued that credit is cheaper in Germany. However, there is no point in comparing interest rates across countries which are largely influenced by macroeconomic factors. It would also be misleading to compare net interest income as a percentage of assets because universal banks of the German type have a larger share of their productive assets in non-interest earning investments (stocks) and hence their share of net interest income is biased downwards. More revealing is a comparison of spreads between lending and borrowing rates. This is the purpose of table 3.1 above which lists spreads between prime rates and money-market rates as a measure of spreads between market-oriented rates.

It should be recalled that non-banks have no access to money market rates in Germany. Hence competitive pressure on bank spreads should be more limited. This is confirmed by the data of Table 3.1, showing spreads for Germany that are mostly a multiple of UK spreads for the last ten years. We are therefore led to believe, in spite of the fact that such data are not entirely comparable, that a bank-based financial system has not been more favourable for the non-bank sector. Savers cannot invest in money-market instruments and must be content with lower interest rates on savings deposits. Borrowers are confined to bank lending. This conclusion on the pricing policies of German banks is in line with the estimates of Price Waterhouse (for the European Economic Commission) which suggest strong potential decreases in financial product prices across the board as a result of completing the internal market. For German banking products the average of prices in excess of competitive prices is estimated at 33 per cent. Only Spain, where large banks are also universal banks, matches Germany in non-competitive pricing.

It is not easy to see whether there is superior efficiency of German universal banks which could compensate for non-competitive behaviour. A clue is provided by a recent study comparing profitability and costs of banking systems in OECD countries (Conti, 1990). The stylised observations from comparisons at OECD level reveal that:

- differences in profitability of banks are strongly related to differences in intermediation margins, defined as the sum of interest margins and income from services (fee-earning activities);
- there is a positive correlation between margins and operational costs;
- there is no clear association between income structure (or productive specialisation as reflected in the relative importance of interest income and non-interest income) and cost structure (i.e., the importance of personnel expenses in total costs);
- higher profitability does not reflect higher operational efficiency and the expense preference theory might hold;
- inter-country differences in banking systems' performances are related to differences in regulation, market segmentation and, needless to say, macro-economic conditions.

In order to shed some light on the pros and cons of universal banks of the German type, we compare the operating results of German banks with similar magnitudes for the banking systems of other OECD countries within Conti's statistical framework. To see whether large size combined with universal banking is associated with particular performances (economies of scope, market power), we also compare the results for the three largest German banks (Deutsche Bank, Dresdner Bank and Commerzbank) with the largest banks of other countries. The results are displayed in Table 3.2.

Universal banking of the German type does not appear to lead to strongly different performances when compared with other forms of banking organisation (mainly commercial banks in the mould of non-German banks used as a benchmark for the comparison). German banks have slightly lower operating expenses and higher interest margins, but also lower net incomes because of strikingly smaller non-interest incomes. In other words, these data do not support the hypothesis of smaller intermediation margins and suggest that German banks, taken as a whole, are less engaged in fee-earning activities.

More interestingly, the three big German banks display higher profit margins. This stems from larger margins – both interest and non-interest margins – despite higher operating expenses. This suggests that large size combined with universal banking does not allow the reduction of costs by strong economies of scope, but allows the extraction of high interest margins.

TABLE 3.2 Operating results, margins and costs (a); Banking system (b); Largest banks (c)

Net interest income (RM)	OECD	2.31	2.19
	FRG	2.38	2.90
Non-interest income (SM)	OECD	1.07	1.07
	FRG	0.61	1.20
Gross intermediation margin (GI)	OECD	3.38	3.26
(GI = RM = SM)	FRG	2.99	4.10
Operating expenses (OE)	OECD	2.17	2.00
	FRG	1.84	2.72
Net income (NI)			
(NI = GI-OE)	OECD	1.21	1.26
	FRG	1.15	1.38

Notes: (a) Data are averages for the years 1985–6 and (when available) 1987. Incomes and expenses are expressed as percentages of banks' total assets.
(b) For OECD countries: mostly commercial banks. For FRG: all universal banks.
(c) For OECD countries: 5 largest banks in each country. For FRG: 3 largest universal banks (Deutsche Bank, Dresdner Bank and Commerzbank).
Sources: OECD, Bank Profitability, statistical supplement, financial statements of banks; V. Conti (1990) and own calculations.

Against these drawbacks it is often claimed that universal banking enjoys risk diversification and hence greater stability. Indeed, in the post-war period the United States has been plagued by a much higher frequency of bank failures and systemic instability. The figures in Table 3.3 below provide a somewhat crude test of the stability hypothesis by comparing the standard deviation of profits during the eighties (unfortunately strictly comparable figures do not extend beyond 1986).

The figures of Table 3.3 do not support the hypothesis of greater stability. The three big German banks display a higher standard deviation for both their operating surplus and their gross income (as do the large Spanish banks for their gross income). However, it is difficult to see whether the greater volatility of performance is related to their universal character as the profit variability of all German banks, taken as a whole, is not statistically significantly larger than for the other banking systems considered (the main reason is, however, the low degree of freedom provided by only seven years of observations).

Another aspect of the stability argument is the impression that universal banking avoids 'short termism' in the allocation of resources and thus fosters stability for the affiliated industrial companies. Such an argument suggests some failure of the

TABLE 3.3 Variability of operating results (1980–6)

	Net income		Gross income	
	Mean	Standard deviation	Mean	Standard deviation
Germany				
Big 3	1.24	0.29	3.85	0.42
All banks	1.13	0.19	2.93	0.21
Is variance greater for big banks?		No	Yes at 0.10 level	
UK (only 5 main clearing banks)	1.53	0.19	4.93	0.26
USA				
Big banks	1.29	0.22	4.05	0.49
All banks	1.39	0.13	4.33	0.31
Difference in variance significant?		No		No
France				
Big banks	0.98	0.09	3.11	0.18
All banks	1.01	0.08	3.17	0.15
Difference in variance significant?		No		No
Spain				
7 big banks	1.96	0.12	5.58	0.34
All banks	1.58	0.10	4.72	0.21
Difference in variance significant?		No	Yes at 0.10 level	

Notes: As to difference in variance of income between German banks and their counterparts in other countries, only the difference with French big banks is statistically significant (at level of 0.1).
Germany: all banks are universal banks; big banks are Deutsche Bank, Dresdner Bank and Commerzbank.
UK: banks are the five main London clearing bank groups.
USA: all commercial banks; big banks are commercial banks having total assets of 1000 m USD or more.
France: all commercial and mutual banks; big banks are the 8 biggest commercial banks.
Spain: big banks are the 7 largest commercial banks.
Source: OECD.

capital markets. Well-developed capital markets should allow for the separation of the responsibility for the capital flow requirements of investments from the risk-bearing responsibility for these investments. Capital markets also provide information (interest rates, security prices) for the selection of firms' investment projects. One may wonder why the firms' long-term allocations should be more efficient when they are shaped in integrated structures like German universal banks, Belgian holding companies or Japanese keiretsu. These forms of integration can fulfil several functions:

1. to help industrial firms specialised in mature sectors to diversify into new activities by external growth and to reduce the variance of their profits;
2. to accompany the long-term development of their affiliated corporations by a long-term financial policy which avoids useless and costly takeovers and limits myopic speculation.

Here again the argument of acquisition of information emerges. Commercial banks making loans do not have perfect information about their borrowers. As it is difficult to identify 'good borrowers' by screening devices, the interest rate which a firm is willing to pay may act as one such screening device. However, the interest rate a bank charges may itself affect the riskiness of its loan portfolio by either sorting potential borrowers (the adverse selection effect: firms who are willing to borrow at high interest rates may, on average, be worse risks), or by affecting the action of borrowers (the incentive effect, as described by Stiglitz and Weiss (1981): higher interest rates charged to firms induce them to undertake projects with lower probabilities of success but higher payoffs when successful). The special link which universal banks of the German type enjoy with their corporate clients might allow them to avoid the failures (adverse selection, incentive effect and the resulting credit rationing) usually associated with imperfect information on the loan market.

These considerations lead to several tentative conclusions concerning the merits of universal banking. First, the importance of universal banks may lead to underdevelopment of the securities market because the shareholders' agency problem is not well resolved. Second, and as a result, resource allocation statically and over time is bound to suffer from inefficiencies because managers of banks and non-banks have large free cashflows and are not subjected to strict board and market controls. Third, outside financial resources (equity and debt) may be expensive in a system based on universal banking. Equity financing is expensive because, due to large free cashflows, stocks are undervalued by the market. As a result of underdeveloped short- or long-term securities markets for the private sector, firms must rely on bank credits. In Germany these credits are more costly than securitised debt and intermediation margins are more comfortable.

4. Universal banking and 1992: a summary

In spite of the current worldwide tendency in favour of universal banking, the picture that emerges from theoretical considerations and the experience of countries such as

Germany is mixed. Universal banks are said to enjoy advantages from economies of scale, economies of scope and from the possibility of reallocating resources internally in response to demand trends. *Empirical verification of these alleged advantages is extremely difficult* and, to date, no conclusive evidence exists.

On balance, we arrive at the *conclusion that the alleged advantages of universal banking tend to be overemphasised.* Economies of scale are not an outstanding feature in banking and, when they exist, can be better exploited by specialised firms (e.g., payments systems, investment banking). For example, computer systems do generate important economies of scale, but they need to be designed specifically for payments systems, loan processing, securities analysis, etc. Hence, although economies of scale exist for some areas of banking, there are no positive economies of scale for a widely diversified bank. Thus, economies of scale are a weak justification for universal banks.

The concept of economies of scope is more appropriate, but empirical evidence fails to provide support. Economies of scope are likely to be bounded by the increased difficulty of managing efficiently a complex, non-focused organisation. There is also a problem of quality, well-known from other service sectors: supermarkets and boutiques cater to different customers. Only for standard financial products is convenience the overriding consideration; corporations and wealthy clients are ready to make an additional trip to deal with a high value-added supplier. Finally, markets internal to the firm have their own problems and escape the invisible hand of market control. Only in very efficiently organised firms are internal markets competitive with external markets. So the argument is circular: internal markets are efficient if the firm is efficient and what makes the firm efficient?

What historical evidence cannot illuminate is the challenge posed for hitherto protected markets by internationalisation of banking in the context of European financial integration. Are universal banks better equipped than specialised institutions to take advantage of the larger and more competitive European market?

If so, can newly created universal banks catch up in a short period of time with universal banks that have evolved through history? Available evidence suggests that the answer to the first question is already unclear. Germany seems to be the world's largest importer of financial services in spite of its leading role in world trade, its large current-account surpluses and the international role of the DeutschMark.

What the German experience shows is that the major historical reason for universal banking, namely provision of long-term financial resources to the economy in the absence of well-developed securities markets, is not a decisive consideration any more. Furthermore, the market power of universal banks needs to be checked by competitive conditions both among universal banks and through specialised institutions. This concern is weighty in small protected markets but less so in a well-diversified European market. Our view is that *specialised institutions will remain highly competitive through excellency and economies of scale so there will be no scope for some universal banks to dominate the market.*

In addition, *internationalisation of specialised firms appears considerably easier than that of universal banks.* It would be a formidable challenge for a specialised, national bank to develop simultaneously into an international and universal bank. Even after 1992 Europe will retain national characteristics and, therefore, organisational and managerial integration of a European universal bank seems quite difficult. The objectives of an integrated corporate culture and adaptation to different national markets are bound to create conflicts. Nor is there scope for marketing a universal bank brand name throughout Europe and thereby achieving economies of scale. Whilst the name of a reputed German bank has household value for a German customer, it may not exert the same attraction in foreign markets. In line with this observation, acquired foreign banks tend to retain their names.

In those countries where universal banking has not existed in the past it would have to be created through ex novo expansions into new territories or through mergers and acquisitions, in the home country and elsewhere. *This is a frightfully difficult and also risky undertaking.* The history of mergers and acquisitions suggests that, more often than not, the ultimate result falls short of expectations. This is particularly true for newcomers and when one or both parties involved suffer from X-inefficiency. Management attention tends to get diverted from traditional tasks for long periods of time. The European context is less favourable to restructuring, cost savings and management changes than the American context. Costs of mergers are therefore higher and the scope for improvements lower. All the more so if transnational operations are involved.

Potential problems posed by universal banks are embracing control over customers, possible conflicts of interest and risk-bundling. These concerns would be further enhanced if the universal bank itself were controlled by a corporation or an individual and thus not subjected to stockmarket control. In Germany this did not happen: the shares of major universal banks are held by a wide public, although insurance companies have held, and are increasing, their participations. It would be reassuring to have regulatory dispositions preventing control of, at least, larger universal banks by particular interest groups. Furthermore, effective anti-trust policy and strict enforcement of competitive market conditions for financial and non-financial markets seem necessary. Bank control of firms with market power multiplies the risks and costs of local monopolies.

From a regulatory viewpoint it would seem possible to preserve the potential advantages of universal banking without being fully exposed to its major dangers. The already existing 'Chinese walls' separating different activities within the universal banks should be transformed into brick walls through corporate separateness. This would allow the bank holding company to operate a span of activities similar to the universal bank. It would, however, break up risk-bundling and thus facilitate risk management; it would facilitate regulations and allow less arbitrary regulatory rules in the interest of banks; and it would reduce the potential conflicts of interest.

To this corporate separation should be added *regulation of investments*, as already mentioned. Bank investments in non-bank corporations, combined with proxy-voting, may yield inefficient and unwarranted control over firms. This could be substantially reduced by *restricting proxy-voting* which, in the German context, provides banks with more voting rights than does share ownership. Participations themselves need to be regulated for prudential and anti-trust reasons. In practice, this regulation can be largely ineffective, as is the case in Germany, if there are no strict accounting conventions for evaluation of stock ownership closer to underlying real (market) values.

According to the European Second Banking Directive (Article 11), share-holdings of a single firm are not to exceed 15 per cent and overall holdings are not to exceed 60 per cent of a bank's capital. To represent an effective constraint, these shareholdings would have to be *evaluated more realistically* and, from an anti-trust point of view, *holdings of the group should be consolidated*. Article 11 remains mute on these problems. Also from an anti-trust viewpoint, the exclusion of financial sector firms from the restrictions of Article 11, including insurance companies, should be evaluated carefully.

Finally, we have attempted to assess some of the *economy-wide gains or inefficiencies* (externalities) that may derive from a universal banking system. Such a system is prone to contribute significantly to the stability of financial markets at the cost of restricting efficiency of the market for corporate control. As a result the allocation of resources in a modern economy requiring drastic corporate and sectorial reallocations, is not subjected to close efficiency monitoring. It gives incumbent corporate managers excessive discretionary freedom, unhampered by shareholder control or by contesting outside raiders. Free internal cashflow in banks and non-banks can therefore be used in ways not compatible with value maximisation. Two results follow: *inefficient static resource allocation and reduced and inefficient invest-ment patterns*. Because it does not provide access to free cashflow, equity ownership outside of the control group is less attractive. *The underdevelopment of German securities markets can thus be seen, to some extent, as a consequence of a finan-cial system* that is anchored in banking. But efficiency is only one consideration; greater stability of the banking market and of the overall economy appears in-creasingly desirable as the more efficient US financial markets go through a period of excessive, and surely unnecessary, instability at the expense of investors and tax-payers.

References and bibliography

Abraham, J.P. and **Lierman, F.** (1990), 'European banking strategies in the nineties', *Revue de la Banque*, 8–9.

Akerlof, G. (1970), 'The market for lemons': quality uncertainty and the market mechanism', *Quarterly Journal of Economics*, 84.

Aoki, M. (ed.), (1984), *The Economic Analysis of the Japanese Firm*, New York: North Holland.

Baumol, W.J., Panzar, J.C. and **Willig, R.D.** (1981), *Contestable Markets and the Theory of Industry Structure*, Harcourt Brace.

Cable, J. (1985), 'Capital market information and industrial performance: the role of West German banks', *The Economic Journal*, March.

Cable, J. and **Dirrheimer, M.J.** (1983), 'Hierarchies and markets: an empirical test of the multidivisional hypothesis in West Germany', *International Journal of Industrial Organisation*, (1).

Caves, R. (1989), 'International differences in industrial organisation', in R. Schmalensee and R. Willig (eds), *Handbook of Industrial Organisation*, vol. II.

Chang-Lee, J.H. (1986), 'Profit pur et q de Tobin dans neuf pays de l'OCDE', *Revue Economique de l'OCDE*, n.7/Automne.

Clark, J.A. (1988), 'Economies of scale and scope at depository financial institutions: a review of the literature', *Economic Review*, Federal Reserve Bank of Kansas City, September/October.

Colenutt, D. (1977), 'Economies of scale in the United Kingdom ordinary life insurance company', *Applied Economics*, 9.

Commission of the EC (1988), 'Creation of a European financial area', *European Economy*, No. 36, May.

Conti, V. (1990), 'Concorrenza e redditività nell'industria bancaria: un confronto internazionale', Banca Commerciale Italiana.

Cummins, J. (1977), 'Economies of scale in independent insurance agencies', *Journal of Risk and Insurance*, 44(4).

Daems, H. (1978), *The Holding Company and Corporate Control*, Leiden: Martinus Nijhoff.

Dermine, J. (1990), 'The specialisation of financial institutions, the EEC model', in A. Porta (ed.), *The Separation of Industry and Finance and the Specialisation of Financial Institutions*, Milan.

Diamond, D.W. (1984), 'Financial intermediation and delegated monitoring', *Review of Economic Studies*. 51

Doherty, N. (1981), 'The measurement of output and economies of scale in property-liability insurance', *Journal of Risk and Insurance*, 48(3).

Dubois, P. (1988), 'Estimation d'une fonction de coût hédonique: compagnies d'assurance I.A.R.D.', Laboratoire d'Etudes et de Recherches Economiques, Université de Caen.

Gilligan, T., Smirlock, M. and **Marshall, W.** (1984) 'Scale and scope economies in the multi-product banking firm', *Journal of Monetary Economics*, 13.

Grossman, S.J. and **Hart, O.D.** (1988), 'One share-one vote and the market for corporate control', *Harvard Law School*, Discussion Paper, 36.

James, Ch. (1987), 'Some evidence on the uniqueness of bank loans', *Journal of Financial Economics*, 19.

Kasuya, M. (1986), 'Economies of scope: theory and application to banking', *BOJ Monetary and Economic Studies*, October: pp. 59–104.

Kolari, J.W. and **Zardkoohi, A.** (1987), *Bank Costs, Structure and Performance*, Lexington: Massachussetts.

Mayer, C. (1990), 'The influence of the financial system on the British corporate sector', in A. Porta (ed.), *The Separation of Industry and Finance and the Specialisation of Financial Institutions*, Milan.

Mester, L. (1990), 'Traditional and non-traditional banking: an information-theoretic approach', paper for conference on bank structure and competition, Federal Reserve Bank Chicago, May.

Monopolkommission, (1980), *Hauptgutachten III : Fusionskontrolle bleibt vorrangig*, Baden-Baden: Nomos Verlag.

Muldur, U. and **Pacolet, J.** (1990), 'Economies of scale in European financial institutions', paper presented for the symposium on *The New European Financial Marketplace*, Centre for European Policy Studies (CEPS), Brussels.

Muldur, U., Pacolet, J. and **M. Sassenou,** (1989), 'Structure des coûts et efficacité des banques françaises', *Analyse financière*, 4.

Pacolet, J. (1987), 'Schaalvoordelen en voordelen van diversificatie in de Belgische banksector, 1976–1985', *Tijdschrift voor Economie en Management*, 4.

Pallage, S. (1990), 'Une estimation des économies d'échelle et de gamme dans le secteur bancaire en Belgique', unpublished Master's thesis, Liège.

Porta, A. (ed.) (1990), *The Separation of Industry and Finance and the Specialisation of Financial Institutions.*

Revell, J. (1990), 'Mergers and acquisitions in banking – are they really worthwhile?', paper presented for the symposium on *The New European Financial Marketplace*, Centre for European Policy Studies (CEPS), Brussels.

Slovin, M.B., Sushka, M.E. and **Hudson, C.D.** (1988), 'Corporate commercial paper, note issuance facilities, and shareholder wealth', *Journal of International Money and Finance*, 7.

Steinherr, A. and **Gilibert, P.L.** (1989), 'The impact of financial market integration on the European banking industry', Centre for European Policy Studies (CEPS), Brussels, *Research Report*. No.1.

Steinherr, A., and **Huveneers, Ch.** (1990), 'Universal banks: the prototype of successful banks in the integrated European market: a view inspired by German experience', Centre for European Policy Studies (CEPS), Brussels, *Research Report*, No. 2.

Stiglitz, J. and **Weiss, A.** (1981), 'Credit rationing in markets with imperfect information', *American Economic Review*, June: 393–410.

Tachibanaki T., Mitsui, K. and **Kitagawa, H.** (1990), 'Economies of scope and intercorporate share ownership in the Japanese banking industries', paper presented at the EARIE (European Association for Research in Industrial Organisation) Conference, Lisbon, September.

CHAPTER FOUR

Regulation and financial market integration

Patrick Van Cayseele

1. Introduction

In anticipation of realising an integrated European financial market by 1992, steps have been taken by the European Commission towards national deregulation together with European 're'-regulation. More precisely, the Second Banking Coordination Directive adopted on 15 December 1989 (Dir. 89/646) entering into force on 1 January 1993 adheres to the 'home country control' or HCC-principle.[1] Therefore, the bank licence delivered by any single country is a passport to deploy banking activities in all other member countries, and the home country controls are recognised as a sufficient means of supervision (mutual recognition). On the other hand, another directive adopted three days later (Dir. 89/647) introduces a minimum obligatory solvency ratio.[2] Therefore, the circumvention of national barriers to entry by the Second Directive, and hence the *de facto* deregulation of anti-competitive legislation is backed by re-regulation at the European level.

This approach towards the creation of a single market for financial services reflects a vision held by the European Commission on the working of financial markets. Some aspects of this vision already have been documented extensively. For example, Steinherr and Huveneers (1990) discuss the possibilities opened for universal banking as well as the conditions necessary for this model to work successfully. Still other visions underlying the Community's approach remain less documented. An attempt to identify some characteristics of the 'model' as well as a test of the appropriateness of the model against known facts from banking strategy are presented here.

To be more specific, it will be argued that the Community's approach is consistent with the view that national regulations can be explained by public choice (capture) theory. In addition, the idea is that banks compete according to strict minima regarding solvency. Hence the adherence to the HCC principle but with minimal standards.

Particularly the view that banks if left alone will tend to locate into countries with low solvency requirements will be challenged. Therefore, it is appropriate to ask whether the minimal standards imposed upon solvency are necessary to achieve financial integration. Among other things, the arguments in favour of and against such a system are discussed in the fifth section. Before that, however, the next section briefly overviews some theories of economic regulation while also giving a brief outline of the goals of the Commission in making 1992 happen. A third section then investigates the view that national regulations can be manipulated by regulators, which are captured by the domestic banking industry. This is very relevant in explaining the abandonment of the First Directive and the host country preference (HCP) principle in favour of the Second Directive and the HCC principle. However, the minimal standards that accompany the Second Directive might again create room for the creation of an entry barrier. Therefore it is appropriate to ask what minimal standards are good for, which will be done in the fourth section. Section 5, as already mentioned, brings together the conclusions and topics for further research.

2. Financial market integration: some views on regulation

Financial market services tend to be regulated in all countries for a variety of reasons. Some of the goals to be achieved by regulation include monetary stability, protection of depositors, and others.

In the pursuit of these goals, countries establish regulatory agencies which control the establishment of market participants as well as the ways in which they operate. Often the result is that, in order to compete, financial institutions have to meet certain criteria. The financial market therefore cannot be contested freely and hence from the theory of contestable markets (see Baumol, Panzar and Willig, 1982) it follows that some inefficiencies might result.[3] The regulators then face a trade-off between stability on the one hand and efficiency on the other.

In the public interest approach to regulation, the authorities attempt to strike a balance between these goals. That is the market outcome is efficient but too low a level of stability exists. The regulators succeed in enforcing an outcome that is 'balanced'.

In the capture theory approach, however, the regulatees through lobbying are able to reduce competition from rivals, by obtaining 'appropriate' regulation. For instance, licences can be misused to block entry from efficient competitors from outside the countries' borders. If it were true that banks monitor each other on the safety of the financial system (reasons why this might be the case will be given below), then in the capture theory view it is the unregulated market that attains a balanced outcome and not the regulated.

At the level of the European Commission, the financial market integration programme certainly aims at increasing efficiency within the Community, while maintaining simultaneously a sufficient degree of stability. Harmonisation, (national) deregulation and (supranational) re-regulation then are not goals as such, they merely serve the purpose of integration as will be shown. Nonetheless, it is appropriate to ask whether the EC policy is effective and efficient, that is whether the goal of integration will actually be achieved and whether this goal was unattainable by means of a different, perhaps laissez-faire policy. In the context of this chapter, only a few ideas can be given on these matters.

3. Host country preference, captured regulators and banking competition in a segmented world

The First Banking Coordination Directive of 1977 was already designed to facilitate the establishment of foreign (Community) branches in member countries. The branch however operates under the supervision of the host country. It can be required to compete on equivalent standards as the host country's own banks. The range of activities deployed by the branch is limited by the host country's legislation (see also Zavvos, 1988).

Although the branch is subject to the controls of its home country, the host country's standards (if different) may be preferred to the provisions prevailing in the home country. Hence the 'host country preference' terminology.

One implication of this principle would be that, in the same territory, local banks and branches of foreign banks compete according to the same rules. In this respect, there are no competitive distortions. Another implication is that, between territories, the rules of the game can be different. How this can lead in some cases to pressure towards more regulation is analysed formally in Van Cayseele and Heremans (1991). The results together with the intuitive arguments underlying these conclusions are presented next.

In reality, several factors affect the competitive position of a financial institution, see Gilibert and Steinherr (1989). In a segmented banking market, the entry barriers that prevent rivals from outside entry are important. If such barriers can be erected so as to avoid new competition, incumbents can improve upon profitability. Hence, the strategic management literature documents the creation of barriers to entry as an important factor in competition (see Van Cayseele and Schreuder, 1988).

In the banking industry, the market is segmented in different ways. First of all, there is the distinction between the wholesale and the retail segments. Second, there is the segmentation between the national markets. The legal entry barriers which follow from the market authorisation procedures are particularly relevant in this respect, and they exist virtually everywhere (see Dale, 1986). Therefore, competition in the pre-1992 era can best be understood along the lines of the legal entry barriers that existed, like solvency requirements that banks had to fulfil in order to obtain a banking licence.

If the solvency ratio (often defined as equity funds/total assets) in one country exceeds this ratio in another country, it will be impossible for the banks in the latter country to enter the former financial market, unless additional capital to meet the solvency requirements is raised. But banks in the country with the highest solvency ratio will be able to enter the other market. This situation raises incentives to increase the solvency ratios in both countries. This deserves some further explanation.

First, consider the incentives to raise the solvency ratio in the country with the initially low ratio. What will happen if they do not succeed in raising the capital? Foreign banks then are able to enter their market. This will imply a loss of profits. Hence, it might pay to attract costly capital and to increase the solvency ratio to an extent that enables them to bank abroad, or even slightly higher. Thus, rather than sitting passively and waiting for foreign banks to take over part of their domestic banking market, the domestic banks now prevent this from happening (foreign banks do not meet the higher domestic solvency ratio). In addition, the domestic banks can now enter the foreign market. Positions have shifted completely: the domestic banks now are no longer in the defence, they are the ones able to invade foreign markets.

Incentives to raise capital now exist in the country which initially had the highest solvency ratio. If they do not increase the ratio in their country, they now run the risk of losing their domestic market. Of course, they are comfortable if the initial low ratio country stays where it was – everything depends on the rival country's actions. Also for the low ratio country, raising capital makes little sense if in the high ratio country a defensive increase is carried out.

In the formal model, Van Cayseele and Heremans show that on the average the outcome in this environment will be that each country increases its solvency ratio. More specifically, if the cost of the additional capital to be raised is exactly offset by the profits that can be made in the foreign market, in 75 per cent of the cases either one or both of the countries will increase the solvency ratio. Harmonisation, which would lead to fully integrated financial markets, has no appeal in this environment. As soon as some country requires slightly higher solvency ratios, it prevents entry by foreign banks while the domestic banks still can bank abroad.

Of course, if some country feels it is disadvantaged, it can easily take action to bridge the gap and even raise the solvency ratio. But then the other country could raise the solvency ratio even further and this process would continue until it is realised that a further increase in capital leaves no room for profitable banking. The 'losing' party then might as well reduce the solvency ratio to the lowest level, in order to avoid bearing excessive costs of capital. If this has been carried out, however, the 'winning' party might as well reduce the solvency ratio to a level just above the position taken by the 'losing' party. They then remain in a winning position but also save on capital costs. But then again the positions can easily be changed, that is, one is back to the situation described at the beginning of this paragraph. The result is a highly unstable situation with solvency ratios increasing steadily then dropping substantially (see Varian, 1980 or Stahl, 1988 for details).

The conclusion to all this is that, while the First Directive allowed in principle for integration, market forces in general and the competitive strategies in a segmented market in particular don't stimulate an integrated outcome. On the contrary, increased regulation without harmonisation or integration is a likely outcome. Therefore, the Commission, in the pursuit of integrated financial markets, has designed further legislation.

4. Home country control, minimal standards and banking competition with less regulation

In the 1985 White Paper, the Commission aimed at the creation of a unified banking market. As documented in the previous section, the restriction on branches to bank according to domestic legislation is a serious obstacle to the realisation of this goal, if legislations can be manipulated to act as barriers to entry. The aim of the Second Banking Coordination Directive was to eliminate these obstacles by adhering to the home country control principle.

The crucial feature of this principle is mutual recognition, implying that the home country controls offer sufficient regulatory guarantees. Even if legislation is different, the controls imposed by the home country offer enough protection against unstable outcomes. With this approach, the *ex ante* rules of the game can be different, competitive distortions can exist.

There are then two competing views regarding what will happen *ex post*. In one view, presumably the one held by the Commission, the competitive distortions will be reinforced, finally leading to competition between regulators and the lowest conceivable standards. Another view, the one defended here, holds that the differences will disappear to an important extent. Both visions are now explained.

4.1 MINIMAL STANDARDS, THE REINFORCEMENT OF COMPETITIVE DISTORTIONS AND THE DOWNWARD SPIRAL

Suppose a banking environment characterised by mutual recognition, as perceived by the Second Banking Coordination Directive. Since a bank licence obtained in any one member country is sufficient to enter any other member country, banks will relocate towards countries with the lowest solvency requirements. The reason is that banks operating from countries with high solvency ratios will face a competitive disadvantage: they have higher capital costs. *Vis-à-vis* their competitors in low solvency ratio countries, they will have to charge higher service fees, pay less interest on deposits or settle for lower profits.

It then might be very difficult to maintain the required capital, since, as banks make less profit, dividends will be lower *vis-à-vis* abroad. In order to pay the same dividends to their shareholders, banks will then relocate to countries with low solvency ratios. But then high solvency ratio countries will lose banking activity and hence they will be tempted to reduce their solvency ratios. This is the downward deregulatory spiral which some are afraid of. Therefore, the Commission has, together with the mutual recognition principle, enacted minimal standards. These minimal standards exceed the current solvency ratios, and hence deserve further attention (see section 5).

4.2 SELF-REGULATION AND REPUTATION

In order to understand why counteracting forces to the downward spiral exist, a simple example from a different sector might be very helpful. In Germany, the 'Reinheitsgebot' requires beer to be brewed according to specific standards, while only a limited number of ingredients can be used. In order to preserve the tradition of high quality beer, only if these standards are met, can the brewer sell it under a specific name. Recently, US brewers started to brew according to the same standards, while mentioning on the bottles: 'brewed according to the Reinheitsgebot'. While the 'Reinheitsgebot' does not prevail in the US, brewers nevertheless try to achieve the German outcome through this kind of promotion. Quality differentiation must be a successful strategy.

Now consider the banking industry and its environment. Quality differentiation in this sector is likely to take on the form of safety guarantees for deposit holders. The view that banks will compete by offering ever higher deposit interest rates and ever lower loan interest rates is mistaken. Competition will be both in price and in quality, especially since deposit insurance schemes are not the same, see Table 4.1, and (perhaps) will not be harmonised. As a matter of fact, the EC only recommends the introduction of deposit guarantee schemes to the member countries, but certainly does not order the implementation of a harmonised deposit guarantee system.

Normally, deposit insurance schemes provide cover for the losses to depositholders, citizens and foreigners alike. That is, member countries that have a deposit insurance system have to watch that the system covers for the potential losses of both the deposits collected by domestic banks inside the country and the foreign branches of domestic banks that collect deposits in countries that don't have a deposit insurance system. Deposit schemes within a country also cover for losses of citizens occurring on deposits held with foreign branches. Or, if a deposit insurance scheme

TABLE 4.1 Deposit insurance systems in different countries

Belgium	Yes up to BeF500,000
France	Yes up to FF400,000
Germany	Yes up to per cent of bank equity
Italy	In study
Netherlands	Yes up to fl.35,000
Spain	Yes up to Pts 1,500,000
United Kingdom	Yes up £10,000
Switzerland	Yes up to SF30,000
US	Yes up to $100,000
Japan	Yes up to ¥10,000,000

Note: Differences in funding, equally important for the robustness of the scheme, exist but are not reported here.
Source: Center for Economic Studies, K.U. Leuven, see also Baltensperger and Dermine (1987) for a different source.

exists, it works for deposits held both with domestic banks or foreign branches, but if it doesn't exist in a country, the depositholders with a foreign branch can appeal to the scheme prevailing in the home country.

The prevalent deposit insurance schemes probably will not suffice to cover all losses from a major bankruptcy, if the system exists at all. Therefore, the solvency of each individual bank remains an important aspect of competitive strategy. By imposing 'tough' standards, that is high solvency ratios, a country then might provide its banks with a safe appeal abroad. Although, due to the higher capital adequacy requirement, banks of that 'tough' country cannot offer equally competitive deposit interest rates, they will offer safer deposits.

Ceteris paribus the deposit insurance systems in each country, it can then be shown that the branches from the country with the highest solvency ratio will attract most of the clients (see Van Cayseele, 1990). Intuitively, the reasoning is as follows: suppose there are three countries, two of them having similar deposit insurance mechanisms while the third country has no such provisions, or has a system that is inadequate. If the banks of the countries that are covered by deposit insurance mechanisms then enter the market of the third country, where depositholders are uncovered by insurance, they will attract deposits for they offer a deposit interest rate plus insurance; recall that the home country systems have to cover for the foreign branches.

The claim then is that most coverage is provided by the system with the highest solvency ratio. Three reasons exist which can support this claim. First, the higher the solvency ratio, the less probability of any single bank going bankrupt. This is pretty obvious and implies that a high solvency ratio avoids individual banks imposing upon the deposit insurance system. Second, and most important, if the probability of any single bank failing is lower, the probability of the entire banking system collapsing will be drastically lower (see Paroush, 1988, for a formal argument). The reason for this is that externalities (bank runs) account for other banks coming under pressure. If they are more solvent, they can readily absorb this pressure and the probability of a system-wide collapse triggered by a single bank default is less pronounced. Finally, the third argument is one of moral hazard. The bank's owners are only liable up to their net worth. If their involvement is low, they will take more risk, and risky loans may again cause bankruptcy problems.

These arguments become especially pertinent when bank runs are transmitted internationally. Thus when a financial crisis can be avoided in the home country, which is more likely when the solvency ratio is high, the deposit offered is 'safer'. Of course, many other factors such as the role of the central bank as a lender of last resort, are important in this respect. A recent study (see Maxwell and Gitman, 1989), however seems to point towards a reluctance to absorb shocks from abroad by large groups of central banks. Therefore, solvability certainly might be a competitive weapon representing an important dimension of quality.

4.3 QUALITY COMPETITION IN BANKING: EVIDENCE

The importance of quality in retail banking in general emerges from recent studies (see Tschoegl 1987). Often it is found that foreign banks perform very well with middle income customers. The reason is that they offer an appeal of exclusivity: 'A bank with branches on every main street is by definition plebian' (Tschoegl, 1987, p. 77).

In addition, safety in particular is an important advantage. Giddy (1981) reports the advantage a foreign bank's nationality brings if it signals comparative safety of deposits. In the past the arguments given in the previous section seem to have worked. Therefore, it is not likely that a downward deregulatory spiral will monopolise European banking, and hence it is appropriate to ask whether minimal standards are a condition *sine qua non* for mutual recognition to yield a safe outcome.

Important foreign evidence also points towards an increased awareness of bank failures. The increased number of bank failures in the US since 1983 well-covered by the news, has created a certain awareness of unsafe banking. In addition, evidence from interstate banking in the US indicates that bank holding companies (BHC), grandfathering networks across (state) borders, tend to lose market share (Goldberg, 1990, p. 7). This of course could be due to a variety of factors, but does not reject the hypothesis that *ceteris paribus* capital adequacy expansion leads to a less safe appeal.

5. Conclusions: the necessity of minimal standards

At the present, nearly all elements that are needed to evaluate the effectiveness and efficiency of the Second Banking Coordinating Directive are available. The Second Directive relies on mutual recognition together with minimal standards to achieve financial market integration. In section 2, it was pointed out that regulation can occur out of a public interest motive, or out of capture theoretic considerations. While it is certainly the case that the Commission strives towards a true, efficient and safe financial market in 1992, minimal standards have to be handled carefully. In section 3, it became clear how barriers to entry can be used to eliminate rivals. In a fragmented financial market, like the one in the European Community, these legal entry barriers have been a dominant element in banking strategy. Now if the 'minimal' standards are enforced at an high enough level, it will imply that some banks will be unable to participate in the 1992 wave. Hence barriers to entry on the global market are imposed. In this respect it is interesting to recall that in most countries capital adequacy requirements fall short of the required levels. It will not be easy for all banks simultaneously to raise the necessary capital and some might miss the opportunities. Also a gateway is made to takeovers by large Japanese banks with no problems raising capital.

On the other hand, however, minimal standards, especially the format of uniform solvency ratios might help to unify the market, as customers have to worry less about the safety of deposits with branches of foreign banks. It was also argued that different deposit insurance schemes together with the same solvency ratio will imply a quality difference in the product offered. So clearly, harmonisation of the solvency requirements alone is not sufficient to obtain a standardised product. The conclusion then is that mutual recognition together with minimal standards is an effective means to achieve integration. In view of the possibly harmful side-effects (the barriers to competition generated by too high 'minima') the question is whether this policy is efficient. In that respect, it seems to be the case that the market, if left on its own, probably will not end up in a 'downward regulatory spiral'. If that is the case, it is appropriate to ask whether 'high' minimal standards are required.

If banks left on their own have an incentive to engage in self-regulation, banking as such will not become less safe. The only reason one then can think of why the systemic risk might increase is a contagion effect. If more banks adapt to each other and the system breaks down if one component fails, that is the Domino assumption of Paroush (1988) prevails, then the marketplace will be less stable due to a sheer numbers effect. Then, minimal standards, by reducing the number of effective rivals that match each other, could restabilise the situation. At present not enough detailed evidence regarding the validity of this proposition is known, and hence it is regarded as a topic for future research.

Notes

1.	The 'home country control' principle has to be contrasted with the 'host country preference' principle underlying the First Banking Coordination Directive. Under that principle, a foreign bank can enter the national market but it has to operate according to the local provisions and is subject to the controls of the host country authorities.
2.	For an excellent survey of current legislation regarding the single market of credit institutions, see CRF-IMI, 1990.
3.	Contestable market theory provides a yardstick for normative conclusions regarding the performance of a sector. It strongly emphasises the absence of entry barriers. The financial sector however is characterised by licence systems, but also by some features which make contestability less suitable as a benchmark theory. For example, following Broecker (1990) one is able to show that, in order to enter the market, it is necessary to undercut the incumbent bank. Now, the response to this might be to match the lower interest rate but only on the 'good' loan applicants, i.e., those who are known to the incumbent bank as having a high chance of paying back. The 'bad' loan applicants then will turn to the entrant bank who will face a clientéle with which, given the proposed interest rate, it might be unable to break even.

References and bibliography

Baltensperger, E. and **Dermine, J.** (1987), 'Banking deregulation', *Economic Policy*, April: 61–109.

Baumol, W. Panzar, J. and **Willig, R.** (1982), *Contestable Markets and the Theory of Industry Structure*, Harcourt Brace Jovanovich.

Broecker, T. (1990), 'Credit-worthiness tests and interbank competition, *Econometrica*, 58 (2): 429–52.

Centre for research in Finance, I.M.I. Group (1990), 'Current status of the single market of credit institutions and of transferable securities as at 1 January 1990', *Documentation Series*, September, Rome.

Dale, R. (1986), *The Regulation of International Banking*, Englewood Cliffs, NJ: Prentice-Hall.

Gardener, E.P.M. (1989), 'The capital adequacy problem in modern banking', *Research Papers in Banking and Finance*, RP89.2, University College of North Wales, Bangor.

Giddy, I. (1981), 'The theory and industrial organisation of international banking, in R. Hawkins (ed.), *The International Markets and Economic Policy*, New York: JAI Press, pp. 195–243.

Gilibert, P. and **Steinherr, A.** (1989), 'The impact of financial market integration on the European banking industry', *EIB- Papers*, p. 56.

Goldberg, L. (1990), 'Banking competition in Europe after 1992: evidence from American banking', paper presented at the European Association of Law and Economics meeting, Rome, September.

Klein, B. (1974), 'The competitive supply of money', *Journal of Money, Credit and Banking*, 6 (4): 423–54.

Maxwell, C. and **Gitman, L.** (1989), 'Risk transmission in international banking', *Journal of International Business Studies*, Summer; pp. 268–79.

Neven, D. (1989), 'Structural adjustment in European retail banking: some views from industrial organisation', *CEPR Discussion Paper*, 311, London.

Paroush, J. (1988), 'The domino effect and the supervision of the banking system', *The Journal of Finance*, 63 (5): 1207–18.

Stahl, D. (1988), 'On the instability of mixed-strategy Nash equilibria', *Journal of Economic Behavior and Organisation*, 9: 59–69.

Steinherr, A. and **Huveneers, C.** (1990), 'Universal banks: the prototype of successful banks in the integrated European markets?', *Research Report*, 2, CEPS Financial Markets Unit, Brussels.

Tschoegl, A. (1987), 'International retail banking as a strategy', *Journal of International Business Studies*, Summer: 67–88.

Van Cayseele, P. (1989), 'National policy responses to innovative multi-nationals: a club theoretic approach, with an application to the pharmaceutical industry', in AUDRETSCH *et.al.*, *The Convergence of International and Domestic Markets*, Elsevier Science Publishers.

Van Cayseele, P. (1990), Quality Control and Export Promotion in Banking, Mimeo, C.E.S., 10 pp.

Van Cayselle, P. and **Heremans, D.** forthcoming, 'Legal prinicples of financial market integration in 1992: An economic analysis', *International Review of Law and Economics*.

Van Cayseele, P. and Schreuder, H. (1988), 'Strategiebepaling door Ondernemingen een overzicht', *Economisch Statistische Berichten*, 7 December: 1152–59.

Varian, H. (1980), 'A model of sales', *American Economic Review*, September: 651–9.

Zavvos, G. (1988), 'Towards a European Banking Act', *Common Market Law Review*, 25 (2): 263–89.

CHAPTER FIVE

Mergers and acquisitions in banking

Jack Revell

1. Introduction

My research on this subject started about five years ago with a study of mergers between the large commercial banks in Europe, but more recently the same topic has cropped up in my research on savings banks and public banks. The subject thus covers a very wide range of banks from the very large to the small and very small. There are certain aspects that are common to all kinds of bank, but there are equally differences in the reasons for mergers and acquisitions among different sizes and types of bank and among banks from different sizes of country and from countries in EFTA or outside Europe.

There are also very important historical differences between periods. At a time of bank expansion mergers can be carried out with comparative ease, and most of the examples of bank mergers that have clearly achieved their objectives date back to such periods. The present is quite a different period, in which successful mergers are much more difficult to bring about because of greatly increased competition, the weakening of many banks by the requirement to create more capital at the same time as they have to make seemingly endless provisions against Third World and domestic loans, and the pressing need to reduce costs, which for the first time now involve making hundreds or thousands of staff redundant. This chapter cannot be a timeless discussion of theoretical propositions about mergers in general but must bear the background conditions in mind all the time.

The changing structure of the universal bank is essential to the development of my argument. My main thesis is the considerable change in the nature of bank mergers and acquisitions in the past few years from a position in which most mergers were either between large banks or between small mutual institutions to one in which the large banks have been intent on acquiring specialist subsidiaries. To sustain this thesis I must spend most of my time analysing the changed structure of banking systems that has caused the new type of mergers.

2. Large banks

2.1 ORIGINS AND GROWTH

I am going to start by considering mergers between large banks in some detail and only then examining the other mergers. Large banks have an interesting history (Revell, 1987a). Back in the nineteenth century they grew large to serve the needs of large industrial and commercial customers, which were themselves growing bigger all the time. These large customers have played a very important part in banking business, although this is reflected in a very inadequate way in the literature. Their importance can be seen from the fact that competition between banks for the accounts of large customers was never suspended, even when the rest of banking business was conducted on the basis of controlled or agreed interest rates and there were 'no-poaching' conventions. Large customers tend to shop around much more these days, but their custom is still fought over vigorously even in these days of disintermediation and securitisation.

There were two watersheds in the history of large banks. The first was in the second half of the nineteenth century with the birth of heavy industry, which quickly raised the average size of companies in the relevant industries. Banks followed suit, mainly by amalgamations, although in some countries in Continental Europe, such as Germany and France, large banks were established specially to serve the needs of heavy industry. The second watershed was in the first quarter of the twentieth century, by which time the large banks had grown so much, and had been reduced in numbers by mergers to between six and a dozen depending on the size of the country, that they were recognised by both the authorities and the general public as the dominant banks, representing the 'core' of the banking system. These core banks have always been shielded from takeover by the central bank, in return for which they were expected to carry out the wishes of the authorities even when this reduced their profits.

Once this core of large banks had been formed and recognised by the authorities, there was little change in the number of large banks, and for the most part they ceased to absorb smaller banks. In Britain the authorities let it be known that they would not approve further mergers between the core banks. This position lasted until the middle or late 1960s, but then there were mergers in many European countries, reducing the numbers of large private banks to between two for small countries and four or five for larger countries. This merger movement did not occur in Germany or the nationalised banking systems of France and Italy. The mergers were rarely planned. What usually happened was that a merger between two banks of the group, often because the smaller of the pair was in difficulties, sparked off further mergers as the remaining banks sought to redress the balance within the group.

There is something mesmeric about the word mergers to monetary authorities and bankers alike: when troubles appear, this is the sovereign remedy to which they turn. Thus the advent of the single European market led the authorities in some countries to prod their large banks into mergers to put their banking systems in a better position, partly to compete in the enlarged market but especially to fend off unwanted predators. In 1987 and 1988 there was a messy episode in Spain during which there were two failed mergers, one of which was enlivened by a juicy scandal, and only one that came off, that between Banco de Vizcaya and Banco de Bilbao, a merger that had its troubles at the beginning. Later on I shall examine some of the other domestic mergers that took place.

In the evolution of large banks during the past 150 years or so the last stage reached so far is the universal bank, in its modern rather than its original German form.
•

2.2   UNIVERSAL BANK

Much of the discussion on banking is conducted in terms of certain buzz-words. These are coined by bankers, consultants and journalists, and they are rarely defined carefully; if they are defined in the first place, popular usage extends the meaning in unpredictable directions. The term 'universal bank' started life long ago, but its current use in Britain and many other European countries began at the time of the Big Bang in 1986. Today any bank worth its salt and above a certain size aspires to the title of universal bank. It conjures up a picture of a monolithic bank that provides a very wide range of services within a single organisation and in recent years does so in a number of national markets, if not globally. The term differs from many buzz-words in having had a very short life, since the reality in terms of bank organisation is already changing drastically.

In the original German form universal banks are invariably associated with participations in the shares of bank customers. Many of the banking laws enacted after the banking crisis of the early 1930s either withdrew the right of holding participations or limited them drastically, but they still live on in Belgium, Germany, the Netherlands and Spain, if not in some other countries. The German use of participations gave rise to the memorable phrase of Gerschenkron (1962, p.14) about a German bank accompanying an industrial enterprise from the cradle to the grave. The term universal bank in countries outside the four mentioned no longer carries the connotation of holding participations.

These participations have played many roles in banking apart from that of enabling a bank to share in the management of an enterprise. In Germany the fact that they are carried in the balance sheet at cost creates hidden reserves (Dale, 1986). The Spanish bank Banesto has transferred its participations to a subsidiary, Corporación Banesto, and is trying to place securities amounting to one-quarter of the value of its portfolio. This is a novel, if rather tortuous, way of raising the bank's capital ratio by lowering the participations to three-quarters of their former value while retaining full control over the whole portfolio.

Universal banks in the original sense are diversified banks at the heart of which is a deposit bank. All activities are under one direction and firmly controlled by the centre. It is a 'top-down' form of control. They are large, mainly because covering the wide range of activities is outside the capability of smaller institutions but also because bankers still profess to believe that economies of scale are inherent in large banks.

The concept of the universal bank as a monolithic organisation has come under fire in the past two years from many quarters. Those by Abraham and Lierman (1990), Forestieri and Onado (1989), Gardener (1990), McKinsey (1990), Métais (1990) and Shaw (1990) cover most of the field, and many of them were written fairly early in 1989, even if they were published in 1990. The most complete of the attacks on the model of the universal bank is to be found in the two articles listed under McKinsey (1990), and I have chosen to use it as the main example, because already many banks seem to have followed its suggestions, in part if not in whole.

2.3 THE McKINSEY 'FEDERAL BANK'

In these two articles the management consultants advocate the dismantling of universal banks and their transformation into what they call 'federal' (or 'federated') banks. They point out that the history of the banks that form the core of universal banks has left them with a reliance on branches as the principal channel of distribution and hence with a generally low level of skill among their staff. While customer demand for retail services was growing at a high rate, this was adequate because profitability could be secured by maximising the volume of business through acquiring new customers and controlling costs. Increased competition, particularly in the form of ever higher interest rates on deposits, and (although the authors do not make this point) the relative stagnation of retail markets at the present time mean that this model of organisation is no longer sufficient.

The fatal flaw of the universal bank is the large extent of cross subsidisation between different services, products and customer segments. It is this that has enabled new competitors to select as their targets vulnerable markets from which the costs of other parts of the universal banks are being subsidised. Put in theoretical terms, this attack on many fronts means that synergies and economies of scope have disappeared even where they previously existed. Economies of scope occur only when a particular service or product can be produced more cheaply in an integrated organisation than by a specialist.

The new competitors are mainly specialists in one of the separate areas of production, distribution or processing. The house mortgage market provides a good example of the 'unbundling' that is taking place, although it is far from complete. It also illustrates the fact that the new specialist competitors are not necessarily one-product firms; often the various functions are undertaken for other institutions by a bank or building society that has spare capacity in a particular field. These specialists can and do perform more cheaply than the universal banks. Mester (1990) makes a related point when she finds diseconomies of scope between the traditional bank functions of originating and monitoring loans and the non-traditional ones of loan selling and buying.

The answer, according to McKinsey, is to break the bank down into a number of specialist units, each conducted as far as possible as an independent business, in order to regain the advantages of specialisation. The new federal bank would have a holding company and specialist subsidiaries split between product companies and distribution companies. The holding company would be responsible for customer information, strategic management, asset and liability management and fulfilment of regulatory requirements; it would also retain control of the traditional core of a retail bank, the payment system and transaction processing. The subsidiary companies would be divided into product companies, responsible for consumer loans, mortgages, unit trusts and other areas, and distribution companies, each of which would concentrate on a segment of the market (mass market, 'upscale' or private banking, for instance). The underlying principle 'is that specialist units should be responsible for those stages of the business system where a real competitive advantage can be achieved by taking a focused approach. All other functions should either be developed centrally, or outsourced from a third party' (McKinsey, 1990b, p.129). The third party might be either within the federal bank or outside it.

It is the essence of this scheme that federal or group banks should not follow each other slavishly into each segment of the market but should choose those areas in which they have a comparative advantage. Their universality would be curtailed on grounds of effectiveness, a point that will be followed up later. Each of the specialist units of the federal bank should be entrepreneurially managed, using staff that have high skills in a particular area. Every task that the unit could not perform efficiently for itself would be sub-contracted or bought in from a third party.

The McKinsey scheme, or something very much like it, is already being put into practice in some cases, and the articles cite several examples. Among them are Barclays Bank, Compagnie Bancaire in France and the network of German co-operative banks. The last example is interesting because it leads on to a point that I shall make later, that the scheme is applicable to all savings banks and cooperative and mutual institutions that operate with a strong central bank.

Although his paper was first presented nearly a year before the McKinsey proposals, Shaw (1990) begins with a somewhat similar analysis but carries it into an area that is insufficiently emphasised by the McKinsey papers. He defines three stages of bank organisation. The first two are supportive organisations (corresponding to the traditional of the McKinsey analysis) and entrepreneurial organisations (corresponding to federal banks). The third stage, collaborative organisations, goes one step further by stressing the need to harness the entrepreneurial prima donnas (my phrase) of the specialist units into a harmonious team; it emphasises the need to overcome the culture clashes between the different groups that must find a way of working together for the greater good of the whole bank.

The problem can be expressed in a different way by seizing on the fundamental organisational difference between traditional and federal banks: the first are 'top-down' organisations, whereas the second are 'bottom-up'. There is a danger that a specialist unit will refuse to serve a particular customer even though it would be to the advantage of the whole organisation to do so. This can only be overcome by the sharing of information throughout the group and the development of what Shaw calls 'constructive conflict' to resolve differences between the specialist units.

The analysis of Abraham and Lierman (1990) looks at the same general problems but develops many new approaches. It starts by noting a shift in bank strategic thinking from a demand-determined approach to a supply-led one. To some extent this change is a consequence of the experiences of the 1980s and particularly of the last few years. Consumer demand has ceased to grow at the previous rate, bank resource needs have been dominated by the prudential demand for extra capital, and the world has become a more risky and uncertain place. Two quotations show conflicting reactions. S. Mark Roberson, a vice president of Unisys, states: 'There is truly only one way bankers can protect themselves within such an environment – that is to maintain as flexible a posture as possible to respond to and capitalize on changes and opportunities as they arise.' The other quotation is from Sir Kit McMahon of Midland Bank: 'Strategy will be better built up from the bank's existing position – size, franchise, strengths, weaknesses, etc. – than down from the global changes in demography, markets, regulatory frameworks, etc.' There is a difference in current philosophy here that transcends the interest of the first in selling computers and of the second in responding to more than his fair share of troubles.

The authors see the need to strike a balance between the two approaches rather than to opt completely for one side or the other. There is a conflict between the need for long-term investment and growth and the imperative of short-term profitability. They look ahead to the scarcity and higher cost of human capital during the 1990s at a time when reorganisation will create redundancies in some departments. They suggest a consensus at both the top and intermediate levels of the bank on the balance between short-term interventions and long-term development that would give the staff a fair share of profits but avoid sacking them when things went wrong from no fault of their own.

2.4 BANKS AND INSURANCE COMPANIES

The latest development in the changing nature of universal banks is a spate of links between banks and insurance companies (see Chapter 3). These links have taken the form of outright mergers in some countries, such as the Netherlands, where the law was changed at the beginning of this year, and France, where it seems that government permission is necessary in each case. Where either the law or the supervisory authorities do not allow mergers, joint ventures have been formed. In yet other countries, like Spain, banks have long had insurance companies among their subsidiaries. Everywhere separate supervision and separate accounting are required.

The only comment I will make concerns the relevance of the McKinsey analysis to this and other developments outside its own field of purely retail banking. In fact, something like the federal bank approach has been followed by banks, certainly in Britain after Big Bang, to bring investment banks and securities houses within the general fold. The same could doubtless apply to insurance companies, although it is worth noting that the larger ones have already formed holding companies to head groups consisting of subsidiaries, not only in life and general insurance but also in such fields as unit trusts and chains of estate agents.

2.5 LARGE BANKS IN SMALL COUNTRIES

So far I have been implying that all large banks share the same characteristics. While we were thinking only of domestic markets, that assumption caused no difficulties, but the unification of the banking market in Europe as a whole, although it may turn out to be a slow process, means that we must look at the relative sizes of the large banks throughout Europe. Generally speaking the bigger banks come from the larger countries, although there is not a one-to-one relationship between size of country and size of large banks. Already one must begin to think in terms of a pecking order of large banks throughout Europe.

In big countries the number of large banks is something that has been worked out by the market over the years. The optimum number of such large banks has fallen because of changes in the nature of banking and of bank customers, but the authorities do not allow it to fall below the level that they see as necessary to provide adequate competition, taking into account any large savings banks, cooperative and mutual institutions, and public banks. In small countries, on the other hand, with much smaller banking markets, this irreducible minimum has not been allowed to fall below two until 1990, when the merger of ABN and AMRO was allowed to break the informal rule. I am sceptical of applying the economies of scale and scope analysis to large banks, but it is still possible to think of a rather vague optimum size of large bank at different stages of banking development. In the cases of some of the small countries even a single large bank could not operate at an optimum level.

This fact has had a considerable influence on the behaviour of large banks in small countries in recent years. Before 1992 loomed on the horizon, the large banks in small countries were beginning to flex their muscles and to move into neighbouring countries. Thus the two large Irish banks now do something like 25 per cent of their business in Northern Ireland, the Isle of Man and the mainland of Britain. Their own market did not allow them sufficient scope, and so they sought an extension to that market. In the same way the Scottish banks moved down into England and Wales. Strangely enough the strongest example of the 'small country' phenomenon is the United States, where the prohibition on interstate banking similarly constricted the large money centre banks, and this was one of the factors that drove them to set up branches abroad in the 1970s.

The advent of preparations for 1992 led to another type of behaviour by large banks in small countries because it made them fear being taken over by one of the much larger banks on a European-size scale; in many of the smaller countries Deutsche Bank has been cast in the role of the bogeyman. The response has been for large banks to merge, primarily as a defence against hostile acquisition but also in some cases as a preparation for operating in other European countries. The single market was very much in the minds of Spanish bankers and the Bank of Spain when they began to consider reducing the number of large banks from seven to three or four. The motive to expand in Europe must be very strong in the merger between ABN and AMRO because the total size of the merged bank is roughly the same as that of Deutsche Bank. The merger activity of banks in smaller countries has not been limited to members of the European Community; banks in EFTA countries like

Norway and Sweden have gone even further in trying to build up strong commercial banks for the same reasons as the smaller countries within the Community.

2.6 IMPLICATIONS OF THE FEDERAL BANK

To the extent that banks follow the advice given in the various papers to which I have referred, banking systems in developed countries will begin to assume different structures from the present ones. All the pressures have so far tended to make banks more like each other, within each country and between countries, because competition between large organisations works to create a single model in each market: all supermarkets have much the same range of goods on their shelves, and all motor cars in the lower price ranges look much like each other apart from a few cosmetic differences. The McKinsey schema counteracts the tendencies towards uniformity by requiring banks to select their markets, both functional and geographical, according to their comparative advantages – the Abraham and Lierman (or Kit McMahon) supply-side orientation in a different guise.

The first implication is therefore that large banks will begin to be more differentiated in each country and probably that each country's banking system will stop trying to make itself more like those of other countries. In future we shall have to classify banks according to a complicated matrix of functional and geographical characteristics. Following a suggestion by Lafferty, Abraham and Lierman (1990, Table 4, p.15) suggest such a taxonomy. The functional characteristics are universal, commercial, investment and specialised banks. The geographical characteristics are worldwide, international (global player), pan-European, super-regional, national, and regional and local. Several other writers give similar matrices, but usually less complicated.

The second implication is that there will probably be fewer powerful competitors in each of the markets served by the subsidiaries of federal banks. This is not to say that there will be less effective competition because most of the institutions in the market will be specialists, many of them members of a powerful federal bank. We are less likely, I think, to get the phenomenon of overbanking, which plagues European retail banking markets at the present time.

The third implication is that the total number of strong federal groups in the world is likely to be much larger than the forecasts given for the number of global banks when the enthusiasm for universal banks of the traditional model was at its height. Then many were saying that there would be only twenty such global banks, accompanied by the demise of medium sized institutions. Now the word (*The Economist*, 25 June 1988) is that there will be as many as 100 groups, many of them medium sized.

From these three implications I draw certain conclusions. The first is that we are likely to see far fewer mergers between large banks because the days of the battleships of banking, the completely integrated universal banks, seem to be numbered. In their place we shall see the continuance of the phenomenon of banking groups expanding by acquiring specialist subsidiaries, which has meant that there are precious few independent 'niche' players left. This will be accompanied by the other new phenomenon of groups withdrawing from certain markets either because the group as a whole is in difficulties or because a certain market is proving unprofitable. Midland Bank and Standard Chartered Bank are examples of withdrawal for the first reason and the Prudential Insurance Group, with the sale of its entire chain of 500 estate agencies, withdrew for the second reason. What is happening to some extent is that the merger market for entire banks is being replaced by a new market for parts of groups consisting of specialist units in various foreign countries and various forms of banking business. This is a much more flexible mechanism for banks to expand and to contract.

The second conclusion is that there may well be further mergers of banks from the smaller countries. In those countries there is still scope to aim for a larger size of group.

In addition to the implications and conclusions for mergers that I have just listed there are several more general implications about the nature of banks and banking that emerge from the debate about universal and federal banks (see Métais, 1990, pp. 175–7 and Revell, 1987b). The first is the point that we can no longer regard banks as purely financial intermediaries. The large ones have blossomed into full financial services conglomerates, and even other institutions like the larger savings banks and building societies have diversified into most corners of retail and whole-sale banking, although generally with less emphasis on international business. The second is that the new types of bank are not likely both to produce and to distribute financial products to the same extent as they do now. In this they are tending to become more like retail distributors, which may place their own brand names on goods manufactured by others but rarely get involved in manufacturing on their own account.

3. Savings banks, mutual banks and public banks

The discussion so far has been limited to the kinds of bank that attract most publicity and interest, the large, privately owned commercial banks, but for a thorough discussion of mergers it is necessary to bring in some institutions of a different sort. These are savings banks (which are usually owned by a self-perpetuating foundation), co-operative banks, mutual banks (like the British building societies and credit coopera-tives) and public banks. In the past few years there have been more mergers in this group of institutions than among commercial banks. They have become important in several ways and cannot be ignored.

This whole group shares certain characteristics. The first is that there are many small and very small institutions among all the groups except public banks, although some of the larger ones, like CARIPLO, Westdeutsche Landesbank, the

Halifax Building Society, Crédit Agricole and Rabobank, are equal in size to many of the larger commercial banks, even though their participation in international and corporate business may be inferior in most cases. The numbers of institutions have been declining since the 1920s by mergers, either because small institutions were in trouble or in a conscious effort to secure a critical size. This merger movement has generally intensified in recent years

The second characteristic is that they have all been immune to hostile take-over, but this immunity is wearing thin in some cases. There have been several cases of large savings banks and public banks being allowed to convert themselves into limited companies, generally with all the shares retained by the state or the foundation as the case may be, and then merging with a private sector institution, thus moving completely away from their original sector; a good example is NMB/Post-bank in the Netherlands, which has further merged with the largest insurance company. British building societies are now permitted to convert themselves into full commercial banks, and the way in which the first conversion took place shows the vulnerability of depositors to bribes of capital gains and free shares. Because the branch network and house mortgage business of building societies would be very attractive to a universal or a federal bank, the press is waiting for the first bid, probably by a foreign bank.

The third characteristic is that savings banks and some of the other types have remained local or regional and have not competed against each other in the same territory. This characteristic has largely disappeared in practically all European countries except France, Germany and the Scandinavian countries, with the largest institutions competing throughout the country against the big commercial banks. This has been accompanied by merger movements designed to create regional savings banks. To my mind much of this is unnecessary, to make savings banks and others competitive. They have always cooperated closely with each other, and much of this remains. In most cases there is a central bank of the movement, which handles group liquidity and foreign business for the smaller institutions, and carries out 'financial engineering' and many other tasks. If this central bank were strengthened, all but the very smallest institutions could survive as distributors, obtaining the more sophisticated products from the central bank of the movement. In many countries the groups of savings banks or credit cooperatives, unified in this way, could rival the very largest commercial banks in size and effectiveness.

Public banks are rather a different kind of animal. There are two main types, of which the first is a postal savings bank and postal giro, often united into a single postbank, and the second a variety of what are normally called special credit institutions – export–import banks, mortgage banks to finance subsidised housing and banks for subsidised lending to local government authorities and certain industries. The first type is blossoming in most countries, and many of them have aspirations to become full-scale retail banks. The business of the second group has largely disappeared with the removal of subsidies and the spreading of the business in which the public banks had a monopoly throughout the banking system. But they are not lying down. Often each of them starts a retail business – IMI in Italy is the prime example – or even tries to become a universal bank in its own right. Several countries, usually those with social democratic governments, have considered combining the various public banks into a single public universal bank, which would often, as in Spain, be the largest bank in the country or among the largest.

Far from being a digression, these examples of what is happening among banks that are not privately owned commercial banks show that the shape of many European banking systems may well look somewhat different in the next few years. In many cases new large banks are being created from sectors other than that of commercial banks.

4. Conclusions

I have chosen to present an argument rather than to list a number of the mergers that have taken place in the past three or four years as 1992 approaches.

My main conclusion is that the arguments advanced in the two McKinsey (1990) articles and in many of the other papers listed at the end of this paper have been borne out by events. In many cases the universal bank model has been tried for a year or two and then dropped in favour of the federal bank; in other cases banks have chosen or been forced by law and regulations to establish a holding company and group right from the start of diversifying their services into many new areas. This is not to say that the federal bank has been adopted in its entirety because the essential development in retail banking of a divorce between production, distribution and processing is still lacking in most cases. The market process of 'unbundling' will probably be the engine to bring this about by creating further independent niche players to be gobbled up by the federal banks in due course. The process of withdrawing from unprofitable functional or geographical markets does not seem to have got very far.

With regard to cross-border mergers that could be sparked off by the approach of 1992 I have expressed scepticism about the possibility of the core banks in any country being attacked from across the borders because of the opposition of national governments, and in that I was proved right.

The mergers of the past two or three years have been of three main types. Firstly, there have been acquisitions of relatively small banks, mainly by the large banks from the four largest countries, Germany, France, Italy and the United Kingdom, although only a handful of large banks have been involved. Muldur (1990, pp.162–5) sees in many of the mergers a move by banks in the north of Europe towards the south. Secondly, there has been a preponderance of mergers within national boundaries, mainly defensive but sometimes with an offensive element, particularly in the smaller countries. Thirdly, many of the mergers and acquisitions have not been between pairs of banks but between a bank and a specialist institution, such as a fund manager or a merchant bank. This third group of mergers is exactly in accord with the movement towards federal banks, this time outside the country of origin of the bank: banks are being selective in the way in which they start operations in other countries.

Finally a quote from Abraham and Lierman (1990, p.5) seems apt. It refers, of course, to the period before banks began to follow the precepts of McKinsey by being selective in their choice of markets:

> with the advice of bank economists and management consultants, bankers once again practised their familiar game of overshooting. . .

It only illustrates how niches which first attract everybody very quickly degenerate into dirty stables.

References and bibliography

Abraham, J.P. and **Lierman, F.** (1990), 'European banking strategies in the nineties: a supply side approach', *Revue de la Banque*, no. 8–9 November (in English; pagination in text from typescript).

Dale, Richard (1986), 'Universal banking: the German model', *The Banker*, 136 (725) July: 14–20.

Forestieri, Giancarlo and **Marco Onado** (1989), 'Il sistema bancario italiano di fronte alle trasformazioni strutturali', section I in Forestieri and Onado (eds), *Il Sistema Bancario Italiano e l'Integrazione dei Mercati: un Confronto delle Strutture e degli Ordinamenti dei Principali Paesi*, Milan: Università Bocconi and E. Giuffrè Editori.

Gardener, Edward P.M. (1990), 'A strategic perspective of bank financial conglomerates in London after the Crash', *Journal of Management Studies*, 27 (1) January: 61–73.

Gerschenkron, Alexander (1962), *Economic Backwardness in Historical Perspective: a Book of Essays*, Cambridge, MA: Harvard University Press.

Khatkhate, Deena R. and **Klaus-Walter Riechel** (1980), 'Multipurpose banking: its nature, scope, and relevance for less developed countries', *IMF Staff Papers*, 27: 478–516.

McKinsey, von Löhneysen, Eberhard, Viana Baptista, Antonio and **Walton, Adam** (1990), 'Emerging roles in European retail banking', *The McKinsey Quarterly*, (a) Winter: 142–50; (b) Number 3: 127–135.

Mester, Loretta J. (1990), 'Traditional and nontraditional banking: an information-theoretic approach', paper read at Conference on Bank Structure and Competition sponsored by Federal Reserve Bank of Chicago, May.

Métais, Joël (1990). 'Towards a restructuring of the international financial services industry: some preliminary and theoretical insights', chapter 10 in Edward P.M. Gardener (eds), *The Future of Financial Systems and Services: Essays in Honour of Jack Revell*, London and Basingstoke: Macmillan.

Muldur, Ugur (1990), 'Restructurations et stratégies dans le secteur financier européen', *Revue d'Economie Financière*, no. 12–13, spring–summer: 155–93.

Revell, Jack (1987a), *Mergers and the Role of Large Banks*, Research Monographs in Banking and Finance no. 2, Bangor, Gwynedd: Institute of European Finance.

Revell, Jack (1987b), 'Towards a microeconomic theory of financial institutions', Institute of European Finance Research Papers in Banking and Finance RP 87/10 (first published in Italian in *l'Industria* and *Ban caria* in 1980).

Shaw, E.R. (1990), 'Changes in organisational structure in banking', Institute of European Finance Research Papers in Banking and Finance RP 90/21 paper read at meeting of European Association of Teachers in Banking and Finance, Dublin, September 1989.

CHAPTER SIX

Competition between banks and insurance companies – the challenge of bancassurance

Geoffrey Nicholson

1. Introduction

Since the late 1980s the financial landscape has been undergoing major changes all over Europe. Under the banner of Allfinanz or Bancassurance, banks and insurance companies have blurred the once sharp boundaries between their industries. They are experimenting with three different approaches – start-ups, acquisitions and alliances (in the forms of joint ventures, mergers or cooperation agreements). The provision of a wider range of financial services defined by the potential to create competitive advantage rather than by regulation is seen as the key to adding value to the customer relationship. This chapter will review the major combinations which have happened, assess the economic logic for these combinations and summarise the key steps for successful implementation.

2. Background

The trend towards Bancassurance has been most pronounced in France and Germany, but other countries are following. The speed of the process is largely determined by the speed with which the regulatory environment loosens, as well as the degree of clarity of vision which the leading financial institutions have. There are three approaches to building an institution which markets both insurance and banking products: start-up, acquisition or an alliance.

One of the most successful examples of the start-up approach is Crédit Agricole whose life insurance company Predica has grown over three years to the second largest life insurance company in France. Their success is partly due to their large branch network – 6000 life insurance agents sell Predica products through Crédit Agricole's network of ninety regional banks – as well as certain tax advantages and their sophisticated customer relationship management techniques. Other banks who have adopted the start-up approach include Deutsche Bank with Deutsche Bank Lebensversicherung, and in the UK, the TSB, who have had a life insurance subsidiary for a number of years. While there are many examples of banks starting *de novo* insurance companies, there are fewer examples of insurers starting up a bank – RAS in Italy and AGF with Banque Générale de Crédit being the only ones which come to mind.

Examples of the acquisition route include the French state-owned insurer GAN who bought the bank CIC, and the purchase of Abbey Life by Lloyds Bank in the UK, to add to its own small life insurance operation Black Horse Life. Aachener und Münchener, one of the leading German insurers, acquired the trade-union Bank für Gemeinwirtschaft. Some of these acquisitions have been largely integrated while others have been left as essentially standalone investments.

Allianz AG, Europe's largest insurance group, and Dresdner Bank, Germany's second biggest bank represent the most recent major alliance example. However, their agreement to cooperate only covers about half of their respective networks, mainly in Central Germany, with Dresdner selling insurance products through about 600 branches, and Allianz offering savings and loan products through 3800 full-time and 18,000 part-time agents. A further example of two major European players who have allied is the agreement between UAP and BNP in France to cross-sell each other's products, albeit with some complaints from the agents' side. In the Netherlands Nationale-Nederlanden, the largest Dutch insurer, merged with NMB Postbank, the country's third largest bank.

This whirlwind of activities began to slow down in 1990. Some institutions have experienced less success than they had hoped in combining banking and insurance. Indeed, some still question whether there are real synergies and opportunities for new business growth, or if the combinations are simply another version of the 'financial supermarket' which has been somewhat discredited in recent years. It is thus worth reviewing the economic logic of these combinations and offering some thoughts on which is likely to be the most successful model, and the best way to execute the logic.

3. The economic logic

The economic logic for these combinations relates to:

> Natural customer 'capture points';
> Opportunities to add value for a customer

3.1 WHAT IS A 'CAPTURE POINT'?

Our review of the logic for these combinations starts from the perspective that financial product demand is generally derived from a more fundamental consumer need.

For example, consumers do not want mortgages – they want to buy houses. They do not want savings accounts – they want a secure source of money for their children's education or old age. Understanding and effectively addressing these underlying needs will be critical to successfully selling financial products in the 1990s.

The outlet where the consumer need is expressed early on is what we label the 'capture point'. This notion of capture points also implies that traditional distribution channels become disadvantaged as the retail outlets, where the consumer need is first expressed, develop the ability to sell financial products. The capture point is rich ground for establishing new customer relationships. Timely satisfaction of customer needs at the capture point leads to additional business at high price premia. To take one traditional example, Henry Ford realised early on that he could build a very profitable auto lending business by sourcing business through his retail car dealerships. These dealers were the natural point to sell car loans, and car loans were a useful additional weapon to sell cars.

Demographic changes imply rapid future growth in life insurance and pension products which, together with their relatively high profitability and low risks, make this an attractive market to be in. Bank channels are generally better capture points for these quasi-savings products than are traditional insurance channels. They also have the need to sell more products through their expensive branch networks.

Also, banks' positions as mortgage providers give them the opportunity to sell both life and house insurance. For example, in the UK nearly 50 per cent of house structure insurance is distributed through the bank or building society channel, while only about 25 per cent is distributed through an insurance agent or company. Similarly, life insurance products are often bundled with mortgages. Hence, for some insurance products the capture point logic is a powerful driving force of the convergence of banking and insurance.

3.2 OPPORTUNITIES TO ADD VALUE

Not only are banks a natural capture point, the combination of bank and insurance products can add customer value in several ways. The three most significant sources of value are:

- reducing distribution costs;
- improving investment capabilities; and
- improving operational effectiveness.

First, these combinations can dramatically reduce distribution costs. Distribution costs are of the order of 15–20 per cent in both life and general insurance (see Figure 6.1). New policy commissions are higher, so for new business distribution costs play an even bigger role. Our work has shown that distribution costs can be reduced by two-thirds when insurance is sold to a bank customer base. Banks achieve higher productivity by using their warm customer base. These powerful economics are often masked for the insurer by the high commission rates paid to financial intermediaries. These commission rates in fact demonstrate the strong position of the intermediary.

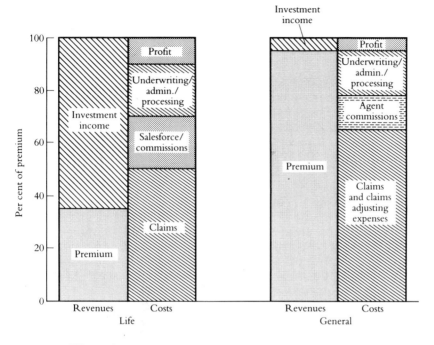

FIG 6.1 Insurance value structures

A second source of value-added can relate to investment management improvement. Figure 6.1 also shows that a major source of value-added in insurance is investment returns. The improvement of these returns from combinations will vary by country because of the different insurance product preferences in different countries. In some countries' life insurance products are largely based on fixed income instruments, while in others they are based on equities. Retail banks have a mostly fixed income management orientation. Thus, the compatibility of insurers' and banks' investment know-how varies from country to country.

For example, investment departments of UK insurers have strong equity capabilities – skills one would not typically find in the treasury area of a UK clearing bank which would tend to be fixed-income oriented. The UK insurer's investment capabilities, therefore, are quite different from those of a UK clearing bank. Thus, in the UK, there is likely to be little synergy on the investment portion of value-added in the combination of a clearing bank and a life insurance company.

Conversely, in Germany, France and the USA, the fixed-income orientation of insurers means that there is potentially an easier fit with the banks' capabilities. In this case combining the capabilities could result in substantial productivity improvements, better risk management, or enhanced return. Hence, value may also be added in a combination by partly merging the investment functions.

The third potential area in which value may be added relates to improving operational effectiveness. Banks and life insurance companies process large transaction volumes, most often at higher cost and lower quality standards than necessary. Some institutions have developed important insights into reducing the cost and improving the quality of this processing. For example, our recent work has shown that many life insurance companies can substantially improve the quality of new policy processing while reducing unit costs by over 40 per cent. Using similar methodology we have also helped banks to reduce unit costs in cheque processing by over 30 per cent. While it would be naive to pretend that processing of bank and insurance products is similar in a superficial sense, it is clear that industrial cost reduction methods and insights may be applied to both industries. In this sense, an institution which has developed or purchased such insights might apply them to another institution. Particularly as systems expenditures grow, these insights will be an important source of competitive advantage. Thus, this area, in which synergy is often dismissed, is, we believe, potentially an important source of cost reduction.

Having reviewed the economic logic of combinations of banks and insurers, we conclude that the logic does hold true where the capture point potential exists or in those examples where other substantial value can be added for the customer. Generally speaking, retail banks can be successful when combining credit insurance, life insurance, household insurance and financial advice products with their banking products. This is where the strongest logic holds. Now we will examine how to implement the logic most successfully.

4. Implementation

Banks and insurance companies have demonstrated a variety of different approaches to implement the economic logic. Three key questions must be considered:

1. What type of institution is in the best position to drive the consolidation?
2. What is the best vehicle (start-up, acquisition, alliance) for development?
3. What are the capabilities required for success and how should institutions build them?

4.1 TYPE OF INSTITUTION

We would argue that in most situations there must be one player driving the combination. It will be hard to create value through distribution channels, systems, and operational rationalisation where one partner does not clearly control the combination. This one partner will tend to be the bank. Banks typically sell their customers a range of products, often starting with money transfer and credit, and later adding home

Customer added-value	Institution core product offering			
	Bank	Life insurance/ Pensions	General Insurance	Insurance broker/adviser
Investment	●	●		○
Credit	●	○		
Money transfer	●			
Risk reduction	○	●	●	○
Financial advice	●	○		●
Home-related products*	●	●	●	●

* Real estate agency, mortgages, household insurance

FIG 6.2   Retail financial services products

related products and investment and savings products with financial advice (see Figure 6.2). This gives them a high degree of consumer loyalty and potentially a strong cross-selling performance as they are more likely to identify the appropriate capture points and act upon them.

Conversely, insurance companies often sell only one or two products to their personal customers, frequently via brokers. This lack of distribution control and direct market presence means that in many countries insurance companies are less well placed to realise value from combinations with banks, than are their bank partners.

In a recent client study conducted in Germany it was found that after four years of cooperation between a bank and an insurer, cross-sales of insurance products to the bank's customers were eight times as successful (measured in sales volume) as cross-sales of bank products to the insurer's customers. In addition consumers were found to be far more loyal to their bank than to their insurance company. Thus, in general insurance products aimed at individuals, the banks have many advantages. Nevertheless, in life insurance, banks still have a long way to go to convince customers of their capability to give good investment advice. Life insurers which are excellent at building customer relationships, especially via a highly capable salesforce, will remain in a strong position to drive the combination.

4.2 VEHICLE

Deciding on the best vehicle to execute the logic will depend greatly on the individual players involved. Executing an acquisition well it could be argued is the best and fastest route for becoming an integrated Bancassurance player, providing there is strategic insight as regards the synergies attainable in distribution channels, investment performance and operational effectiveness. An acquisition adds many capabilities rapidly and should leave no room for doubt as to who is driving the combination.

Although acquisitions appear the easiest route, the other vehicles do have advantages and can be made to work. Start-ups ensure there is minimal cultural clash and profit stays with the company, rather than being lost in commission or acquisition premia. The long development times inherent in setting up such an operation, especially in achieving underwriting and new product development capabilities, can make this a less attractive option.

However, Crédit Agricole, as mentioned already, has been extremely successful with its life subsidiary Predica. It claims its success is due to several reasons. These include a policy of limiting the product range to no more than ten different products and keeping products relatively simple. Crédit Agricole has an extensive training programme which to date has involved thousands of staff who had to take an exam on completing the training. This is not the only way the bank monitors the standard of knowledge – most recently it conducted a voluntary test of knowledge throughout the entire network which it claims was successfully completed by one-third of trained staff. Crédit Agricole thus seems to have been successful in developing a method which has enabled the bank to identify itself with insurance products. Most interestingly the implementation does not rely on incentives – Predica does pay the bank around 2–3 per cent of sales as commission, however, neither the individual outlets nor the salespersons are compensated directly.

Alliances would seem to be the most difficult structure for creating shareholder value. In many cases the process of reaching an agreement on the structure of the cooperation has been very slow and problematic, e.g., specifying the commission structure, who does how much of the processing, whether or not the insurance salesperson sits in the branch, what to do about products which are already being offered by both partners, and other issues. The closer the two partners are in size the more difficult it may be to realise value from synergies.

Alliances, however, are successful when implementation is superb. Figure 6.3 shows the results of successful versus unsuccessful implementation. Bank X was found to be very successful in selling life products through its branch network. This was due to offering a standardised product, with own branding and IT support. Most importantly the bank gave in-house training which was linked to target volumes. This ensured the branch staff were able to identify warm leads when they came to the branch and there were incentives for them to convert these leads into sales. There was close management control.

In the case of Bank Y, the management placed little emphasis on the insurance sales volume and any training took place via the partner without linkage to target volumes. The bank could not identify itself with the insurance products.

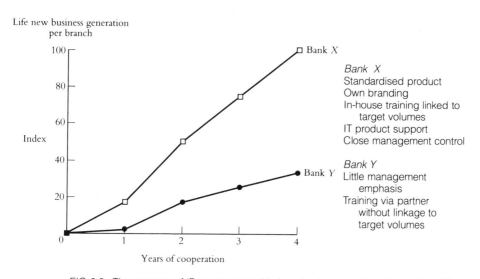

FIG 6.3 The success of 'Bancassurance' is heavily dependant on the quality of the implementation

4.3 CAPABILITIES

In order to create real shareholder value, superb implementation is required, including putting in place a new organisation, and effective and rapid rationalisation, systems integration training and management targeting and control. Organising the institution effectively will be the major implementation task, mainly because of the cultural issues and the need to preserve capabilities. The combined institution faces several choices in reorganising itself. By thinking through the institution's core capabilities in distribution, treasury/investment, risk assessment/underwriting and administration and processing, management may choose structures which fit with the strategic challenges (see Figure 6.4).

On organising the distribution, the institution must choose among:
- branch staff selling insurance;
- placing insurance salesperson in branches;
- direct response; or
- rationalisation of channels.

The practical organisation at branch level is going to be critical for either of the first two choices. The organisation must overcome the numerous cultural differences between bank and insurance staff. The branch manager should be encouraged to ensure insurance policies are sold. Placing insurance salesperson in branches sometimes leads to uncooperative behaviour by the bank staff. The staff want to protect 'their' customers from the hard-selling techniques often associated with insurance salesperson. There is often envy as well. On the other hand, in the case of

	Choices	Challenges
Distribution	Direct response Insurance salesmen in branches Branch staff sell insurance Rationalisation of channels	Insurance vs Bank culture Customer protectiveness Identifying leads
Treasury/investment	Separation of instruments Profit vs cost centres	Managing own money/reserves Managing others' money/reserves Pay/status of units
Risk assessment/underwriting	Centralised vs. decentralised Expert systems	Preservation/pooling expertise Analytical systems implementation
Administration/processing	Separate vs combined processing Centralised vs decentralised	Customer service delivery Transferring effectiveness insights

FIG 6.4 Organising appropriately: some choices and challenges

branch staff selling insurance, there is the challenge of being able to identify warm leads when they come into the branch.

Opting to distribute insurance products through a bank's network requires the insurance company carefully to think through how this fits in with existing distribution channels. The Nat–Ned example demonstrates clearly that this strategy can cause severe conflicts with the intermediary channel.

In organising the treasury/investment department of the combined institution, decisions on the separation of instruments will have to be made. Whereas in a bank the treasury department may be seen as a cost centre, the investment department of an insurer is often a profit centre. Managing the institution's own money and reserves needs to be balanced against managing others' money and reserves. Different fiduciary requirements prevail. Furthermore the often significant differences in pay and status between bank treasurers and insurance company investment officers will create friction if not managed appropriately.

The main choice in the structure of the risk assessment/underwriting capabilities is between centralisation or decentralisation. The organisation needs to pool expertise but also preserve it – is there added-value if the underwriters are located with the commercial lenders? The decision here will have important implications on how information technology is applied.

On the administration/processing side of the combination, the key strategic challenge is to realise economies of scale and transfer effectiveness insights which should lead to an improved customer service delivery. While we have found that approaches to operational effectiveness in banks and insurance companies can be similar, we have also found that there are few advantages in combining bank and insurance processing operations. Again the key choices to be thought through are between separate versus combined processing and a centralised versus a decentralised structure.

5. Conclusions

The blurring of the boundary between banking and insurance will accelerate. New types of institution will emerge, with new economically defined niches replacing the niches founded on regulation. Combinations will be successful where they are founded on strategic insight and superb implementation. The insights will relate to the logic of capture points and other opportunities to add value for customers. Many deals will fail because of poor implementation.

Banks are at the moment in a better position to be the drivers of the combined organisation and thus to add value for the customer. Acquiring is likely to be the best and fastest strategy. Banks may exploit their capture points to sell personal insurance, particularly credit insurance, life insurance, household insurance and financial advice products. They will also identify opportunities in insurance to apply their distribution, investment and operational effectiveness skills. Real synergies appear attainable. Insurance companies are likely to have a more difficult time realising economic benefit from such combinations.

PART TWO

TOWARDS PAN-EUROPEAN CAPITAL MARKETS

CHAPTER SEVEN

Ten years of innovation in Europe: development of markets and change in financial behaviour

Christophe Belhomme, Claude Dupuy, Nada Matta and Raoul Salomon

1. Introduction

The 1970s witnessed an upheaval in the old economic order, with the scrapping of fixed parities and the growth of current-account imbalances induced by repeated oil shocks. The western banks' recycling of oil-producing country surpluses created a world-scale intermediation phenomenon that rapidly came up against the challenges of external debt sustainability and explosive inflation. Financial innovation in the 1980s emerged as a necessary alternative to the predominance of bank credit in the preceding decade.

The first signs of financial change can be discerned in the birth of the Euromarkets as deregulated international financial spheres. For national economies, these developments were useful for dealing with external imbalances. To finance their external and fiscal imbalances, countries had to open their domestic financial markets to foreign investors and introduce reforms that met the need for greater international capital mobility (Artus, 1990a,c). In the background, higher real interest rates also promoted the financial innovation process: both because lenders demanded higher returns on their savings and because borrowers sought cheaper sources of funds. In either case, agents were aiming at managing their finances more efficiently. Meanwhile, the increased volatility of interest rates since the late 1970s necessitated the creation of rate-risk hedging instruments. The conjunction of these various elements fuelled the surge of financial innovations – such as investment instruments bearing unregulated interest, financial assets covering the entire range of maturities and markets for managing interest-rate and exchange-rate risks.

US innovations served as a model for the financial changes implemented in Europe since the late 1970s. London was unquestionably the first European money centre to be swept by the wave of reform. Next came France and Italy, where the pace of change was brisk. West Germany responded later and more moderately.

The Euromarkets – attracted to London by its historical importance and the concentration of its financial services – propelled the City to global capital market dominance. To preserve its leadership, and under the pressure of both a sustained budget deficit in the first half of the decade and increased foreign competition, the

City was the first European marketplace to deregulate.

The British experience, in turn, accelerated innovation in other European countries. In France, innovation began spreading very swiftly in the early 1980s, prompted by the need to maintain the external competitiveness of the country's financial system. The financial system's inability to meet agents' needs acted as a decisive stimulus for market reform. After several years of credit and exchange controls, the French financial markets could no longer satisfy the ever-larger borrowing requirements of government and business. Market liberalisation and an easing of regulations had therefore become essential.

In countries such as Italy, the public debt surge in the mid-1980s made the existing financial market organisation obsolete. The government had to diversify its funding sources and to reorganise the secondary market – improved liquidity in the government securities market being one of the prerequisites for attracting foreign capital.

At first, West Germany did not feel the need to modernise its financial markets. This may have been because its current-account surpluses eliminated the problem of external financing. In addition the monetary authorities were reluctant to encourage financial innovations that would diminish their control over monetary policy. However, once they became convinced of the need to set up a financial marketplace comparable to those of its partners, they eventually implemented such a programme. The process was fairly slow because of the relative looseness of financial system regulations and because of decentralisation – the regional financial centres hindering the rise of the Frankfurt exchange.

The objective of this chapter is to analyse European financial innovation as illustrated by four major countries: United Kingdom, France, West Germany and Italy, representing the heterogeneous evolution of the financial innovations across Europe. The first section outlines the reforms implemented in the four countries over the past decade and presents the resulting changes in the financial markets as a whole. In section 2 the effects of innovations on borrowing and investment strategies of economic agents – households, non-financial enterprises, banks and governments – are assessed. The closing section collects the main points of the study and attempts to answer the following question: Did innovations ultimately produce a better allocation of resources among European countries and economic agents, and at what cost?

1.1 REFORMS

Table 7.1 lists the main reforms of the securities markets, secondary markets and money markets in the UK, France, Italy and Germany. These reforms were also accompanied by the increase in the collective management of savings, by securitisation, and by a tightening of supervisory regulations. Ahead of all these reforms, the gradual lifting of exchange controls was a prerequisite to the modernisation and internationalisation of Europe's financial markets.

TABLE 7.1 Financial innovation in Europe: highlights and chronology

UNITED KINGDOM

...   Earlier reforms: unit trusts (mutual funds); certificates of deposit (CDs)

1979   Abolition of exchange controls.

1980   Creation of unlisted securities market.

1982   Opening of London International Financial Futures Exchange (LIFFE) and London Traded Options Market (LTOM). Lifting of consumer credit controls.

1985   Introduction of interest-paying current accounts.

1986   Stockmarket reform (Big Bang):
Implementation of a negotiated commission system and easing of brokerage rules.
Abolition of regulatory separation between brokers and jobbers.
Deregulation of access to stock exchange membership.
Introduction of electronic trading system.
Establishment of Stock Exchange Automated Quotations System (SEAQ) for international securities and reform of gilt-edged market.
Issuance of commercial papers.

1987   Implementation of the Building Societies Act (1986).

1991   Launching of futures and options on the FT-SE Eurotrack 100 index (created in 1990), tracking movements of major European bourses.

GERMANY

1986   Creation of bond options market to complement existing share option market. German banks allowed to issue DM paper with CD characteristics.

1987   Opening of unlisted securities market.

1988   Introduction of DAX stock index and continuous quotation system. Brokerage fees lowered.

1989   Establishment of securities distribution system outside of official trading hours.

1990   Creation of Deutsche Terminborse (DTB), a futures and options market: trading of DAX index futures contracts and public-bond contracts.

FRANCE

...   Earlier reforms; bond and equity mutual funds (SICAVs)

1979   Introduction of Fonds Communs de Placement mutual funds.

1983   Creation of unlisted securities market ('second marché').

1984   Abolition of credit controls.

1985 and 1986   Issuance of negotiable credit instruments: CDs in francs and foreign currencies by banks, commercial paper by non-financial firms and Treasury bills by the government. Establishment of a computerised continuous quotation system (CAC).
Growth of money-market mutual funds.
Abolition of stock brokerage monopoly and creation of securities houses ('maisons de titres').
Reform of government securities market: creation of government bonds (OATs) and primary dealers (SVTs).
Creation of financial futures market (MATIF), trading in instruments such as 10-year Treasury bond contracts and 3-month PIBOR contracts.

1987   Creation of stock options market (MONEP).

1988   Opening of a MATIF options market, and launching of CAC-40 stock index futures and options contracts.

1990   Last phase of removal of exchange controls.

ITALY

1978   Creation of unlisted securities market.

1982   First CD issues.
Creation of interbank market for overnight funds.

1983   Lifting of credit controls.

1984   Creation of mutual funds.

1987   Progressive implementation of securities market reform programme:
Full computerisation and integration of quotation, information dissemination, order execution, clearance and settlement.
Centralisation of all securities transactions.

1988   Reorganisation of secondary government-bond market and appointment of primary dealers in government securities.

1990   Last phase of removal of exchange controls.

1.1.1 Securities markets

Since the mid-1980s, the European securities markets have undergone a sweeping reorganisation, mainly aimed at improving their efficiency while preserving their stability and protecting investors (Haberer, 1988; Naouri, 1986). The following trends have been observed:

Abolition of monopolies and fixed commissions

In London, as part of the thorough reorganisation of the stockmarket known as the Big Bang, financial and non-financial institutions, both domestic and foreign, were allowed to acquire equity stakes in specialist brokerage houses or to set up their own entities (OCDE, 1987). This reform was combined with the abolition of the single-capacity rule separating brokers from jobbers, replaced by the market-makers' function and by the introduction of negotiated commissions. Italy and France went through a similar process with the abolition of the stockbroker's monopoly and the establishment of securities houses. Several European countries, including France and West Germany, also adopted the principle of negotiated commissions, leading to lower brokerage fees.

Reorganisation of government securities markets

Government securities markets were modernised and internationalised under governmental impulse: the secondary markets in these securities were revamped to meet investors' needs. In the UK, the essential change in the gilt-edged market at the time of the Big Bang (Bronk, 1989) was the introduction of the market-making function. It replaced the single capacity structure by dual capacity gilt-edged market-makers (GEMMs). The new structure witnessed an increasing number of new firms operating as GEMMs and has undoubtedly improved market liquidity, efficiency and enhanced participation of international firms. France and Italy also appointed government securities primary dealers to act as market-makers and ensure market liquidity. In West Germany, innovation in government securities markets has been inhibited by the bank syndication system for government bonds.

Creation of unlisted securities markets

To complement the official exchanges, Italy (1978), Britain (1980), France (1983) and West Germany (1987) all set up unlisted securities markets. These offer an equity-raising facility for medium-sized firms that are unable to meet big-board listing requirements.

Computerisation

Computerisation of bourses and market transactions has intensified throughout Europe since 1986. This technological innovation has improved market liquidity by providing a fuller and quicker circulation of information.

1.1.2 Markets for derivative products (futures and options)

The efficiency of securities markets has been enhanced by the creation of new financial markets such as futures and options markets – LIFFE and LTOM in London (1982), MATIF and MONEP in Paris (1986, 1987), and DTB in Germany (1990) – all of them modelled on the Chicago Treasury Bond Futures Market. These institutions are designed to provide participants with a means of hedging against interest-rate, exchange-rate and market-price risks. Their trading volumes have expanded rapidly.

The transactions cover futures contracts on Treasury paper ('notional' bonds on the MATIF, British gilts, German Bunds, and US T-bonds on LIFFE), short-term rates (MATIF 3-month PIBOR contract), stockmarket indices and currencies – including ecu on LIFFE (since 1989) and MATIF (since 1990). In addition to firm futures contracts, the markets offer options contracts on some of the products traded on the futures markets. Table 7.2 shows the growth in trading volume on LIFFE and MATIF measured by the number of financial contracts. In 1990, these two markets were ranked as the world's fifth and sixth largest futures and options exchanges respectively.

In Germany, the persistence of relatively heavy taxes on financial transactions and the slowness of innovation have diverted a share of German securities trading to London.

TABLE 7.2 Number of financial futures contracts (millions of contracts)

	1986		1988		1990	
	LIFFE	MATIF	LIFFE	MATIF	LIFFE	MATIF
Futures contracts	6.5	1.2	13.8	12.9	29.8	20.0
Options contracts	0.5	–	1.8	3.4	4.4	8.2
Total	7.0	1.7	15.5	16.3	34.2	28.2

Source: Matif s.a.

1.1.3 Changes in money markets

All four countries surveyed have carried out a major reform of their money markets: it is possible for borrowers to issue negotiable paper in domestic markets in local currency and, in some cases, foreign currencies. In the UK, both the government and banks have had this possibility since the 1970s, followed by companies in 1986. France set up a unified money market open to all economic agents – government, banks and non-banking firms in 1985. As a result, companies can issue commercial paper, banks can issue certificates of deposit, and the Treasury can issue easily tradeable notes. In Germany and Italy, firms have a narrow access to the money market because of a limited issue of commercial papers.

TABLE 7.3 Net assets of UCITs (billions of ecu)

	W.Germany	France	UK	Italy	Total EEC
1985	23	96.8	32.9	13.3	196
1986	29.4	142.0	44.0	45.1	304
1987	32.4	157.4	52.0	39.0	328.7
1988	43.5	202.9	64.2	33.5	423.1
1989	52.3	247.7	79.8	32.6	518.2

Source: ASFI

1.1.4 Rise of collectively managed instruments

Undertakings for collective investment in transferable securities or UCITs appeared in Europe in the late 1970s and have enjoyed a brisk growth in countries where demand deposits earn little or no interest. Table 7.3 shows France's lead in UCIT growth since 1985. In France, time deposits are very strictly controlled – interest is unregulated on deposits of over FF500,000 frozen for a minimum of six months – and demand deposits do not bear interest. French UCITs (called SICAVs) have thus provided an attractive short-term alternative. Between 1985 and 1989, net SICAV assets accounted for half of total EEC UCIT assets, and soared by more than 150 per cent over the same period. Although UCIT assets have grown significantly in the other countries as well, their levels have remained low there owing to the rigid attitude of German authorities and the availability of interest-bearing demand deposits in the UK and Italy.

1.1.5 Securitisation

Securitisation has been a major innovation allowed by money market evolution (Ducos, 1989). It is largely drawn on the US and British examples, and has been applied in France but not in Germany or Italy. Securitisation enables financial institutions to dispose of assets they have originated to other agents – such as institutional investors, insurers and private individuals. For this, the institutions repackage the assets in the form of securitised asset funds, thereby spreading the related risks to be born by final investors and forcing part of the institution's capital into new ventures.

1.1.6 Tighter supervision

In a deregulated environment, it has become indispensable to impose new rules or pursue the existing ones in order to preserve the financial system's stability and increase investor protection. Thus capital market supervision mechanisms have been reinforced. The Financial Services Act of 1986 in the UK extended the scope of direct control to financial futures and options. This responsibility is entrusted to the Securities and Investments Board (SIB), which, in turn, may delegate some monitoring tasks to Self-Regulating Organisations (SROs). In Italy, the powers of the Commissione Nazionale per la Società de la Borsa (CONSOB) and the Bank of Italy have been augmented as in France with the extension of the investigative power of the COB (Commission des Opérations de Bourse), the self-regulatory organisation of the futures market and the SICAV managers' association. At the same time, the monetary authorities have reinforced the prudential control on financial institutions (liquidity ratio, solvability ratio, new international norms).

Having reviewed the process of deregulation and financial innovation in European domestic markets, the following section analyses their consequences for financial flows.

1.2 CHANGES IN FINANCIAL FLOWS

Financial innovation in 1980s has deeply modified the structure of domestic financing channels. The emergence of direct markets has allowed a diversification and marketisation of finance by challenging the near-monopoly previously enjoyed by banks.

1.2.1 The diversification of finance

In the early 1980s, the financial flows that met national borrowing requirements were concentrated on banks' credits – a pattern fostered by the relative atrophy of the financial markets (De Boissieu, 1986). The expansion of the latter during the decade changed the situation to varying degrees in each country. The reorganisation of secondary markets for securities, the simplification of issuance procedures in the primary markets and the creation of options and futures markets allowed businesses and governments to raise funds directly in order to build up their equity, improve liabilities management or develop bond issues. Meanwhile, the diversification of money-market maturities enabled those agents to modify their debt structure. European firms, mainly in France and the UK, were now able to resort to direct financing by issuing commercial papers which represented an alternative to short-term bank borrowing, whereas governments took advantage of an improved money-market liquidity and a more important participation of foreign investors.

1.2.2 Disintermediation or financial competition?

The restructuring of non-financial agents' liabilities raises the issue of disintermediation (Rapport du Conseil Economique et Social, 1988). Table 7.4 presents an in-

TABLE 7.4 Structure of overall financial flows of non-financial sectors (% of total gross borrowing requirement)

	1983	1984	1985	1986	1987	1988	1989
West Germany							
Bank credits (a)	65.9	62.9	54.9	50.2	58.1	61.2	56.7
Direct financing (b)	19.9	21.0	27.4	43.0	33.7	27.0	19.1
Other (c)	14.2	16.1	17.7	6.8	8.2	11.8	24.2
France							
Bank credits	72.0	63.0	56.8	38.0	52.4	64.5	48.8
Direct financing	25.8	34.7	39.6	50.0	24.7	27.3	35.3
Other	2.2	2.3	3.6	12.0	23.0	8.2	15.9
Italy							
Bank credits	27.9	35.4	31.9	22.1	19.4	29.2	31.9
Direct financing	59.8	53.2	57.8	66.5	54.9	50.1	40.2
Other	12.3	11.4	10.3	11.4	25.7	20.7	27.9
United Kingdom							
Bank credits	53.0	72.0	72.0	73.0	68.0	85.0	72.0
Direct financing	43.0	26.0	36.0	35.0	36.0	14.0	22.0
Other	4.0	2.0	-8.0	-8.0	-4.0	1.0	6.0

Notes: (a) Commercial loans, short- and long-term credit.
(b) Money-market securities, stocks and bonds.
(c) Adjustment and/or external financing
Sources: Bundesbank, Bank of France, Bank of Italy, Central Statistical Office, Bank of England.

termediation rate defined by the ratio of (a) the increase in the indebtedness of non-financial agents (government, enterprises, households) towards the financial system to (b) their gross annual borrowing requirements.

Over the period 1983–6, an overall deterioration of the intermediation rate was observed to varying degrees in all countries except Britain. The sharpest decline occurred in France, where this rate was halved from 72 per cent to 38 per cent; this disintermediation trend is initiated by firms only, as the French government is not indebted to banks.

Germany does not appear to have escaped the disintermediation movement. Despite the fact that its intermediation rate remained high, it shrank over the period. The bank credit share of total financing fell from 66 per cent in 1983 to 50 per cent in 1986. A distinguishing factor, however, is the German government's borrowings from financial institutions, which still today account for nearly one-third of the public debt outstanding. Changes in government borrowing behaviour are thus a major determinant of the intermediation rate.

In Italy, the large size of the public debt as a percentage of all agents' gross borrowing requirement makes it hard to draw international comparisons. In the 1983–6 period, Italy did not join the financial innovation movement. The change in the intermediation rate was simply the result of the increase in the public debt and in Treasury bond issues.

In Britain, the intermediation rate held stable at 72 per cent despite the intensive financial innovation. Competition among banks emerged very early in the UK – later spreading to France and Germany, but on a lesser scale. As a result, the British banks increased their outstanding loans by a discount policy on existing markets or by moving into new segments – notably loans to individuals and unincorporated enterprises. Competition has resulted in maintaining a high rate of intermediation in the UK despite the boom in the financial markets.

Over the period 1987–8, one can discern a trend of reintermediation amid the diversity of individual country patterns. The summer 1987 bond-market crisis and the October stockmarket crash depressed the volume of direct financing transactions. This triggered a reintermediation movement; this movement was amplified by the diversification of loans to individuals and small businesses in order to limit earlier losses of market share. The readjustment was sharp in the UK and France, where the intermediation rate moved from 68 per cent to 85 per cent and from 52 per cent to 65 per cent over the same period respectively. In Germany, the rise was more moderate and was largely influenced by a sharp increase in government borrowing from banks.

In the final year surveyed, 1989, the renewed attractiveness of the financial markets resulted in a visible shift towards disintermediation (except in Italy). It should be noted that, in the most recent periods, external financing – statistically listed under 'other' financial flows in Table 7.4 – became significant especially in Italy and France. The rise in cross-border financing is naturally correlated with the gradual deregulation of foreign-exchange transactions and the improvement in market liquidity (mainly for government securities) offered to non-residents.

An analysis of Table 7.4 demonstrates the existence of a disintermediation trend in the 1980s. But the phenomenon is not irreversible. A stockmarket collapse, as in 1987, can reverse the process. It would therefore be more accurate to speak of the emergence of competition between intermediated financing and direct financing systems. Agents choose between the two sources on the basis of many criteria (interest rates, liquidity, market stability...) each one offering a comparative advantage at any given moment.

1.2.3 The rise of securitisation

The earlier measurement of intermediation in ratio form is restrictive, as it reduces the concept to credit allocation alone. In reality, the banks did not stay on the sidelines of financial innovation. For example, the growth of money markets and bond markets entailed a restructuring of bank liabilities in favour of CDs and bonds. On the assets side, the expansion of those markets caused the banks to shift their portfolios towards investment securities and bonds or negotiable commercial paper issued by non-financial agents. Thus the banks as well took an active part in the growth of financial markets through issues and acquisitions, initiating a widespread trend towards the marketisation of finance.

We can therefore suggest a broader definition of intermediation as the set of financial flows channelled through bank balance sheets. A broad intermediation ratio would accordingly have as numerator the increase of non-financial agent borrowings from banks and net purchases of financial assets (shares, bonds, money-market securities) by financial agents (all banks + UCITs + insurance companies). The denominator would be the gross borrowing requirement of non-financial agents.

Does this broader definition of intermediation modify the analysis of the disintermediation–reintermediation cycle described earlier? Table 7.5 paints a very different picture from Table 7.4.

TABLE 7.5 Intermediation rate (broader definition) (% of total gross borrowing requirement)

	1985	1986	1987	1988	1989
West Germany	59.7	64.1	75.8	54.1	78.3
France	na	46.9	51.0	70.5	54.0

Sources: CDC, OECD.

TABLE 7.6a: Equity capitalisation (at 31 December, billions of local currency units and US dollars)

	1982			1986			1989		
	Local curr.	Dollar	%GDP	Local curr.	Dollar	%GDP	Local curr.	Dollar	%GDP
W. Germany	163.9	67.5	10.0	480.2	221.1	25.0	563.9	299.4	24.9
Paris	199.4	30.3	5.0	990.3	143.0	20.0	1700.0	266.9	33.1
London	121.6	212.2	44.0	320.7	470.2	85.0	480.0	786.9	90.0
Milan	na	na	na	na	na	na	48707.5	35.4	16.4

Source: OECD.

TABLE 7.6b Change in real capitalisation (deflated by the stockmarket index)

	1982		1986		1989	
	Index	Real capital	Index	Real capital	Index	Real capital
West Germany (Commerzbank)	763.4	163.9	2046.4	204.9	1826.63	335.9
France (CAC)	100.2	199.4	397.8	398.6	489.16	923.2
United Kingdom (FT-SE 30)	596.7	121.6	1308.6	176.3	1781.35	238.3

Source: OECD.

The overall intermediation rate in Table 7.5 is higher, and it reverses the 1985–6 disintermediation trend observed in Table 7.4. The adjustment is more clear-cut in France, where the surge in UCITs has caused a greater expansion of the financing process in which firms issue short- and long-dated negotiable paper subsequently purchased in the market by financial institutions.

The broader ratio, however, is unstable because of its sensitivity to the restructuring of financial institution liabilities. In 1988 in West Germany and 1987 in France, financial institutions as a whole issued more securities than they purchased. CD issues by French banks and bond issues by German banks were particularly abundant. Nevertheless, this alternative measurement of intermediation emphasises the need to replace the distinction between intermediation and direct financing by the concept of securitisation.

1.3 THE FINANCING VOLUME EXPLOSION

Finance marketisation and the competition between intermediated and direct financing owe their emergence to the large-scale expansion of the financial markets. Capitalisation, equity and bond issues, and transaction volume have soared in all stockmarkets.

1.3.1 Increase in stockmarket capitalisation

In all four countries, the gradual modernisation of financing techniques has gone hand in hand with a rapid increase in capitalisation. Measured in percentage of GDP, equity-market wealth more than doubled in West Germany and London between 1982 and 1989. In Paris, the capitalisation volume boomed from 5 per cent to 33.1 per cent of GDP over the same period (Table 7.6a).

Comparing on the basis of a single currency, the dollar, Paris witnessed the biggest rise in capitalisation between 1982 and 1989. Far behind Germany in 1982, it had climbed up to nearly second rank in Europe by 1989. The City, however, has not lost its supremacy, since its capitalisation remains almost equal to all the continental European centres put together. Milan remains far behind the main European places, its capitalisation did not exceed 35.4 billion dollars in 1989.

The growth of market capitalisation may, however, be misleading if one attempts to analyse market activities, as it is partly due to a purely nominal phenomenon: the increase in asset market values. The evolution of the stock exchange indices must therefore be considered (Table 7.6b). The real increase in market capitalisation, deflated by the stockmarket index rise, remains impressive. From 1982 to 1989, real capitalisation doubled in Germany and the UK, and increased fourfold in France.

Bond-market growth (Table 7.7), while less spectacular than stockmarket growth, was nevertheless significant. The share of bond capitalisation in GDP

TABLE 7.7 Bond capitalisation (at 31 December, billions of local currency units and US dollars)

	1982			1986			1989		
	Local curr.	Dollar	%GDP	Local curr.	Dollar	%GDP	Local curr.	Dollar	%GDP
W. Germany	na	na	na	na	na	na	955.0	508.0	42.0
Paris	779.2	118.6	21.0	1870.6	270.0	37.0	2353.0	369.4	45.9
London	144.7	252.5	52.0	303.4	444.9	80.0	310.0	508.2	60.0

Source: OECD.

TABLE 7.8 Gross securities issues (billions of local currency units)

	1982	1983	1984	1985	1986	1987	1988	1989
Equities								
W.Germany	46.8	7.3	6.3	11.0	16.4	11.9	7.5	19.4
France	33.7	49.7	59.2	84.3	137.8	160.9	156.6	317.0
UK	33.7	2.4	1.6	4.4	7.6	15.9	5.8	6.9
Italy	6.9	12.5	11.8	14.9	23.8	13.3	10.8	19.8
Bonds								
W.Germany	969.2	225.4	226.8	260.2	256.4	244.5	208.0	251.7
France	154.7	193.7	241.6	304.2	344.9	285.3	333.1	327.2
UK	61.3	16.9	16.1	17.2	17.1	16.7	10.3	5.2
Italy	346.2	376.5	361.2	407.6	431.2	438.6	558.6	617.5

Source: OECD.

doubled in France in 1982–9, and rose from 52 per cent to 60 per cent in the UK, which seems to have suffered more heavily from the 1987 crisis than its continental neighbours.

1.3.2 Gross securities issues and transaction volume

It is convenient to view the growth of market capitalisation in parallel with the rise in gross securities issues. The latter, combined with the rise in transaction volumes, represent a way of assessing the increase in market liquidity. Table 7.8 shows that, between 1985 and 1987, equity issues climbed by an annual average of 65 per cent in West Germany, 40 per cent in France and 110 per cent in Britain. The growth in securities issues was enhanced by a favourable economic context such as robust GDP growth and lower nominal interest rates However, the market crisis and the depressed state of the equity market in 1988 slowed the pace of new issues, which recovered with the 1989 turnaround. Bond-market trends were identical despite significantly lower growth rates.

Transaction volume, on the other hand, increased on all stock exchanges. In 1982, the transaction volume/GDP ratio stood at 6.7 per cent in London, 2.5 per cent in West Germany and 1.3 per cent in Paris. By 1986, it had reached 24 per cent, 17 per cent and 7 per cent respectively. The growth in transaction volume is correlated with the enhanced professionalism of these markets – notably the rise of mutual funds and other institutional investors, as well as the emergence of primary dealers to organise secondary markets for government securities.

2. Changes in economic agents' behaviour in response to innovation

The growth of financial markets has led to a change in agent behaviour. Households seek the highest return on their deposits, firms aim for the lowest cost of capital and governments look for optimal debt management. Banks have adapted to the changes in non-financial agents' behaviour and have also derived direct advantage from the buoyancy of financial markets. The interest rate has therefore become the discriminant variable in finance and investment choices.

2.1 CHANGES IN HOUSEHOLD FINANCIAL INVESTMENTS

The 1980s witnessed a reorientation of household financial investment in the four largest European countries (Table 7.9). In France, West Germany and Italy, liquid instruments (non-negotiable deposits) fell sharply, whereas the opposite trend was observed in Britain. At the start of the decade, acquisition of liquid assets made up more than half of the investment flows in France, West Germany and Italy; by the end of the 1980s, they had dwindled to roughly one-third of annual household financial investments.

2.1.1 The growth of UCITs

The fall in the share of liquid assets was particularly significant in France, where the 1984–5 deregulation offered households access to a wider range of financial investments – especially through the rise of mutual funds (UCITs, under the heading of short-term securities in Table 7.9). In the other countries, they remain relatively

TABLE 7.9 Household investment flows (% of total investments)

		Liquidity	Short-term securities*	Bonds	Shares	Life insurance
France	80	63.5	–	19.0	6.6	5.3
	86	30.0	39.3	4.3	5.8	20.4
	87	47.1	14.4	2.9	11.7	23.7
	88	40.7	18.9	0.7	9.3	30.3
	89	33.6	17.7	1.1	5.2	42.3
West Germany	80	48.3	0	20.5	-0.7	29
	86	52.5	0	5.8	2.6	34.8
	87	39.6	0	18.3	4.0	34.7
	88	29.3	0	30.7	1.6	34.6
	89	27.5	2.1	36.9	-4.0	32.8
Italy	80	55.1	29.7	-2.50	1.5	13.2
	86	30.6	3.30	26.7	2.7	8.5
	87	31.0	20.7	37.4	0.6	8.8
	88	34.8	23.8	38.7	0.0	8.7
	89	36.2	24.3	30.9	0.3	12.2
United Kingdom**	83	50.2	–	2.3	-1.7	49.7
	86	54.8	–	4.2	-7.7	49.4
	87	57.7	–	4.1	-9.9	50.1
	88	82.7	–	-7.5	-21.6	47.0
	89	81.0	–	-6.4	-37.9	63.5

Notes: *Money-market funds + mutual fund shares
**Bonds: public sector (gilts).
Shares: includes unit trusts.
Life insurance: includes life assurance and pension funds.
Sources: Bank of France, Bank of Italy, Central Statistical Office, OECD.

undeveloped and have therefore had little influence on household investment flows.

Whereas mutual fund holdings by French households were virtually non-existent in 1980, by 1986 they accounted for 40 per cent of investment flows. This change bears witness to the very high mobility in household saving management patterns and to a deep shift in investor behaviour. Individuals are no longer settling for low-yield or non-interest-bearing instruments – such as French demand deposits – but seek a more active management, accepting a measure of risk in exchange for a higher return.

2.1.2 Stockmarket phenomena

The shift in household stockmarket behaviour is very conspicuous in France, where individuals have been investing 5–10 per cent of their annual saving in equities since

1980. Admittedly, this attraction to the Bourse is not only due to financial innovation, but also to favourable market and interest-rate trends. In fact, the French government set up tax incentives to promote household investment in securities. Such measures include the 'Monory' mutual funds (1978), the share-invested savings account (Compte d'Epargne en Actions) (1983) and tax relief on investment income. A further stimulus came in 1986 with the privatisation of major state-owned enterprises. Since 1989, however, equity investments have become less popular. The intrinsic weakness of share-purchasing motivation is no longer offset by tax incentives.

West Germany, Italy and Britain offer a different picture. Households have invested very little in the stockmarket – or have actually pulled out of it. Although large-scale privatisation in the UK has increased the number of individual British stockholders, institutional investors remain the key players on the stockmarket, and the share of household direct equity ownership remains minimal.

2.1.3 The growth in life insurance

Collective management is very widespread in European countries. In the UK and France, the fall in direct bond purchases by households over the past ten years indicates that it has become less attractive for individuals to engage in such transactions. It is simpler for a household to own bonds via mutual funds or insurance companies than to hold them directly. They offer personal investors a return often comparable to that of the bond market, and a better management of risk through collective management. The share of life insurance in Germany remains high, although retirement policies have not grown as significantly there as in France during the past decade. This difference can be explained by two factors. First, the French life-insurance industry had long lagged behind its counterparts in other major industrialised countries. Secondly, French households, covered by a pension system financed almost exclusively from public funds, previously displayed little interest in private retirement plans. Moreover, French retirement plans have enjoyed major tax relief – such as partial deductibility of premiums from income tax and exemption from estate duties – and have succeeded in offering complementary services that have ensured their robust expansion. Investment flows into endowment life insurance products increased eight-fold between 1980 and 1989, rising from 5 per cent to 40 per cent of total flows.

2.1.4 Liquid investments

The fall in liquid investments in France stems chiefly from the move out of demand deposits, tax-exempt savings accounts (Livret A and Livret Bleu) and taxable instruments such as time deposits and passbooks. These products offer little or no yields – and, when they do, their yields are generally well below the return on new products with similar characteristics, such as money-market mutual funds. The share of time deposits and bank notes in French household financial assets fell from 18.4 per cent in 1979 to 10.8 per cent in 1989. Tax-exempt savings accounts and other non-negotiable but taxable accounts moved down from 17.1 per cent and 7.2 per cent respectively in 1979 to 11.3 per cent and 2.3 per cent in 1989.

In West Germany, the decline in demand deposits, essentially due to their low yield (0.5–2 per cent), was mainly offset by larger bond purchases. In reality, German investment behaviour is determined less by financial innovation than by the yield spread between foreign and domestic assets. The relative stability of the European Monetary System (EMS) over the past five years has driven the Germans to invest in higher-yielding foreign securities. In 1980, foreign bonds accounted for 12 per cent of total bond holdings of German non-financial agents. By 1984 the share had climbed to 32 per cent; by 1987 to 67 per cent. Thus, while the comparative lack of financial innovation in Germany cannot explain the shift in personal financial investment, it is likely that German households took advantage of financial innovation abroad – even in France the authorities have sought to attract foreign investors by reforming the public debt financing system.

The apparently contradictory pattern observed in Britain, where liquid assets climbed from 50.2 per cent in 1983 to 81 per cent in 1989, is explained by the high yields on demand deposits and time deposits – between 5.5 per cent and 10.5 per cent. The 'liquidity' item of Table 7.9 also includes bank CDs, an instrument that we were unable to quantify separately.

2.1.5 The Italian case

Government bonds account for most of the large bond component of Italian household financial portfolios (Banca d'Italia, 1987–9). The short-dated securities held by Italian households consist mainly of Treasury notes. These instruments have proliferated with the modernisation of the country's government securities market. Private investors have preferred them to bonds, which are perceived as riskier owing to the growth in public debt and the danger of an inflationary spiral. In shifting towards government securities, Italian households have drawn down their bank deposits. In the ten years to 1987, the share of deposits in household financial assets has fallen by 20 percentage points to 40 per cent, while the proportion of government securities has soared from 4.5 per cent to 30 per cent.

The government has encouraged these shifts by applying a total tax exemption on government securities income for individual investors from 1978 to 1986. In 1988, the banks reacted to this competition by offering more attractive yields on all their deposits. As a result, the share of non-negotiable deposits in total investment flows has stopped declining since 1988.

2.1.6 The gains from investment shifts

Two features common to all countries emerge from Table 7.9. First, by reducing their investment flows towards liquid instruments, households have sought higher returns on their savings – with the paradoxical result, in Britain, of a return to demand and time deposits. In France, the search led to the supply of new financial products; in Germany, to investments in higher-yielding foreign assets; in Italy, to increased investment in government securities. These portfolio shifts testify to the high mobility of household saving patterns.

The second feature, observed in all countries, is the growing role of collective management institutions – mutual funds, life insurance companies and pension funds – as financial product suppliers. This phenomenon has allowed households to gain cheap access to the advantages of portfolio management. These investment shifts can safely be said to have raised the average return on households' financial assets, but also their exposure to interest-rate fluctuation.

2.2 CHANGE IN CORPORATE DEBT STRATEGY

In addition to global financial reforms and modernisation, innovations especially adapted to the corporate sector were introduced. This was particularly the case in the UK and France.

For British and French companies, the most important reform was the authorisation to raise funds directly on the money market by issuing commercial paper. This measure encourages firms to act with greater autonomy *vis-à-vis* the banking system. As a short-dated instrument and therefore largely insensitive to interest-rate fluctuations, commercial paper is relatively independent of market trends. It constitutes a source of stable financing for firms, often cheaper than bank funds. In France, commercial paper outstandings jumped from FF24 billion at the end of December 1986 to FF146 billion three years later. Such vehicles are still insignificant in the UK, virtually non-existent in Germany and unknown in Italy.

The evolution in corporate debt strategy has been heterogeneous; in France, restructuring of corporate financing has entailed a fall in the percentage share of bank loan flows between the early and late 1980s (Table 7.10). In the other countries, by contrast, the share of bank borrowings increased over the decade. In 1989, bank loans accounted for 85 per cent of funding sources in West Germany and Italy, and nearly 60 per cent in Britain. The relative disintermediation observed in France is therefore an isolated instance. This is partly the result of the growing success of commercial paper.

2.2.1 Raising funds on the market

Of the four leading European economies, France was the country with the largest share of market financing, followed by the UK. In Italy and Germany, market funding still plays a limited role, accounting for no more than 10–25 per cent of total financing. The very tight regulations applied to the entire German financial system

TABLE 7.10 Corporate financing flows (% of gross borrowing requirements)

		Bonds	Shares*	Short-term securities**	Total market-raised funds***	Bank loans
France	80	8.2	25.2	–	33.4	61.3
	86	18.5	74.1	9.3	101.9	-6.6
	87	4.2	45.7	4.3	54.2	39
	88	9	32.5	4.0	45.5	50.7
	89	5.7	31.5	8.9	46.1	53.1
West Germany	80	1.3	8.6	1.5	7.5	79.5
	86	16.5	29.8	0	46.3	53.6
	87	24.8	20.4	-1.1	44.1	55.9
	88	5.6	8.7	0.1	14.3	86.5
	89	0	14.5	-0.2	14.3	85.9
Italy	83	5.4	6.7	0	12.1	65.1
	86	10.4	21.4	0	31.8	61.3
	87	8.1	14.3	0	22.4	72.0
	88	0.3	8.1	0	8.4	88.5
	89	-0.2	9.1	0	8.9	91.3
United Kingdom	83	51.6	–	12.0	63.6	33.7
	86	40.8	–	4.4	45.2	49.2
	87	49.8	–	8.4	58.2	35.4
	88	17.5	–	8.5	26.0	68.6
	89	13.4	–	12.5	26.0	59.0

Notes: *Shares and other equity investments.
**Commercial paper. For the UK, also includes public grants and loans and other non-bank borrowings.
***Bonds, equities, and short-term securities.
Sources: Bank of France, Bank of Italy, Central Statistical Office, OECD.

forced local companies to go abroad, especially to London, in search for more developed financial markets such as Euromarkets. However, Germany is catching up with the rest of Europe in offering innovations to corporate financiers. In 1991, the Bundesbank will abolish its requirement for prior authorisation for the issue of domestic bearer bonds. This will allow companies to issue securities without maturity restrictions. Firms will thus be able to float short-dated commercial paper as a complement to the existing range of medium- and long-dated DM Europaper. Despite the introduction of an unlisted securities market, which broadened the scope for equity issues, and despite the many modernisations of financial markets in all the countries studied, this innovation wave does not appear to have revolutionised corporate financing practices. This must, however, be qualified because of the obviously close link between market funding and financial market trends – particularly interest-rate movements. In 1986 and 1987, all countries with the partial exception of Britain experienced a considerable increase in equity and bond financing, which then contracted sharply after the 1987 crash. The 1986–7 market performance allowed companies to strengthen their equity base and restructure their long-term debt, but this ability was impaired by less favourable market conditions in the late 1980s. Therefore it is difficult to analyse the impact of financial innovation on businesses based on securities issues. However, the high mobility of financing flows during the 1980s shows that the reforms unquestionably made it easier for companies to choose between bank credit and market funding.

2.2.2 Preference for bank credit in 1988–9

Corporate financiers' sharp swing back to bank credit in 1988–9 is linked not only to poor stockmarket performance, but to other changes as well. First, the period coincided with a phase of vibrant economic growth in which investment spending – and therefore corporate funding requirements – climbed briskly. Secondly, the fall in stockmarket prices triggered intensive mergers and acquisition activity, requiring the formation of large reserves. Mergers and acquisition by industrial and commercial companies were particularly important within the UK where total expenditures jumped from £7 billion in 1985 to £27 billion in 1989. These transactions were largely financed by bank credits.

The third basic reason for the shift to bank loans was the banks' reaction to the competitive pressures of direct financing, to which they had been subjected. To win back their customers, the banks mainly brought their lending rates into line with market rates. The challenge was particularly tough for French banks because of the commercial paper market boom. More generally, banks have also been seriously threatened by the new financial units set up within large corporations. These entities aim to optimise financial strategy by taking direct advantage of market opportunities. Generally, to a lesser extent in Germany, small and medium-size companies have also benefited from interbank competition. It has had the effect of reducing small- and medium-size companies' borrowing rates towards those of large companies which have access to the money market.

2.2.3 Cross-border financing

The liberalisation of capital movements, with the gradual lifting of exchange controls, allowed companies to borrow in foreign currencies. This new funding source was all the more attractive because of the persistence of wide rate spreads among EEC countries coupled with smaller volatility of parities inside the EMS. In Italy for instance, the exchange control reform of October 1988 came as a major innovation for local firms. They became strongly motivated to borrow abroad particularly because long-term rate spreads were in their favour of over 250 basis points with France and over 450 points with Germany. Thus the share of foreign financing in total financing jumped from 1.6 per cent in 1983 to 13.6 per cent in 1989. Similarly, overseas

TABLE 7.11 Corporate investment flows (% in total investments)

		Liquid assets	Short-term securities	Shares*	Bonds**
France	80	58.3	0	23.7	11.7
	86	21.1	36.5	37.6	0
	87	13.7	42.4	41.8	0
	88	10.7	40.1	44.8	2.7
	89	14.0	41.4	37.0	6.8
W.Germany	80	51.1	0	46.5	0
	86	96.3	0	-1.9	-2.4
	87	72.7	0	8.8	7.9
	88	66.4	0	22.8	5.9
	89	84.2	0.5	0	5.6
Italy	80	61.9	16.7	20.8	-2.3
	86	35.4	-1.8	7.8	47.3
	87	32.5	18.2	13.7	39.5
	88	31.5	10.8	-10.2	61.7
	89	38.4	5.0	8.4	43.4

Notes: *And other equity investments.
**Includes purchases of foreign securities.
Sources: Bank of France, Bank of Italy, OECD.

borrowing by UK industrial and commercial companies represented 5 per cent in total sources of funds in 1983 and 15 per cent in 1989.

2.2.4 More efficient investment management

Financial system reforms enabled businesses to implement a new investment management policy.

Once again, the most sweeping changes occurred in France. Prior to the reforms, French companies were allowed to deposit cash balances on non-interest- or regulated interest-bearing accounts. In addition, the rapid growth of short-term mutual funds since 1985 has represented an interesting alternative. In 1980, nearly 60 per cent of French corporate investment flows went into liquid assets such as demand and time deposits. This percentage has fallen significantly and a correspondent rise in short-term securities has been observed since 1986 (Table 7.11).

The existence of interest-bearing demand deposits in the three other countries explains the more limited scope of changes in corporate financing patterns; German and Italian firms have mainly increased their foreign-currency investments. However, the scrapping of the stockmarket transaction tax will facilitate securities investments and give a boost to Germany's financial markets. Money-market investment funds – which still remain forbidden by law – are expected to be allowed at a later date.

2.3 FINANCIAL INNOVATION AND THE BANKING SECTOR

As shown, financial innovation has altered household portfolio structures and corporate financing practices. Such changes have a direct link with the balance-sheet structure of banks (Artus 1990b). Tables 7.12 and 7.13 list the liability and asset aggregates compiled from balance-sheet data (such data were unavailable for the UK, the growing competition between banks and building societies in the UK is, however, analysed in 2.3.3).

2.3.1 Banks' liabilities

The main feature of the changes in banks' liabilities is the rise in the cost of funds, which are increasingly indexed on market rates. Across countries, the movement in banks' liabilities depends on whether or not demand and time deposits are interest bearing. In France, where interest on deposits is low (indeed non-existent for demand deposits), the share of non-negotiable deposits in banks' liabilities has progressively fallen over the decade (25 points in less than ten years). In contrast, in Germany and Italy, their share has remained roughly stable. French bank liabilities offer an interesting example of the financing problem facing the banking industry since the emergence of new products. French households seek an attractive return on their savings but they want enough flexibility to keep their savings liquid. They have therefore turned to mutual funds. To offset the corresponding fall in deposits, the banks have issued CDs.

There has been a considerable growth in bond issues and equity increases as a source of bank financing. Most countries have followed a rather similar pattern, with the combined share of bonds and stocks in the banks' total liabilities rising between 1980 and 1989 (Table 7.12), except Italy where banks do not issue bonds. While the 1987 crash temporarily halted the climb, 1988–9 saw a recovery. One of the main causes of the expansion in bond financing is that it is not subjected to required-reserves regulations. French and German banks have accordingly given preference to bond issues. It should be recalled here that German banks do not issue CDs. The Bundesbank has consistently opposed money-market mutual funds in order to preserve its control over monetary policy.

2.3.2 Banks' assets

On the assets side (Table 7.13), French and German banks offer a roughly similar picture. About 80 per cent of their assets outstanding consist of loans. In France, the share of long-term loans dropped 15 points between 1980 and 1986. This decline, largely due to disintermediation, was accompanied by a move into new credits markets mainly consumer credits – hence the increase in short-term loans. The second half of the decade witnessed a slight reintermediation trend, as noted earlier.

TABLE 7.12 Bank balance-sheets Liabilities (% of total liabilities)

		Deposits	Short-term securities	Bonds	Equities
France	80	78.9	0.8	12.7	7.4
	86	64.2	0.9	19.0	15.7
	87	65	4	18.5	12.3
	88	58.1	6.4	19.3	16.1
	89	54	9.5	17.8	18.4
West Germany	80	76.9	0	21.2	1.8
	86	69.7	0	26.8	3.3
	87	70.8	0	26.5	2.5
	88	72.0	0	24.9	3
	89	71.5	0	24.6	3.8
Italy	80	93.9	–	–	6
	86	89.7	–	–	10.2
	87	90.2	–	–	9.7
	88	89.6	–	–	10.3
	89	na	–	–	na

Notes: France: members of Association Française de Banques (AFB).
West Germany: regional, commercial, mortgage, and savings banks, cooperative credit institutions and private bankers.
Italy: deposits and short-term securities of cooperative banks. Savings, rural, and small business banks, and central credit institutions.
UK statistics are not available due to difficulties in combining banks' and building societies' data.
Sources: OECD, CDC, CSO.

In West Germany, long-term loans constituted more than 75 per cent of assets over the entire period. This phenomenon is related to the traditionally close links between German banking and enterprise. Virtually all German medium-sized or large corporations have at least one banker on their boards. These privileged ties result in massive corporate financing through bank loans.

Despite these similarities, the basic difference between French and German banking assets is the volume of bond investment in Germany. It is commonly stated that banks 'make' the German bond market – both as issuers and subscribers: they hold 40 per cent of bonds outstanding and originate 60 per cent of domestic bond issues.

In Italy, the massive public debt largely influences the bank asset structure: Italian banks hold a very large government bond portfolio, over 35 per cent of their assets throughout the 1980s.

2.3.3 Growing competition between the building societies and the banks

In the UK, the building societies sector represents an interesting case as it has faced a radical change in the mortgage and savings markets since the early 1980s (Callen and

TABLE 7.13 Bank balance-sheets Assets (% of total assets)

		Short-term securities	Bonds	Stocks	Loans Short	Long
France	80	3.8	5.4	4.1	18.2	68.3
	86	5.0	7.5	7.1	26.2	53.8
	87	4.6	9.3	5.4	27.2	53.2
	88	3.2	8.5	5.3	28.1	54.6
	89	2.6	7.5	6.3	28.9	54.4
West Germany	80	0.3	11.8	0.1	9.3	76.8
	86	0.3	15.9	2.7	7.1	73.7
	87	0.2	16.5	2.2	7.1	73.7
	88	0.2	16.9	2.5	5.3	74.8
	89	0.2	16.1	3.5	5.0	75.3
Italy	80	13.7	36.4	0.4	35.6	9.3
	86	5.9	37.8	10.4	36.7	8.9
	87	4.8	39.4	8.2	37.5	9.9
	88	3.9	35.4	8.0	42.1	10.4

Notes: See Table 7.12.
Sources: OECD, CDC.

Lomax, 1990). Until 1980, British legislative restrictions on bank lending – the 'corset' – segmented the market to the advantage of building societies, which enjoyed a virtual monopoly on mortgages. The lifting of these controls has blurred the difference between banks and building societies. The banks have become involved in mortgage lending, while building societies have gained access to new sources of funds. In 1986, the Building Societies Act officialised these changes by greatly broadening the range of products that building societies were allowed to handle. Meanwhile, the Building Societies Association surrendered a part of its authority in mortgage interest-rate setting, and the rates became much more sensitive to market fluctuations.

All these changes influenced the structure of the building societies' balance sheets. On the liabilities side, the creation of new savings instruments triggered a spectacular rise in deposits. While bank deposits rose 160 per cent between 1985 and 1989, building society deposits tripled over the same period. Their share of total deposits jumped from 60 per cent in 1985 to 75 per cent in 1989. Like banks, the building societies are allowed to issue bonds and certificates of deposit. Between 1985 and 1990, building societies' CD issues increased roughly sevenfold.

On the assets side, the building societies have doubled their investment activity in less than a decade, although the liquid assets share in their total assets declined from 20 per cent in 1983 to 15 per cent in 1989. The main change in their investment portfolios has been the shortening of maturities: the share of government securities has fallen from 40 per cent to 15 per cent between 1980 and 1989, whereas the share of CDs has soared from 20 per cent to 75 per cent over the same period. The shift was caused by the introduction of a tax on bond income, but it is also linked to the yield-curve inversion since 1988. The removal of the 'corset' and the existence of profit opportunities have allowed the banks to compete against the building societies in the latter's traditional mortgage business. The banks' share of mortgage allocation rose to 40 per cent in 1987. However, thanks to product diversification and the British residential-property boom, the building societies were able to double the volume of their mortgage allocation between 1985 and 1989. Product diversification also augmented the power of building societies to the point where they were allowed to open branches in EEC countries.

In sum, building societies underwent both legislative and structural changes during the 1980s. Although these institutions lost their mortgage monopoly, they successfully adapted by creating new savings vehicles that boosted their share of total deposits. Finally, a rise in intra-sector takeover activity was observed throughout the decade. The number of societies was reduced by half between 1980 and 1989. Merging has resulted essentially in a more efficient use of capital and lower average operating costs, leaving the purpose and the distinct identity of building societies unchanged and the societies' share in the mortgage market high by historical standards.

2.4 GOVERNMENT FINANCING

We have seen that governments have been a powerful engine of financial innovation. It is hard to define typical budget-deficit financing behaviour – the main distinguishing factor here is the size of the deficit (or surplus).

2.4.1 Innovations triggered by the French government

The French government's budget-deficit evolution and innovation policy witnessed two different periods. The first phase began by an enlargement of the public sector and a policy of demand stimulation, inflation and high nominal interest rates. The French Treasury appears to have responded 'passively' to 'lenders' demands, notably as regards the characteristics of the securities issued. In the second phase, the Treasury continued to borrow but asserted its determination to preserve the option of modifying its debt structure through market intervention (Du Parquet, 1989). Moreover, it became heavily involved in product innovation.

The French Treasury's first major innovations concerned products. Some were ill-designed (borrow index-linked gold), others more sensible (zero coupon). In 1982, the Treasury made a decisive move by launching renewable bonds (Obligations Renouvelables du Trésor or ORTs). These instruments – a hybrid between bonds and Treasury notes – are based on the principle that interest is capitalised at the paper's nominal rate. The Treasury soon began floating four quarterly issues a year. By 1983, each issue comprised a fixed-rate tranche and a floating-rate tranche.

In 1984, the Treasury realised that constant product innovation might make France lose control of its debt structure. To prevent this, the Treasury began, for example, to buy back ORTs at every new auction. Of the six ORT lines issued, only two are still active but they represent very small volumes.

TABLE 7.14 General government: main financing instruments (billions of local currency units)

| | | Short-term securities** | | Bonds | | |
		Total	of which rest of world	Total	of which households +corporates	Loans from banks
France	80	-5.9	0	27.6	-	-
	86	38.3	0	111.7	-	-
	87	60.4	8.9	20.6	-	-
	88	15.6	18.5	62.2	-	-
	89	70.0	42.4	76.4	-	-
Italy	80	30.1	0	-0.8	0	0.7
	86	9.7	0	87.8	35	1.5
	87	27.5	1.7	57.8	45.3	3.4
	88	42	4.7	62	53	4.8
	89	40	na	53	na	7.3
W.Germany*	80	-2.1	-	2.1	-	30.3
	86	-1.8	-	51.2	-	3.2
	87	-3.2	-	49.9	-	19.1
	88	0	-	42.9	-	25.1
	89	7.2	-	26.2	-	5.2
UK	84	0	0.1	8.6	7.4	0
	86	0.2	0.2	6.8	4.8	0
	87	2.2	1.1	4.6	2.3	0
	88	1.3	0	-5.0	-4.1	0.2
	89	2.9	0.9	-18.3	-11.9	0.4

Notes: *Central and state government.
**In local currency.
Sources: OECD, CDC.

In 1985, the Treasury returned to active debt management by introducing the fungible bond (Obligation Assimilable du Tréesor or OAT) system. The government created credit lines on which it can reissue paper indefinitely. The system allows the Treasury to intervene on both the supply side and the demand side, which offers a considerable liquidity advantage. Table 7.14 shows that in 1986 the French Treasury used the OAT system a lot: 111 billons francs. In contrast with Germany, the French government does not run into bank debt. The creation of the MATIF futures market has also turned government debt into a financial market stimulus. In 1985, the Treasury standardised all its paper: BTANs (Bons du Tresor Annuels Normalisés) carry two- or five-year maturities, and their interest is paid at the end of each term. The share of floating-rate notes is steadily declining. The government can thus use the OAT system to take advantage of yield-curve inversions. An example of this is the early 1991 'reverse auction', in which the French Treasury will buy back its short-dated paper by issuing long-dated paper.

2.4.2 Coping with the Italian budget deficit

In Italy, we observe the same innovation sequence. In the opening phase, the wide-ning public deficit forced the Treasury to implement financial innovations. Because of the involuntary nature of its decision, the Treasury was relatively unable to master the process. In the second phase, however, the move towards innovation became more purposive with the opening of financial markets, the search for liquidity and other measures. Until 1980, the Italian government had used a monetary-based fin-ancing procedure, obtaining advances on an open credit line from the central bank. By early 1980, the increase in the public borrowing requirement had made that sys-tem incompatible with anti-inflation monetary targets. The government turned to do-mestic saving as an alternative source of funds. But high inflation expectations led it to issue short-dated securities and to open Treasury note auctions to non-banks. These initiatives, backed by tax incentives, proved successful since households bought up half of the short-dated paper (Table 7.14). In 1980, households held no government bonds, whereas in 1987 they purchased almost 80 per cent of total bonds issued. The average maturity of government debt fell, forcing the authorities to put an enormous volume of securities on the market. By 1983, the lengthening of debt maturity had become a top priority.

The Italian Treasury therefore had to devise innovations that would encour-age investors to purchase long-dated securities without driving interest rates up too high. The main innovation was to issue medium- and long-dated securities – called Treasury Credit Certificates – indexed on short-term paper. Once again, the innova-tion provided a short-term solution to the debt financing problem, but quickly came up against its built-in limits. In summer 1987, the Banca d'Italia raised short-term interest rates to preserve fixed exchange rates creating a conflict between monetary and fiscal targets. The explosion of debt service charges led the Italian Treasury to take quick remedial action. The old method of short-term securities financing was reintroduced, naturally reviving the acute problem of maturities. The second innova-tion phase did not get under way until the end of the decade. Broadly speaking, Italy took as its example the French modernisation of public debt financing.

2.4.3 More reasonable deficits in Germany and the UK

In the 1980s, the federal and state governments of West Germany were in a very different situation from the French and Italian authorities for several reasons. German budget deficits stayed within reasonable limits, the share of public debt in GDP also remained limited, and – most important – West Germany was running large current-account surpluses. Unlike its European partners, West Germany therefore remained largely closed to product innovation. Government departments continued to borrow extensively from banks, while meeting the balance of their borrowing requirements with conventional bond issues.

The UK situation is a mix of Germany and the other countries. The UK public sector witnessed a persistent deficit in the early 1980s. The public sector began running fiscal surpluses in 1987 and used them to repurchase its debt in the following years. On the other hand, in the continuing competition between financial market-places, London sought to overtake Paris as the leading ecu centre. In October 1988, the British government began issuing ecu bonds for that purpose – hence the increase in short-term paper issues since 1988 (this is not shown in Table 7.14, which includes only local currency issues).

3. Conclusions

After ten years of financial innovation, disparities are still observable in the reform process underway in Europe. Overall, the financial changes helped internationalise the capital markets and benefited all countries. The implied capital mobility, however, was obtained at the price of high real interest-rate levels. At the microeconomic level, the impact of innovation appears to differ considerably for each category of economic agent.

The introduction of domestic reforms and the liberalisation of capital movements have allowed a better allocation of resources between countries with net lending capacity and those with net borrowing requirements. Countries have therefore managed to finance both internal and external deficits, avoiding immediate structural adjustments, which would have inevitably weighed on growth. It is not surprising, therefore, to find governments and deficit countries largely responsible for pioneering financial innovation.

In the European Monetary System, the increase in capital mobility has been achieved in a framework where central and peripheral currencies remain imperfectly substitutable. To attract capital denominated in currencies such as lire, pesetas or French francs, the countries concerned have had to lift domestic interest rates and pay a risk premium in order to induce non-resident investors to raise the percentage of local currency assets in their portfolios.

Financial innovation has lowered the efficiency of quantitative monetary policy, forcing the monetary authorities to use interest rates as their main regulatory instrument (Easton and Brierley, 1990). The maintenance of fixed parities in the EMS has therefore amplified the variability of short-term rates and that of the entire yield curve. These fluctuations have engendered an additional premium to offset the instability of asset prices.

Households and firms have largely profited from innovations in their investment and financing policies. The wider range of investment vehicles offered at home and abroad has led non-financial agents to adopt more active cash management methods and to demand higher returns on their assets – playing competitors off against one another. Non-financial lenders have thus been rewarded by higher average returns.

On the financing side, firms have reduced the cost of their funds by putting the market and the banking system in competition against each other. Like governments, firms have also taken advantage of the many available financing solutions to rationalise their indebtedness policy. Meanwhile, with the lifting of credit controls, banks have focused their marketing efforts on households to make up for their losses in the corporate lending segment. As a result, the broader access to the loan market has also benefited households. Easier borrowing was not risky as long as economic growth remained buoyant. But, in a cyclical slowdown, the financial constraint reasserted itself and the debt crisis triggered a readjustment in the real economy. That has been the pattern of the 1990–1 crisis, marked by a sharp increase in interest payments by non-financial agents, notably governments and firms.

The debt rise has aggravated the risk of borrower default – with repercussions on banks' liabilities. Banks have therefore had to set aside loan-loss provisions. At the same time, faced with competition from new investment products, the financial institutions have been obliged to offer higher-yield instruments in order to keep their customers. This investment shift, coupled with the increased recourse to market financing, has inevitably driven up the banks' cost of funds. The banking system has emerged somewhat weaker from the innovation period. They have seen their profit margins shrink on their established intermediation business, and have therefore developed new lucrative activities directly tied to financial innovation. Innovations have forced the banking sector to redefine its functions as financial intermediary and to adapt to the new economic environment.

Bibliography

Artus, P. (1990a) 'La politique monétaire dans les années 1980', *Document de travail 1990-04/E*, Service des Etudes Economiques, Caisse des Dépôts et Consignations.

Artus, P. (1990b) 'Les résultats des banques françaises sont-ils en danger?' *Document de travail 1990-10/E*, Service des Etudes Economiques, Caisse des Dépôts et Consignations.

Artus, P. (1990c) 'Marchés financiers: internationalisation, mécanismes, risques et politiques', *Document de travail 1990-01/E*, Service des Etudes Economiques, Caisse des Dépôts et Consignations.

Banca D'Italia, *Annual report*, 1987–9.

Bronk, V. (1989), 'The gilt-edged market since Big Bang', *Bank of England Quarterly Bulletin*, February, London.

Callen, T.S. and **Lomax J.W. (1990)**, 'The development of the building societies sector in the 1980s', Bank of England Quarterly Bulletin, November, London.

De Boissieu, C. (1986), 'Les innovations financières en France', *Revue d'Economie Politique*, 5, 585–600.

Du Parquet, L. (1989), 'Innovation financière du trésor dans les années quatre-vingt', *Innovation financière et déréglementation GDR monnaie et financement*, 5, September, Orléans.

Ducos, P. (1989), 'Les conséquences de la titrisation', *Revue d'Economie Financière*, 10, July–September, 107–25.

Easton, W.W. and **Brierley, P. G.** (1990). 'The interest rate transmission mechanism', *Bank of England Quarterly Bulletin*, May, London.

Haberer, J.Y. (1988), 'La globalisation des marchés de capitaux', *Revue d'économie financière*, 5/6 June – September.

Naouri, J. C. (1986), 'La réforme du financement de l'Économie', *Revue Banque*, March.

OCDE (1987), 'Royaume-Uni', *Etudes économiques*, July.

Rapport du Conseil Economique ét Social (1988), 'Economie réelle et sphère financière', *Journal Officiel*, 17.

CHAPTER EIGHT

Monetary integration versus financial market integration

G. Majnoni, S. Rebecchini and C. Santini

1. Introduction

The scope of this chapter is twofold. First, to demonstrate that monetary integration and financial integration cannot be pursued exclusively through market forces but require active intervention by the authorities to coordinate the two processes and maximise the net benefits of economic and monetary union. Second, to show that coordination of the two types of integration will become crucial as we enter Stage 2 of EMU, the transition phase, and that if the two processes go ahead at different speeds the overall EMU objective may be jeopardised.

In section 2 of the chapter we argue that public policy intervention is justified on two scores: because monetary integration and financial integration generate public goods and because the two processes interact and produce externalities, so that they need to be closely coordinated. In section 3, we review the progress achieved so far in the field of monetary integration and financial market integration and highlight the asymmetry in the objectives and procedures for the two processes: monetary integration is characterised by clearly defined final objectives and vague methods, while well-defined methods and hazy final objectives characterise financial market integration. In section 4, we contend that proper coordination of the two processes requires that this asymmetry be corrected, and that it is actually being corrected by specifying the content of the transition phase of EMU and the design of the integrated financial system.

2. Some preliminary definitions

Building a monetary union involves a process of integration of national financial markets and of monetary policies to which we commonly refer using the comprehensive term of monetary and financial integration. The financial aspects are generally identified as those of a microeconomic nature (the behaviour and regulation of intermediaries, the organisation of markets) while the monetary aspects tend to relate to the macroeconomic sphere (price levels and exchange rates). The two aspects are interrelated and the importance of their interaction for monetary union can hardly be overstated: it affects the speed and efficiency of the overall process. In addition, this conceptual distinction often corresponds to differences at the institutional level, where 'different legislative procedures, negotiating fora and, to some extent, competent authorities' tend to generate different timetables for the integration of markets and for the integration of monetary policies (Padoa-Schioppa, 1990a).

The fact that the monetary union will include integrated markets and integrated monetary policies does not mean that it can be achieved by meeting only one of the two conditions, with the other being obtained as a residual. Such an approach would hardly prove satisfactory. The presence of public good aspects in both the making of monetary policy and the orderly working of financial markets means that the switch from national to supranational structures has to be carefully coordinated. In the absence of a unified approach, the interaction between the monetary and financial sides of the integration process would be left to the impulses coming from the market, from different authorities and from different countries, and there is no reason why this should lead to an optimal outcome.

In order to clarify the discussion that follows, we start by providing a concise definition of the monetary and financial aspects of the integration process. This will help to identify the nature of the interaction between the two and the scope for their coordination.

The term monetary integration, in particular, will refer to the process of coordination of national monetary policies and can be viewed as the progressive achievement of irrevocably fixed exchange rates and uniformly low inflation rates within the European area. More generally, though, the coordination involves the whole set of procedures through which monetary policy is implemented: the definitions of the intermediate and operational targets, the use of the information set and the nature of the intervention techniques.

Financial integration, on the other hand, is more a question of the integration of markets. It is the process through which common investment opportunities are made available across countries and yields equalised on homogeneous assets. This process results from the interaction of public policies with the behaviour of private intermediaries. The role of the authorities in this area appears to be twofold: the removal of existing constraints, such as capital controls, and the creation of the regulatory and technical structures required to make capital mobility effective.

If we accept these definitions, the positive externalities that monetary integration generates for financial integration are mainly given by the reduction in the number of sources of uncertainty in the economy. As regards nominal variables, monetary policy coordination can reduce inflation and exchange risk premiums, thereby freeing resources for investment. More generally, as regards real variables, the integration of national macropolicies can be expected to diminish the importance of country-specific risks, thereby eliminating the need to hedge against them through portfolio diversification. This in turn will bring additional savings in portfolio management costs.

The coordination issue comes to the fore when we consider how traditional sources of uncertainty will be compounded by those associated with institutional change. In view of the possibility for financial market participants to make mistakes or bad judgements in a period of prolonged but rapid and complicated change pro-moting the stability of nominal variables (monetary integration) can significantly lower the cost of decision-making by reducing the noise component in price forma-tion. In addition, the saving on information costs in connection with the reduction of national-specific risks should facilitate the distribution of financial resources across countries, thereby widening the access of foreign saving to profitable investments.

The externalities that financial integration generates for monetary integra-tion are related to the positive effects of increased asset substitutability on the trans-mission of monetary impulses across markets. For instance, a common European monetary policy would hardly be feasible if it required a coordinated set of proce-dures for intervention on variously segmented national markets. Therefore the devel-opment of financial integration, especially in the markets for government securities and banking products, is a prerequisite for the transition from a coordinated to a common monetary policy. The speed of market integration depends on how long it takes market forces to exploit the broader investment opportunities to the full and the authorities to reduce transaction costs by standardising both the regulation of markets and intermediaries and clearing and settlements procedures.

Moreover, the interaction between monetary policy and financial market integration affects not only the 'quality' but also the speed of the overall process of monetary union. Recognition of this fact underlies the whole strategy of convergence towards monetary union: the recently completed liberalisation of capital movements provides a strong incentive to proceed with monetary coordination, which, in turn, will speed the integration of financial markets by promoting greater stability of relative prices in the area. However, two aspects of this 'chain reaction' cannot be determined accurately: the speed at which market forces adjust to changes in the institutional framework and the amount of regulation needed to control the reaction process itself.

So far financial integration and monetary integration have proceeded in a relatively close fashion, following the blueprint of the White Paper and the Delors Report. However, some problems have already surfaced, pointing to the need for close coordination of the speeds of the two processes. Coordination is also necessary in view of the procedural asymmetry that characterises monetary and financial inte-gration. We will briefly review the nature of this asymmetry and the macroeconomic problems that have emerged in the next two sections.

3. Methods and objectives of the integration process: an underlying asymmetry

If one looks at the substantive decisions and commitments of the authorities regard-ing monetary integration and financial market integration, one cannot fail to be struck by the asymmetry between the two processes. While the final stage of monetary integration is defined in detail in the Delors Report, the procedural aspects of achieving a single monetary policy and a single currency in the Community are left broadly undetermined. By contrast, on the issue of financial integration the authorities have agreed to the detailed procedure defined in the Commission's 1985 'White Paper', but no description exists of the desired outcome of the process.

Let us examine these aspects more closely, starting with financial market integration. The 'White Paper' establishes a detailed operational programme, including 300 Directives, a deadline for 1992 and two fundamental principles for market integration: first *mutual recognition*, whereby all member states agree to recognise the validity of the laws of all other members and accept not to exploit differences between regulatory systems to protect their national markets; second *minimal harmonisation*, intended to ensure Community level regulation that will safeguard basic public interests. These two principles are supplemented by that of *home-country control*, which attributes supervisory responsibility to the authorities of the member state in which a financial institution was originally authorised to operate.

There appear to be two reasons why the final outcome of the process of financial market integration has been left undetermined: first, there is no unanimous agreement among authorities, academics and practitioners on the 'optimal' financial structure for advanced industrial economies (Nardozzi, 1990). The natural evolution approach (embodied in the works of Gerschenkron) envisages a tendency for financial systems to shift from banking-oriented to market-oriented or strongly market-oriented, but does not appear to be borne out by the facts, which point to a convergence between the various types of financial system: i.e. more banking in 'market-oriented' systems and more market in 'bank-oriented' systems (Nardozzi, 1990).

The second reason is that detailed definition of the final outcome would have undermined mutual recognition, which implies that the national rules in force in the twelve member states will all coexist in the single market. This in turn implies, as underscored by Padoa-Schioppa (1990a), that 'the outcome will not necessarily be complete convergence . . .' and systems with different features and advantages, in terms of prudential controls or regulation, will coexist in order to satisfy the preferences of investors regarding protection and the regulation of financial institutions.

As for the process of monetary integration, the Delors Report (paragraph 22) clearly states the final objectives: full currency convertibility and the irrevocable locking of exchange-rate parities. These conditions were already contained in the Werner Report of 1970, but in two respects the Delors Report goes much further than the Werner plan. In the first place, it clearly recognises that the management of monetary and economic union needs a new monetary institution to decide and execute monetary policy at the Community level (paragraph 32). Secondly, the Delors Report envisages the adoption of a single currency, which, 'while not strictly necessary for the creation of a monetary union ..., is a natural and desirable further development of the monetary union' (paragraph 23). A single currency would allow members to reap the full benefits of monetary integration by facilitating monetary management, avoiding the transaction costs of converting currencies and clearly demonstrating the irreversibility of the move towards monetary union.

While the ultimate objectives of monetary integration are clearly recognised, the procedures for achieving them are less clearly defined with respect to both timing and content. There are two notable areas of vagueness. The *first* concerns the transition to monetary union. According to the Delors Report, the transfer of monetary decision-making powers from national authorities to a Community institution should take place gradually. However, the Report recognises the 'fundamental difficulty inherent in this transition' and when it was written did 'not consider it possible to propose a detailed blueprint for accomplishing this transition' (paragraph 57). Even as late as last July, the Report prepared by the EEC Monetary Committee on economic and monetary union (Monetary Committee, 1990) recognised that the features of the transition phase, Stage 2 of the Delors plan, had not been fully examined by the Ministers (paragraph 41, Monetary Committee, 1990). The *second* area of haziness concerns the single currency for EMU. The Delors Report only makes passing reference to the fact that the ecu 'has the potential to be developed into such a common currency' (paragraph 46), reflecting member states' different attitudes towards the ecu. The role of the ecu in the final stage of monetary union was clarified to some extent in the European Council meeting in Rome in October 1990, when it was agreed that the Community will make the ecu the currency of the union, although the procedures for achieving this were left undefined.

4. Problems surfaced in progressing towards EMU

A first difficulty concerns the *sustainability of the current-account imbalances* among member states, which have been rising steadily. In the last three years, following the removal of restrictions on capital movements, substantial capital flows have occurred within the EMS from low-inflation to high-inflation countries, fuelled by expectations of stable exchange rates (Giavazzi and Spaventa, 1990). This has allowed domestic demand to grow rapidly in high-inflation countries, while current accounts, overfinanced by capital inflows, have deteriorated. It has been argued, particularly by the authorities of surplus countries, that current-account disequilibria should not matter in a monetary and economic union, just as current-account imbalances between Texas and California do not. While such disequilibria may not matter in the final stage of EMU, we view mounting current-account imbalances in the transition stage with great concern, as they affect the formation of exchange-rate expectations and the level of interest rates for the deficit countries. In a system increasingly committed to fixed exchange rates such as the EMS, a current-account deficit that is continuously financed rather than corrected can lead to the rapid expansion of that country's external debt and cause the interest-rate burden to become potentially explosive. On the one hand, mounting imbalances and the consequent misalignment of exchange rates with respect to fundamentals, can undermine the credibility of the authorities' commitment to exchange-rate stability. On the other, such imbalances could lead to more active management of nominal exchange rates in the EMS at the expense of the anti-inflationary function of the system: this course was advocated several times by the Bundesbank in the second half of 1989. In our view these imbalances point to the need to accelerate, rather than reduce, the pace of integration. The most effective way to correct them would be by promoting changes in the real exchange rate through the adjustment of internal costs and price dynamics. In turn, this objective should be supported by further stressing the authorities' commitment to exchange-rate stability, so as to reduce inflationary expectations and, by maintaining the time schedule for the completion of the 1992 objectives, help to make money wages and prices more flexible (Frenkel and Goldstein, 1990; Viñals, 1990).

A second problem raised by integration, and highlighted by the debate in countries like Italy with large public debts, is the so-called '*high interest-rate problem*'. This refers to the fact that long-term interest-rate differentials between EMS countries are still fairly large, despite the narrowing of inflation differentials and the recent stability of EMS exchange rates. (There have been no realignments since early 1987, apart from the technical variation of parities when Italy adopted the narrow fluctuation band.) This is because financial markets are not convinced that exchange rates are fixed for ever, so that a risk premium is added to the interest rates of the currencies of higher-inflation countries. As Dornbusch (1989) pointed out with reference to Ireland, this is the worst possible situation for countries with high debt ratios, with uncertainty over exchange-rate policy exacerbating fiscal problems, since high real interest rates build up debt relative to GDP. This situation calls for policy action to cut budget deficits in the first place and, in addition, to reduce uncertainty over the future course of exchange-rate policy by stepping.

5. Completing the EMU process

As already argued, monetary integration and financial integration need to be closely coordinated. This need becomes all the more important as we move to Stage 2 of EMU (the transition stage) during which the speed of financial integration will be largely dictated by market forces. Meanwhile the speed of monetary integration will be determined by the authorities through institutional changes, notably the establishment of the European Central Bank, the conduct of a single monetary policy and the adoption of a single currency.

The recent European Council meeting in Rome has clarified some important features of Stage 2, stating that the new Central Bank of the Community will be created at the beginning of Stage 2 (January 1994) in order to:

● strengthen the coordination of monetary policies;
● establish the instruments and procedures for the future conduct of a single monetary policy;
● supervise the development of the ecu.

Each of these objectives in turn calls for the settlement of a number of fairly complex issues.

We shall start with the first of these: *strengthening monetary policy coordination*. This objective requires that a common decision-making structure be built in the transition phase, *without* this implying any transfer of national sovereignty to the Community institution (Monetary Committee, 1990, paragraph 45). This in turn implies designing a procedure to define monetary policy at the Community level *before* it is defined at the national level, a task complicated by the fact that during Stage 2 no legal basis exists for asserting the primacy of the Community policy over the policies of individual countries (Papadia, 1990). As part of the preparatory work of the Delors Report, Governor Ciampi put forward a proposal for a system that would reinforce policy coordination during Stage 2. This system would operate on three levels: a central monetary institution would control the liquidity of national monetary authorities by regulating the supply of ecu reserves, while national central banks would be responsible for managing the liquidity of the commercial bank system in each country (Ciampi, 1989).

The second point concerns the *creation of instruments and procedures* for the conduct of a single monetary policy. This implies defining a common analytical framework and harmonising national monetary systems and instruments. To this end, work is progressing to implement a scheme for setting standardised national monetary targets. This involves identifying the aggregates to be used as intermediate objectives in the coordination exercise and establishing the procedure for preparing *ex ante* and *ex post* exercises, including the method for calculating the statistics. However, Stage 2 will require a more advanced exercise of monetary policy coordination than that agreed so far; an exercise in which not only procedures but also monetary aggregates and instruments are harmonised. For *monetary aggregates*, this will require eliminating the differences between member countries regarding the liquidity of assets counted as money, their institutional frameworks and the treatment of cross-border holdings of monetary assets. As for *instruments*, harmonisation implies narrowing the substantial differences in the use of open market operations and refinancing facilities. Although the former have gained in importance recently, the latter continue to play a major role in some countries. Moreover, differences still exist in the use of compulsory reserve requirements with respect to the aggregates to which they apply, the remuneration, and the reference period. These differences can be considered as creating tax differentials between national banking systems that affect their competitive positions and encourage the shift of business to the least regulated international financial markets, with a consequent reduction in the effectiveness of domestic monetary policy.

The final point, on which the debate is still wide open, is the supervision of the *development of the ecu* in Stage 2. An important question to be addressed is what is meant exactly by the 'currency of the EMU'. Padoa-Schioppa (1990b) has noted that three definitions of this concept are currently being floated in the debate. The *single currency*, which would entirely replace all member states' currencies and be the only one allowed to circulate in the Community. The *common currency*, which would be utilised by the market in place of existing currencies but would not imply the creation of additional money. The *parallel currency*, which would be created by a

Community institution independently, and in addition to member states' currencies, with which it would compete. In addition, during the transition stage and until exchange rates are irrevocably fixed, the official value of the currency of the EMU in relation to national currencies could be determined by a 'basket' mechanism, such as the one currently used for the ecu, or by a 'parity' mechanism, which would fix an official exchange rate with other currencies.

The hard ecu recently proposed by the UK could be viewed as a 'common' currency whose official value would be determined by a 'parity' mechanism. This proposal is a useful contribution to the current debate, serving to clarify the unresolved aspects of the transition stage, but is not an alternative to the objective of monetary unification. In-depth analysis of the technicalities of the British proposal is currently under way. At this stage it does give rise to some concern, mainly in connection with its effects on monetary policy coordination in the Community, the stability of the interbank market for the currencies included in the present ecu and the prospects for the existing private ecu market.

The 'macroeconomic agenda' just reviewed is paralleled by a 'microeconomic agenda' more closely related to the integration problems of intermediaries and financial markets.

With respect to the first type of problem, the Community has responded to the lack of agreement on the optimal structure of *financial intermediaries* by taking a neutral position in order to foster conditions of 'fair competition' among different categories of intermediaries in the European marketplace and left the task of selecting the optimal outcome to the operation of competitive forces. The Community's position has nonetheless been modified somewhat in recent years: initially, the approval of the Second Directive on banking coordination gave a competitive edge to universal banks over specialised institutions. Subsequently, the proposed Directive on financial services revised this position by extending home country control to securities houses. Apart from institutional difficulties, the definition of conditions of fair competition proved no easy task. As an example of the conceptual problems it is sufficient to recall the recent discussion on the capital requirements for securities houses. It became apparent that equalising regulatory costs (in terms of capital requirements) for different suppliers of the same financial service might not level the playing field if the different intermediaries do not face the same risk of failure.

From a conceptual viewpoint, the design of an optimal regulatory framework will therefore require more precise definitions and measurements of the relevant categories of risk. Different risks, such as credit and position risk, need to be dealt with using different prudential measures in order to avoid distortionary effects. In addition, different theoretical models exist for financial risk measurement, whose empirical validity should be tested to evaluate their fitness for regulatory purposes.

From an institutional point of view the task will be that of adjusting the prudential framework to offset the potential costs arising from an integration process that, as recalled in previous chapters, relies to a certain extent on competition between systems. The possibility of unexpected distortions or stability problems will therefore require careful monitoring, coordinated at the international level, in order to improve the present regulatory structure. Such a coordinated approach can be expected to permit a better understanding of the cost of alternative methods of regulation (outright prohibition of specific activities as opposed to effective supervision) and a progressive convergence of opinions on the related issues of separation and optimal regulatory structures (Carosio, 1990).

Finally, let us consider the financial integration aspects related to *market organisation*, generally referred to as market globalisation. This process consists in the ability of financial intermediaries to branch across countries and to supply financial products in several markets, and in the possibility of markets themselves expanding worldwide.

The creation of the single market has relied mainly on the first two aspects of the financial integration process. By the middle of 1990 the liberalisation of capital movements had been completed and by 1993 the freedom of establishment of financial enterprises will extend liberalisation to financial services, thereby marking a second decisive step towards the equalisation of the investors' opportunity set. The third element of financial integration has so far played only a minor role and will need to be more carefully considered in the future.

The notion of market has always had local connotations: markets were generally named after the location where traders congregated in order to meet each other and carry out exchanges. The development of low-cost telecommunications services will modify this feature in the financial area. Markets will move to reach traders at their different locations, raising a whole new set of regulatory and technical problems if undesired forms of price instability are to be avoided.

As a result of the ongoing process of financial integration intense regulatory arbitrage can be expected. In addition, the presence of substantial market externalities, or external economies of scale as they are often defined (Grilli, 1989), will undoubtedly result in some shift of the financial industry towards the more developed centres. This will lead to large cross-border flows of funds, which will vary between banking and non-banking financial markets and, within each market, according to the liquidity of assets. In the not so distant future, however, the creation of a continental computerised system for several financial markets may make the issue of the geographic distribution of trade largely irrelevant. The first steps in this direction are already being taken, as is shown by the proposal to interconnect national central-depository schemes put forward by the International Federation of Stock Exchanges and accepted by several exchanges (Pagano and Roell, 1990).

6. Issues to be addressed

The interactions between developments in the macropolicy area and in market structures raise a number of issues. Among them we have identified two different groups: the first is related to the impact of these interactions on the speed of the overall process leading to the EMU; the second pertains to the potential problems arising from the lack of adequate coordination between monetary policy and developments in the areas of financial supervision, fiscal integration and market organisation.

The debate on the desirability of a 'gradual' versus a 'rapid' approach to full monetary unification falls within the first group.

The proponents of the gradual approach point to the need to maintain national and supranational authorities in parallel for some time, to permit 'learning by doing', the running in of policy instruments and procedures and the adaptation of private sector behaviour: a mistake in the conduct of monetary policy is likely to be more dangerous and disruptive if it occurs at the central level than at the national level. A second argument is that gradualism is necessary because economic structures and conditions in Europe still differ greatly, thus making monetary union very vulnerable to exogenous asymmetric shocks, as the recent Gulf crisis has reminded us.

The proponents of the rapid approach to monetary unification argue, on the other hand, that a gradual transition involves substantial costs, some of which are becoming more and more apparent (growing current-account imbalances, high nominal interest rates) and could endanger the process. An independent monetary policy conducted at the national level is clearly incompatible with increasing capital mobility and the commitment to fixed exchange rates. Accordingly, a rapid switch would increase the credibility of the unification process, thus reducing uncertainty about exchange-rate stability and facilitating the adaptation of microeconomic behaviour to the new standards (Frenkel and Goldstein, 1990). It would also avoid the negative externalities associated with beggar-my-neighbour policies during the transition stage (Papadia, 1990) and might make monetary policy more effective, since the demand for money in the Community area may be more stable than the demand in individual countries (Kremers and Lane, 1990).

As for the debate on the *propulsive factors* (private versus public), the arguments often overlap with the 'gradual versus rapid' debate. Gradualists support the view that unification should be fuelled by the competitive behaviour of market forces, which will lead monetary standards to converge at the 'best' equilibrium level and avoid the risk of collusive behaviour (United Kingdom Treasury, 1989). Proponents of the rapid approach argue that the process of monetary unification, particularly currency unification, should not be left exclusively to market forces, in view of the risk of systemic instability and sub-optimal equilibrium and they claim that public intervention is needed to provide the necessary institutional set-up and guide the transition process (Padoa-Schioppa, 1990b).

In our opinion the key to successful monetary and financial unification lies in the close coordination of market forces and public policy. The aim should be to ensure that the speed of monetary integration, controlled by the public authorities, is kept in line with progress in financial market integration, determined mainly by market forces providing a solution to the 'gradual versus rapid' debate.

The issue of the relationship between the supervisory and regulatory functions and the objective of price stability in an integrated European financial market falls within the second group of questions. As clearly illustrated by Friedman (1990), monetary authorities may be constrained in their ability to conduct an anti-inflationary policy because of concerns regarding the stability of the financial system as a whole. The constraint arises not only because authorities have to provide 'lender-of-last-resort' assistance in cases of financial crisis but also because they may want to avoid any tightening of macroeconomic conditions that may make such a crisis more likely.

This issue is particularly relevant to the EMU process for two reasons. First, because the financial industry in general is suffering from considerable overcapacity which in Europe is likely to be aggravated by the process of financial market integration. This overcapacity will have to be reabsorbed and the problem for the monetary authorities in Europe is how to do this without incurring serious systemic risks and at the same time without reducing their credibility with respect to the objective of price stability. Second, because according to the draft Statute of the ESCB approved by the EEC Governors, in the final stage of EMU, while the conduct of monetary policy will be centralised in the ESCB, the regulatory and supervisory functions will remain within the domain of national authorities, some of which are not central banks. In practice, this set-up introduces an additional constraint to the potential conflict between the objectives of price stability and market stability due to the national and supranational dimension of the problem.

An additional set of problems pertains to the conduct of monetary policy in the absence of integrated fiscal treatment of financial assets. The increased mobility and substitutability of assets, when not matched by progress in tax equalisation, tends to induce unwarranted capital flows. In relation to monetary assets, this determines changes in both the degree of controllability and the informational contents of monetary aggregates. In the absence of agreement on the treatment of capital income and reserve requirements for banks, harmonisation may be left to market forces: competition between fiscal regimes may shift banking intermediation towards markets with lower regulatory costs and yield a sub-optimal allocation of resources.

Finally, consideration should be given to the effects on financial markets and intermediaries that could be generated by the changes in techniques for monetary management associated with the shift to a single monetary policy in Europe. Pending the convergence of national financial systems towards a common structure, the conduct of a single monetary policy will require careful balancing of the different intervention techniques utilised (refinancing facilities versus open market operations) as well as of the geographic location of such interventions. The implementation of the common monetary policy influences the financial structure at the national level by enhancing the role of markets in which official interventions are performed and of intermediaries acting as counterparties to monetary authorities.

7. Conclusions

The extensive interaction between monetary policy integration and financial market integration affects both the costs and the speed of progress towards monetary union. Close monitoring by public authorities is therefore needed to evaluate whether and when corrective intervention is necessary to stabilise the overall process. The benefits of a carefully coordinated approach include greater ability of integrated monetary policy to achieve price stability and more stable integrated markets.

The pace of progress towards monetary union depends very much on the 'chain reaction' generated by market developments and policy decisions. In some cases the authorities must take the initiative: for instance, it was important that they should clearly state and define the final objectives of monetary integration in order to speed financial market integration through changes in private market behaviour; yet steps towards a more closely integrated monetary policy should not be taken in advance of progress towards the integration of financial markets. The relation between financial market developments and monetary policy decisions is by no means easy to define: the latter must stimulate market reactions while, at the same time, depending on them.

The importance of monetary and financial coordination will grow in the next few years as the cross-border substitutability of financial assets increases. From the economic viewpoint, it will be necessary to counter some of the distortions in current-account imbalances, interest rates and competitive conditions, to which the integration achieved so far may have contributed. In addition, the emergence of additional negative externalities will need to be prevented. From the institutional point of view there is the need to revise the coordination procedures adopted in the past and reduce the asymmetry in the definitions of objectives and methods that has so far been a feature of the monetary and financial aspects of integration.

References

Carosio, G. (1990), 'Problems of harmonization of the regulation of financial intermediaries in the European Community', *European Economic Review*, 34.

Ciampi, C.A. (1989), 'An operational framework for an integrated monetary policy in Europe', *Report on Economic and Monetary Union in the European Community*, Brussels.

Commission of the EC (1990), 'One market, one money', *European Economy*, 44, October.

Committee for the Study of Economic and Monetary Union (1989), 'Report on economic and monetary union in the European Community', Luxembourg, 17 April.

Dornbusch, R. (1989), 'Credibility, debt and unemployment: Ireland's failed stabilization, *Economic Policy*, 8.

Frenkel, J. and **Goldstein, M.** (1990), 'Monetary policy in an emerging European economic and monetary union: key issues', *Working Paper* 73, International Monetary Fund, Washington, August.

Friedman, B.M. (1990), 'Implications of increasing corporate indebtedness for monetary policy', *Occasional Paper*, 29, Group of Thirty, New York and London.

Giavazzi, F. and **Spaventa, L.** (1990), 'The "new" EMS', *CEPR Discussion Paper*, 369, Centre for Economic Policy Research, London, January.

Grilli, V. (1989), 'Financial markets', *Economic Policy*, October.

Kremers, J.M. and **Lane, T.** (1990), 'Economic and monetary integration and the aggregate demand for money in the EMS', Washington, International Monetary Fund, *Working Paper*, 23, March.

Monetary Committee of the EC (1990), *Report on Economic and Monetary Union beyond Stage One*, Brussels, 23 July.

Nardozzi, G. (1990), 'The structural evolution of financial systems in the '80s: from its determinants to its possible outcomes', *BNL Quarterly Review*, 172, March.

Padoa-Schioppa, T. (1990a), 'Financial and monetary integration in Europe: 1990, 1992 and beyond', *Occasional Paper*, Group of Thirty.

Padoa-Schioppa, T. (1990b), 'Unione e concorrenza monetaria: note per un dibattito', *Politica Economica*, 3.

Pagano, M. and Roell, A. (1990), 'Stock markets', *Economic Policy*, April.

Papadia, F. (1990), 'La Banca centrale europea: una nuova istituzione per l'Europa', *Mondo Bancario*, 4, July–August.

United Kingdom, H.M. Treasury (1989), *An Evolutonary Approach to EMU.*

Viñals, J. (1990), 'The EMS, Spain and macroeconomic policy', *CEPR Discussion Paper*, 389, Centre for Economic Policy Research, London, March.

Capital adequacy and European securities markets*

Richard S. Dale

The European Commission's Second Banking Coordination Directive, which was formally adopted in December 1989, will allow banks to engage in securities, as well as banking, activities throughout the European Community. The Commission's draft Directive on Investment Services is designed to give the same opportunity to non-bank investment firms. In support of this programme the Commission in April 1990 published a Proposal for a Council Directive on Capital Adequacy of Investment Firms and Credit Institutions. The proposal aims to harmonise capital adequacy requirements for securities business in the same way that the Solvency Ratio Directive together with the Own Funds Directive provides a common regulatory framework for banking.[1]

In examining the European Commission's latest capital adequacy proposal this chapter will consider first why it is that we need to regulate securities firms, secondly the different regulatory objectives and techniques applicable to securities firms as compared with banks, third the EEC's approach to capital adequacy and, finally, potential systemic risks in the post-1992 financial market regime which the EEC approach may not have adequately addressed.

1. The need to regulate securities firms

It is possible to identify three separate reasons for regulating securities firms: the protection of retail investors, the protection of counterparties and the stability of the financial system.

The traditional approach to regulating securities markets has focused primarily on the risk to investors.[2] Broadly, the idea here is that investors should be free to incur whatever risks they choose, provided that they are made fully aware of those risks and provided also that those risks do not include losses arising from the insolvency of the securities firm itself. In order to cover the latter eventuality it has been

---

*This chapter is based on an article published in the *Journal of International Securities Markets*, Vol. 4 Autumn 1990, pp. 211–25

the practice in many countries to establish an investor protection scheme that compensates investors up to some maximum figure. The proposed EEC Directive on Investment Services follows this practice by requiring that an investment firm 'is either a member of a general compensation scheme designed to protect investors who are prevented from having claims satisfied because of the bankruptcy or default of the investment firm or makes individual arrangements which provide investors with equivalent protection'.[3] This provision is buttressed by the further requirement that investors' securities and cash be held separately from the investment firm's own assets.[4] Given these safeguards it may be doubted whether there is an additional need for capital adequacy requirements simply to protect investors against default.

There is, however, a second rationale for regulating investment firms – namely, the need to reassure counterparties, including banks and other creditors, who might otherwise be reluctant to deal with such firms. The suggestion here is that the market could not operate efficiently without regulation because the financial condition of investment firms cannot be effectively monitored by market participants. This argument was, for instance, advanced by the Technical Committee of the International Organisation of Securities Commissions in their recent study[5] of the capital adequacy problem. On the other hand, it might reasonably be argued that in the absence of regulation investment firms would simply be forced to become less reliant on short-term unsecured borrowing and more dependent on secured and medium-term borrowing. Indeed, it appears that an adjustment of this kind is now taking place within the US investment banking industry in the wake of the Drexel collapse.[6]

The third and most persuasive case for regulation is based on the view that the default of unregulated securities firms could destabilise the financial system. Official concern over the potential for systemic disturbances of this kind have increased following the global stockmarket crash of 1987. A recent OECD study expressed these concerns as follows:

> the rising importance of securities markets in the financial systems of OECD countries, the growing concentration in the securities industry, the effects of new technologies, the nature of the risks now being born by securities market intermediaries and the links between the securities market and the banking and payments system all suggest that the occurrence of serious misfunctions in the securities markets would have the potential to destabilise the entire financial system.[7]

It might be objected that the collapse of Drexel without any serious financial ripple effects provides contrary evidence. However, it must be recalled that Drexel's failure was very carefully managed by the US regulatory authorities with a view to ensuring that the holding companies' broker-dealer subsidiary was given the opportunity to wind down its business in an orderly manner. The SEC Chairman has since stated in Congressional testimony that, by maintaining the broker-dealer's solvency immediately following the parent company's collapse, the authorities were able to protect other broker-dealers and their customers from defaults on trades involving billions of dollars in securities, and that 'a sudden collapse of a major broker-dealer such as Drexel Burnham Lambert could have had extremely adverse consequences on confidence in the marketplace, and on the smooth functioning of our clearance and settlement system'.[8] Of course, it is hardly necessary to emphasise that the failure of a major *bank-related* investment firm in a universal banking country would be a more serious matter still – a point to which I shall return later. Suffice it to say here that concerns over financial stability, rather than investor protection, seem to be the main driving force behind recent initiatives to strengthen the regulation of investment firms.

2. Differences between bank regulation and the regulation of securities firms

Before examining the EEC's approach to regulating securities firms it is helpful to consider the main differences between bank regulation and the regulation of securities activities.[9] In order to make such a comparison it is necessary to identify those key differences between securities and banking business that have implications for regulatory policy.

The most fundamental difference is that securities firms have a much shorter commercial time horizon than banks. Banks typically hold loans on their balance sheet until maturity, whereas securities firms experience rapid asset turnover as a result of their underwriting, market-making and trading activities. The difference in time horizon is reflected in the liquidity characteristics of the assets which the two types of institutions hold. That is to say, a large proportion of bank assets are in the form of unmarketable commercial loans, whereas the assets of securities firms are by definition highly marketable. This means that the main business risk for securities firms is market risk, whereas for banks it is credit risk. Also, because of their differing time horizons, securities firms are evaluated on a liquidation basis and their accounting is mark-to-market whereas banks are evaluated as going concerns and their accounting is based on original cost.

A closely related point is that securities firms can adjust their balance sheets rapidly to changing circumstances whereas the composition of a bank's loan portfolio changes only slowly. Similarly, while the market risk profile of a securities firm can be adjusted very quickly, the credit risk associated with a bank's commercial lending can be modified only gradually.

Arising out of their ordinary business operations, securities firms also experience large fluctuations in their balance sheet size and in their capital ratios. Banks, on the other hand, have relatively stable balance sheets and their capital ratios change relatively slowly.

Finally, on the liabilities side, securities firms are entirely dependent on wholesale money markets for their non-capital funding whereas for banks an important contribution to funding may come from retail deposits. History suggests that wholesale markets are more fickle than a captive retail deposit base but against this it has to be recognised that a large proportion of securities firm's borrowing is secured.

As the recent Drexel collapse demonstrates, it is the *unsecured* component of securities firms borrowing – notably in the form of commercial paper – that is most liable to sudden contraction. Overriding these considerations, however, is the fact that banks' deposit liabilities are uniquely vulnerable to contagious panic withdrawals owing to the illiquid and non-transparent nature of banks' assets and related uncertainties concerning net worth.

These differences in the business characteristics of banks and securities firms have important regulatory consequences. The most important of these concerns the way in which the two types of institution are expected to respond to financial difficulties. A securities firm with impaired capital is expected to shrink its balance sheet immediately in order to comply with its regulatory capital requirement. This it can do so long as its assets are in readily marketable form. Hence the regulatory emphasis on securities firms' 'liquid capital'. In the extreme a securities firm is required to wind down its business completely. For instance, the SEC's capital adequacy rules for US broker-dealers are explicitly designed to ensure that such firms can wind down their activities, while protecting their customers, within a time-frame of one month. The targeted wind-down period for UK securities firms, under the Securities Association's (TSA's) regulatory framework, is somewhat longer, at three months.

By way of contrast, a bank is most emphatically not expected to respond to financial problems by going out of business since if it were to do so its non-marketable assets could be sold quickly only at a heavy discount which would leave depositors and other creditors exposed to losses. Therefore the main objective of bank regulators is to sustain banks as going concerns and in the event of capital impairment to allow them time to raise new capital, strengthen management and conserve financial resources by, for instance, cutting dividend payments.

Accordingly, regulatory capital fulfils different functions for banks and securities firms. In both cases it is there to absorb losses but for banks the capital should be permanent – to support the institution as a going concern – whereas for a securities firm it may be temporary, reflecting the latter's ability to scale down its activities as well as its fluctuating need for capital resources. It is also worth noting here that because securities firms' business activities fluctuate so much, they typically operate on a capital base far above the regulatory minimum.[10] The excess capital enables such firms to take immediate advantage of business opportunities, such as underwriting, as they arise and it also advertises to the financial community a firm's ability to serve large customers and to undertake large-scale transactions.

The regulatory emphasis on permanent capital for banks and the more permissive approach to temporary capital for securities firms is therefore the result of divergent regulatory objectives. Because banks are uniquely vulnerable to contagious deposit withdrawals, bank failures involve risks to the financial system as a whole. The capital which a bank must hold is therefore intended to prevent it from going into liquidation. As securities firms, on the other hand, have not generally been vulnerable to 'runs' in the same way as banks, their assets are required to be readily saleable and prompt contraction and liquidation are the regulators' chosen methods of protecting customers and creditors.

One consequence of these differences in regulatory approach is that securities firms are generally entitled to rely heavily on subordinated debt as a source of capital, whereas for banks such financing typically counts only towards secondary capital and is subject to strict limits. Furthermore, to the extent that banks may rely on subordinated debt, it must generally have a minimum term to maturity of several years.[11] In contrast, under SEC rules for broker-dealers, an unusually large underwriting may be capitalised with temporary subordinated debt repayable within forty-five days.

Regulatory differences extend also to the role of deposit insurance and the lender of last resort. Within most banking systems deposit insurance plays an important part in maintaining confidence, thereby stabilising banks' deposit base. At the same time official liquidity assistance is available to sustain solvent banks as going concerns pending any necessary adjustments in their operations or financial structure. But because securities firms can generally contract their way out of trouble, they do not have the same need for a lender of last resort. Moreover, investor protection schemes have the limited purpose of providing protection to retail customers who are not in a position to monitor the financial condition of those with whom they deal.

In a sense, therefore, securities firms are much easier to regulate than banks even though the risks they incur may be as great, or greater.[12] The net worth of securities firms can be more readily ascertained, because their assets are saleable and marked to market; their liabilities are less vulnerable to contagious withdrawal; and the scale of their operations can be rapidly contracted in the event of capital impairment. Indeed, forced contraction and, in extreme cases, shut-down, are the regulators' main weapons in dealing with financially troubled securities firms, whereas troubled banks call for longer-term remedial programmes involving management restructuring, capital infusions and, as final measures, official liquidity support and even nationalisation.

The above differences in the regulation of banks and securities firms have led to serious difficulties for EEC policy-makers in their attempts to establish an appropriate regulatory framework for the single European financial market. The problems here arise from the prevalence of universal banking in Continental Europe, the related fact that the Second Banking Coordination Directive gives a broad definition of banking which includes securities activities, and the perceived need to maintain competitive equality between specialist and bank-related securities firms.

3.   The EEC's approach to regulating investment firms

3.1 DEFINITION OF CAPITAL

The EEC proposal for a Directive on the Capital Adequacy of Investment Firms and Credit Institutions (CAD) allows alternative definitions of capital for the supervisors of non-bank investment firms. These supervisors may choose either the definition of capital applied to banks in previous EEC Directives, or they can adopt an alternative

definition which is 'purpose-built' for securities businesses. In this alternative definition the emphasis is on liquidity rather than solvency, so that (a) all illiquid assets
must be deducted from capital while (b) subordinated debt with an initial maturity of
at least two years is allowable as regulatory capital up to a ceiling of 2½ x equity
capital. This alternative definition is broadly in line with that currently applied to
investment firms by the US, UK and Japan – although the limits on subordinated debt
are more restrictive. Under the EEC rules the implied time-frame for winding down
an investment firm follows the three month target adopted by the TSA so that, for
instance, bank deposits repayable within ninety days are included as liquid assets.

Under the CAD rules, supervisors of banks which undertake securities activities are also given alternative definitions of capital. They may continue to apply to
all of the bank's business the 'bank definition' of capital set out in earlier Directives,
or they may permit an alternative definition which allows the risks on the bank's
trading book[13] (only) to be covered by additional subordinated debt. This subordinated capital is subject to the same maturity and quantity constraints as under the
alternative capital definition for non-bank investment firms, but in addition the use of
the alternative definition must not add more than 25 per cent to the regulatory capital
that would be allowed under the 'bank definition'. Banks are not required to deduct
illiquid assets when applying the alternative definition of capital, since their trading
book, by definition, is made up entirely of marketable securities.

These alternative definitions of capital are, of course, intended to meet the
policy objective of ensuring a level playing field as between banks and non-bank
investment firms. However, the question that must be asked is whether these capital
rules can be justified on prudential grounds.

The official thinking behind the proposed definitions of capital was indicated in a recent speech by the Vice-President of the European Communities, Sir
Leon Brittan. Sir Leon stated that non-bank investment firms should be allowed a
larger amount of subordinated debt than banks since subordinated debt provides adequate protection for investors and counterparties. However, he went on to say that
such debt does not provide adequate protection in the case of banks:

> Their buffer [against potential losses] needs to be mainly in the form of
> equity so that losses may be absorbed without their net worth turning
> negative. In this way depositors can be confident that their credit
> institution will remain solvent. If this confidence was lacking, a panic
> withdrawal of funds would rapidly lead to a liquidity crisis for a bank given
> the long-term illiquid nature of its assets. Non-banks do not face the same
> problem, for their assets which are held for short periods are, by contrast,
> liquid and readily marketable.[14]

According to this line of reasoning the appropriate regulatory goal for bank
supervisors is to ensure solvency – hence the emphasis on equity capital. For investment firms, however, the stated regulatory objective is more limited: it is to protect
investors and counterparties without necessarily ensuring solvency, a goal that can be
achieved with more liberal use of subordinated debt.

Given the way securities markets have developed in recent years, this
statement of regulatory objectives may be questioned. In particular, the Drexel

episode suggests that investment firms, too, can suffer a collapse in confidence in much the same way as banks. It will be recalled that the Drexel group had over $1 billion of short-term unsecured borrowings, mostly in the form of commercial paper, but when the rating on Drexel's paper was downgraded in December last year it became impossible to roll over these borrowings.[15] The Chairman of the US Federal Reserve, Mr Alan Greenspan, subsequently referred to this funding collapse as the equivalent of a 'bank run'.[16] The Drexel affair also highlights the importance of a reliable funding base and the interconnections between solvency, asset liquidity[17] and the liquidity of liabilities. Yet the proposed EEC Directive, in common with the SEC's capital rules, says nothing about investment firms' non-capital liabilities.

If one does accept the EEC's divergent regulatory objectives for banks and investment firms, it is difficult to justify the alternative definition of capital available to banks. As explained, the alternative definition allows more liberal use of subordinated debt to support the bank's trading book. But to this extent the burden of absorbing losses on the trading book may have to be borne by the equity capital that supports the rest of the bank's business. The risk of insolvency is therefore increased.[18]

Furthermore, there is a danger that publicised losses on the trading book may trigger deposit withdrawals: if these withdrawals were to exceed the funding needed to support the trading book, the bank itself could be placed in jeopardy. For these reasons it seems inappropriate to try to segment a bank's securities and conventional banking business and to apply different capital rules to each.

There is also a danger that in its efforts to secure competitive equality within Europe between banks and non-bank investment firms, the proposed CAD Directive will create competitive distortions between European investment firms and those outside. For instance, under the TSA's capital rules for UK investment firms subordinated debt qualifies as regulatory capital up to a ceiling of $4 \times$ equity capital so long as it has an initial maturity of at least two years, while the SEC permits subordinated debt repayable within forty-five days to be used to capitalise unusually large underwritings. Given the stated objective of ensuring solvency, it is understandable that the proposed EEC Directive applies more stringent capital criteria than these to banks – indeed, as indicated earlier, the proposed rules may already be too permissive on this count. On the other hand, by applying to investment firms similar restrictions on the use of subordinated debt the EEC proposal arguably deprives the latter of needed flexibility and may place them at a disadvantage *vis-à-vis* their US counterparts, particularly when competing for large-scale underwriting business.

Of course, problems of this kind are inescapable so long as securities firms are subject to a dual regulatory regime – that is, a European regime designed to accommodate universal banking, and a US regime which separates banking and securities business.

3.2 POSITION RISK

I turn now to the various categories of risk against which investment firms are required to maintain capital. These are identified by the proposed EEC Directive as position risk – a broad concept embracing market, credit and liquidity risks – settlement or counterparty risk, foreign exchange risk and 'other' risks. I will focus briefly on the most important of these, namely, position risk and settlement risk.

The risk weights included in the fixed interest position risk requirements differentiate between only three categories of issuer: essentially, central government, other public sector plus listed grade corporate, and the rest. Furthermore, there is no differentiation by currency denomination of the issue. These risk categories are much cruder than those currently applied by the UK Securities Association which has identified significantly different price volatility as between, for instance, US Treasuries and Yen Sovereign issues.[19] Similarly the standard 10 per cent risk weighting for qualifying equities proposed by the EEC is much cruder than the present UK arrangements which differentiate between equities on the basis of the volatility of the stockmarkets where they trade.[20] The difficulty associated with the simplified EEC approach is that it may lead to inefficient use of capital, unacceptably high risks for investment firms specialising in volatile securities, as well as competitive disadvantages for lower risk markets.

This important consideration apart, the EEC capital requirements for position risk appear to be broadly in line with, albeit somewhat lower than, those currently applied in the US, UK and Japan. The EEC proposal states that, so far as equities are concerned, the position risk requirements are intended to cover a firm against a 10 per cent change in the general level of equity prices on its main markets, but it is not clear over what period the movement is to be measured. Put another way, it is unclear how quickly a firm is expected to be able to dispose of its equity position and how long it is therefore assumed to be exposed to market risk. The same uncertainty applies to interest-rate risk in relation to a firm's holdings of fixed interest securities.

The chief danger for regulators in assessing position risk is that the characteristics of particular securities markets can change dramatically due to unforeseen developments, as happened with the seizure of the markets in junk bonds (see note 6) and perpetual floating rate notes.[21] That is a risk which cannot easily be guarded against but there is a case for penalising investment firms whose activities are focused on a particular sector of the market, even if there is diversification within that sector. After all, it was Drexel's specialisation in the junk bond market that led to its downfall.

One other qualification needs to be made. As with the definition of capital, it is difficult to see how interest-rate risk, as captured by the EEC's proposed fixed interest position requirements, can be usefully applied to a bank's trading book. A bank's interest rate risk can be viewed only in the context of *all* its assets and *all* its liabilities: it surely cannot make sense to isolate some portion of one side of the balance sheet and use it as a basis for determining the market risk associated with interest-rate movements. This is just one of the many difficulties that may arise when applying the trading book option to banks' capital adequacy requirements.

3.3 SETTLEMENT RISK

So far as settlement or counterparty risk is concerned, there are two types of exposure. The first arises where there is 'free' delivery and money is paid away, or securities are delivered, prior to the other party fulfilling its side of the transaction. Here the exposure takes the form of full credit risk. The second type of exposure occurs under a cash against delivery transaction where the counterparty defaults: here the risk is that of replacement cost, which can be measured by the difference between the agreed settlement price for the security and its current market value.

The proposed EEC Directive makes explicit provision only for the second type of risk. This it does by specifying a capital requirement, measured as a percentage of the difference between the settlement and current market price, for transactions which remain unsettled after the due delivery date. The percentage capital requirement increases with the lapse of time, reaching 100 per cent forty-six days after due settlement date.

As indicated, no special provision is made for the full credit risk that arises under free delivery. However, this is covered indirectly by the ordinary capital adequacy rules in so far as unsecured receivables are illiquid assets that have to be deducted from capital. Arguably, this is unnecessarily severe, and it might have been better to follow the SEC in allowing routine receivables to count towards capital to an extent based on their age.

4. Systemic risks and 1992

The real difficulty with the EEC proposals for regulating securities activities lies not so much in the way that particular risks are dealt with, but rather in the attempt to establish competitive equality between banks and non-bank investment firms. There is a fundamental policy dilemma here which can only be properly understood by examining the way in which modern banking systems have evolved. For this purpose I shall use the US as an example simply because the relevant data are more readily available.[22]

In 1840 the average equity-capital-to-total-assets ratio for US banks was around 50 per cent. Over the next seventy-five years this ratio declined but by the late 1920s the average was still around 12 per cent. These high ratios – as they now seem to us – were the consequence not of any regulatory action but of market forces. That is to say, visibly high equity capital ratios were necessary to maintain depositors' confidence. Yet by 1989 the equity-capital-to-total-assets ratio of the 25 largest US banks was only 5 per cent – despite a decade of regulatory action aimed at strengthening US banks' balance sheets.

The markets have accommodated this dramatic decline in banks' capital ratios mainly because deposit insurance and access to the official discount window have drastically reduced the risks born by depositors. However, because the riskiness of a bank's assets is no longer reflected in the cost or availability of its funding, the propensity for risk-taking by banks has greatly increased. Hence the need for stringent regulation of the banking industry.

Against this background, the mingling of banking and securities activities under the EEC's 1992 regulatory programme presents some formidable policy problems. First, banks may be infected by their securities activities, whether these be conducted within the bank itself of through separate subsidiaries. The issue here is not one of 'firewalls'[23] since, as the Drexel collapse has demonstrated, a well capitalised entity, such as Drexel's government securities subsidiary, can have its funding cut off if questions are raised about the health of its parent company.[24] The same problem was highlighted, albeit on a much smaller scale, by the forced closure of a highly capitalised UK bank, British and Commonwealth Merchant Bank, simply because of its association with a troubled affiliate. The clear message for regulators is that, if *any* part of a financial conglomerate gets into difficulties, then any other part that depends on short-term unsecured funding can be put in jeopardy.

More broadly, it is reasonable to concur with the Chairman of the US Federal Reserve Board, Mr Alan Greenspan, that 'as financial institutions engage in more and more similar activities, disruption and pressures in non-banking financial markets may create systemic risk similar to that faced in earlier years in a narrower banking system'.[25] If national authorities respond to these pressures by extending the official safety net to non-bank financial activities, including securities business, then the problem of subsidised, and therefore excessive, risk-taking will be widened beyond the banking sector to securities markets. That development will in turn lead to demands for even more stringent regulation of investment firms.

By focusing its efforts on establishing a smooth path between banks and non-bank investment firms, and failing to address this more fundamental policy dilemma, the proposed EEC approach to regulating investment firms could achieve the worst of all possible worlds. The 'trading book' option allows banks to dilute the quality of their capital, while at the same time the risk of cross-infection from securities activities is increased. On the other hand, the competitive position of European-based investment firms may be weakened by the application of more stringent tests of capital adequacy than would be strictly necessary for self-standing securities houses.

5. Conclusions

The intensified competition between financial intermediaries that will inevitably accompany the 1992 liberalisation of European financial markets must be viewed against a background of existing surplus capacity in the global financial services industry.[26] The combination of a highly competitive environment, associated declines in lending margins and risk premia, and a European-wide change in the regulatory regime could create the kind of conditions after 1992 that in the past have led to financial instability.[27]

It is therefore important that the European Commission's capital adequacy proposals should be designed to ensure that financial institutions can cope with the difficult business climate that is in prospect. Unfortunately, the Commission's task has been made more complicated by a tight time schedule and the absence of any parallel global coordination of securities market regulation of the kind that exists in banking. The proposed capital adequacy rules for investment firms are intended to achieve a number of objectives: namely, to protect investors, counterparties and the stability of the financial system while simultaneously ensuring competitive equality between banks and specialist securities houses and also between European financial institutions and their non-European rivals. The danger is that in giving undue emphasis to establishing a smooth path between banks and securities houses, the Commission's proposals could jeopardise these other objectives.

Notes

1.   The directives referred to are discussed in Chapter 1.
2.   See 'Arrangements for the regulation and supervision of securities markets in OECD countries', OECD, Paris, 1989, p.20.
3.   Article 11 (1).
4.   Ibid.
5.   'Capital Adequacy Standards for Securities Firms', Report of the International Organisation of Securities Commissions, August 1989, p.6.
6.   See 'Morgan Stanley Files $1bn Shelf Registration', *Financial Times*, 9 June 1990, p.12. Drexel sought protection under Chapter 11 of the federal bankruptcy code in February 1990. The firm faced a liquidity crisis because it had acquired a large portfolio of unmarketable 'junk bonds' financed largely through short-term bank borrowings. Evidently US brokerage houses have been attempting to reduce their reliance on short-term bank borrowing, partly because banks have become much more cautious about lending to such firms since the Drexel collapse.
7.   'Arrangements for the regulation and supervision of securities markets in OECD countries', p. 20.
8.   See Statement of Richard Breeden before the Committee on Banking, Housing and Urban Affairs, US Senate, Concerning the Bankruptcy of Drexel Burnham Lambert Group Inc., February 1990, p.33.
9.   For an excellent analysis, see Gary Haberman, 'Capital requirements of commercial and investment banks: Contrasts in regulation', Federal Reserve Bank of New York, *Quarterly Review*, Autumn 1987, pp. 1–10.
10.   For instance, at year end 1986, sixteen US securities firms reported average net capital 7.3 times larger than minimum requirements. See Ibid., p. 6.
11.   Under the Basle capital adequacy rules for international banks, subordinated debt is allowable as supplementary capital up to a maximum of 50 per cent of core capital, subject to the condition that it must have a minimum original fixed term to maturity of over five years.

12.   Thus the US Securities Investor Protection Corporation, which was set up in 1970 to insure the accounts of customers of broker-dealers, has been able to operate with a low level of reserves on a minimal $100 per firm annual premium (1987): Haberman 'Capital requirements', p.6. In comparison the US Federal Deposit Insurance Corporation, which insures bank deposits, has in recent years experienced large claims on its resources, reflecting bank failures running at over 200 per annum.

13.   Article 2 of the CAD Directive defines a bank's 'trading book' to include 'its proprietary positions in transferable securities or derivative instruments, which are taken on by the [bank] in order to benefit from actual or expected differences between their buying and selling prices, or in order to hedge other elements of the trading book'. Such a definition, which is based on intention, may lead to some ambiguity in the classification of a bank's securities holdings.

14.   Speech to the Overseas Bankers Club, Guildhall, London, 5 February 1990, p.6.

15.   Following the reduction in Standard and Poor's rating on its commercial paper from A-2 to A-3 in December 1989, Drexel's outstanding commercial paper shrank from around $600 million to $180 million. See Statement of Richard Breeden, p. 24.

16.   See Testimony before the Subcommittee on Economic and Commercial Law, Committee on the Judiciary, US House of Representatives, 1 March 1990, p.4.

17.   The key problem for Drexel was that its approximately $1 billion holding of junk bonds became progressively less marketable as the junk bond market collapsed. By early 1990 these bonds could not be readily disposed of, nor could they be used as collateral for bank borrowings. See Statement of Richard Breeden, pp. 21–5.

18.   This, presumably, explains the additional constraint placed on banks' use of subordinated debt under the alternative definition, i.e., the 25 per cent rule referred to in the text. However, it is surely unwise to accept a higher insolvency risk for one particular group of banks, namely those which undertake securities business and whose supervisors choose to apply the alternative definition of capital.

19.   Thus the risk weight applied to 1–2 year US Treasuries is 1.50 per cent and for 1–2 year Yen Sovereign issues only 0.75 per cent. See TSA, *Financial Regulations*, Appendix 13, February 1988.

20.   For instance, the Percentage Risk Addition (PRA) applicable to equity holdings is 21 per cent for Australia compared with 10 per cent for Switzerland. See TSA, *Financial Regulations*, Appendix A, February 1988.

21.   The market in perpetual floating rate notes (FRNs), developed rapidly in the mid-1980s, reflecting banks' desire to raise debt capital in this form, and the market's willingness to absorb such paper on a low spread above short-term interbank rates. However, in 1986/7 the FRN market suffered a crisis of confidence, prices collapsed and the secondary market seized up.

22.   These data were presented by the Chairman of the US Federal Reserve Board, in a recent speech. See Alan Greenspan, 'Remarks before the Annual Conference on Bank Structure and Competition', Federal Reserve Bank of Chicago, 10 May 1990.

23.   'Firewalls' are a regulatory mechanism designed to insulate one part of a financial group from difficulties experienced in another part. Typically, firewalls

consist of strict limits on intra-group financial transactions – as, for instance, applied to US banks and their non-bank affiliates, under the US Federal Reserve Act.

24.   See Alan Greenspan, 'Testimony before the Subcommittee on Economic and Commercial Law', Federal Reserve Bank of Chicago, 10 May 1990.

25.   'Remarks before the Annual Conference on Bank Structure and Competition', Federal Reserve Bank of Chicago, 10 May 1990.

26.   As one prominent central banker put it recently: 'There is ... undoubted over-capacity in the financial sector which is leading to unrealistic undercutting of fees and margins in much the same way as we saw very low spreads being offered to Third World borrowers in the 1970s.' See Huib Muller, Executive Director, De Nederlandsche Bank, 'Risk Management', Remarks before the International Monetary Conference, San Francisco, 4 June 1990, p.7.

27.   See E.P. Davis, 'Instability in the Euromarkets and the economic theory of financial crisis', Bank of England, *Discussion Papers*, 43, October 1989.

PART THREE

FINANCIAL   INTERMEDIATION AND ECONOMIC GROWTH

CHAPTER TEN

Financial innovation, regulation and investment: international aspects*

José Viñals, Angel Berges and Francisco J. Valero

1. Introduction

In recent years, Western countries have undergone an intense process of financial innovation which has changed quite considerably, and in some instances perhaps lastingly, the functioning of their financial markets. Although this has generated an abundant literature on the factors causing financial innovation, and its effects for financial stability and monetary policy effectiveness,[1] it is not clear, however, how much all these financial developments have influenced the real sector of the economy – namely, production, saving and investment decisions.

That this is likely to remain an open and controversial issue in the near future can be explained by the following reasons: first of all, the difficulty in being precise about what is meant exactly by financial innovation, since this encompasses not only new financial instruments but also changes in the very nature of financial markets due to securitisation, global integration, etc.; second, the lack of a well-defined conceptual framework which clearly establishes the linkages between financial innovation and production, saving and investment decisions; finally, the scarcity of solid empirical evidence on the effects of financial innovation on the real sector of the economy.

The above problems notwithstanding, the more modest aims of this chapter are to provide a relatively simple conceptual framework that can be used to stimulate thought about the effects of the new financial instruments on capital formation, and to assess how important these effects have been in Europe. In the above sense, it is clear why this issue is of critical importance for the European Community countries. On the one hand, the integration of financial markets resulting from the establishment of free capital mobility and the liberalisation of banking activities will certainly significantly affect the process of financial innovation. And, on the other hand, the integration of goods markets will probably lead to changes in national production structures which, in turn, need substantial investments. Therefore, it seems of great policy relevance to analyse how the new financial instruments can be expected to influence, if at all, decisions regarding the volume and composition of private capital formation.

*Translation of paper published in *Monida y Credito*, 190.

The chapter is organised in five sections. Section 2 examines the true meaning of financial innovation, and the conditions under which its effects spill over to the real sector of the economy. Section 3 looks at the various theoretical determinants of private investment and discusses how important they are likely to be in practice. Section 4 surveys the most significant new financial instruments and analyses their potential and actual contribution to investment financing. Section 5 focuses on the implications that follow for financial regulation policy. Section 6 ends the chapter with a summary of the main conclusions obtained and with a discussion of the main implications for financial policy.

2. Financial innovation: its nature and meaning

Financial markets have become a key element in the functioning of modern economies. In turn, the existence of financial markets themselves can be traced back to two elements: time and uncertainty.

Regarding the *time* dimension, saving and investment decisions are made by households and firms after solving complex constrained multiperiod optimisation problems. Thanks to financial markets, they are allowed to transfer purchasing power from the present to the future and vice versa in such a way as to allow saving to be channelled into the most profitable investment opportunities thus improving resource allocation.

Regarding the *uncertainty* dimension, the presence of risk in economic life can be a serious impediment to the efficient allocation of resources unless there exists a complete set of contingent commodities markets. However, as shown by Arrow (1964) and Debreu (1959), even when the number of available markets is smaller than the number of contingent commodities (which equals the number of goods times the number of states of nature: $nös$), an efficient allocation of resources is made possible by the existence of enough financial instruments.[2] Specifically, there will be an efficient allocation of resources through the market whenever the number of independent marketable securities equals the number of states of nature (s). In such cases, it will be possible to reproduce exactly the allocation of resources obtained with ($nös$) contingent commodity markets by instead purchasing appropriate amounts of the (s) distinct securities, each of which pays a given sum of money when a particular state of nature occurs, and then using the proceeds to buy the desired quantities of goods in the (n) spot markets available. In sum, in an uncertain world a complete set of financial markets is critical to the achievement of an efficient allocation of resources.

In reality, nevertheless, financial markets seem to be quite different from the above ideal cases in several important respects. First, financial markets are *incomplete*, in the sense of the number of financial instruments falling quite short of the number of contingencies; as explained, this leads to serious economic inefficiencies. Second, there are *operational inefficiencies* associated with the high transaction costs of channelling savings into investment, which are reflected in the gap between the return most individuals earn on assets and the costs they pay as borrowers.

In short, the lack of markets for many financial instruments and the imperfect functioning of the markets for many existing instruments produces an unsatisfied demand for financial services which, if appropriately filled, can yield economic profits. Therefore, as Levich (1987) has stressed, the market will be ready to pay for those financial innovations which reduce the transaction costs of doing things that were already possible, and for those which allow a better spreading of risk in the economy by allowing people to do things they could not do before. In this respect, Van Horne (1985) has proposed to define as *financial innovations* all those new products or processes that 'make the markets more efficient in an operational sense and/or more complete', therefore helping achieve a better allocation of resources.

It may be useful to recall at this point that the financial innovation process does not only encompass new products (i.e., interest-rate futures) or new processes (i.e., electronic fund transfers), but also major changes taking place in the financial framework. In a recent study, the Bank for International Settlements (BIS, 1986) lists these major changes as: (a) the trend towards securitisation associated with the growing role of capital markets to the detriment of credit markets, (b) the increasing importance of off-balance-sheet activities by banks and (c) the global integration and internationalisation of financial markets.

Keeping this in mind, the definitional criterion for financial innovation can be usefully applied to the debate about whether such innovations are no more than a zero-sum game played exclusively within the financial sector and leading just to more transfers and transactions without benefiting the real side of the economy or, on the contrary, such innovations spill over to affect favourably real economic decisions like saving, investment and production. In this regard, those things which are sold in the market as financial innovations but which do not either lower financial transaction costs and/or contribute to a better spreading of risks, will not have favourable effects either on the operational efficiency and/or completeness of financial markets. Consequently, they will not help – but may actually hurt by diverting scarce resources from truly productive activities – the real sector of the economy. As indicated by Van Horne (1985), Miller (1986) and the BIS study (1986) among others, this is not to say, though, that there will not be profits for those introducing the pseudo-innovations, at least until the market finally recognises that nothing really new is being offered.

In the sections that follow, rather than trying to answer normative questions regarding economic welfare, we focus on the more limited but still important positive issue of how the recent wave of innovation in financial instruments can affect private capital formation.

3. Economic and financial determinants of investment

3.1 CAPITAL FORMATION, PROFITABILITY AND FINANCIAL CONSTRAINTS

It is firmly established that the rate of capital formation is a key element in determining the growth rate of the economy. Nevertheless, when studying the effects of financial innovation on capital formation it is best to distinguish between the long run and the short run.

In the *long run*, competitive profit-maximising firms have a demand for capital that depends on the costs of capital and of the other factors of production. Given that some of the new financial products are usually credited with lowering the financial cost of capital to firms, it is clear how the new financial instruments could affect the long-term capital stock of the economy through this channel. Since the aggregate capital stock depends negatively on the cost of capital, a drop in this cost will raise the capital stock in a proportion that depends on the production technology of the economy. To get an idea of the order of magnitude involved, it may be useful to take a stylised example not too far removed from reality. In the case of a Cobb–Douglas, constant returns to scale, production function with a share of labour in total income of 2/3, the elasticity of the long run aggregate capital stock of the economy with respect to the rental cost of capital is -1.5. That is, a 1 per cent reduction in the cost of capital increases the long run capital stock of the economy by 1.5 per cent, which is a very substantial effect.

It would be inappropriate, however, to conclude from the above that cost of capital reductions induced by financial innovation will have as large effects on investment in the *short to medium run*, which is most relevant for policy purposes. The basic reason – supplied by the modern theory of investment – is that capital is durable and firms are subject to the increasing costs of changing the capital stock. Therefore, firms will carefully take into account the present and expected future consequences of adding a new unit of capital before embarking in a new investment.

Investment depends positively on the present discounted value (to the firm) of the extra unit of capital (q). In turn, q will be larger when the '*marginal efficiency of capital*' (i.e., the stream of expected earnings generated by the extra unit of capital) is higher, and when the financial '*cost of capital*' to the firm (i.e., the discount rate used in the present value calculation) is lower. As a result, when firms have ready access to external finance (debt and equity) as well as to internal finance, their investment decisions will be fully determined by the evolution of q dictated by the behaviour of the marginal efficiency of capital and the cost of capital.

Consequently, new financial instruments which (a) change the financial cost of capital to the firm, (b) help the firm cover contingencies, or (c) provide new and more flexible financial arrangements, will affect investment by affecting

q. While the first effect works through the cost of capital channel, and the third through the marginal efficiency of capital channel, the second works through both channels.[3]

Finally, there is another channel through which new financial products may have an effect on investment in addition to the 'profitability' q channel. This happens whenever financial market imperfections make firms' investment decisions depend on their financial structure.

The issue of the relationship between investment and financing decisions has been a controversial one in the financial literature for the last thirty years. The debate, too well known to reproduce at any length here, started with Modigliani and Miller (1958) showing that, under the assumption of perfect capital markets and given firms' investment policies, financial structure is irrelevant to the value of the firm. Most of the following controversy has centred on how financial structure can become relevant – even if investment policy continues to be exogenously given – due to market imperfections.[4] Our main interest here, rather, is on those financial market imperfections which make investment decisions depend on financing decisions.

The most important of these imperfections is the asymmetry of information between providers and users of funds, which can cause severe financial constraints to the firm.[5] Given that potential suppliers of funds cannot always screen 'good' from 'bad' firms, new shareholders and debtholders will want to be compensated by charging all firms with a premium to cover the losses made from inadvertently financing 'bad' firms. This will then increase the cost of external finance to the firm. At the same time, recent work regarding the existence of asymmetric information in loan markets shows that if lenders are unable to distinguish 'good' from 'bad' borrowers they will behave optimally by setting credit limits.[6]

The above problem has quite unfavourable implications for the ability of modern firms to make the types of investment that the changing industrial structure demands. On the one hand, small and new firms – probably the most dynamic and adaptable to the changing industrial demands – are most likely to face financial constraints or higher costs due to the difficulties they have in showing the market 'how good they are'. On the other hand, high technology firms, and in general firms intensive in intangible assets, also face large informational asymmetries, as well as uncertainty regarding the liquidating value of assets in the event of bankruptcy. As Long and Malitz (1986) have shown, they are also likely to suffer from severe external financing constraints.

In sum, when asymmetric information prevails in financial markets firms may suffer from *external financial constraints* and limited possibilities of substituting new equity for debt. This is consistent with firms' investments depending not only on the existence of good profit opportunities (reflected in q) but also on the availability of internal finance. In this regard, a variable like current profits or cash flow, which proxies for internal finance conditions, may also be an important determinant of investment. An implication of the above is that new financial instruments that alter the degree of informational asymmetries in financial markets, or have an impact on the current profits or cash flows generated by firms, will also affect investment.

3.2 EMPIRICAL EVIDENCE ON INVESTMENT EQUATIONS

Before drawing any implications about the overall effects of financial innovations on investment, it is necessary to review the evidence regarding the effects of q and financial constraints on investment. Table 10.1 summarises in chronological order several of the most relevant recent empirical studies on investment functions for the United States, major European countries and Japan. The overall impression we have from looking at the international evidence, both at the aggregate and firm level, is the following: first, the q-channel is not very powerful for explaining investment behaviour, the effects of q on investment being generally small and slow. Second, those studies[7] which separate the marginal efficiency of capital from the cost of capital components of q find that the first component generally has larger and more significant effects on investment than the second. And third, variables like current profits, cash flow and sales also seem to matter for investment, often dominating the role of q.[8] To summarise, Figure 10.1 graphically illustrates the main determinants of investment and their empirical role.[9]

In sum, the lessons we learn from the theoretical and empirical literature on investment reviewed in this section are the following: while the new financial instruments are likely to have only a limited effect on investment by lowering the cost of capital to the firm, they may nevertheless have a significant effect on investment by helping firms' profitability and by relieving their financial constraints.

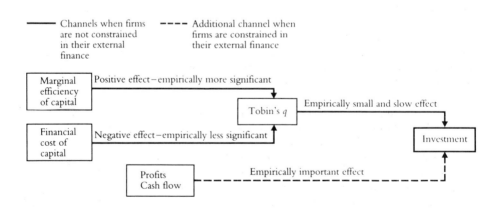

FIG 10.1 The determinants of capital investment

TABLE 10.1 Recent empirical evidence on investment equations

Studies	Country	Data	Main findings
Abel (1980)	US	Aggregate	The elesticity of investment to q is significant and ranges between 0.5 and 1.1
Meese (1980)	US	Aggregate	Insignificant relative price effects, very significant lagged dependent variables
Summers (1981)	US	Aggregate	q has extremely low effects
Hendershott and Hu (1981)	US	Aggregate	Insignificant effects of the cost of capital on equipment investment
Chappell and Cheng (1982)	US	Firm	q not significant
Salinger and Summers (1983)	US	Firm	q significant in half the firms
Poterba and Summers (1983)	UK	Aggregate	Very mixed results
Mairesse and Dermont (1985)	France Germany US	Firm	Current and past output, and profits, have significant effects; not very significant effect of the cost of capital
Dinenis (1985a, b)	UK	Aggregate	Current and past q have significant effects on investment
Abel and Blanchard (1986)	US	Aggregate	q significant but: large, serially correlated residual, the marginal efficiency of capital component has larger and more significant effects than the cost of capital component, profits and output variables also matter
Chirinko (1986a)	US	Aggregate	Even when separation between structure, equipment and inventories is made q-effects are still extremely low, lagged variables matter and there is serial correlation of residuals
Bruno (1986)	(*)	Aggregate	Large effects of profits, insignificant effect of the cost of capital
Chirinko (1987)	US	Aggregate	Very small q-effects, serial correlation, cash flow enters but not robust to estimation technique, past investment and current output also have important effects
Hayashi and Inoue (1987)	Japan	Firm	Significant but very weak effect of q; profits and past values of q also matter
Fazzari et al. (1987)	US	Firm	Investment sensitive to q but also to cash flow in firms likely to be financially constrained

Note: Bruno (1986) runs ad hoc investment equations for US, Canada, Japan, UK, France, Germany, Italy and Sweden.
Source: Most of the studies are discussed in Chirinko (1986b).

4.   An analysis of the new financial instruments

Having defined in the previous two sections the nature and meaning of financial innovation and the main economic and financial determinants of investment, we now analyse in detail the new financial instruments and how they can contribute to investment. This contribution can be in terms of: (a) making available new external financial sources previously unavailable to firms (financial constraint effect), (b) providing cheaper sources of investment finance (cost of capital effect) or (c) allowing the firm a better financing of working capital or a better covering of the risks arising from investment or financing decisions[10] (efficiency of capital and cost of capital effects). To complete the analysis, we also examine how large are these potential effects likely to be, given the actual use firms make of the new instruments, and given the relative size of the latter in financial markets.

It must be pointed out at the start that any review or classification of innovations in financial instruments risks omitting some which may be of interest to market participants. Our purpose here, however, is not to give an exhaustive coverage of all the new financial instruments, their origin or degree of success,[11] but rather to focus on those which – at least potentially – are more closely related to investment decisions of non-financial firms.

Our analysis takes as its starting point the distinction usually made in corporate finance theory between debt and equity as the available sources of external finance to the firm. As is well known, debt and equity differ in terms of the kind of financial obligations they impose on the firm. While straight debt implies payment obligations which are invariant with respect to both the firm's performance and future financial conditions, equity, on the other hand, allows a lot more financial flexibility to the firm, since it is paid out of the funds remaining after the firm has met all its contractual costs.

This simple but theoretically attractive distinction can be used to classify the main new financial instruments as in Table 10.2. The first three categories of instruments in the table represent recent modifications of traditional debt and equity instruments to finance investment, while the last one includes those instruments which facilitate the coverage of investment or financing risks. Each of these categories of new financial instruments is discussed in detail in what follows.

4.1   SPECIAL DEBT INSTRUMENTS

The first group in this category – floating interest-rate debt instruments – includes those instruments whose financial charges are not fixed in advance but rather vary according to financial market conditions. Floating rate debt instruments were originally introduced in the early 1970s by financial institutions seeking to avoid interest

TABLE 10.2 Classification of the main financial innovations

Special debt instruments
   Variable rate loans ⎫
   Floating rate bonds ⎬ Floating rate debt
   Note issuance facilities ⎭

   Zero-coupon bonds ⎫
   Junk bonds ⎬ Special fixed rate debt

Debt-equity hybrid instruments
   Convertible bonds
   Bonds with warrants
   Prêts participatifs

Special equity instruments
   Euro-equities
   Venture capital

Risk-covering instruments
   Swaps
   Futures/forward rate agreements
   Options

---

rate risk in a period of increased volatility in financial markets. The first major development was the generalisation of *variable rate loans* (VRLs), specially in the Euromarkets. In this type of loan, the interest paid by the borrower is the sum of some known spread plus a variable base interest rate representative of the financial institution's cost of financing. The use of variable interest rates has also extended more recently to *bond issues* (Floating Rate Notes or FRNs), where the interest payment is also linked to some representative base interest rate.[12]

A mixture of the two instruments just described (VRLs and FRNs) are the so-called NIFs or *Note Issuance Facilities*, probably one of the clearest signs of financial innovation in the present decade. NIFs are basically equivalent to commercial paper programmes with the added feature that a financial institution guarantees the borrower the availability of short-term financing (three to six months) over a medium term (five to seven years) horizon. The paper issued by the borrower is either placed with investors (similar to FRNs) or kept by the guaranteeing institution (similar to VRLs). Interest payments of NIFs are generally linked to the interbank rate, usually with a discount since NIFs are issued by high-quality borrowers with sometimes even better risk ratings than many banks.

Having briefly reviewed the nature of the main floating debt instruments, we now focus on how they can potentially contribute to capital formation through any of the three channels previously mentioned.

By their very nature, floating rate debt instruments do not provide completely new sources of finance, although they have a comparative cost advantage with respect to previously existing financial sources. On the one hand, relative to traditional long-term (straight) debt, they have the cost advantage embedded in the liquidity preference hypothesis: average expected costs of short-term financing are generally found to be lower than known average long-term costs. Moreover, they constitute a particularly attractive source of financing whenever a firm's revenues are positively correlated with interest-rate movements (ie, due to the inflation component of both nominal interest rates and cash flows, etc.). On the other hand, relative to straight short-term debt, floating rate debt is in principle equivalent, in terms of finance availability, to the rolling-over of short-term debt. Nevertheless, there are two important advantages to the former. First, by receiving the guarantee that finance will be available in the future – at the then prevailing market interest rates – the firm suppresses the risk of being rationed out of the credit market in the future. Second, even if there was no future credit rationing, the cost of short-term financing to the firm may still increase whenever its credit rating deteriorates. This risk is avoided with the new instruments since the spread (or discount) is usually set in advance for the entire life of the instrument.[13]

Summarising, it seems that floating rate debt instruments can be potentially very useful to finance working capital at lower costs – which increases the net profitability of the firm for any given investment project – and also to finance physical investment projects whose returns are closely correlated with interest rates. In terms of the main determinants of investment discussed in section 3 of this chapter, the existence of floating interest-rate instruments can help increase the firm's q by increasing the marginal efficiency of capital and by lowering the financial cost of capital.

But to assess how important are these q-type effects likely to be in practice, we must first answer two questions: how large is the size of the market for the new instruments relative to the overall market for financial sources; and, how much are these instruments used by non-financial corporate borrowers as opposed to financial institutions themselves?[14] If the answer to both questions is favourable, then it is important to ask whether there has really been a lowering of the financial costs with the new instruments relative to the previously existing ones. We address now these questions subject to the constraints imposed by data availability.

Starting with market size, most of the available data correspond to international financial markets. Table 10.3 summarises the volume of funds raised by borrowers of major European countries and the US between 1986 and 1989. The most salient feature in the table is the strong increase of VRLs after 1986, leading to a triplication in volume in 1989. In contrast, there has been a marked reduction in the issue of bonds, and especially of floating rate bonds, probably as a result of the higher interest rates existing in recent years.

Regarding the recent increase of VRLs, the simplest financing modality in international markets, this is probably connected with the shifting towards traditional banking instruments following the stockmarket crash of 1987. In that respect, it could even be said that the crash stopped, or even inverted for a time, the tendency towards financial disintermediation.

A similar conclusion is obtained regarding the recent evolution of NIFs, whose use has been more erratic and which certainly has not increased by as much as that of VRLs. In any case, the volume of funds obtained through this instrument can

TABLE 10.3 Flow of funds raised in the international financial markets (US$ billion)

Country	1986 Loans		1986 Eurobonds		1987 Loans		1987 Eurobonds		1989 Loans		1989 Eurobonds	
	Total	NIF	Total	FRN	Total	NIF	Total	FRN	Total	NIF	Total	FRN
Germany	0.8	0.2	11.1	1.0	1.3	0.1	7.8	0	3.0	0	0.9	2.0
France	7.2	2.5	13.4	4.0	9.7	4.9	.4	0.5	8.9	0.2	12.2	0.7
UK	17.3	8.8	19.0	12.4	52.4	26.4	9.3	1.1	77.3	0.4	19.8	8.4
Italy	6.6	1.5	5.4	2.0	5.9	0.5	6.7	2.0	6.7	0	9.5	1.4
Spain	7.9	0.7	1.7	1.4	3.4	1.4	0.2	0	3.3	0	0.6	0
Netherlands	0.4	0.1	2.8	0	0.1	0	2.8	0	2.3	0	2.4	0.1
US	47.6	5.5	44.7	10.7	123.7	11.2	20.2	2.9	167.4	0.9	15.5	2.0
TOTAL	87.8	.3	98.1	31.5	196.5	44.5	54.4	6.5	268.9	1.5	69.0	14.6

Notes: All loans are variable rate loans.
FRN: floating rate loans.
NIF: note issuance facilities.
The total amounts shown correspond to the contries listed and may differ from world totals.
Source: Euromoney Syndication Guide and I.F.R. Global Financing Directory.

TABLE 10.4 Worldwide commercial paper (issues outstanding in US$ billion)

Market	1986	1987	1989
US	323.0	420.0	523.0
Canada	11.4	15.4	
Sweden	7.4	4.8	
Spain	5.4	3.3	
Australia	4.3	6.2	
France	4.0	10.5	
Hong Kong	1.2	0.6	
UK	1.0	5.0	
Euromarkets (NIFs)	35.0	55.0	79.0

Source: Bank of England (1987a) and Euromoney Corporate Finance (1988).

be considered to be rather small, since it is no more than 1–2 per cent of the total financing in the countries analysed.

One may wonder how much these numbers change when we add to the international market data the national market data. The answer is that generally they do not change much, at least for those instruments for which we have been able to find data.[15] Table 10.4 shows an estimate of the worldwide volume of commercial paper issues outstanding in recent years. Among the EEC countries only Spain, France and the United Kingdom have a domestic commercial paper market, and only in the first country does its volume represent a significant share of the total flow of funds of the economy.

But to make things even worse, it is not only the case that the market size of the most dynamic new variable rate debt instrument (FRNs and NIFs) is small, it also happens that they are used to a large extent by the financial institutions them-

TABLE 10.5 Financial institutions' share of total FRNs and NIFs (% issued in international financial markets)

	1982	1985	1988	1989
FRNs	38.8	52.7	n.a.	n.a.
Total bonds	15.3	26.4	44.3	47.3
NIFs	29.3	27.5	3.5	n.a.

Source: BIS 1986) and analistas Financieros Internacionales.

selves as a way of finding resources. As Table 10.5 shows, both in the case of bonds and NIFs, the weight of financial institutions among the issuers has increased systematically during recent years, being at present approximately less than half in the first case (bonds), and a bit more than a third in the second (NIFs).

Moreover, since according to the BIS (1986) study, at most 20 per cent of the total NIFs arranged have actually been drawn, this means that NIFs are mainly used as a back-up facility and not as a direct source of funding. As a result, this makes their effective use by firms as a method of finance far lower than what the table suggests.

In sum, the limited evidence available seems to indicate that floating rate bonds and NIFs generally play a minor role in the financing of non-financial corporate institutions. On the other hand, the outlook does not seem too optimistic either when we look at price rather than quantity data. To take an example, in the discussion of the new financial instruments of the variable interest-rate category, NIFs were singled out as being potentially very useful as a source of financing to firms. But, if we look at the average discount in NIF rates with respect to the interbank rate, it can be seen that it goes down from more than 1.2 per cent in 1980 to 0.15 per cent in 1988. We interpret this as indicating that as the increase in NIFs issues took place in the period (Table 10.3) lower quality borrowers came to the market, wiping out the financial cost advantage of NIFs relative to traditional sources of finance. Both because of the very low market size of NIFs in European countries and their vanishing cost advantage, we conclude that this new instrument has had in general a minimal effect on the financing of firms. Variable-rate loans, on the contrary, seem to be quite important in size – if one adds to the international issues the domestic issues – and intensely used by firms (see note 15).

Our main conclusions regarding the potential and actual contribution of floating-rate debt instruments to investment are summarised in the first rows of Table 10.6.

A second class of special debt instruments included in Table 10.2 are pure fixed interest-rate debt instruments issued either with a very delayed or flexible repayment schedule, or with a high subordination to other debt issues, so that their risk characteristics are more like those of equity.

A typical example of the first are *zero-coupon bonds*. These are medium to long-term bonds without any interest or principal payment before maturity. The return to the investor (cost to the issuer) comes from the difference between the face value

TABLE 10.6 The new financial instruments and investment

Type of instruments	Economic contribution to investment (a)			Usable/ used by firms (b)	Practical importance (c)
	1	2	3		
Variable rate loans		X	X	S	S
Floating rate bonds		X	X	W	W
NIFs/commercial paper		X	X	W	W
Junk bonds	X		X	W	W
Zero-coupon bonds	X		X	S	W
Leasing	X		X	S	S
Convertible/warrants		X	X	S	S
Participating loans	X		X	S	W
Euroequities		X		S	W
Venture capital	X			S	W
Swaps	X	X	X	S	S
Futures - FRAs/options			X	W	W

Notes:
(a) 1 Offering finance not previously available
2 Previously available finance, but at cheaper cost.
3 Adding flexibility or hedging facilities for financial obligations.
(b) The extent to which main users are firms as opposed to financial institutions.
(c) Weight of the particular instrument in total European non-financial business finance.
'S' and 'W' indicate strong and weak respectively.

of the bond (to be returned at maturity) and the issuing price. Such absence of intermediate payments makes this type of instrument very attractive to finance investment, specially in heavy industries or research oriented ones with a long maturity period before investments start paying back.

Without doubt, the most representative exponents of low grade (or no grade at all) debt issues are the *junk bonds* used in the US mainly to finance leveraged takeovers. Their ultimate goal, very often unrelated to the financing of real investment,[16] and their virtual absence in the European financial markets mean that junk bonds can be expected to have little impact on helping finance European (or US for that matter) investment.

A final type of special debt instrument detailed in Table 10.2 is *leasing*. Although it has been around already quite a long time to be considered a recent financial innovation, its relation to real investment is, nevertheless, probably the closest of all the instruments considered so far. This is because virtually 100 per cent of the finance provided by leasing is tied to the use of physical equipment (which is not acquired and financed, but rather leased). The way leasing helps investment is by creating a source of finance previously unavailable. Additionally, it is a flexible source not in relation to the repayment schedule – which is fixed in advance – but in the sense that it does not alter the borrowing capacity of the lessee as long as neither the equipment nor its associated liabilities appear in the financial statements.

Table 10.7 shows the importance of leasing in total capital formation of

TABLE 10.7   Penetration of leasing in capital formation (a) (%)

Country	1982	1987
Germany	3.0	14.0
France	8.5	13.0
UK	13.0	17.5
Italy	6.8	12.0
Spain	4.5	14.0
Netherlands	5.1	12.0
Europe	6.9	
US	27.9	

Note: (*a*) Leasing investments as a percentage of total capital formation.
Source: OECD (1986) and Euromoney.

major European countries, as compared to the US. As can be observed, there has been an important growth of leasing as a source of financing in recent years in European countries and, furthermore, leasing now has a weight regarding total gross investment which exceeds that of the rest of the financial innovations analysed in the present section. It must be noted here that an additional advantage of leasing over the other instruments – although hard to quantify –, is that, while only a few larger and highly rated companies can have access to most financial innovations, leasing is available to virtually every manufacturing company, regardless of size or age. The corresponding rows of Table 10.6 summarise the likely contribution of special fixed interest rate debt instruments and leasing to investment.

4.2 DEBT–EQUITY HYBRID INSTRUMENTS

A large number of financial instruments, mostly in the form of securities, have been developed with some mixed features between debt and equity financing. This category of instruments can be characterised as adding flexibility to the financial obligations of the issuing firm. They are issued formally as debt but their remuneration incorporates some features which make them enjoy some equity advantages.

The main exponent of hybrid instruments are *convertible bonds* and *bonds with equity warrants*. The difference between them is that convertibles disappear after conversion, while a bond with an equity warrant can remain as a straight bond after the warrant is exercised. In both cases, the bond carries a given interest (usually fixed) lower than the equivalent on a similar straight bond. This smaller interest is compensated for through the possibility of realising important capital gains at conversion, or warrant exercise.

In studying how these instruments can help investment through the three channels previously mentioned at the beginning of the section, both convertibles and warrants have several interesting features. On the one hand, they provide finance similar to that provided by straight debt but at a lower cost.[17] On the other hand, if

TABLE 10.8 National stockmarkets comparison

	Trading as % of market value		Market value % of GNP		Market concentration	
	1985	1989	1985	1989	1985	1989
Germany	20	152	21	40	45	47
France	n.a.	34	14	45	24	25
UK	30	65	58	180	28	25
Italy	10	23	15	40	54	46
Spain	10	22	10	28	52	45
Netherlands	25	60	25	80	n.a.	67
US	40	56	50	70	15	15

Note: (a) Percentage of total market value accounted for by the ten largest listed companies.
Source: Euromoney Syndication Guide, OECD (1986), Berges (1989)

TABLE 10.9 Hybrid instruments in the international financial markets (US$ billion)

	1984	1986	1988	1989
Convertible	4.2	6.5	10.3	5.0
Bonds with warrants	2.6	15.3	28.6	66.9

Convertible and warrant bonds: breakdown by issuing countries

Germany	0.1	1.8	0.5	1.0
France	0.1	0.6	0.8	0.6
UK	0.3	1.4	0.5	1.5
Italy	0.0	0.8	0.1	0.2
Spain	0.0	0.0	0.4	0.3
Netherlands	0.1	1.1	0.1	0.0
US	2.0	13.4	0.7	0.8

Source: Euromoney Syndication Guide and I.F.R. Global Financial Directory.

the bond is converted into equity, the new financial obligations for the firm are much more flexible than before. Finally, in certain cases, they may allow indirect equity financing to firms which otherwise might find it very difficult – or impossible – to raise equity financing in the stockmarket. This last aspect is, however, doubtful since unlisted firms (in stock exchanges) could hardly place convertibles or bonds with warrants given that the conversion or exercise is usually dependent upon the issuer's stock prices. For all these reasons, such hybrid instruments can only expect to have a significant weight in firms' financial sources when they are backed by a deep and liquid stockmarket.

According to the data in Table 10.8 this now seems to be the case in most European countries. As shown, both total stockmarket capitalisation and trading in the European countries listed have increased spectacularly in recent years. It should

TABLE 10.10 Share and convertible bond issues in the Spanish market (billion pesetas)

Year	Share issues	Convertibles
1985	150.6	49.5
1986	110.8	271.8
1987	389.2	189.1
1988	273.8	613.3
1989	131.2	332.5

Source: Asesores Bursátiles and C.N.M.V.

be noted, however, that the existence of cheap and wide stockmarkets is a necessary but not a sufficient condition for the effective utilisation of hybrid instruments as financing sources by firms.

Actual data on convertibles and warrants issues are only available for the international financial markets, and are shown in Table 10.9. The table indicates that issues of bonds with warrants are expanding rapidly, mostly due to Japanese institutions, stimulated by the Tokyo Stock Exchange boom of recent years. Yet, a breakdown of issuing activity by European countries shows how insignificant is the market size for convertibles when compared to other sources of finance, like floating debt instruments (shown in Table 10.3) or, even more, relative to total financial needs.

Before concluding that the role played by those hybrid instruments is limited, it would also be necessary to gather evidence on their use in national markets. In this regard, although we do not have homogeneous evidence for different countries, there are grounds to believe that their utilisation has grown rapidly in recent years, following the 1987 stockmarket crisis, as a substitute for the issue of shares.

Table 10.10 clearly shows the above-mentioned phenomenon in the Spanish case, where the issue of convertibles in 1988 and 1989 has been more used as a source of financing than share issues. Indeed, most of these convertible issues are really nothing but share issues effective at a later point in time. If we extrapolate this behaviour to other financial markets, it could be concluded that the importance of convertibles in the financing of firms is more than considerable. Nevertheless, this conclusion ought to be amended once it is taken into account that the new source of financing is clearly crowding out another, like share issues.

In addition to convertibles and warrants, there is another hybrid instrument with a very reduced degree of use. The '*prêt participatif*', introduced first in France and then in Spain, is a mixed debt–equity instrument whose remuneration consists of a fixed part (debt feature) plus a variable part linked to some measure of the earnings of the borrower. Since it has seldom been used other than to substitute for former problem loans to almost bankrupt firms (and in many instances imposed as the only alternative to a complete default) it can hardly be considered as an important financial innovation regarding investment.

The corresponding rows of Table 10.6 summarise the likely contribution of hybrid instruments to investment.

TABLE 10.11 Euroequities issues (US$ billion)

Country	1986	1987	1988	1989
UK	1.6	5.9	1.3	–
US	1.7	2.6	0.9	0.9
Spain		0.2	0.4	0.2
Australia	0.2	0.2	0.3	0.2
Germany	0.4	0.9	0.2	0
Switzerland	0.9	0.8	0.2	0
Canada	0.4	0.9	0.1	0.5
France	1.4	2.4	–	1.0
netherlands	0.2	0.4	–	1.2
Others	1.2	1.2	1.1	1.1
TOTAL	8.0	15.5	4.5	5.3
Privatisations	1.8	7.5	1.4	1.7

Source: OECD, Financial Market Trends

4.3 SPECIAL EQUITY INSTRUMENTS

This category of instruments refers to those forms of equity which are issued outside traditional stock exchanges. Two main types of instruments of a very different nature can be included in this category, as seen in Table 10.2.

The first one are the so called *Euroequities*, whereby firms of large size and well-known name place shares in different countries, not through the stockmarkets, but through the underwriting and placing network of the Euromarkets. In terms of the three channels outlined at the beginning of the section, the potential influence of Euroequities on investment is clearly in terms of reducing the cost of financing. It cannot be considered as providing a previously non-existent financing source because what the issuer gets is just pure equity denominated in its own currency. By issuing it in several markets, however, the firm can have access to a wider spectrum of investors without pushing down too far its share price (equivalent to pushing up the cost of capital). Table 10.11 shows the quantitative importance of Euroequities issues: after a remarkable growth between 1983 and 1987, there has been a spectacular reduction, probably as a result of the 1987 stockmarket crash, with investors thus seeking refuge in less risky and, above all, more familiar instruments in national markets.

Regarding the utilisation of this instrument by firms, empirical evidence is far from conclusive. Indeed, although, it is certainly the case that practically all the issues in the market are non-financial firms, the number of companies benefiting from this new instrument is very small, with a dozen large European companies tapping over 70 per cent of the market. It seems, therefore, that access is restricted to large well-known companies. And, on the other hand, as Table 10.11 shows, between a third and a half of the issues have been made by firms in the process of privatisation.

A completely different story lies behind the second special equity instrument: *venture capital*. Contrary to Euroequities, it was originally designed to meet the financing needs of new and small companies unable to issue equity in traditional

TABLE 10.12 Availability of venture capital

Country	US$ billion		In % of GNP	
	1984	1988	1984	1988
Germany	0.25	0.16	0.04	0.03
France	0.15	0.38	0.03	0.05
UK	3.0	1.20	0.70	0.30
Italy	0.15	0.08	0.04	0.02
Spain	0.08	0.08	0.01	0.01
Netherlands	0.55	0.11	0.5	0.01
EEC	4.3	n.d.	0.2	n.d.
US	15.0	n.d.	0.4	n.s.

Source: Financial Times.

stockmarkets. Nonetheless, the high risk involved in investing in shares of new and little-known small companies – usually with not much more than 'good ideas' as assets – makes it necessary to have some sort of government support to the development of the venture capital market. In most European countries, this support has been of an institutional and fiscal type. The first type has been exemplified by the starting of parallel or unlisted security markets to provide liquidity to ventures. The second has involved granting some kind of fiscal relief to the return obtained by venture capital investors. It is also quite common to provide venture capital in complex packages, including some loans, and specially managerial support agreements, to help reduce the uncertainty and lack of information faced by investors.

Despite the efforts made by most European governments and the potential attractiveness of venture capital markets in providing a new form of finance not previously available, its actual penetration is still extremely low. As Table 10.12 indicates. For the EEC as a whole, venture capital is estimated to represent no more than 0.5 per cent of GNP; that is, one-hundredth of the value of stockmarket capitalisation shown in Table 10.8. Even in the United States, where it started five years earlier, it is no more than 1.0 per cent of GNP. Consequently, venture capital markets have played a minor role in the financing of European – and United States – investment.

The corresponding rows in Table 10.6 summarise our views on the role of the special equity instruments in financing investment

4.4 RISK COVERING INSTRUMENTS

The final class of innovations considered in this section are those capable of facilitating hedging against risk. In this group we include swaps, financial futures (and forward rate agreements) and options.

The first type of instrument to consider are *swaps*. Taken to be one of the main exponents of financial engineering, swaps are a technique whereby two parties agree to exchange two streams of interest payments. These can be: (a) in the same

TABLE 10.13 Estimated volume of the swap market (US$ billion)

	Interest rate swap (outstanding national value)		Currency swaps (flows)
	Dealer/ end-user	Dealer/ Dealer	
1982	3	n.a.	3
1983	20	n.a.	6
1984	80	n.a.	13
1985	142	28	24
1986	250	57	45
1987	683	n.d.	83
1988	669	341	317

Source: Bank of England (1987b) and BIS.

currency but with a different interest-rate base (interest-rate swap, for example between a fixed rate and a variable rate based interest payments); (b) in the same base interest but in different currencies (currency swap); or (c) in different base interests and different currencies (cross-currency interest-rate swap).

Consequently, swaps are not only risk-covering instruments, but also true sources of finance as long as they enable the borrower to raise funds in the market in which he has a comparative advantage – i.e., due to some kind of market segmentation – and swap the proceeds into his preferred type of liability.

It can be concluded, therefore, that swaps have the potential to stimulate investment. Specifically, swaps can give (indirect) access to a given financial source which wasn't available before; they may reduce the cost of previously available financial sources;[18] and, finally, they can provide hedging for interest-rate and/or exchange-rate risk.

Turning to the data, it must be noted that measuring the volume of swap markets or the degree of involvement of non-financial firms is an almost impossible task, as a whole chain of interbank operations can develop between two end-users and as banks are not required to report regularly their swap activities (off-balance sheet). All the available statistics are just estimations like those shown in Table 10.13. As can be seen, volume has skyrocketed in the seven years of market existence in currency swaps, and specially in interest-rate swaps where outstanding notional value has grown by a factor of 200. These numbers should be taken with caution, however, as in interest-rate swaps there is no exchange of principal but only of the associated interest payments, while in currency swaps it is not uncommon to exchange the principal.

But perhaps the most interesting aspect of Table 10.13 is that dealer–dealer swaps – the interbank portion of the swap market – as opposed to end-user–dealer swaps represent between 20 per cent and 50 per cent of the total market. This is not to say that all the remaining volume has gone to finance non-financial firms, since end-users can also be financial institutions. But with no alternative evidence it is not possible to deny that swaps may actually be used in financing real investment either. In addition, despite the tremendous increase in swap market activity during recent

TABLE 10.14 Volume of major financial futures and options markets (US$ billion)

	Open interest			Daily trading volume		
	1980	1985	1989	1980	1985	1989
Futures	81	254	838	25	86	160
Interest rate	79	236	780	24	73	130
Stock index	–	10	32	–	3	16
Currency	2	8	26	1	4	14
Options	–	138	785	–	24.5	155
Interest rate	–	89	650	–	11.5	73
Stock index	–	37	85	–	12	68
Currency	–	12	50	–	1	14
Total	81	392	1,618	25	111	315

Source: Levich (1987) and Wall Street Journal.

years, average swap spreads relative to Treasury bond yields have only slightly increased in recent years. Extrapolating the trend, we conclude that the market could still allow a good deal of lower quality new borrowers before spreads go up substantially, therefore eliminating the cost advantage of swap operations.

The two other financial innovations available to facilitate hedging are financial futures and options. In a *futures* contract, buyer and seller agree to exchange a prespecified amount of the underlying asset at a given future date at a price set today. An essential aspect of the futures trading mechanics is the role of the Clearing House as intermediary between the buyer and the seller. Another is the marking to market, whereby the value of the outstanding contract is adjusted daily to movements in the futures prices. These two aspects facilitate the cancellation of contracts prior to their expiration date by simply entering a reverse contract. The extension of futures trading to financial instruments was initiated in 1975 in Chicago and today they cover a wide range of financial instruments (as underlying assets) among which Treasury bonds and bills, Eurodollars, Stock Indexes, and the major currencies, account for over 90 per cent of the total (financial) futures market share, well ahead also of traditional commodity futures.

An *option*, on the other hand, gives the holder the right, but not the obligation, to buy (call option) or sell (put option) a prespecified amount of the underlying asset at a predetermined price within a given period. Trading mechanics are very similar to those in futures markets and, besides the heavy and well-established – specially in the United States – trading of options on shares, the main underlying financial assets are the same as in the financial futures.

Let us turn now to the issue of investment and how financial futures and options could help finance it. As is clear from the description of these instruments, they do not directly contribute to generating new or cheaper financial sources for firms. Because futures and options are traded only in secondary markets, they cannot be used as a source of funds for any type of borrower. The only possible channel potentially open to influencing investment directly is through the risk reduction obtained by hedging against adverse interest-rate or exchange-rate movements.

To get an idea of how important this effect is likely to be, we look now at market size. As Table 10.14 shows, the size of the financial futures and options markets has increased dramatically during the present decade, both in terms of open interest (market value of outstanding contracts) and trading volume. How much of that volume is risk-covering' and how much is speculation is hard to know as most exchanges don't have any information about the basic purpose for entering contracts. There is, though, some indirect but suggestive evidence that can be obtained by simply relating the open interest and trading volume data shown in the table. Open interest indicates the market value of all contracts existing at a given point of time (year-end, in Table 10.14) and is a stock-type measure. Trading volume indicates, on the other hand, the average daily purchases – and sales – of contracts at market value, and is a flow-type measure. Dividing the latter by the former measure we obtain an estimate of the liquidity of the market, given by the percentage of existing contracts which change hands daily. Conversely, dividing the stock (open interest) by the flow (daily trading volume), we obtain an estimate of the average holding period of contracts. When such calculation is done, it turns out that the average holding period is three to four days, which illustrates the very high degree of liquidity of options and future contracts.

The above finding can have two alternative readings. From the point of view of the major users of the market, such a quick turnover – which implies that most contracts are cancelled before maturity – seems to suggest the predominance of speculative over-hedging activities. Nevertheless, it is possible to identify hedging situations in which contacts need not be maintained until maturity, and therefore it is not totally correct to assign a speculative nature to all contracts cancelled before maturity.

The above notwithstanding, from the viewpoint of the transparency of prices, it is clear that this increases with the liquidity of the market. Yet, taking into account the rigidity implied by fixed-date expiration of contracts, it is not evident at all that futures and options are intensely utilised by firms. Nevertheless, the market is used by financial firms when covering the risks associated with the joint management of their assets and liabilities. This, in the last instance, should lead to an improvement in their capacity to render financial services to firms.

It is thus on the basis of the second indirect channel rather than on the basis of the first direct channel that we assign to options and futures contracts a rather reduced importance regarding their utilisation by firms to hedge against the risks derived from the real investment process.

Risk-covering instruments similar in many regards to financial futures are *forward rate agreements* (FRAs), whereby two parties (mainly banks) agree on the interest of a (notional) deposit to be made at a future date. Given that they are tailored to meet the two parties needs regarding both the quantity and the future date of the contract, FRAs have more flexibility for hedging purposes than futures, where both the quantity and maturity date of the contract are set by the Futures Exchange. Still, the actual use of FRAs as hedging instruments by firms can be also considered marginal, with a total estimated trading volume in international markets of 1 per cent that of the interest-rate futures, and most of it being of an interbank nature according to BIS (1986).

The last rows of Table 10.6 summarise our views about the effects of risk-covering instruments on investment.

4.5 SUMMARY

Having reviewed in this section the potential usefulness of the new financial instruments in stimulating capital formation (columns 1, 2 and 3 of Table 10.6), their relative importance in overall financial markets, and their use by firms (last two columns of Table 10.6), it is our impression that, among them, variable-rate loans, leasing, convertibles and warrants, and swaps are likely to have the most significant effects on investment. Moreover, as the evidence on the main determinants of investment contained in Table 10.1 and Figure 10.1 indicates, the direct effect of these financial innovations on investment will be more significant whenever they help increase the profitability of the firm – e.g., by providing better hedging devices – or make available external financial sources not previously available that relieve the financial constraints suffered by firms. As columns 1, 2 and 3 of Table 10.6 show, one or both of these features seem to be present in the five instruments singled out. On the contrary, the other instruments reviewed do not seem to have the capability or market size to play a significant role in influencing investment, at least until now.

5. Implications for financial regulation

Regulation has often been regarded as one of the most important explanatory factors behind financial innovations (Miller, 1986). If these latter are positively valued, it would therefore seem logical to conclude that an appropriate use of regulation might encourage some specific innovations and, through them, the desired increase in investment.

There are, however, some caveats behind this casual relationship. If real investment is the goal, it is not clear at all that financial innovation is the best way to achieve it. As a counter example, some countries like Japan and West Germany have witnessed in the past a lower rate of growth of financial innovations, and despite this their rate of investment has been larger than in other countries with faster financial innovation.

It is not surprising, therefore, that the link between financial innovation and regulation has progressively weakened, forcing the need for other explanatory factors.

5.1 FINANCIAL INNOVATION AND REGULATION FROM THE SINGLE EUROPEAN MARKET PERSPECTIVE

Regulation, as an explanatory factor for financial innovation, has often rested on tax loopholes arising from some inconsistencies in fiscal regulations. Given the current fiscal differences between EEC countries, not likely to be eliminated soon, they make up for important tax arbitrage flows in the context of free capital movements. This is so without any need for new financial innovations. A similar fact, also linked to other regulatory advantages besides fiscal ones, explains the emergence and growth of the European offshore financial centres.[19]

A good example of the aforementioned fiscal differences, and their effects on capital flows, can be taken from Germany in relation to the withholding tax on interest earned by foreigners on government bonds. After realising how big an impact it was having on foreign investment flows, the German authorities decided to eliminate the tax, in an attitude that makes the move to a fiscal harmonisation within the EEC more difficult.

5.2 THE ROLE OF FINANCIAL INTERMEDIATION

Additional scope for the link between financial innovation and regulation lies upon the issue of financial intermediation. The evidence observed in section 4 emphasised the rebirth of traditional syndicated loans in international financial markets. This backward movement in the overall disintermediation trend can be possibly related to Ross's opacity argument.[20] In essence, innovations can be explained as an attempt to fill up the continuum of possibilities between transparency and opacity in the observability of institutional investors adopting those innovations.

The heavy competition between lending banks, especially in the international markets where other types of borrowers have a more difficult access, has probably precluded the demand for opacity to become a clear source of competitive advantage for those banks.

From here, a point can be made that the main contribution of financial intermediation rests upon bringing the financial sources closer to the specific needs of the borrower. It is not surprising, in this context, that swaps, whose main objective is to overcome market barriers, is one of the financial innovations with a more direct effect on capital formation, as was discussed in section 4.

Financial marketing and innovation, then, entails not only financial intermediation in itself, but also the ability to demonstrate its ability to fulfil the financial objectives of both parties. From the viewpoint of both parties, this function is more valuable the less transparent is the transaction in question.

5.3 REGULATION AND THE PROMOTION OF NEW FINANCIAL MARKETS

The desire for transparency and the existence of transactions costs may, in some stage of the development of a financial instrument, justify the setting up of an organised market. The question is whether it should be promoted by some type of favourable regulation.

This issue is especially relevant lately in most European countries in relation to futures and options markets. These have been rated in section 4 as the financial innovations with the least direct impact on investment. There is an important function that the markets for these instruments can play, normally that of price formation. As long as risk hedging instruments – as futures and options – have special difficulties for price calculation, the need for organised markets becomes more apparent. These markets need to be extremely liquid, otherwise the price setting mechanism would not be trustable.

Regulation might be addressed, as an example, to improving the quality and speed of the transactions processing, or reducing the risk of 'excessive' competition.

This 'protective' regulation has been implemented in several countries, and not always by the public regulators, as is the case with self-regulation in many financial centres, especially in the Anglo-Saxon countries.

A case like France is especially relevant; with its more conservative legal approach – the Napoleonic code – to financial markets, France has been able to participate in the race of financial regulation. It shows how public support, in the form of protective regulations, can be an important source of stimulus to innovation.

5.4 FINANCIAL MARKETS AND INTERNATIONAL COMPETITION

The example of France uncovers the attempt to regain prestige and market share in international finance, against the traditional British advantage. In cases like this, regulation may attempt to help introduce financial innovations already established in other countries or markets.

Since most financial innovations need a learning and adapting period by the users – especially firms – it appears that regulation must have a permissive character towards the usage of those innovations, at least in the early stages.

The 'demonstration effect', whereby innovations already in place in a country are rapidly spread to many other countries, is one of the main reasons for the convergence observed among the dynamics of the financial systems in the main developed countries. The use of regulation in this direction has some potential problems. As long as the price-setting function is better done in those markets with higher liquidity, the remaining markets lose some of their rationale. A temptation to defend by any means their own domestic markets may conflict with the main objective: to guarantee the most appropriate price-setting process.

In conclusion, it appears that regulation is neither the only, nor probably the best, incentive for innovations to affect real investment. Regulation can, however, play an important role in promoting new innovations as well as guaranteeing the appropriate safety mechanism for them.

6. Conclusions and policy implications

The recent wave of financial innovation taking place in Europe is generally credited with increasing the efficiency of financial markets and, often, with facilitating the channelling of saving into the most profitable investment opportunities.

In this chapter, we have explored the relationship between innovation in financial instruments and capital formation, with special emphasis being placed on the European context. The main questions raised and discussed have been whether there are any direct channels through which the new financial instruments may affect investment, whether these channels are wide enough in practice and whether innovation in financial instruments has been a sizeable phenomenon in Europe. The tentative answers we come up with are affirmative in the first case, and only partially affirmative in the second and third cases.

Although it is true that all of the new financial instruments reviewed can potentially affect real investment decisions either by making available to firms cheaper or more flexible external finance sources, or by allowing them a better covering of finance or investment related risks, the available empirical evidence indicates that these potential direct effects have not been very important in practice. The reasons why this has happened, we think, are mainly two. On the one hand, the empirical evidence on investment functions suggests that new financial instruments which mainly reduce the cost of capital to the firm are likely to have a very limited impact on the firm's investments in the short to medium run, while the opposite seems to be the case with those new instruments which help relax the firm's external financial constraints. On the other hand, even for the last type of instruments, it is often the case that they are neither very significant in terms of market size, nor much used by firms. Among the instruments reviewed, only variable rate loans, swaps, warrants and convertible bonds, and leasing operations seem to meet all the requirements needed to be actually useful for the firm's investments.

The implications for financial policy are several. First of all, policy-makers must realise that some of their moves to deregulate and free financial markets may sometimes lead, if not properly implemented, mainly to a proliferation of interbank transactions, and to secondary market speculative trading without really helping firms finance their investment projects. Second, given that the problem with many of the new instruments is not lack of potential for helping firms with their investments, but rather one of market size and low use by firms, there seems to be some room for financial and tax policies in helping promote the growth of the potentially most useful markets. This seems to apply most of all to products – like venture capital – which can best meet the financing needs of small and new firms, high-tech firms, and generally those firms investing in intangible assets. A final implication is that, if the ultimate main problem is how to promote investment, there is perhaps a lot more to be done through appropriate macroeconomic supply and demand policies than through financial policy.

Finally, we must insist that our tentative conclusions refer only to the new financial instruments and to their direct effects over real investment, not to the financial innovation process itself. At the same time, it must be noted that, since financial innovation has supplied savers with a wider array of assets and firms with more effective cash management techniques, this may have led to changes in the saving rate of the economy, and in the mix between physical and financial investments of firms, which may have also indirectly affected investment. In addition, many of the interbank transactions observed in the market may have improved risk spreading and lowered costs within the banking sector which, in turn, may have benefited ultimate borrowers through lower cost of new and traditional credit lines. These issues, which exceed the scope of this chapter, are important enough to deserve careful future investigation.

Notes

1.   See, for example, Dufey and Giddy (1981), Mayer (1982), Silber (1983), Van Horne (1985), Kaufman (1986) and BIS (1986).
2.   This assumes perfect foresight regarding future spot commodities prices.
3.   It is assumed that whatever improves the certainty of the firm's operations also improves q.
4.   Among the imperfections considered, are corporate taxes (Modigliani and Miller, 1963), bankruptcy costs (Kim, 1978; Scott, 1976, Haugen and Senbet 1978) or personal taxes (Miller, 1977).
5.   See the papers by Myers (1976), Myers and Majluff (1984), Greenwald, Stiglitz and Weiss (1984) and Fazzari, Hubbard and Petersen (1987).
6.   See Stiglitz and Weiss (1981).
7.   This is done explicitly in Abel and Blanchard (1986). The studies by Mairesse and Dermont (1985) and Bruno (1986) also distinguish between profit and cost of capital effects, finding that the second is not generally statistically significant.
8.   See for example Mairesse and Dermont (1985) and Chirinko (1987)
9.   For the Spanish case, see the recent papers by Andres et al. (1989), and Mato (1989).
10.   An example of risk arising from investment decisions would be when an investment project yields an output whose price is uncertain. An example of risk arising from financing decisions would be a firm suffering from exchange-rate risk and/or interest-rate risk as a result of financing the investment project through certain channels.
11.   For an analysis along those lines see Dufey and Giddy (1981), Silber (1983), Van Horne (1985) and BIS (1986).
12.   A special form of this last instrument are perpetual FRNs, whereby the principle is never recovered; only interest is paid – on a floating basis – forever.
13.   In NIFs, however, bank usually have the right to opt out if borrowers' credit standing deteriorates.
14.   Interbank dealings of some instruments can also have an effect on investment, as long as they allow financial institutions to lower their costs, and the savings are passed on to firms. This channel seems much more indirect than directly providing finance to firms.
15.   Although we have not found internationally homogeneous data on domestic VRLs for the European countries studied, it seems that they are about 80 per cent of total loans in countries like Italy, France and the United Kingdom,

according to Akhtar (1983). Regarding FRNs, the figures are 80 per cent of total bond issues for Italy and 20 per cent for France, with no figures for other European countries.

16.   Although it is true that junk bonds are most often used for leveraged buyouts, it might still be argued that the increased risk of takeovers – caused by the existence of junk bonds – can discipline managers in their searching for the optimal investment policy.

17.   This is so initially, since the total implicit cost can be larger if conversion causes a large earnings dilution. This is the reason why in the corresponding row of Table 10.6 there are marks in columns 2 and 3, although, in practice, only one will apply depending on conversion exercise.

18.   This is so as long as the two parties share the total cost saving produced by the swap operation, which is not uncommon.

19.   See Berges, Ontiveros and Valero (1989).

20.   Transparency and opacity are the two extremes of a continuum which attempts to measure the degree of observability by external agents of the behaviour of financial institutions. Thus, an opaque financial transaction would not be detectable and observable except by the parties directly involved. In contrast, a transparent transaction would be easily detected and observed by the market.

References

Abel, A.B. (1980), 'Empirical investment equations: an integrative framework', *Carnegie-Rochester Series on Public Policy* 12: 39–91.

Abel, A.B. and **Blanchard O.J.** (1986), 'The present value of profits and cyclical movements in investment', *Econometrica*, 54 (2): 249–273.

Akhtar, M.A. (1983), 'Financial innovations and their implications for monetary policy: an international perspective', *BIS Economic Papers*, 9.

Andrés, J., Escribano A., Molinas, C. and **Taguas, D.** (1989), 'La inversión en España', *Moneda y Crédito*, 188.

Arrow, K.J. (1964), 'The role of securities in the optimal allocation of risk-bearing', *Review of Economic Studies*, 31: 91–6.

Bank of England (1987a), 'Commercial paper markets: an international survey', *Quarterly Bulletin*, February: 46–53.

Bank of England (1987b), 'Recent developments in the swap market', *Quarterly Bulletin*, February: 66–79.

Bank for International Settlements (1986), *Recent Innovations in International Banking*, BIS, Basel.

Berges, A. (1989), 'La financiación de la empresa en los mercados de valores', *Informes y Estudios*, 51.

Berges, A., Ontiveros, E. and **Valero, F.J.** (1989), *La internacionalización de la banca*, Espasa-Calpe, Madrid.

Bruno, M. (1986), 'Aggregate supply and demand factors in OECD unemployment: an update', *Economica*, Supplement, 53: 35–53.

Chappell, H.W. and **Cheng, D.C.** (1982), 'Expectations, Tobin's q, and investment: a note', *Journal of Finance*, 37: 231–6.

Chirinko, R.S. (1986a), 'Investment, Tobin's *q*, and multiple capital inputs', National Bureau of Economic Research, *Working Paper*, 2033.

Chirinko, R.S. (1986b), 'Will the neoclassical theory of investment please rise? The general structure of investment models and their implications for tax policy', mimeo, University of Chicago.

Chirinko, R.S. (1987), 'Tobin's *q* and financial policy', *Journal of Monetary Economics*, 19: 69–87.

Commission of the European Communities (1988), *Research on the 'Cost of non-Europe in Financial Services*, Brussels.

Debreu, G. (1959), *Theory of Value*, New York: Wiley.

Dinenis, E. (1985a), 'Adjustment costs, Q, taxation, and investment in the U.K.', Center for Labor Economics, L.S.E., *Discussion Paper*, 235.

Dinenis, E. (1985b), 'Q, gestation lags and investment: is the flexible accelerator a mirage?', Center for Labor Economics, L.S.E., *Discussion Paper*, 236.

Dufey, G. and **Giddy, I.A.** (1981), 'Innovations in the international financial markets', *Journal of International Business Studies*, Fall: 33–51.

Fazzari, S., Hubbard, R.G. and **Petersen, D.C.** (1987), Financing constraints and corporate investment, mimeo.

Greenwald, B., Stiglitz, J.E. and **Weiss, A.** (1984), 'Information imperfections in the capital market and macroeconomic fluctuations', *American Economic Review*, 74: 194–9.

Haugen, R. and **L. Senbet** (1978), 'The insignificance of bankruptcy costs to the theory of optimal capital structure', *Journal of Finance*, 33: 383–93.

Hayashi, F. and **Inoue, T.** (1987), 'Implementing the Q-theory of investment in microdata: Japanese manufacturing 1977–1985', mimeo, Osaka University.

Hendershott, P.H. and **Hu, S.** (1981), 'Investment in producers' equipment', in H.J. Aaron, and J.A. Pechman (eds.). *How Taxes Affect Economic Behavior*, Washington: The Brookings Institution.

Kane, E. (1986), *Technology and the Regulation of Financial Markets*. Lexington: Lexington Books.

Kaufman, H. (1986), *Interest Rates, the Market, and the New Financial World*, New York: Times Books.

Kim, E.H. (1978), 'A mean-variance theory of optimal capital structure and corporate debt capacity', *Journal of Finance* 33: 45–63.

Leland, H. and **Pyle, D.** (1977), 'Informational assymetries, financial structure, and financial intermediation', *Journal of Finance* 32: 371–87.

Levich, R.M. (1987), 'Financial innovations in international financial markets', National Bureau of Economic Research, *Working Paper*, 2277.

Long, M., and **Malitz, I.** (1986), 'Investment patterns and financial leverage' in B. Friedman (ed.), *Financing Corporate Capital Formation*, National Bureau of Economic Research, pp. 325–351.

Mairesse, J., and **Dermont, B.** (1985), 'Labor and investment demands at firm level: a comparison of French, German, and US manufacturing, 1970–79', *European Economic Review*, 28: 201–232.

Mato, G. (1989), 'Inversión, coste de capital y estructura financiera: un estudio empírico', *Moneda y Crédito*, 188.

Mayer, C. (1987), 'New issues in corporate finance', Center for Economic Policy Research, *Discussion Paper* 181.

Mayer, Th. (1982), 'Financial innovation-the conflict between micro and macro optimality', *American Economic Review*, 72 (2): 29–34.

Meese, R. (1980), 'Dynamic factor demand schedules for labor and capital under rational expectations', *Journal of Econometrics*, 14: 141–58.

Miller, M.H. (1977), 'Debt and taxes', *Journal of Finance*, 32: 261–75.

Miller, M.H. (1986), 'Financial innovation: the last twenty years and the next', *Journal of Financial and Quantitative Analysis*, 21 (4): 459–71.

Modigliani, F. and **Miller, M.H.** (1958), 'The cost of capital, corporation finance, and the theory of investment', *American Economic Review*, 48: 261–97.

Modigliani, F. and **Miller, M.H.** (1963), 'Corporate income tax and the cost of capital: a correction', *American Economic Review*, 53: 433–43.

Myers, S. (1976), 'Determinants of corporate borrowing' *Journal of Financial Economics* 5: 147–76.

Myers, S. and **Majluff, N.** (1984), 'Corporate financing decisions when firms have investment information that investors do not', *Journal of Financial Economics*, 13: 187–220.

Nickell, S.J. (1978), *The Investment Decisions of Firms*, Nisbet/Cambridge.

OECD (1986), 'Financial resources for industry's changing needs', Background Paper, April.

OECD (1989), *Economies in Transition: Structural adjustment in OECD countries*, Paris.

Poterba, J.M. and **Summers, L.H.** (1983), 'Divident taxes, corporate investment, and Q', *Journal of Public Economies*, 22: 135–67

Ross, S.A. (1989), 'Institutional markets, financial marketing and financial innovations', *The Journal of Finance*, 44 (3), July.

Salinger, M. and **Summers, L.H.** (1983), 'Tax reform and corporate finance: a microeconomic simulation study', in M.S. Feldstein (ed.), *Behavioral Simulation Methods in Tax Policy Analysis*, Chicago: Chicago University Press.

Salomon Brothers, Inc. (1986), *Prospects for Financial Markets in 1987*, New York.

Scott, J.H. (1976), 'A theory of optimal capital structure', *Bell Journal of Economics*, Spring: 33–53.

Silber, W.L. (1983), 'The process of financial innovation', *American Economic Review*, 73, (2): 89–95.

Stiglitz, J.E. and **Weiss, A.** (1981), 'Credit rationing in markets with imperfect information', *American Economic Review*, 71: 393–410.

Summers, L.H. (1981), 'Taxation and corporate investment: a q-theory approach', *Brookings Papers on Economic Activity*, 1: 67–127.

Van Horne, J.C. (1985), 'Of financial innovation and excesses', *Journal of Finance*, 40: 621–631.

CHAPTER ELEVEN

Savings, financial innovations and growth

M. Aglietta

1. Introduction

The more competitive the financial system, the better the world economy. This view has become commonplace since the sweeping wave of financial liberalisation has gathered momentum. When they say competitive, the advocates of the present trend of financial innovations mean the broadest opportunities of arbitrage between types of assets and between currencies. Such an opinion is generally rooted in macroeconomic arguments: a more efficient allocation of savings, more complete markets and better diversified risks, tighter profit margins for financial firms and lower costs of credit for non-financial borrowers.

This most popular view has been challenged on the grounds of systems risks. The financial system does not operate under conditions of perfect information. When uncertainty is brought into the picture, the stability of a deregulated financial system can be seriously questioned. Competitive behaviour can create disruptive dynamic externalities both in securities and credit markets: speculative bubbles, overlending and excessive risk taking are not only formal possibilities, they are sheer realities. The wild appreciation of property market prices in Japan and in the UK, the Third World Debt Crisis, the collapse of thrift institutions in the US are not fortuitous accidents. They are indicators of a fundamental mismatching between a global financial system and an inadequate financial safety net.

The issue of overall financial stability is getting growing acceptance and has begun to be tackled by the regulatory authorities of the main industrial countries. There is yet another perspective to gauge the performance of the deregulated financial system of the 1980s. This is the macroeconomic issue of savings and growth. Declining savings rates, persistently high real interest rates, unimpressive average growth rates, are phenomena wedded into the legacy of the 1980s. They need a sober inquiry if the financial system is to fulfil the hopes of steadier and better balanced growth by its proponents.

In the first part of this chapter, I will make an assessment of the changes in private savings which occurred in the 1980s. In the second part, I will analyse the relationships between these structural changes and the pervasively high real interest rates which impede the financing of growth in the world economy. I will conclude by pointing out the unique role of banks and the necessity of a proper supervisory

framework if financial innovation is to deliver its promises of a more efficient allocation of capital.

2. Inquiry into the development of savings.

Let us begin with empirical evidence about private savings, its overall decline
relative to GDP and its structural transformations over the last decade.

2.1 CHANGES IN PRIVATE SAVING RATIOS

It is well known that savings and investment ratios have substantially declined since
the heydays of high growth in the 1960s. It is no surprise considering the slow-down
of growth itself. With constant capital–output and wealth–income ratios, both savings
and investment rates would be proportional to the growth rate. More disturbing and
largely responsible for international financial imbalances, is the mismatching between
changes in savings and investment across the largest OECD countries. Table 11.1
shows that, in the US alone, private savings declined more than private investment
relative to GDP. As comparisons between levels of savings are meaningless because
of different accounting procedures, only time changes are suitable for international
comparisons.

In all countries but the US, private savings ratios declined more than private investment ratios, improving net financial positions of the private sectors in
those countries. Furthermore, the ranking of countries according to the decline of the
growth rate matches their ranking with the change in private investment ratios, not
with private savings. These results suggest that capital–output ratios have been more
stable than wealth–income ratios, in spite of large changes in relative prices between
factors of production. One can easily admit that lower growth is a common cause for
the decline of both ratios. But conventional wisdom, which points to the crowding
out of investment by the weakening of savings as the primary factor, is much more
debatable and has to be investigated further.

2.2 CHANGES IN THE COMPOSITION OF PRIVATE SAVINGS

The first dimension of the composition of private savings is the distinction between
business and household savings. One can argue that it is unimportant; only the total
matters if the development of one component is automatically offset by the opposite

TABLE 11.1 Private savings, private investment and output growth

	Changes from the 1984–7 to the 1964–72 average			GDP growth rate		
	Private savings/ GDP	Private investment/ GDP	Gap	1960–73 average	1973–87 average	Change
United States	−2.4	−2.1	−0.3	4.0	2.5	−1.5
Japan	−8.0	−12.4	4.4	9.6	3.7	−5.9
Germany	−3.2	−7.2	4.0	4.4	1.8	−2.6
France	−6.4	−9.7	3.3	5.4	2.1	−3.3
Italy	−4.0	−5.2	1.2	5.3	2.8	−2.5
United Kingdom	0.6	−2.6	3.2	3.2	1.7	−1.5

Source : OECD National Accounts 1989

development of the other. It is an argument formally similar to Barro's neutrality of national savings, between their public and private components. Yet, we know the latter is far from complete. What about the former?

Since the statistical handling of individual businesses, varies widely from one country to another, the gap between business and household savings only carries meaning in terms of net financial savings. It is not far-fetched because, in the long run, households are the exclusive holders of privately owned wealth. Their time preference is a fundamental parameter of long-run equilibrium.

The composition of net financial savings is given in Table 11.2 for the three largest OECD countries. In the US, the double offset does not apply. True in the beginning of the 1980s, the deterioration in public savings was offset by a matching increase in private financial savings. But the reason was the recession with a slump in investment; it had nothing to do with Ricardian equivalence. When growth resumed in 1983, private savings weakened much more than public savings improved, deteriorating current accounts. Furthermore, business and household financial savings declined together; there was no offset at all within private savings. Opposite features can be drawn from Japan and Germany. The improvement in public savings was not matched by an equivalent decline in private savings in either country. In Germany, both improved together in the 1980s. Business and household savings partially offset each other, but it was far from complete. A big and continuous increase in business financial savings from the late 1960s went with a moderate decline in household savings.

Thus different configurations are possible for the composition of private savings. Looking back to the 1980s for EEC countries, one can say that whatever happened in business savings to offset the decline of household savings, it was a reflection of the big change in the distribution of income. The share of profits increased and the share of wages decreased in GDP with disinflation. Since macroeconomic policy was restrictive and, since the real burden of past debt was heavier, business was selective with investment expenditure. Larger profits were carried into better financial positions.

TABLE 11.2: Net financial savings in terms of GDP percentage

Countries	Business*	Household savings	Total Private	Public	Total National
United States					
1965–74 average	–2.0	2.8	0.8	–0.4	0.4
1975–81 average	–1.1	2.7	1.6	–1.3	0.3
1982	–0.5	4.1	3.6	–3.6	0
1985	–0.7	1.1	0.4	–3.4	–3.0
1987	–1.0	0.1	–0.9	–2.5	–3.4
Japan					
1965–74 average	–7.7	7.9	0.2	0.6	0.8
1975–81 average	–5.6	10.0	4.4	–4.1	0.3
1982	–4.5	8.8	4.3	–3.6	0.7
1985	–5.0	9.5	4.5	–0.8	3.7
1987	–5.4	8.4	3.0	–0.6	3.6
Germany					
1965–74 average	–6.2	7.4	1.2	–0.3	0.9
1975–81 average	–4.3	7.5	3.2	–3.3	–0.1
1982	–3.5	7.1	3.6	–3.3	0.1
1985	–2.5	6.1	3.6	–1.1	2.5
1987	–0.8	6.4	5.6	–1.8	3.8

Source: CEPII, MIMOSA database.
Note: * Business includes non-financial and financial corporate sectors.

However, it is clear that the shift in income distribution was the counterpart of very high levels of unemployment. It is a transitional phenomenon from high to low inflation, and is not a permanent drift of income distribution due to a peculiar type of technical progress biased against labour. Therefore, household savings trends are the driving force of private savings in the long run. The structural and institutional factors which shape those trends impinge upon the growth process and welfare of the economy.

2.3 STRUCTURAL CHANGES IN HOUSEHOLD SAVINGS

From 1980 to 1987, the savings rate of households declined the most in France and in the UK where it lost respectively 8.9 per cent and 7.5 per cent. On the contrary, the fall was very moderate in Germany (–0.8 per cent) and in Italy (–0.3 per cent). The development in the US and in Japan was intermediate, respectively –2.5 per cent and –2.3 per cent. There is no agreement about the set of factors able to explain both the general decline and the differences among countries. For instance Germany and Italy have in common a conservative approach to financial innovations, but widely different records about inflation. I will not attempt here a detailed comparison between countries. But I will point out the determining factors of household trends according to available studies and their possible relationships with financial innovations. There are short-run and long-run factors which can explain different aspects of household savings. However, they stem from the same assumption. Households have a consumption target: *in the short run, savings are the transfer of income in the life cycle. The flexibility of savings in performing both functions depends on the financial structure.*

2.3.1 Savings as a shock absorber

In all industrial countries the evolution of total consumption per capita exhibits inertia. Whether it is their will or a social constraint, households try to meet their consumption target when they undergo a slow-down of their current real income. The sharper the kink in real income growth, the larger the fall in the savings rate. Households discount more the future.

The looser the liquidity constraint, the larger the room for the adjustment in savings. Households can lower their savings rate, by spending more out of current income, by spending out of liquid assets or by spending out of the proceed of rising debt. Financial deregulation substantially loosened liquidity constraints in the 1980s. Securitisation expanded the range of quasi liquid and near liquid financial instruments available to small investors. Competition between banks and non-banks enhanced the last development of consumer credit. Personal loans became available to any income strata with the relaxation of restraints on maturities, funding, collateral and finally the suppression of credit rationing in some countries. Lending against the appreciation of asset values became common practice. It amounts to a wealth effect in nominal terms which was vastly increased in real terms by disinflation in the years 1982–7.

The above factors directly or indirectly appear in the econometrics of the consumption function. The usual regressions in macroeconomic models always show a strong influence of real disposable current income. The elasticity of consumption to income is less than one in the short run and equal to one in the long run (MIMOSA, 1990). It fits with the theory of savings as a shock absorber in the short run. If the change in income becomes a change in the permanent income path, consumption has to adjust so that the income–wealth ratio gets back to its desired level. The real wealth effect appears indirectly through the positive influence of inflation rates on savings rates in any country but Germany where the trend and the volatility of inflation have always been low (Bosworth, 1990). The direct effects of financial variables are much more difficult to display. Nominal wealth effects are not robust because there is no satisfactory measure of capital gains. It is only in Germany, the US and the UK, that the level of the long-term interest rates seems to have some positive influence on the savings rate.

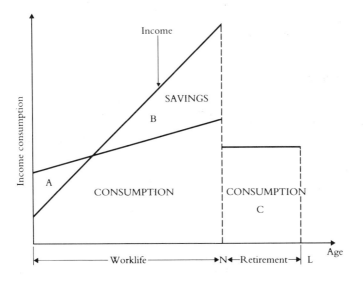

FIG 11.1   Age profile of consumption

2.3.2   The savings rate in the life cycle

Long-run factors, like the development of demographic structures, do not show up easily in standard regressions explaining the savings rate. But simulation models of the life cycle, over a long enough period of time allowing capture of the turnover of generations, can give an estimate of the consequences of big demographic changes across countries (Aglietta, Brender and Coudert, 1990).

An analytical framework was built to study the effect of sharply different demographic structures on the household savings rate of the US, Japan and Germany. The main assumptions are gathered in Figure 11.1. Three age groups were distinguished. Young households (aged twenty to forty) consume more than they earn and borrow against future income. Mature households (aged forty to sixty-five) get increasing income out of which they save to redeem their debt and to accumulate wealth for their retirement. Retired households (aged over sixty-five) consume out of their wealth until they die. It is assumed that there is no net bequest: people transmit no more wealth to their descendants than they got from their ascendants.

Contrary to the standard life cycle model, our framework puts financial institutions into the picture. Young households cannot borrow freely against expected future income. Their ability to borrow is limited by liquidity constraints which are different from one country to another. Consumption therefore depends not only on permanent income, but also on current income. With these assumptions, *financial deregulation has the effect of lowering the savings rate.* It reduces the liquidity restraints for every age income profile. Thus, the propensity to consume out of current income is diminished and the savings rate of young households is reduced. This direct effect is less than offset in the aggregate savings rate by the supplementary savings required later for the reimbursement of a higher debt. Finally, *a decrease in the rate of interest has a more ambiguous consequence on the savings rate than the relaxation of credit rationing.* Such a decrease changes the age profile of consumption. Young people can borrow and consume more. But mature households have less interest income and consume less. The aggregate effect depends on the age structure. If the proportion of young people is high, a lower interest rate will reduce the aggregate savings rate; the reverse happens if the proportion of mature adults is larger.

Putting together the different factors in the model, one gets the simulation described on Figure 11.2. The simulation of savings rates is obtained under the following assumptions: the retrospective and prospective development of demographic structures comes from UN statistics and projections; the rate of growth of real income is taken in the future as the average rate over the last twenty years in each country; the propensity to consume out of current income in each country expresses the degree of liquidity restraint reached in 1985 and is supposed to be unchanged in the future. Figure 11.2 essentially features the impact of long-term changes in demographic structures on the trend of the savings rate. The main results are: the maturing of the working population in the US which would substantially raise the savings rate up to the year 2005, everything else remaining the same; the growing importance of the retired population in Japan beginning in 1985 which would involve a slow decline of the savings rate; the slow and steady rise of the savings rate in Germany, and for that matter in Western and Northern Europe (Mediterranean countries excluded) as long as the large generation of the 60s is growing older in its working life.

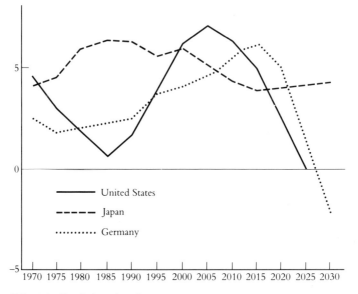

FIG 11.2 Simulation of savings rates
Source: CEPII

TABLE 11.3 Uses of savings funds as a per cent of French households' savings

Items	1970	1975	1980	1985	1989
Capital account					
Housing investment	52.8	52.0	60.3	55.0	63.4
Miscellaneous items					
and adjustment	15.7	7.9	10.2	2.1	15.4
Financial accounts					
Fixed & non-fixed					
savings deposit	49.5	61.9	43.7	35.7	22.0
Securities & contractual	6.5	7.4	21.6	40.0	50.4
Savings*	–24.5	–29.2	–35.8	–32.8	–51.2
Minus new consumer credit	31.5	40.1	29.5	42.9	21.2
Net financial savings					
– savings rate as per cent of					
disposable income	18.7	20.2	17.6	14.0	12.3

Source: INSEE, P. L'Hardy (1990) from flow of funds tables.
Note: * Bonds, equities, shares of mutual funds, life insurance contracts.

2.3 CHANGES IN THE ALLOCATION OF SAVINGS

Changes in the use of savings funds by households have been more pronounced than changes in the savings ratios. They bear the full impact of financial innovations. But OECD financial accounts are not harmonised and they are published with much delay. It is necessary to resort to national sources which depend on specific classifications of financial items and make systematic international comparisons a huge task, especially for retrospective data covering a long time span in the past. However, qualitative conclusions are similar for all large countries which have felt the full impact of the wave of financial deregulation and innovations. This is why, for the purpose of the present chapter, I will limit myself to illustrating the qualitative changes with quantitative data for the French financial system.

Table 11.3 shows the allocation of household savings in France over twenty years.

The drastic change brought about in the 1980s by securitisation stands out. All kinds of securitised financial instruments have soared: bond holdings were stimulated by the increase in yields (the real long-term interest rate jumping from an average of 1 per cent in the years 1976–80 to 6 per cent in 1986–8); shares of mutual funds were lured by huge capital gains in the equities market from 1982 to the crash of October 1987; and life insurance contracts increased at a fast and steady pace as an attractive instrument to accumulate wealth for future retirement. The counterpart of the active net purchase of securitised instruments, while the savings rate itself declined severely, was a near collapse of new deposits. Commercial banks lost their core deposits and were under pressure to finance their assets with costly borrowed funds. Housing is still a serious reason for saving. But the market for newly built housing is plagued by high financial costs that low- to middle-income families can no longer afford. Then, new consumer credit, though a volatile item, represents a rising proportion of savings and an important source of funds, as mentioned before.

The financial system has one basic characteristic: institutions dealing with contractual savings (mutual funds, pension funds, life insurance companies) collect an increasing share of savings at the expense of banks. But they do not allocate funds according to the same rationale as banks do. Institutional investors have basically the same risk aversion as an average wealth owner. They diversify their portfolios conservatively according to well-established risk minimising rules in the long run. However, since they collect large amounts of cash, they are lured by short-term capital gains and they indulge in myopic and mimetic behaviour when they arbitrage in financial markets. On the contrary, the function of banks is to transform risks since they make risky loans out of deposits convertible at par into fiat money. In principle, banks control their risks microeconomically by monitoring individual investments.

Therefore, the financial trends acknowledged above raise a structural problem in the financial system. Let us suppose that institutional investors get the major part of savings and that they invest funds in proportions only marginally affected by differential yields, between *existing* assets (land, property, shares, gold and the like) and claims on low risk debtors (public and blue chip securities). Banks are left to finance the bulk of productive investment with a shrinking deposit base. Such a financial system will be seriously flawed. The part of savings invested in existing assets will only circulate ownership rights without any new production. Since the stock of existing assets is fixed, excess demand will induce capital gains on the market prices of these assets, wealth appreciation and more consumption for their sellers. The result is bound to be higher interest rates for bank credit. First, a higher cost of funds will force banks to undertake more risky loans to preserve their profit margins. Secondly, the rise of wealth–income ratios shifts the aggregate demand schedule outwards so that the real interest rate is higher at any level of income. Thirdly, arbitrage between capital markets makes speculative appreciation on existing assets set the tune, laying a threshold that the yield on productive investment has to meet. *If the financial system works that way, financial innovation hardly fulfils its promised efficiency.*

3.   High real interest rates: what are the reasons? What are the consequences?

High real interest rates have been a striking feature in the world capital markets of the 1980s. They are puzzling because of their coincidence with slow growth and more competitive markets. One can safely reject the contention that high interest rates are a statistical artefact due to our ignorance of expected inflation. It is true that current inflation overestimates expected inflation when the pace of inflation is slowing down. However, it is possible to make up for the inertia of expectations. Building self-regressive formula upon past inflation, using inflation forecasts given by surveys or by econometric models, extracting a measure of expected inflation from the comparison between straight bonds and indexed bonds with otherwise identical characteristics, are well-known devices. Whatever measure of expected inflation is chosen, the conclusion remains: in every country but the UK, the average level of real long-term interest rates on Treasury Bonds was 2 per cent to 4 per cent higher in the 1981–5 period than in the 1976–80 period (Bismut, 1990). Moreover, from 1986 on, inflation rates were sufficiently stable to entail no further systematic error when measuring expected inflation, so that it is not incorrect to directly compute *ex post* real interest rates. Although they abated somewhat until 1989, they generally remained above 3 per cent.

A simple explanation currently in fashion is to attribute the persistently high level of interest rates to a world-wide disequilibrium between savings and investment. This explanation is part of the so-called real business cycle theories and denies any bearing of the financial system on real variables. In that view low savings come from intertemporal preferences of individuals and high investment demand stems from new technology. Since capital markets are perfect and, since money is neutral, the real interest rate is truly real and real funds are allocated worldwide. The real interest rate is the equilibrium rate which equalises the stock of capital required by technology and the desired wealth of individuals. If a technological shock raises the return on real assets above the current return expected on financial assets, the rate of investment to GDP moves up. It induces a rise in the real interest rate until the higher stock of capital leads to a reduction of its marginal productivity. The technological shock is finally absorbed when the marginal return on capital is again equal to the real interest rate paid on funds.

It is an explanation seemingly grounded into hard theory. But neither does it fit the facts, nor does it stand upon acceptable assumptions.

If the real interest rate were set on a world capital market, the adjustment would proceed from a market mechanism allocating world savings by equalising rates of return on capital invested in every part of the world. At least in the OECD countries where capital controls have been removed, one might expect a tendency for real interest rates to converge towards a single level. Yet, no such tendency does exist. Real long-term interest rates remain significantly different from one country to another. There are some contemporaneous correlations within variations of real long-term interest rates indicating that they fluctuate together (Artus, 1990b). But the disparities in their levels point to imperfect capital markets (risk premia) and goods markets (deviations from P.P.P.).

Furthermore, the recourse to technological shocks in explaining the high real interest rates of the 1980s is theoretically a call for a *deus ex machina* and is empirically erroneous. If a technological shock were a common exogenous cause, there would have been an increase of real interest rates and of rates of investment. But we observed, in Table 11.1 above, that the investment rates declined substantially in every large OECD country. In so far as the 1980s are a decade of drastic changes, these are financial and monetary. The objectives and procedures of monetary policy changed abruptly in the early 1980s. Financial deregulation removed institutional obstacles to capital mobility. But it made it plain that markets are incomplete, risk assessment suffers from an asymmetrical flow of information, monetary policy is not neutral in the short to medium term. There are multiple financial causes for the high level of interest rates; they interact sequentially and, being non-independent, are impossible to weigh quantitatively.

3.1 MONETARY POLICY IS NOT NEUTRAL

In Europe, one could contend that, unlike in the US, monetary policy never ceased being restrictive after 1983. For, the stance of German monetary policy was accepted by other EMS countries through tighter exchange-rate rules. On the whole, one cannot assert that monetary policy was a permanent cause for high real interest rates; but it certainly was a major cause for different countries at different times throughout the decade.

The real effects of a tight monetary policy on real interest rates and savings operate through the rigidity of prices and the adjustment of income. The restriction of liquidity provokes a sharp rise in nominal interest rates. Since prices are not flexible in the short run, the real interest rate jumps simultaneously. With sticky prices, the shortage of liquidity leads to a reduction of effective demand. Income has to adjust to a lower absorption and the economy falls into recession. Since savings work as a shock absorber, lower income involves more than proportional lower savings. The rise in real interest rates and the decline in the private savings rate are twin results of a common cause, i.e., the policy induced shortage of liquidity. But one is not the consequence of the other. *In the short run, the predominance of income adjustment precludes the working of price adjustment.* Then the recession runs its course and prices decelerate with the increase of unemployment. If monetary policy keeps being restrictive, the nominal interest rate declines more slowly than inflation. The *ex post* real interest rate keeps going up for a while and reverses with considerable inertia. Therefore, the sequential reaction of nominal interest rates and prices to the initial liquidity shortage spreads the real effects over several years if the initial tightness is severe.

3.2 CAPITAL MARKETS ARE IMPERFECT

At least three factors play a part in sustaining real interest rates higher than they would otherwise be. It is remarkable that the three factors are all offsprings of financial liberalisation.

The first one is *higher volatility in interest rates and securities prices.* With deregulation, stronger competition, and capital mobility, the volatility of short-term interest rates has spread to other market segments as well. Moreover, more and more governments have wanted to keep the instability of foreign exchange markets in check, in order to maintain their struggle against inflation or preserve the competitiveness of their business sector. They had to indulge in monetary policies which transmitted the volatility from exchange rates to interest rates. Whatever the reasons, volatility of interest rates makes the holding of securities with long maturities riskier. Depending upon their risk aversion, bondholders demand *higher risk premia*. They are wedded into the level of interest rates, both nominal and real, which are permanently higher than before the deregulation of financial markets.

The second factor is *the intrinsic instability of equity and property markets* which are sensitive to destabilising speculation. Those markets have peculiar characteristics. The future yields of the assets they trade are uncertain and their fundamental determinants are at least as difficult to assess as the prices of the assets themselves. They are assets with quite a rigid supply; i.e. new issue or new production is insignificant in the short run compared to existing supply. Therefore the secondary market for those assets sets the price as the result of a dynamics that can be largely autonomous from general economic conditions. They are markets for capital gains. Some market participants know those characteristics. So they know that the relevant expectations are linked to the opinions of others concerning the development of the future price. Other participants just follow the direction of the price whatever it is. Markets which are driven by this kind of behaviour are conducive to *self-fulfilling prophecies*. They are powerful but fragile dynamics, very sensitive to news which is likely to break up the convergence of opinions which sustains a particular path of price appreciation. Consequently, those markets exhibit high volatility, short-lived but sharp speculative bubbles, sudden breakdowns; these oddities modulate long trends of capital appreciation or depreciation, depending upon the pattern of the allocation of savings.

As was mentioned above, institutional investors allocated huge amounts of savings on secondary markets for equities and properties in the 1980s. Large excess demand was absorbed by price appreciation which drove more savings in the expectation of further appreciation. I already mentioned that this wealth accumulation stimulated consumption. It also influenced interest rates in more direct ways. Credit on margin by banks procured high leverage to the wealth accumulation process. This credit demand added up to consumer credit. Depending upon the stance of monetary policy, fast growing credit demand induced higher levels of interest rates charged by banks or fuelled future inflation. Another linkage operated through interaction between the bond and the stockmarket. In the US, junk bond financing of LBOs and MBOs substituted debt to equities. More generally, the attractiveness of stocks, while the bond market had to absorb large issues of public debt, created tensions on long-run interest rates.

The last factor of market imperfection that has contributed to high real interest rates comes from the situation of the banking system in several countries, as a consequence of financial deregulation. Banks have been affected by the higher cost of funds, on the liability side of their balance sheets, by slower growth and higher credit risks on the assets side. The average cost of funds is higher because many commercial banks have been obliged to finance their assets with an increasing share of borrowed funds, at (or near) market interest rates, in their total liability. Slower growth of yielding assets means that banks find it more difficult to cover their operating costs with a large fixed component. Heavy fixed costs lay a floor for the level of the prime rate charged by banks when market interest rates move downwards. Then, financial innovations and competition from non-bank institutions have deprived banks of their previous long-standing relationships with their best business customers. To cover their higher funding costs and to keep their market shares, they resorted to riskier loans. The deterioration in their ranking, the multiplication of troubled banks, the increase of provisions against non-performing loans, are all signs of the substantially higher levels of risks taken by banks. The increase in risks is reflected in the structure of interest rates charged to all but their best customers. It means that the main part of business investment, i.e., the part undertaken by firms which do not have direct access to securities markets, bears higher costs of financing.

3.3 HIGH REAL INTEREST RATES AND THE SAVINGS–INVESTMENT BALANCE

The role of real interest rates in macroeconomic adjustment is not straightforward. We have already stated some reasons that impair the effectiveness of price adjustments to regulate the savings–investment balance. In the short run, price stickiness and consumer behaviour combine to make high real rates and low savings rates twin outcomes of money shocks without any functional relationship between those two variables. Therefore, one cannot infer that high real rates will induce a rise in future savings rates from the observation of their apparent contemporaneous relative evolution (Artus and Kaabi, 1990). In the longer run, it has been shown, using the life cycle model, that there are as many reasons for the savings rate to fall as to rise, following an increase of the real interest rate.

   With these results in mind, one can sum up what has already been said under the following line of argument. For the structural and institutional reasons stated in the first part of the paper, there has been a prolonged decline of the private savings rate, especially in the US. In that country, the *ex ante* savings–investment gap was aggravated by large public deficits. Because of the structural imbalance, magnified by the whole range of imperfections in the capital markets, real interest rates have been unusually high. International capital mobility, coupled with the will of governments to avoid too large real exchange-rate misalignments, have partially transmitted the high real interest rates from the US to other OECD countries. Econometric studies have shown that long real interest rates, if they stay high for several years, can have a negative influence on real investment (Artus, 1990a or b). However, since those high real rates coincide with low savings rates, the impetus on consumption offsets the inhibition to invest. As long as the savings rate declines, the overall growth rate can be protected from the negative effect of the real interest rate.

   It cannot be the end of the story however. If capital accumulation has been stifled, it can impede either the growth rate itself or the level of consumption per capita in long-run equilibrium. But it is also possible that excessively low production capacities in the short run would reignite inflation. Higher inflation would produce a long-run equilibrium 'à la Kaldor'. With real wage flexibility in the long run, inflation lowers the real interest rate and generates enough savings out of profits to sustain the required rate of investment. But this arguement assumes that all savings are productive. We have seen that this is not always the case when households save in the life cycle, and when they transfer ownership rights on existing assets between generations.

4. Conclusions

Financial innovations have attracted a lot of attention in the 1980s. But much was directed towards increased competition in financial services and towards new financial instruments to diversify risks provoked by higher volatility in financial variables. Pervasive distortions in assets prices, though much more important in their macroeconomic consequences, were underestimated by the proponents of financial liberalisation.

The most fundamental trend in the structure of the financial systems of developed economies stems from household savings. Savings rates have declined, but the composition of savings has also undergone drastic change. Regarding the liabilities of the financial system, there has been a prolonged shift out of bank deposits towards institutional savings. On the assets side, more savings have been allocated to wealth accumulation based upon price appreciation of speculative assets and less on the financing of productive investment. The consequences of this structural change are numerous and have just begun to be felt.

The first and foremost consequence is a higher interest rate and a less stable financial environment. It can be demonstrated to happen even with perfect capital markets when productive investment has to compete for funds with speculative assets markets and with deregulated markets for consumer credit.

If markets are imperfect, which is always the case with default risks, lending on expectation of asset prices appreciation as collateral aggravates whatever financial fragility has built up in credit institutions. It has been rather serious for banks already plagued with an adversely shifting deposit base, with higher cost of funds and squeezed profit margins.

The turnaround of price inflation in assets markets indicates that the euphoria of easy-going wealth accumulation is over. But the legacy of the excesses of the past decade can be most unfavourable, especially if monetary policy is kept tight in fear of a spillover of inflation into goods and labour markets. A collapse of highly inflated assets prices transmitted to other segments of a densely integrated market, would induce a credit crunch that would spur a world recession. Even if such an adverse outcome does not show, a tightening of bank credit is likely to happen as banks struggle to meet their capital adequacy standards. Therefore, high real interest rates are here to stay for a while and future growth might be stifled with dire consequences for employment in developed countries, for the reconstruction of the Eastern economies, and for indebted developing countries.

This is a matter of serious concern, in particular because banks have a unique position in the financing of the economy when financial markets are imperfect. When productive investment in fixed capital is irreversible because of sunk costs and a long phase-in period, firms need finance in advance to undertake their projects. Since they are able to supply credit in anticipation of *future* savings, banks release investment plans from the availability of *current* savings. It was Keynes's basic insight: *ex post* investment expenditures, identical to *ex post* savings, alone determine the level of productive activity because *ex ante* investment plans are independent from *ex ante* savings. But the macroeconomic function of bank credit can sustain long-run non-inflationary growth only if banks are able adequately to monitor the solvency of borrowers at the microeconomic level. In this respect too, banks which transform risks between their liability and their assets sides are different from institutional investors which transmit the risk aversion of their average customer into their portfolio diversification.

In the face of mounting risks, national monetary policy cannot reach all the objectives if financial deregulation and integration are to be preserved. Additional instruments are to be found in much more strengthened prudential regulation and international coordination. By promoting securitisation of their assets, banks can manage to hold on to their unique function in the distribution of credit and shift the risks to stronger institutions. But it will not lower the overall financial fragility if prices of assets are still subject to huge misalignments. Finding ways to curb self-fulfilling speculation in sensitive assets markets is a challenge for monetary authorities. Another unresolved issue is to acknowledge that finance can lead to excess competition and overcapacity in the supply of credit. These structural imbalances are partly responsible for the inadequate assessment of risks and for the feverish attempt to secure high short-term yield for funds. A more sober view of the credit process needs tighter bank supervision and careful reorganisations to get rid of surplus capacity in the financial industry in an orderly manner. Building up a stronger financial structure and keeping an internationally steady monetary policy might keep real interest rates on a lower track and help finance the huge prospective demand for investment.

References and bibliography

Aglietta, M., Brender A. and **Coudert, V.** (1990), *Globalisation Financière : l'aventure obligée*, Economica.

Artus, P. (1990a), 'Epargne nationale, investissement et intégration internationale', *CDC, Service des Etudes Economiques et Financières*, Doc. N° 1990–17/T, May.

Artus, P. (1990b), 'Equilibre épargne-investissement au niveau mondial : évolutions et problèmes', *CDC, Service des Etudes Economiques et Financières*, Doc. N° 1990–8/E, September.

Artus, P. and **Kaabi, M.** (1990), 'Taux d'intérêt réels élevés : peut-on identifier les causes et les conséquences en longue période?', *CDC, Service des Etudes Economiques et Financiéres*, Doc. N° 1990–09/E, May.

Atkinson, P. and **Chouraqui, J.C.** (1985), 'Les origines du niveau élevé des taux d'intérêts réels', *Revue Economique de l'OCDE*, 5, October.

Bentzel, R. and **Berg, L.** (1983), 'The role of democraphic factors as a determinant of saving', in R. Hemming (ed.), *National Saving and Wealth*, London: MacMillan.

Bernheim, B. (1987), 'Ricardian equivalence: an evaluation of theory and evidence, in Stanley Fisher (ed.), *NBER Macroeconomics Annual 1987*, Cambridge MA: MIT Press.

Bismut, C. (1990), 'Pourquoi les taux d'intérêt restent-ils élevés?', *Economie et Statistique*, 232, May.

Blanchard, O. and **Summers, L.** (1984), Perspectives on high world real interest rates', *Brookings Papers on Economic Activity*, 2.

Bohm, V. and **Fuhakka, M.** (1988), 'Rationing and optimality in overlapping generations models', *Scandinavian Journal of Economics*, 90.

Bordes, C. (1987), 'Interprétation théorique du mouvement d'intégration du marché des capitaux', *Cahiers Economiques et Monétaires*, 31, Banque de France

Bosworth, B. (1990), 'International differences in savings', *American Economic Review Papers and Proceedings*, May.

Buiter, W. (1981), 'Time preference and international lending and borrowing in an overlapping generations model', *Journal of Political Economy*, August.

Dean, A, Durand, M., Fallon, J. and **Hoeller, P.** (1990), 'Savings trends and behaviours in OECD countries, *OECD Economic Studies*, 24, Spring.

Feldstein, M. and **Bacheta, P.** (1989), 'National saving and international investment', NBER Working Paper, 3164, November.

Feldstein, M. and **Horioka, C.** (1980), 'Domestic saving and international capital flows', *Economic Journal* 90 : 314–29.

Graham, J.W. (1987), 'International differences in saving rates and the life cycle hypothesis', *European Economic Review*, 31.

L'Hardy, P. (1990), 'Epargne des Ménages': Montée des Placements, INSEE Première, 105, October.

Oliveira Martins, J. and **Plihon, D.** (1990), 'L'impact des Transferts Internationaux d'Epargne sur les Déséquilibres Extérieurs,' *Economie et Statistique*, 232, May.

Shields, J. (1988), 'Controlling household credit', *National Institute Economic Review*, August.

Stiglitz, J. and **Weiss, A.** (1981), 'Credit rationing in markets with imperfect competition', *American Economic Review*, 71.

CHAPTER TWELVE

The allocation of savings in a liberalised European capital market

Jørgen Mortensen

1. Introduction

Alongside the free movement of goods, persons and services, the free movement of capital within the Community is one of the basic freedoms laid down by the Treaty establishing the European Economic Community as from January 1958. The initial objective of the Treaty was to have eliminated restrictions on the movements of capital in the course of the transitional period of twelve years, that is by 1970. However, the lifting of restrictions in this field proved to be less of a priority for member states than initially envisaged and at the start of the 1980s there was in fact relatively little mobility of capital within the EC as compared to the considerable progress made in the field of intra-EC trade and in view of the spectacular growth in international financial transactions particularly through the Euromarket.

This situation changed radically in the course of the 1980s, with the adoption of the Single Act, the decision to eliminate as from the beginning of 1993 all remaining non-tariff barriers to trade within the internal market and the decision taken in 1988 to eliminate as from 1 July 1990 the last restrictions on capital movements. This chapter focuses on the allocation of saving in the European capital market in the 1990s. After a preliminary analysis of the level and evolution of the rates of return on various assets it examines more systematically the inward and outward capital flows of the member states and their possible causes and explanations. On this basis it presents some speculations with respect to the pattern of capital movements within the EC in the 1990s.

2. Return on assets and capital mobility in the EC

2.1 RETURN ON ASSETS

The total stock of fixed capital of an economy will typically amount to around four times the value of a year's GNP. If we exclude land and forests and other non-reproducible parts of this capital stock the figures will be somewhat lower but still appreciable. The rate of return on these assets is defined normally as the gross or net operating surplus of the sector as a per cent of the capital stock at replacement cost. The operating surplus, in itself, is the balance of large national accounts aggregates.

Estimates of rates of return for the total economy or for the business sector thus represent a synthesis of very large components and under normal conditions tend to change only relatively little from one year to the next. In the recent history of the EC-member states there are nevertheless a few examples of an explosion of domestic labour costs which over just a few years practically wiped away the net operating surplus of the economy and reduced the net rate of return of fixed capital for the whole economy to almost nil according to estimates by the EC Commission. This was the case in Portugal in the early 1970s, with the rate of return (on the same definition) falling from almost 12 per cent in 1970 to close to 2 per cent in 1975 and in Greece in the late 1970s with the rate of return falling from more than 12 per cent in 1973 to around 4 per cent at the end of the decade. It should also be stressed that the rise in the price of oil in 1974, the resulting recession and the accompanying increase in the real labour cost reduced the rate of return on capital for the EC on average by more than 2 points from 8.5 per cent in 1973 to less than 6 per cent in 1975.

The theory of investment, and by extension, also the theory of capital movements, attaches an explanatory value to the ratio of the rate of return on investment to the cost of capital. This ratio is most often termed the 'q' ratio. Financial market analysts, however, also frequently make use of another, but conceptually rather similar indicator: the yield gap, which is defined as the difference between the rate of return on stocks and the rate of return on bonds. From the point of view of pure theory, only the expected future return on assets should be taken into account. However, since expected values are not subject to direct observation, it is assumed in the following that the observed, recent values of these variables under normal market conditions may offer some guidance as to what markets may expect for the near future in terms of return on assets.

As seen from Table 12.1, the gross rates of return in EC-member states, the United States and Japan, as calculated for the business sector by the OECD Secretariat, appear for 1990 to lie within a relatively wide range, from around 9 per cent in Ireland and the United Kingdom to more than 19 per cent in the United States. Within the Community the highest rates of return are recorded for Belgium and Spain. The degree of convergence in this respect, moreover, appears to be particularly large between the closely integrated economies of the founding member states: Belgium, Germany, France, Italy and the Netherlands.

A closer examination of the development through time of the rates of return of the respective member states in fact shows little long-term tendency towards a reduction of divergence in response to the integration of the new member states into the Community framework of trade and capital movements. As seen from Figure 12.1, the divergence of rates of return (measured as the unweighted coefficient of variation) among the present member states of the Community, with the exception of Greece and Luxembourg, has been relatively stable since 1975 and even rose somewhat in the early 1980s. The closely knit founding member states did record some

TABLE 12.1 Rate of return and real rate of interest in the individual EC countries, US and Japan

	Gross rate of return OECD-def. business	Real rate of interest	q-ratio OECD-def. business sector	Yield gap OECD-def. business sector
		1989		
B	17.2	4.9	3.5	12.3
DK	10.5	7.4	1.4	3.1
D	13.9	3.8	3.7	6.7
GR	9.2	2.5	3.7	6.7
S	16.7	6.6	2.5	10.1
F	14.0	5.3	2.6	8.7
IRL	8.4	5.4	1.6	3.0
I	15.1	6.3	2.4	8.8
L	–	4.2	–	–
NL	15.2	5.5	2.8	9.7
P	–	1.7	–	–
UK	10.0	2.2	4.5	7.8
EC	13.6	4.5	3.0	9.1
US	19.6	4.3	4.6	15.3
J	15.1	3.6	4.2	11.5
		1990		
B	17.4	6.2	2.8	11.2
DK	10.6	8.3	1.3	2.3
D	14.4	4.9	2.9	9.5
GR	9.8	4.2	2.3	5.6
S	16.5	7.7	2.1	8.8
F	14.2	6.5	2.2	7.7
IRL	9.1	7.4	1.2	1.7
I	14.9	6.4	2.3	8.5
L	–	5.1	–	–
NL	15.3	6.1	2.5	9.2
P	–	2.1	–	–
UK	9.3	3.9	2.4	5.4
EC	13.6	5.6	2.4	8.0
US	19.4	3.8	5.1	15.6
J	14.9	5.7	2.6	9.2

Note: (1) Real rate of interest calculated as the nominal low less the rate of increase of the GDP-deflator over cur. the following year.
Source: EC Commission and OECD.

increase in the divergence of profitability in the first half of the 1980s but subsequently have moved closer again, to the lowest level of divergence recorded since 1976.

Thus, while, the degree of homogeneity among the founder members of the Community is rather large in the field of rates of return on fixed capital, a significant diversity remains in the field of interest rates. In fact, even in 1990 Italy recorded an average long-term rate of interest of 13.4 per cent, 4½ points above the level in Germany. With respect to interest rates, a high degree of homogeneity has, on the

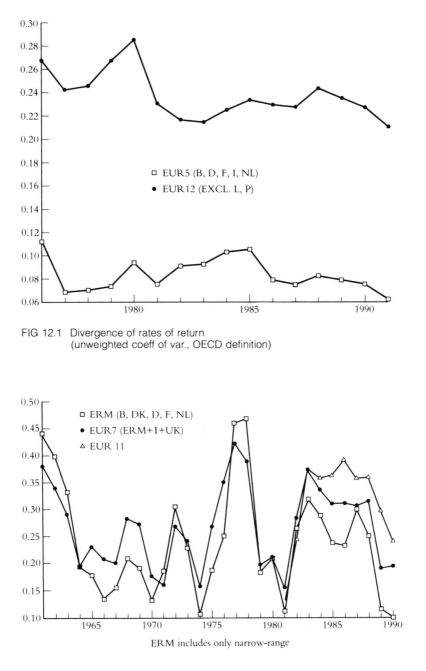

FIG 12.1   Divergence of rates of return
(unweighted coeff of var., OECD definition)

FIG 12.2   Divergence of interest rates
(unweighted coeff of var. (Short term))

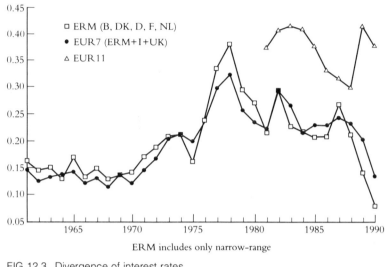

ERM includes only narrow-range

FIG 12.3 Divergence of interest rates
(unweighted coeff of var. (Long term))

other hand, been realised between countries observing the narrow-band within the
ERM independently of the date of their adhesion to the Community. As seen from
Figures 12.2 and 12.3, the coefficient of variation of, notably, short-term rates within
this group has, with a brief interval in 1987, been declining markedly since 1984 and
was by 1990 lower than at any other point in time since 1960 and substantially lower
than in the wider grouping of ERM plus Italy and UK or the whole of the Community. For long-term rates the reduction in divergence within the ERM has also
been pronounced during the latter half of the 1980s, but the development in this area
has been closer in line with trends in Italy and the UK.

As already underlined the figures for the rates of return in the various
countries constitute the balance of very large economic aggregates, and only small
errors or omissions in the aggregates may result in substantial changes in the calculated rate of return. The same reservations are therefore appropriate with respect to
figures for the macroeconomic yield gap, that is the difference between the rate of
return and the real rate of interest. For what they are worth, these figures, shown in
Figure 12.4, nevertheless appear to shed some light upon the evolution in the Community relative to the United States and Japan.

A particularly striking feature of Figure 12.4 is the steep fall in the yield
gap in the United States from 1979 to 1982. The rise in the dollar and the recession
in 1981/2 entailed a fall in the operating surplus of the economy and the tightening of
monetary policy resulted in a pronounced rise in real interest rates. During the sub-
sequent period, however, the profitability of the US economy improved, partly as a
result of the fall in the value of the dollar, and the yield gap rose to a level comparable to the one observed in the late 1970s. The position of the Community did not
deteriorate as much as that of the United States in the early 1980s but neither has it

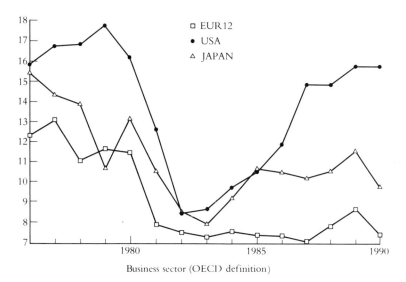

Business sector (OECD definition)

FIG 12.4 Yield gap in the main areas

improved much in recent years. As far as can be judged the yield gap in Japan has remained significantly lower than the one calculated for the United States and showed some decline in 1990 in response, notably, to the rise in real interest rates. The yield gap in the Japanese economy nevertheless even in 1990 is seen to lie significantly above the level recorded in the EC.

2.2 CAPITAL MOVEMENTS IN THE EC

Against the background of the powerful shocks in the international economy, notably the external imbalances of the United States and Japan, the direct investment and portfolio investment flows in and out of the EC member states look comparatively small in absolute terms and hardly liable to seriously modify the basic conditions in the countries concerned. Yet in some cases the amounts involved are quite large as compared notably to the level of current-account deficits or surpluses of the same countries. Total direct investment recorded by the EC member states in 1988 thus amounted to more than 56 billion ecu or 1.4 per cent of GDP as far as the outgoing and to 41 billion ecu or 1 per cent of GDP as far as the incoming direct investment was concerned. Moreover, in proportion to the level of domestic investment the figures look even more impressive: 7 per cent and 5 per cent of domestic investment respectively for outgoing and incoming direct investment on average for the EC in 1988.

Looking at the outgoing direct investment of the individual EC member states, the United Kingdom appears to be in a class of its own. As seen in Table 12.2 direct investment from the United Kingdom to abroad in 1988 and 1989 amounted

TABLE 12.2 Direct investment in EC countries

	1981	1982	1983	1984	1985	1986	1987	1988	1989
Direct investment abroad, % of GDP									
B	-0.1	0.1	-0.4	-0.4	-0.3	-1.5	-1.9	-2.5	- 4.4
DK	-0.2	-0.1	-0.3	-0.2	–	–	–	–	–
D	-0.6	-0.4	-0.5	-0.7	-0.8	-1.1	-0.8	- 0.9	-1.1
S	-0.1	-0.3	-0.2	-0.2	-0.2	-0.2	-0.3	- 0.4	-0.4
F	-0.8	-0.5	-0.3	-0.4	-0.4	-0.7	-1.0	- 1.5	-2.0
IRL	0.0	0.0	0.0	0.0	0.0	0.0	0.0	0.0	–
I	-0.3	-0.3	-0.5	-0.5	-0.4	-0.4	-0.3	- 0.7	-0.2
NL	-3.4	-2.4	-2.8	-4.1	-2.6	-2.5	-4.1	- 1.6	-4.5
P	-0.1	0.0	-0.1	-0.1	-0.1	0.0	0.0	-0.1	–
UK	-2.4	-1.5	-1.8	-1.8	-2.5	-2.9	-4.5	- 3.3	-3.8
Direct investment from abroad									
B	1.4	1.7	1.6	0.5	1.3	0.6	1.6	3.3	4.6
DK	0.2	0.2	0.1	0.0	–	–	–	–	–
D	0.0	0.1	0.2	0.1	0.1	0.2	0.2	0.1	0.6
GR	1.4	1.1	1.3	1.4	1.3	1.2	1.5	1.7	–
S	0.9	1.0	1.0	1.1	1.2	1.5	1.6	2.1	2.2
F	0.4	0.3	0.3	0.5	0.5	0.4	0.6	0.9	1.1
IRL	1.2	1.4	1.0	0.7	1.0	-0.2	0.3	0.3	–
I	0.3	0.2	0.3	0.3	0.2	0.0	0.5	0.8	0.3
NL	1.3	0.8	1.0	1.4	1.1	2.4	1.6	1.6	2.8
P	0.7	0.6	0.7	1.0	1.2	0.8	0.9	2.1	–
UK	1.2	1.1	1.1	-0.1	1.0	1.3	2.0	1.7	3.8

respectively to 3.3 per cent and 3.8 per cent of GDP or a figure practically equivalent to the current external deficit of the United Kingdom in that year. Among the other EC member states, Belgium, France and the Netherlands also recorded a high outflow while, somewhat surprisingly, the direct investment abroad by Germany appears to be at a low level in proportion to the strength of the German economy.

Turning to the inflow of direct investment from abroad, the figures appear to correspond more neatly to expectations. As seen from the lower panel of Table 12.2, Belgium/Luxembourg in 1988 attracted amounts corresponding to as much as 3.3 per cent of GDP, no doubt as a reflection of the boom in the construction sector in this economy and of a regain of popularity as 'the plaque tournante' and the capital of Europe. The inflow rose to an unprecedented 4.6 per cent of GDP in 1989. No doubt the central geographical location is also the explanation of the persistent high inflow of direct investment into the Netherlands. Apart from the Benelux countries benefiting from their strategic position, the inward direct investment in recent years has clearly been directed towards to less developed member states: Greece, Spain and Portugal. In these countries inward direct investment in recent years has amounted to

TABLE 12.3 Portfolio investment in EC countries, net (% of GDP)

	1981	1982	1983	1984	1985	1986	1987	1988	1989
B	-0.7	-2.3	-4.5	-5.1	-7.3	-5.7	-1.7	-2.8	-1.9
DK	0.1	-0.3	0.6	0.2	–	–	–	–	–
D	1.2	-0.1	0.5	0.2	0.3	2.6	-0.2	-3.6	-1.1
GR	0.0	0.0	0.0	0.0	0.0	0.0	0.0	0.0	–
S	0.1	0.0	0.0	0.0	0.1	0.5	1.3	0.7	1.6
F	-0.1	1.3	1.1	1.4	1.2	0.3	0.5	0.8	2.4
IRL	2.8	1.0	2.2	7.3	6.1	7.7	-0.7	3.4	–
I	-0.1	-0.1	0.1	0.0	0.1	-0.2	-1.0	0.0	-1.0
NL	0.8	-0.1	0.2	0.0	0.3	-2.7	1.1	1.5	1.5
P	0.0	0.1	0.1	1.2	0.5	1.4	2.2	4.3	–
UK	-1.7	-2.6	-1.7	-2.6	-3.4	-4.7	2.7	-1.5	-5.0

Source: IMF and OECD and, for 1989 data, BIS

around 2 per cent of GDP or some 10 per cent of gross fixed asset formation and has thus provided a very significant supplement to domestic saving and to the financing of the external deficit. It is on the other hand somewhat surprising to see that Ireland, which was one of the champions of inward direct investment in the 1970s and the early 1980s, no longer seems to attract much capital from abroad. Is this due to the stiffer competition from the new EC member states or to a certain saturation after a long period of building-up of foreign investment?

While the flows of direct investment seem to be rather stable and to correspond broadly to a pattern compatible with our assessment of the fundamentals of the economy, portfolio investment appears to be much more volatile, subject to strong fluctuations from one year to the next, and also to exhibit larger differences as between countries. As seen from Table 12.3 the net outflow of portfolio investment reached a figure as high as 7.3 per cent of GDP in Belgium in 1985 while Ireland recorded a net inflow of 7.7 per cent of GDP in 1986. The latter was, however, followed by a net outflow of 0.7 per cent of GDP the following year and this is by no means the only case of year-to-year fluctuations of this order of magnitude.

Taking a deeper look at the data contained in the IMF balance of payments statistics one is led to the conclusion that a large part of the swings in portfolio investment tends to be compensated for by swings in the other direction in other categories of capital movements. As seen in Table 12.4 the strong outflow of portfolio investment in Belgium in 1985 is largely compensated for by an inflow of other long- term and short-term capital of the same order of magnitude. Similarly, the pronounced shift in German portfolio investment from an inflow corresponding to 2.6 per cent of GDP in 1986 to an outflow of 3.6 per cent of GDP in 1988 is compensated for by a shift in other capital movements from an outflow of 6 per cent of GDP in 1986 to one of only 1.3 per cent in 1988. Furthermore the large outflow of portfolio investment from the United Kingdom in 1989 is counterbalanced by a record-high inflow of other long- and short-term capital.

Emerging from this brief and somewhat impressionistic examination of the

TABLE 12.4 Other long- and short-term capital, net (% Of GDP)

	1981	1982	1983	1984	1985	1986	1987	1988	1989
B	2.9	2.9	3.9	5.6	6.1	4.1	1.6	0.4	-0.4
DK	2.3	4.6	4.0	3.5	7.7	5.0	7.5	3.0	–
D	0.0	0.4	-1.4	-1.7	-2.6	-6.0	-1.5	-1.3	-0.7
GR	3.4	2.2	5.6	4.9	7.5	5.0	2.9	1.8	–
S	1.5	0.4	1.1	1.0	-2.1	-2.7	0.8	0.5	-0.6
F	0.8	0.6	0.6	-0.9	-0.9	-0.2	-0.6	0.1	0.2
IRL	9.7	10.9	4.6	-0.6	0.2	0.5	2.7	-3.7	–
I	2.2	0.5	1.3	0.8	0.2	1.1	1.9	1.4	2.8
NL	-1.3	0.2	-1.3	-1.9	-0.9	1.9	1.3	-1.8	-2.9
P	4.2	8.9	4.0	2.6	2.4	-2.9	-3.4	-6.0	–
UK	-0.2	3.3	0.7	-0.5	1.9	3.8	-2.9	3.1	8.7

Source: IMF and OECD and, for 1989 data, BIS.

key statistics on capital movements within the EC is thus an extremely complex image of flows which are very large in proportion to GDP and relative to the current account balances. We see relatively stable flows of direct investment mainly in favour of the Mediterranean countries and huge but often volatile flows of portfolio investment and other long- and short-term capital with no stable geographical pattern. This volatility of monetary capital in the wider sense is an indication of a high degree of substitutability both between various subgroups of this broad category of monetary assets and between monetary assets of various origins. No doubt this conclusion is not new to people with inside knowledge of the operation of financial markets but may come as surprise to some researchers such as Feldstein and Horioka[1] who, on the basis of more aggregate econometrical analysis of the swings in domestic saving and investment and in current external accounts, have argued that fundamentally the degree of mobility of capital among the industrial countries is relatively low.

Having concluded that the degree of mobility of capital within the EC despite a certain segmentation of markets and remaining transactions costs and exchange risks is already quite high, we are left with the central question: what are the driving forces? To what extent can these capital movements be explained simply by the differentials with respect to rates of return and rates of interest and to what extent should other (temporary) factors be taken into account?

Although the global picture of capital flows appears to be somewhat bewildering, the flows of direct investment, as already suggested, do seem to reflect to some extent at least the underlying macroeconomic conditions. The plotting of the net flows of direct investment against the gross rate of return on capital as observed in the late 1980s (three year averages) – see Figure 12.5 – in fact shows that for a group of highly developed OECD countries (US, J, B, D, F, I, NL, UK)[2] the level of the rate of return (expressed as the difference between the national level and the EC average) goes a surprisingly long way towards explaining the net flow of direct

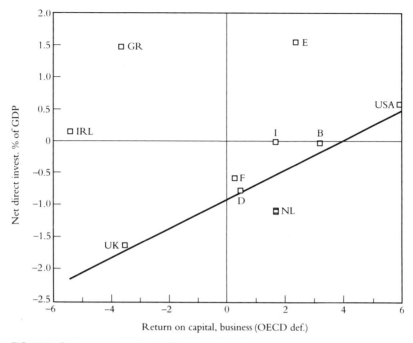

FIG 12.5   Return on capital and direct investment

investment of these countries (the straight line drawn in the figure indicates the linear regression of the observations for these countries).

     Figure 12.5 however also shows that net inward direct investment for Greece, Ireland and Spain, is substantially above the level corresponding to the relation found in the group of more developed OECD countries included in the regression. The flow of direct investment into these three countries (and probably also into Portugal) thus seems to respond not just to differences with respect to profitability but to other factors, among which could be found, presumably, the absolute level of labour cost in comparison with the more developed countries, special fiscal incentives liable to influence post-tax rates of return and/or the special incentives resulting from the ECs regional aid programmes (the 'structural funds'). The latter, in fact, for countries like Greece, Ireland and Portugal provide subsidies which are large enough to significantly influence the profitability of the investments benefiting from these programmes and may therefore go a long way towards explaining why the inward flow of direct investment is clearly in excess of the level corresponding to the pre-tax, pre-subsidy level of profitability of investment for the whole business sector.

3. Outlook

Although an outlook for capital movements cannot at present be based on a formal model, some basic features of recent European development are nevertheless emerging and should be of some support in judging trends over the next few years:

- Direct investment flows appear to respond to differences in rates of return on capital. They also reflect differences in labour costs and the impact of investment subsidies granted via the ECs budget (the structural funds).

- The stock of portfolio investment and other long- and short-term capital in the medium term tend to follow a stable pattern, determined by the state of the current account of the balance of payments. In the short run the corresponding flows however respond quickly and often violently to changes in expectations and in rules of taxation, etc.

Turning to the prospects for capital flows within the EC over the coming years, a central question is whether the countries most in need of supplementing national savings with capital imports will be well placed to attract direct investment and certain categories of long-term portfolio investment as during recent years.

As far as direct investment is concerned a key question is whether countries like Greece, Ireland and Spain will continue to offer a sufficiently low level of labour cost and various subsidies for investments from outside to compensate for a comparatively low level of profitability, at least in the case of the two former countries. Their ability to keep the growth of real labour cost low enough to maintain or even improve competitiveness may therefore be of increasing importance, notably in a context of a progressive stabilisation of interest rates.

With respect to portfolio investment, the impact of the choice of the exchange-rate regime will be even more decisive than in the case of direct investment. The process of monetary integration with, notably, a progressive stabilisation of exchange rates between the EC member states will most certainly lead to a further narrowing of interest-rate differentials between member states. On one hand this evolution is likely to considerably reduce the scope for capital movements taking advantage of interest-rate arbitrage. On the other hand, the elimination of the exchange rate movements should allow a substantial reduction of the prevailing high risk premium on investment in government bonds of some member states. All in all we might therefore see a pattern of capital flows much more in line with the fundamentals of the country or region concerned and notably the relative cost of labour, the profitability of capital and the level of saving.

With respect to the claims on saving in the Community, the Delors Report on EMU in fact expressed the fear that a monetary union, due to the equalisation of interest rates, might allow countries with an excessively lax budgetary policy to finance their deficits in the (integrated) capital market at a lower real cost than at present. According to this argument, there would be a risk that certain governments might 'confiscate' a rising proportion of private saving, pushing the real rate of interest to a higher level and crowding out productive investment. Up to recently the main fear was that the Italian authorities through such a procedure absorb a disproportionate part of Community saving. However, the reluctance of the German government to finance the costs of unification through taxes and (sufficient) expenditure cuts and the consequent sharp increase in the government budget deficit may be seen as another example of a policy aimed at covering the costs of certain policies through borrowing in the capital market rather than raising taxes.

Unless the Community member states spontaneously eliminate many or most of the features of present regimes providing incentives to borrowing, the 1990s could therefore well be a period with persistently high real rates of interest. If, in this manner, a climate of competition of claims upon limited financial resources were to prevail, countries and regions with a comparatively low rate of return on fixed capital would be likely to suffer even more than today. Such a development would therefore put even larger emphasis upon the capacity of peripherical and/or underdeveloped regions to ensure an appropriate rate of return on business investment.

Notes

1.   See Feldstein and Horioka (1980).
2.   Since all major OECD countries participate in the international capital market, an attempt to model the flows of direct investment clearly cannot be limited to the EC member states.

Bibliography

Amirkhakhali, S. and **Dar, A.A.** (1990), 'On the degree of capital mobility; an empirical analysis of OECD countries', paper presented at the Fifth Annual Congress of the European Economic Association, Lisbon, September 1990.

Bank of International Settlements, 60th Annual Report, Basle, 11 June 1990.

Barenco, B. (1990), 'The dollar position of the non-US private sector, portfolio effects, and the exchange rate of the dollar', OECD Department of Economics and Statistics, Working Paper No. 76, February.

Bini Smaghi, L. and **Micossi, S.** (1990), 'Managing exchange markets in the EMS with free capital', in Paul De Grauwe and Lucas Papademos (eds), *The European Monetary System in the 1990s*, Longman.

Chan-Lee, J.H. (1986), 'Pure profits and Tobin's q in nine OECD countries,' OECD Department of Economics and Statistics, Working Paper No. 34, April, and Economic Studies No. 7, Autumn.

Chan-Lee, James H. and **Sutch, Helen** (1985), 'Profits and rates of return in the OECD member States', OECD Department of Economics and Statistics, Working Paper No. 20, May.

Dean, A., Durand, M., Fallon, J. and **Hoeller, P.** (1989), 'Saving trends and behaviour in OECD countries", OECD Department of Economics and Statistics, Working Paper No. 67, June.

European Economy, Supplement A, No. 6, June 1990, 'Trends in national saving in the Community'.

European Economy, Supplement A, No. 8/9, August/September 1990, 'Some basic facts about the European financial sphere'.

European Economy No. 36, May 1988, 'Creation of a European financial area'.

European Economy No. 44, October. 1990, 'One market, one money; an evaluation of the potential benefits and costs of forming an economic and monetary union'.

Feldstein, M. and Horioka, C (1980), 'Domestic saving and international capital flows', *Economic Journal*, 90.

Fukao, M. and **Hanazaki, M.** (1987), 'Internationalisation of financial markets and the allocation of capital'; *OECD Economic Studies*, No. 8, Spring.

Funke, M. (ed.) (1989), *Factors in Business Investment*, Berlin Heidelberg: Springer Verlag .

Gros, D. (Rapporteur) (1989), 'Capital-market liberalisation and the taxation of savings', Centre for European Policy Studies (CEPS), Brussels, *Working Party Report*, No. 2.

Hallet, A.H., Minford, P. and **Rastogi, A.** (1990), 'The European monetary system, achievements and survival', Liverpool Research Group in Macroeconomics, Working Paper No. 90/04, Department of Economics and Accounting, University of Liverpool.

Jones, R.W. and **Kenen, P.B.** (1985), *Handbook of International Economics*, Amsterdam: North-Holland.

Laüdy Joëlle (1990), 'Les strategies financières', 'Direction générale des affaires économiques et financières', Commmission des Communautés Européennes (II/181/90).

Mayer, Jörg (1989),'Capital controls in the EMS – a survey', Centre for European Policy Studies, Working Document No. 43, August 1989.

Mortensen, Jorgen (1984), 'Profitability, relative factor prices and capital/labour substitution in the Community, the United States and Japan, 1960–1983', European Economy, No. 20, July 1984.

Mortensen, Jorgen (ed.) (1985), 'Monetary assets and inflation-induced distortions of the national accounts', North-Holland and EC Publications Office.

Mortensen, Jorgen (1987), 'Profitability, real interest rates and fiscal crowding out in the OECD area 1960–1985', EC Economic Papers No. 59, October 1987.

Niehans, Jürg (1984), 'International monetary economics', NY: Johns Hopkins University Press.

OECD Economic Outlook, June 1990.

Stern, R.M. (1973), 'The Balance of payments, theory & economic policy", *Aldine Treaties in Modern Economics*, London: Macmillan.

Turner, Philip (1990); 'Capital flows in the 1980s: a survey of major trends', Bank of International Settlements, October 1990 (unpublished mimeo).

CHAPTER THIRTEEN

International trade in banking services: a conceptual framework*

Sydney J. Key and Hal S. Scott**

1. Introduction

The Uruguay Round of trade negotiations within the General Agreement on Tariffs and Trade that has been under way since 1986 includes discussions on liberalisation of trade in services in addition to trade in goods. The inclusion of services for the first time in GATT negotiations reflects their increasing importance in international trade, especially over the last decade. Financial services in general, and banking services in particular, are now a significant component of international trade in services, in part because of the growing interdependence of national financial markets.

1.1 PRINCIPLES IN USE

The search for principles to govern the provision of financial services by foreign firms, whether located inside or outside the national market of the customers, has taken place in a number of contexts in addition to the GATT negotiations. These contexts have included unilateral national policies towards foreign providers of financial services, bilateral treaties such as the US – Canada Free Trade Agreement, the supranational rules adopted by the European Community (EC), and the multilateral codes of the Organisation for Economic Cooperation and Development (OECD). In the banking sector, the major industrial countries have negotiated informal guidelines covering prudential matters such as minimum capital requirements under the auspices of the Bank for International Settlements (BIS).

In this chapter we focus on the principles for regulating the international provision of banking services because of the unique character of such services and because, despite the increasing internationalisation of financial services and markets, national regulatory systems still differ substantially. The banking sector of a national

*This chapter was first published by the Group of Thirty as Occasional Paper 35, Washington DC, 1991.
**The authors wish to thank Howell E. Jackson, Karen H. Johnson, James S. Keller, Robert W. Ley, Kathleen M. O'Day, Patrick J. Pearson, Fernando Perreau de Pinninck, William A. Ryback, and Alexander K. Swoboda for valuable comments and suggestions. The authors also wish to thank Mendelle T. Berenson for her work in editing the manuscript. The views expressed in this chapter are those of the authors and should not be interpreted as representing the views of the institutions with which they are affiliated.

economy is a particularly sensitive one. Reserves held by banks have traditionally been used as an instrument of monetary policy, and banks play a key role in the payment system and in financing the real economy by intermediating between savers and borrowers. The latter role depends in part on public confidence in the banking system. The failure of one bank can trigger imitative runs on other banks or a chain reaction of failures through the payment system or through default on interbank obligations. This phenomenon is often referred to as 'systemic risk'.

For international trade in banking services, the most generally accepted principle is national treatment, which seeks to ensure equality of competitive opportunity for domestic and foreign firms providing banking services in a host country. Under a policy of national treatment, foreign banks are treated as nearly as possible like domestic banks: they have the same opportunities for establishment that domestic banks have, they can exercise the same powers in the host country, and they are subject to the same obligations. But differences between regulatory and institutional structures in home and host countries can make it difficult to apply the principle of national treatment.[1]

Some of the most intractable problems stem from the lack of agreement among the major industrial countries regarding the permissible activities of banks. For example, the European Community finds it difficult to accept US restrictions separating commercial and investment banking in the United States when the Community does not apply such restrictions to the activities of EC banks. Problems also arise in trying to apply to foreign branches capital adequacy and other requirements developed for the domestic banks of a host country. Moreover, national treatment does not address the extent to which multinational cooperation and agreement are necessary to regulate and supervise financial activities conducted internationally.

Other principles for governing international trade in financial services go beyond national treatment, that is, they presuppose national treatment and seek something more. These principles have been advanced as the basis for requirements imposed by national reciprocity policies or as obligations undertaken in connection with international agreements or supranational regulation. Although these principles, with labels such as mutual recognition and effective market access, are not always precisely defined, they involve explicit or implicit harmonisation of national regulatory structures, with concomitant changes in the regulation of domestic as well as foreign banks.

1.2 THE BANKING MATRIX

In this chapter we develop a conceptual framework for analysing the principles that should govern the provision of international banking services. To do so, we substitute for the conventional terminology more basic, albeit less colourful, terms. National treatment and the principles that go beyond it can be understood in terms of three basic components that can be applied separately or in combination: (1) host-country rules; (2) home-country rules; and (3) harmonised rules that apply in both countries. For example, national treatment requires the non-discriminatory application of host-country rules to foreign banks. By contrast, mutual recognition, which is the basis of

Table 13.1 Banking matrix
Rules to govern international trade in banking services, for combinations of policy
goals and methods of providing services

| Policy goals | Method of providing banking services | | | | |
| | Cross-border | Branches | | Subsidiaries | |
		Entry	Operation	Entry	Operation
Competitive markets	Home-country rules	Home-country rules and harmonized rules	Home-country rules and harmonized rules	Host-country rules and harmonized rules	Host-country rules and harmonized rules
Safety and soundness	Harmonized rules, home-country enforcement of rules	Harmonized rules, home-country enforcement of rules	Harmonized rules, home-country enforcement of rules	Host-country rules	Host-country rules
Avoidance of systemic risk	Home-country rules	Does not apply	Host-country rules with additional requirements for foreign banks	Does not apply	Host-country rules
Consumer protection: Deposit insurance	Home-country rules	Does not apply	Host-country rules with additional requirements for foreign banks, agreement on host-country bankruptcy jurisdiction	Does not apply	Host-country rules
Consumer Protection: Disclosure	Host-country rules	Does not apply	Host-country rules	Does not apply	Host-country rules

the EC internal market programme, involves both harmonisation of essential rules and, in the absence of harmonisation, acceptance by host countries of home-country rules. Even if rules are harmonised, there is the question of who administers the rules – the host country, the home country, or a supranational entity. In the banking sector, this question is particularly important because harmonisation does not by itself guarantee the quality of supervision.

The public policy question is what basic principle or combination of principles – host-country rules, home-country rules or harmonised rules – should govern international trade in banking services. Our analysis suggests that no single rule is appropriate for the provision of all international banking services. The choice of a rule depends on the interaction between two factors: the manner in which the service is provided and the public policy goals underlying the regulation of banking services. A bank located in one country (the home country) can provide services to customers in another country (the host country) in three principal ways: across borders, that is, without establishing a presence in the host country; through branches established in the host country; or through subsidiaries, which must be separately incorporated in the host country. Countries generally have four principal policy objectives that affect their regulation of such services: promoting competitive markets, ensuring the safety and soundness of banks, protecting against systemic risk and ensuring adequate protection of consumers.

In regulating the international provision of banking services, countries must choose from among the basic principles the ones most likely to promote these policy goals, given the forms in which banking services are provided. To help organise thinking about these choices, we have constructed a 'Banking Matrix', which sets forth the combinations of public policy goals and forms of provision of banking services (Table 13.1).

The entries in the cells of the Banking Matrix summarise the results of our analysis. For example, the analysis suggests that the best way to govern the entry of foreign branches so as to promote safety and soundness would be to apply harmonised rules that the home country would enforce. Similarly, consumers would be protected best if subsidiaries of foreign banks operated under host-country rules. The matrix emphasises a major theme of our analysis, namely, that different principles may be appropriate for different forms of provision of services or for different policy goals. Thus, the matrix indicates that, with some important exceptions, home-country rules should be applied to cross-border services, host-country rules to subsidiaries, and harmonised rules or special host-country rules to branches. It also indicates that harmonised rules are particularly important for the goals of promoting competitive markets and ensuring safety and soundness. Although reasonable people may differ over the particular principles we propose for each cell of the matrix, it is still valuable in relating policy goals to methods of providing services.

1.3 THE APPROPRIATE FORUM

Our analysis suggests that a fully satisfactory international framework for trade in banking services would require countries to agree whether host, home or harmonised rules should apply in particular situations, and on the specifics of harmonised rules when harmonisation is the accepted principle. Since that effort would clearly go considerably beyond the one currently under way in the GATT's Uruguay Round, the paper also discusses the characteristics of a forum in which such agreements might be negotiated.

In principle, the forum would comprise primarily the most developed countries; it would have the participation of finance ministry officials and financial service regulators; and it would possess the authority to formulate proposals, monitor their implementation and resolve disputes. No such forum exists at present. However, we suggest that the OECD or the GATT might, with some modifications to their current structure, serve as a broad forum for agreement on appropriate principles and could participate in or coordinate the efforts of other specialised fora, such as the BIS Committee on Banking Regulations and Supervisory Practices, in arriving at harmonised rules.

We begin our analysis by discussing the different, and sometimes conflicting, public policy goals that form the vertical dimension of the matrix. Next, for each of the different forms of international trade in banking services, the horizontal dimension of the matrix, we discuss which of the three basic principles, or combination thereof, best furthers each of the policy goals. We then summarise the results by providing generalisations about the appropriate rule for a particular form of provision of services or for a particular policy goal and identifying the areas in which such generalisations break down. Our analysis makes it clear that the provision of international banking services through branches presents the most difficult public policy choices. Finally, we discuss the forum issue, and draw some general conclusions.

2. Complementary and conflicting policy goals

In this section we review the goals countries generally pursue with respect to banking services and examine how these goals may complement or conflict with one another.

2.1 PROMOTING COMPETITIVE MARKETS

It is generally agreed that free trade results in competitive and efficient markets that maximise consumer welfare. To achieve free trade in banking services, then, what barriers must be removed? Clearly, national rules that discriminate between foreign and domestic providers of banking services constitute barriers to free trade. The principle of national treatment, which applies host-country rules to foreign and domestic firms on a non-discriminatory basis, is meant to ensure equality of competitive opportunity by eliminating such discriminatory barriers. It is generally understood that national treatment must be applied *de facto* as well as *de jure*. For example, the OECD National Treatment Instrument defines national treatment as treatment under host-country 'laws, regulations and administrative practices – no less favourable than that accorded in like situations to domestic enterprises'. The expression 'no less favourable' acknowledges that exact national treatment cannot always be achieved and that any adjustment should favour the foreign firm.

But the appropriate market for achieving equality of competitive opportunity for multinational banking institutions may be broader than a single country. Because such banks compete on a global scale, barriers to international trade in banking services may also result from non-discriminatory differences in national rules, that is, differences in national rules that do not discriminate between domestic and foreign firms. Fundamental differences in rules for permissible activities of banks or for the products they may offer can create significant barriers to trade. Even if they are non-discriminatory, a country's rules may be so much more restrictive than those in other major countries that they create market distortions and inefficiencies. For example, in the view of the European Community, prohibitions on combining banking and securities activities in the United States and limitations on interest rates in Japan restrict the ability of EC banks to compete effectively in those markets.

Although market forces may foster regulatory convergence in the longer run, in the short term removing non-discriminatory barriers among countries may be extremely difficult politically. However, within the European Community, where political agreement on goals for regulatory convergence has already been reached, the elimination of non-discriminatory barriers to trade in banking services is a critical element of the internal market programme.[2] This liberalisation is being carried out in an environment of substantial coordination and of common obligations established through a supranational structure to which the member states have already transferred a significant degree of sovereignty. By contrast, the OECD Codes of Liberalisation and National Treatment Instrument are concerned only with discriminatory barriers, a limitation that reflects the absence of a comparable political consensus or degree of integration among members of that organisation. For this reason, a GATT agreement on trade in services would have even more difficulty in addressing non-discriminatory barriers.

'Reverse discrimination' could occur if foreign banks were to receive treatment better than that granted to host-country banks – if, say, a German bank were permitted to offer a service in France (even when French banks could not do so) on the grounds that Germany permitted the service to be offered. Under the EC internal market programme, powers permitted in the home country (provided such activities are listed in the Second Banking Directive) will govern the provision of banking services across borders and through branches. However, the expectation – indeed, the overall EC strategy – is that any resulting competitive inequalities for a host country's banks will quickly force that country to conform its national rules to those of other member states. Within the Community, such reverse discrimination is essentially a strategy to produce harmonisation and is predicated on political agreement on goals for convergence of national regulatory systems.

Another dimension of national policies to promote competitive markets involves adoption and enforcement of policies to prevent concentrations of market power ('antitrust policy' in the United States, 'competition policy' in the European Community). These policies generally support *de novo* entry by new competitors, and thus do not pose obstacles to foreign banks offering cross-border services or establishing branches or subsidiaries in host countries. They might prevent a foreign bank that already has a substantial presence in a host country from acquiring a bank of significant size in that country, but such restrictions would apply equally to domestic banks.

Other considerations may sometimes modify – or even overrule – the economic goal of promoting competitive and efficient markets. In particular, developing countries often restrict competition from foreign banks out of concern that those banks will dominate their less efficient domestic institutions. To such countries, the efficiency gains achievable through competition are outweighed by the loss in national control of the banking sector. In some cases, such countries gradually open up their markets as they become more confident about the ability of their local institutions to compete. Industrialised countries are not immune to similar considerations: France and Italy in effect protect some of their major banks from foreign ownership through state ownership of these institutions. The governor of the Bank of England has stated that in the United Kingdom, which is generally regarded as having an open and competitive banking market, 'it is of the highest importance that there should be a strong and continuing British presence in the banking system. . . '.[3]

Devising a policy to promote competition in the banking sector through the entry of foreign banks is complicated by the need to ensure the safety and soundness of banks and to protect consumers of banking services. Countries have often justified limits on competition, such as chartering restrictions, ceilings on deposit interest rates, and restrictions on permissible activities, on prudential grounds. Some have argued that less competition means fewer failures. In the international context, countries may fear unfair competition from banks of other countries that regulate their institutions less stringently. Lower home-country capital requirements, for example, may allow foreign banks to operate on narrower margins. Given the significance of financial services to consumers, national legislation to protect consumers is also an important factor. The line between legitimate host-country consumer protection and anticompetitive policies is often hard to draw, particularly when the service provider is foreign and thus may be beyond the reach of the local authorities.

2.2 ENSURING SAFETY AND SOUNDNESS

Because of concerns about systemic risk and consumer protection, countries seek to avoid bank failures through safety and soundness policies. If, for example, capital adequacy requirements provided a 100 per cent guarantee that a bank would never fail, other measures to deal with systemic risk or depositor losses would be unnecessary. If a country has a deposit protection scheme, capital and other requirements to ensure the safety and soundness of banks protect the insurer, and possibly the taxpayer, not just the consumer of banking services. In this chapter, we view deposit insurance schemes as related primarily to the goal of consumer protection. However, such schemes are usually justified also as ensuring the stability of the banking system. By providing safety for the funds of individual depositors, these schemes protect those who are relatively unsophisticated financially and also reduce the systemic risk resulting from withdrawal of depositors' funds not only from troubled institutions but also from other banks. Some might argue that to the extent a bank is experiencing difficulties solely because it lacks liquidity, a deposit insurance scheme contributes to its safety and soundness. But the US experience suggests that the moral hazard of an overly generous deposit insurance scheme can encourage excessive risk-taking by bank owners and managers and thereby, perversely, undermine the safety and soundness of individual banks.

National authorities impose a variety of rules to ensure the safety and soundness of banks. These include capital requirements, limitations on large exposures, liquidity requirements, restrictions on permissible activities, requirements for accounting that accurately reflect the bank's condition and help to prevent fraud, and requirements for reporting and examination for regulatory and supervisory purposes. Ensuring the safety and soundness of foreign banks providing services in its territory poses special problems for a host country because it does not directly regulate or supervise the foreign parent bank.

This issue frequently arises with regard to branches of foreign banks, whose capital is essentially that of the foreign institution and whose condition is monitored and supervised by home-country authorities. To address this situation, host countries often impose special quasi-capital or liquidity requirements on branches of foreign banks. However, these rules can unduly restrict competition. Unlike most countries, the United Kingdom does not impose such requirements and instead relies on procedures for screening of banks, seeking to establish branches in its territory and regular monitoring of branch activities.

One promising approach to ensuring the safety and soundness of foreign banks operating in a host country is to reach international agreement on prudential rules, that is, the harmonisation approach. In general, the internationalisation of financial services and markets has both necessitated and facilitated international cooperation with regard to supervision and regulation. But the coordination and harmonisation of rules have been accomplished by bank regulatory authorities in a relatively limited and informal way. For example, the 1988 Basle risk-based capital framework is an accord among the banking authorities of the major industrial countries rather than a formal international agreement or treaty. It was negotiated under the auspices of the BIS Committee on Banking Regulations and Supervisory Practices, a committee established in December 1974 as a mechanism for regular consultation among the banking authorities of the Group of Ten countries.[4] Two earlier accords had been negotiated in the same way: the 1975 Basle Concordat, which sets forth general principles regarding the relative roles of home- and host-country supervisors in an effort to ensure that all banking organisations operating in international markets are supervised institutions; and the revised Concordat, released in 1983, which incorporates the principle of supervision of multinational banking institutions on a consolidated worldwide basis.[5]

2.3 PROTECTING AGAINST SYSTEMIC RISK

The need to protect against systemic risk arises because prudential controls may be ineffective in preventing liquidity or solvency problems for a particular institution. In that event, the difficulties of one bank may be transmitted to others, and ultimately affect the banking system as a whole. For example, a failing bank may hold substantial interbank deposits, either as a result of placements or through furnishing correspondent payment services. This was a particular concern in the case of the near failure of Continental Illinois Bank in the mid-1980s. Moreover, if a bank that participates in a net settlement payment system, such as CHIPS in the United States or EAF in Germany, is unable to settle its position, other participating banks may incur losses.[6] A chain reaction could also occur through withdrawal of depositors' funds from the troubled institution and from institutions that have claims on it or that are perceived to be exposed to the same risks.

Domestic regulations may limit the participation of foreign banks in interbank markets or national payment systems in order to minimise the possibility that a foreign bank failure could trigger a series of domestic bank failures. The BIS, through its Committee on Interbank Netting Schemes, has recently set out minimum standards for the design and operation of cross-border and multicurrency netting schemes, as well as principles for cooperative central bank oversight of such schemes.[7] The major purpose of such standards is to minimise the possibility of settlement failures and thereby to limit systemic risk.

Many countries seek to avoid systemic risk by rescuing failing banks. They employ a variety of techniques: extensions of credit by the central bank, injections of capital, arrangement of mergers with healthy institutions. Because such measures are designed to restore the solvency of failing banks, they can be viewed as another aspect of policies to promote safety and soundness. However, because they become necessary only when a bank is in danger of failing, it is useful to distinguish them from the normal prudential regulation and supervision that apply to all banks. In countries with a government-operated deposit insurance scheme, such as the United States, measures for dealing with failing banks may be part of that scheme because the insurer has an interest in the comparative costliness of alternative rescue measures. Nonetheless, rescue measures are widely employed by countries without deposit insurance schemes, and thus we consider such measures as furthering the policy goal of avoiding systemic risk.

2.4 ENSURING ADEQUATE CONSUMER PROTECTION

Consumer protection measures in the banking area generally fall into two broad categories. The first – primarily deposit insurance systems – consists of laws and regulations to limit losses of depositors. Host-country branches of foreign banks may be required to participate in such a system, particularly if they take domestic deposits in the host country.[8] The second category of consumer protection measures consists of disclosure rules. They typically apply to terms of credit, interest rates payable on deposits, charges for checks, and so on. Some countries go beyond simply requiring disclosure and mandate certain provisions in consumer contracts; some countries also try to protect the consumer against unwarranted disclosure of personal financial information.

Consumer protection policies are often politically sensitive. In the European Community, where the basic approach to banking regulation consists of a combination of harmonised and home-country rules with home-country enforcement, consumer protection rules could still be adopted by the host country. However, if such rules create barriers to the provision of banking services by banks from other member states, the host country must be able to justify the restrictions as necessary to protect the 'public interest', a stringent standard established by the European Court of Justice. The Court not only requires that host-state restrictions apply equally to foreign and domestic firms, but also prohibits such restrictions if the public interest is already protected by the rules of the home state or if less restrictive rules could achieve the same result.

2.5 MAINTAINING THE EFFECTIVENESS OF MONETARY POLICY

In the absence of a monetary union, domestic monetary policy is, of course, set and implemented by host countries. Although the provision of international banking services cannot change this basic fact, it does raise the question of whether such policy can be effective. In a world of economically interdependent nations, domestic monetary policy cannot be made in isolation. Over the past few decades, in several fora, the major industrial countries have sought to consult and cooperate with regard to the formulation of macroeconomic policies; during the last five years, among the Group of Seven countries, the process has become somewhat more formal.[9]

Theoretically, international banking activity should not interfere with the conduct of domestic monetary policy in a large open economy. Such activity would not render domestic monetary policy ineffective even though it might change the responsiveness of interest rates to a given change in the monetary base or modify the relationship between a change in interest rates and a change in nominal gross national product. The monetary authorities would still be able to achieve their targets; they would, in effect, adjust their decision making to take into account the effect of the offshore activity. Because the offshore activity could, over time, alter these relationships in unpredictable ways, the availability of data on such activity is helpful. Thus, some countries collect and share information: for example, Canada and the United Kingdom provide the United States with aggregate data on US dollar-denominated deposits of US residents at banking offices in those countries.

In any event, host-country rules, with some degree of international coordination and cooperation, govern the conduct of monetary policy. The use of host-country rules is not dependent on the way in which international banking services are provided, and monetary policy considerations thus should not affect our analysis.

3. Principles applicable to different forms of trade in banking services

International trade in banking services, as we use the term, refers to the provision of banking services by a bank whose principal place of business is in one country to customers in another country. Providing banking services to host-country residents from an office in another country – cross-border provision of services – is analogous to trade in goods. But providing banking services may also involve direct foreign investment if it takes place through a branch or subsidiary in the host country. Thus, rules regarding both the establishment and the operation of host-country offices of foreign banks play an important role in international trade in banking services. Because the different forms of providing banking services pose distinct issues in terms of the public policy goals discussed above, we consider each form separately.

3.1 CROSS-BORDER PROVISION OF SERVICES

Cross-border services are those offered by a bank located in one country to customers in another country without establishing an office in the customer's country, the host country. In general, the liberalisation of cross-border services has concentrated on removing exchange controls. In recent years, however, increased attention has been given to barriers in such areas as portfolio management and investment advice; this shift has been particularly apparent within the OECD, where much of the multinational work on international trade in financial services has taken place. Examples of host-country rules that impede the cross-border provision of services include restrictions on particular products or instruments, prohibitions on the solicitation of business by foreign entities, and tax rules that favour transactions with domestic rather than foreign offices.

The OECD principles for treatment of foreign providers of cross-border services depend on whether the transaction takes place in the host country or abroad. In the first case, the transaction may be significantly regulated but only on a non-discriminatory basis; in the second, only advertising in the host country may be regulated, but discrimination is not forbidden. Because services are intangible, however, locating the *situs* of banking services provided across borders is fraught with difficulties. This issue typically arises with respect to tax treatment of cross-border transactions and the choice of law governing a particular transaction. For example, lenders and borrowers can easily adapt to formalistic rules that make tax treatment turn on where a loan agreement is signed.

Competitive markets. In the interest of promoting competitive markets, host countries should allow cross-border provision of services under home-country rules without imposing any restrictions. This practice would permit host-country consumers access to a broader range of services and a larger number of service providers. On the other hand, broader powers, lower capital requirements, subsidies and other advantages offered by foreign governments may make for 'unfair' competition in the context of cross-border services. As discussed below, the Basle risk-based capital accord partially addresses this concern by setting minimum capital requirements for banks in countries party to that agreement. However, if the only consideration were maximising the welfare of host-country consumers (but not producers), it might be preferable to allow them to benefit from, for example, more favourable pricing by foreign banks, even in the absence of additional harmonisation. In any event, for large business customers, host-country limitations on the provision of services would be largely ineffective since such customers have easy access to banking offices located abroad. Thus, we conclude that the goal of competitive markets can best be promoted by applying home-country rules, as the Banking Matrix indicates.

Safety and soundness. The host country has a concern with the safety and soundness of foreign banks offering cross-border deposit services to retail customers, who could be defined as those with deposits of, say, under $100,000. Other customers, it is presumed, can protect their own interests and, in any case, can more easily place funds in the Euromarkets. If a foreign bank taking such retail deposits were to fail, host-country customers would be at risk unless the deposit insurance scheme in the home country protected them.

In any event, prudential rules are the first line of defence against bank failures, and the international harmonisation of these rules is the most promising approach for ensuring the safety and soundness of a foreign bank providing cross-border services. To further the goal of safety and soundness, we therefore envision international harmonisation, as depicted in the Banking Matrix.

Since the service provider is located entirely abroad, only the home-country regulators could enforce the international standards. Ensuring some degree of uniformity in the enforcement of such standards would depend primarily on cooperation and consultation among supervisors. In this regard, it should be noted that the 'home-country' supervisors might include not only those from the place of incorporation or location of the entity providing the service but also those from the country in which the banking organisation as a whole has its principal place of business. This would also be the case with respect to branches and subsidiaries, discussed below.

Avoiding systemic risk. A host country has minimal concern with systemic risk in the provision of cross-border services. The risk for individual domestic banks of holding deposits with foreign banks can be addressed by regulating such exposure directly rather than by imposing restraints on foreign banks. Cross-border services do not directly involve a foreign bank in the payment system of the host country, nor is the failure of a foreign bank likely to trigger imitative runs on domestic banks. If such runs were to occur, they would, in any case, have little relation to the foreign bank's provision of cross-border services. Thus, home-country rules should apply with respect to systemic risk, as noted in the matrix.

Consumer protection. For cross-border services, deposit insurance must necessarily be provided under the home country's scheme. The host country could, of course, best protect its consumers if basic elements of deposit insurance schemes were harmonised among nations. But achievement of this goal, although highly desirable, seems unlikely given the vast disparities in these schemes. Furthermore, the enormous effort that would be required to achieve harmonisation does not seem justified by the host country's policy concern with insurance of its residents' deposits in foreign offices of foreign banks. Therefore, home-country rules, without any harmonisation, should govern deposit insurance for cross-border provision of services.

By contrast, host-country rules can be used for disclosure requirements or mandatory contract terms. For example, host countries could require a foreign bank to disclose whether its deposits are insured and, if so, by whom and on what terms. If the deposit were denominated in a foreign currency, disclosure of the currency risk might also be required. Such rules would not impose extra requirements on foreign banks because they would be associated with the nature of the transaction, not with the nationality of the provider. Thus, domestic banks that offered foreign currency deposits would be subject to the same disclosure rules about exchange risk. In contrast to the OECD approach, determining the *situs* for provision of the service would not be important. If host countries were to impose overly burdensome disclosure requirements or mandatory contract terms, there might be a need to harmonise these measures to avoid an adverse impact on competition. However, for purposes of this chapter, we assume such harmonisation would not be necessary.

3.2 BRANCHES

Traditionally, analyses of issues relating to international trade in banking services have distinguished between providing services across borders, on the one hand, and providing them through the establishment of subsidiaries or branches, on the other. But a further distinction is useful because, unlike a subsidiary, a branch is an integral part of the foreign bank and is not separately incorporated in the host country. Recently, the special characteristics of branches have been given increased attention in international fora such as the OECD. Moreover, the European Community has in effect drawn a line between financial services provided through subsidiaries (which are subject to non-discriminatory host-country rules) and those provided through branches and cross-border services (which are governed by home-country rules and enforcement, based on harmonisation of essential rules). Our analysis seeks to identify the rules that should be applicable to the establishment (entry) of branches and to their operation.

3.2.1 Entry

Only two of the policy goals we have identified seem relevant for the entry of branches of foreign banks: competition and safety and soundness.

Competitive markets. Some countries limit or prohibit entry by branches of foreign banks by, for example, applying quotas or limitations on geographic location that do not apply to domestic banks. Developing countries often impose restrictions out of fear of foreign domination, although developed countries may also restrict branch entry. Canada, for example, prohibits the establishment of branches of foreign banks, although it would justify the prohibition on grounds of safety and soundness.

Because branches can operate on the basis of the consolidated capital of the foreign bank and are often a more efficient method of doing business than operating through subsidiaries, permitting branch entry is important in promoting competition among foreign and domestic banks in a host-country market. This consideration suggests that, for competitive purposes, branches should be allowed to enter under home-country rules; that is, if the home country authorises a bank to establish a foreign branch, the host country would be required to accept that decision. Safety and soundness concerns would be addressed by harmonisation of prudential standards (see discussion below).

A further problem arises with respect to non-discriminatory restrictions imposed by a host country. For example, a host country such as the United States may restrict intranational branching of its own banks and, accordingly, also place geographic limitations on the establishment of branches of foreign banks. Even if they are non-discriminatory, such limitations may be anticompetitive and create barriers to the provision of banking services, both on an intranational and international basis. This type of problem could be resolved through international harmonisation of rules for intranational geographic expansion.

In view of these considerations, home-country and harmonised rules appear to be the best way to promote competitive markets with regard to the establishment of branches, as reflected in the Banking Matrix. Thus, home-country rules would be used to determine whether a foreign bank was permitted to establish branches in the host country. Harmonisation of prudential standards would remove the safety and soundness justification for discriminatory host-country restrictions. Harmonisation is included under the goal of competitive markets to deal with a different issue, namely, the elimination of non-discriminatory barriers to branch entry.

Safety and soundness. Prudential concerns regarding entry of foreign branches cannot be allayed by the non-discriminatory application of host-country law. Allowing entry by a foreign branch is inherently different from permitting a domestic bank to open a branch. Branching by a domestic bank is predicated on initial approval for the establishment of the bank itself, and establishment of a branch is merely incremental. Moreover, domestic banks are subject to domestic (host-country) regulation for safety and soundness, whereas a foreign bank establishing a branch is not. The host country therefore needs to assure itself on this point in permitting entry for a foreign branch.

When a country permits entry by a foreign branch, it is implicitly or explicitly accepting the adequacy of home-country regulation and supervision, including enforcement of those rules. But why should it accept the adequacy of regulation and supervision by all home countries? Some degree of harmonisation of rules – say, by adherence to the Basle accord or other internationally agreed standards – might be required before permitting entry. Even if rules were harmonised, a host country might have reservations about the quality of enforcement in a particular home country; but conditioning entry on the quality of supervision would be extremely difficult unless home-country supervision was extraordinarily lax. The only answer may be sufficient cooperation and consultation among national supervisory authorities to establish an atmosphere of mutual trust.

The approach of harmonisation with home-country enforcement is reflected in the Banking Matrix. By removing the safety and soundness justification for discriminatory restrictions on entry, international harmonisation of prudential rules would enable nations to permit branches of foreign banks to enter under home-country rules, and would thereby promote competitive markets.

3.2.2 Operation

In contrast to entry, the operation of branches raises issues for all four of the policy goals.

Competitive markets. Competition within a host-country market would be promoted by allowing branches of foreign banks to engage in the same activities permissible for domestic banks, that is, by a policy of national treatment. However, competition could be further promoted if branches of foreign banks were allowed to engage in any activities their home countries permitted. If home-country rules were the more liberal ones, host-country banks would suffer reverse discrimination that could be removed only by a change in the host-country rules. However, if home-country rules were more restrictive than host-country rules and the home country applied identical rules to its banks' foreign and domestic activities, branches of home-country banks would be at a competitive disadvantage in the host-country markets.

The European Community is using the home-country approach, but bases that approach on agreement among countries regarding convergence of national rules. Thus, the EC's Second Banking Directive involves both harmonisation and home-country rules.[10] It sets forth a list of activities subject to mutual recognition; a host country is required to permit a bank from another member state to engage, through a branch or through the cross-border provision of services, in any activity on the list that the home country permits. Without implicit or explicit agreement on such a list, it would be politically impossible, either within or beyond the Community, to allow branches of foreign banks to operate under home-country rules for permissible activities.

Home-country rules combined with harmonisation of basic rules for permissible activities would best promote competitive markets for the operation of branches, and this is reflected in the Banking Matrix. Such harmonisation could be explicit, as in the European Community, or it could occur *de facto* through unilateral changes in national rules to conform to the more liberal rules in other countries. However, a broader group of countries may find it difficult to agree on permissible activities, especially securities activities or insurance activities (the latter are not even included on the EC's list). Countries have different traditions and experience in this area. Some view expansion of bank powers as a positive promotion of competition; others have concerns about safety and soundness, potentially anticompetitive concentrations of power, or conflicts of interest.

At present, two major countries with restrictive rules for permissible activities – Japan and the United States – are considering proposals for change. However, adoption of these proposals would not produce the harmonisation necessary to allow branches of foreign banks to operate under home-country rules for permissible activities. The reason is that the proposals envision that securities and insurance activities would be conducted in affiliates of the bank rather than in the bank itself. This approach contrasts with that of the European Community, discussed above, under which securities activities (though not insurance activities) could be conducted in the bank. As a result, a second-best alternative to the entry in the Banking Matrix – that is, home-country and harmonised rules for permissible activities of branches – would be host-country rules for permissible activities of branches combined with harmonised rules for permissible activities of bank affiliates. Such harmonisation would, in effect, require implicit or explicit agreement on a list of permissible activities for bank affiliates. There would also need to be agreement that foreign banks could operate such affiliates in addition to branches in a host country.

Safety and soundness. The issue of safety and soundness with regard to operations of branches of foreign banks in a host country is similar to that with regard to entry.

Once a branch was permitted to enter, its safety and soundness would continue to be determined largely by harmonised standards enforced by the home country. If, in the absence of a more widespread international agreement, adherence to the Basle standards by the parent bank had been a condition of entry, continued adherence should be included as part of the condition. As in the case of entry, the issue of adequate enforcement of harmonised standards could be dealt with through cooperation and consultation among national supervisors. In the extreme case, branch activities could be terminated by host-country authorities.

Systemic risk. Considerations of systemic risk are of particular significance for branches of foreign banks because the failure of a foreign bank necessarily means that its branches cannot continue to operate. The inability of a branch that played a significant role in host-country financial markets to meet its obligations could lead to a chain reaction of failures of other banks through the interbank market or payment and settlement systems or through imitative runs on branches of other foreign banks and on domestic banks. If a home country rescues a failing bank, systemic risk can be avoided; but host countries cannot count on such rescues. The decision of a country to rescue a failing bank depends on a variety of considerations, including the immediate financial cost and the longer-term potential for increasing moral hazard.

If necessary, the interbank market problem can be addressed by prudential regulation of domestic banks, for example, by limiting large exposures to less creditworthy banks, whether domestic or foreign. The risk to domestic banks from the failure of a foreign bank would generally not increase because funds were placed with a host-country branch of that bank rather than with the foreign bank in its home country or with a branch in a third country.

The payment and settlement system of a host country is subject to two risks from foreign branches. First, a foreign branch might default on a settlement position through failure to cover uncollateralised overdrafts on its clearing account with a central bank, incurred in connection with the use of a central bank payment system, such as FedWire in the United States. Such a failure might result in a loss for the central bank. Second, the failure of a foreign branch to meet its uncollateralised settlement obligations in a net settlement system, such as CHIPS in the United States, could expose other bank participants to losses.

Given that the ability of foreign branches to meet their settlement obligations depends ultimately on the solvency of the bank as a whole, which is regulated by the home country, host countries may be reluctant to allow foreign branches to participate in their payment systems on the same terms as domestic institutions. In addition, branches of foreign banks may have more difficulty than domestic institutions do in promptly covering settlement shortfalls: They may be less able to fund themselves quickly in host-country money markets, and home-country markets could be closed. The costs of settlement failure could be avoided if a central bank were to extend lender-of-last-resort facilities to the failing bank. But it is not clear whether any central bank would make these facilities available in such a situation. And then, which central bank would do so – that of the home country of the failing bank or that of the country in which the payment system operates?

The risks that participation by branches of foreign banks pose to a payment system could be controlled by a variety of measures. The BIS Report has formulated minimum standards for the G-10 countries that are designed to minimise the possibility of a settlement failure in net settlement systems. These standards would affect all participants in such systems, whether branches of foreign banks or domestic institutions. Although adoption of these standards will decrease the risk of settlement failure, it will not eliminate it. Moreover, the standards do not apply to use of central bank gross payment systems, such as FedWire, so that other policy measures will still be required.

One approach is to exclude branches of foreign banks from direct participation in the payment system by requiring them to clear payments through domestic participants. France, for example, permits only domestic banks to participate in Sagittaire, its net settlement system for cross-border payments. Alternatively, branches of foreign banks could be subject to special position limits or collateral requirements. Although such requirements could be viewed as discriminatory, they may be the only practical alternative to a system under which the host country's central bank may be forced to act as a lender of last resort for such branches. The Banking Matrix therefore indicates that host-country rules should apply with respect to systemic risk, with the qualification that the rules for branches of foreign banks may be different from those for domestic banks.

Harmonisation might be used to avoid special requirements for branches. For example, the Federal Reserve Board in the United States now allows branches of foreign banks to participate in FedWire on terms closer to those afforded to domestic institutions, provided the home country of the foreign bank adheres to the Basle capital accord. Adherence to the accord would give host-country authorities greater confidence in the safety and soundness of the foreign bank. This approach, however, does not address the issue of systemic risk that arises when a foreign bank with a branch in the host country actually fails. Under our framework, capital requirements would already have been harmonised for purposes of safety and soundness for the entry and operation of branches. Extra measures would be needed to avoid systemic risk if this first line of defence proved inadequate.

Consumer protection. If a branch of a foreign bank accepts deposits of host-country residents, the host country has an interest in protecting the depositors against the possible failure of the foreign bank. To this end, a host country could require branches of foreign banks, or at least those that take 'retail' deposits, to participate in its deposit insurance system. The problem with this approach, that is, using host-country rules, is that the exposure of the host-country insurer is dependent on home-country regulation and supervision of the bank. Harmonisation of rules for safety and soundness could make this situation more acceptable; but because such rules cannot provide a 100 per cent guarantee against failure, the host country might still be required to pay for the ineffectiveness of the home country's supervisory policies.

One solution to the problem of potential losses by the host-country insurer is to permit the host country to require branches of foreign banks to pledge readily marketable assets as a condition for insurance. In addition, the host country might require that branches of foreign banks maintain total assets that exceed total liabilities and that the assets not be excessively risky, a quasi-'capital' requirement. In the event that a foreign bank failed, the pledged assets would be immediately available to host-country authorities to cover or reduce the losses of the insurer, or they would be available directly to uninsured local depositors. Although other branch assets would be subject to host-country liquidation, the 'capital' requirement would help to ensure that such assets were sufficient to cover the claims of branch creditors, including those of the insurer. However, special host-country requirements for branch assets might unduly constrain the ability of the bank as a whole to operate in an efficient manner and, given harmonised capital requirements, would be unnecessary to maintain the safety and soundness of the bank.

Moreover, the effectiveness of these measures assumes that the host-country authorities have the legal power to seize branch assets and control their disposition, either through realising on the pledge or putting the branch into liquidation. This assumption is not free from doubt. It depends on whether a branch is treated as a separate entity in a liquidation (host-country jurisdiction) or whether there is unity of the bankruptcy (home-country jurisdiction). If the home-country receiver asserts a claim to the assets of the entire bank, including the assets of foreign branches, the host country may not be able to dispose of the assets of the branch without causing conflict with the home country.

In practice, host countries may try to liquidate a branch of a failing foreign bank as if it were a separate entity. For example, in the United States, state or federal authorities have seized assets (in one case a building, in another large local interbank deposits) and used them to pay off local depositors and creditors; in one instance, a surplus was sent to the home-country authorities. Nonetheless, the home-country receiver may well consider all of the assets of the failed bank – including those booked at its foreign branches – to be within the jurisdiction of the home country. In the case of the 1974 near failure of Franklin National Bank, US authorities persuaded the UK authorities to allow the US receiver to take control of the London branch of the US bank.

There is no generally accepted international rule in this area. The Basle Concordat deals with supervisory issues (it assigns primary responsibility for solvency to the home country and liquidity to the host country) and does not address assignment of responsibilities in the event of bankruptcy. Financial institutions are not covered by a bankruptcy convention recently agreed upon in the Council of Europe or by a draft EC convention still in long-standing negotiations.

If the home country has the legal power to control the disposition of all of the assets of a failed bank, including those at its foreign branches, the pledge and quasi-capital requirements of the host country would be rendered ineffective. In this situation, a host-country insurer would be fully exposed to the risk of inadequate supervision by the home country. To reduce this exposure, the host country would need to have jurisdiction over the disposition of the branch assets. Thus, the use of host-country rules for deposit insurance requires use of host-country rules for bankruptcy (that is, the separate entity approach).

There are, however, significant drawbacks to this approach. Home-country depositors, or their insurers, may be deprived of claims to assets booked at foreign branches, and it is far from clear why host-country claims to such assets should be superior. Since the bank as a whole has gone bankrupt, fairness suggests that claims should be resolved in one collective proceeding in which similarly situated creditors are treated alike. In addition, dismemberment of the bank through host-country liquidations of branch assets may effectively prevent the home country from restructuring or selling the bank, thus interfering with the preservation of the bank's overall value. Nonetheless, the fact remains that it would be exceedingly difficult to achieve an international agreement providing for exclusive home-country jurisdiction over bank bankruptcies.

As an alternative to host-country deposit insurance, deposits in a branch of a foreign bank could be covered under the deposit protection scheme of its home country. For host countries, this raises the question of what amount of protection provided by the home-country scheme would be acceptable; for example, the level of coverage, the degree of risk-sharing by depositors, the types of deposits covered and the speed and convenience of payouts. This question is further complicated by the fact that the lack of uniformity in deposit protection schemes is not the only factor contributing to differences among countries in protecting depositors. Other factors that can be equally important to host countries include government ownership of banks and central bank lending to or government recapitalisation of private banks.

The concerns of the host country about the adequacy of depositor protection afforded by the home country could be resolved only by harmonisation of deposit protection schemes. Indeed, the EC Commission is now considering whether to propose the home-country approach for Community branches of EC banks and, if so, what harmonisation such an approach might entail. Beyond the Community, whether sufficient harmonisation of deposit protection schemes exists or could ever be agreed upon is far more uncertain.

If harmonised and home-country rules were used for deposit insurance, home-country rules could then be used for bankruptcy. Because host-country authorities would not be providing insurance for deposits at branches of foreign banks, the host country would no longer need to have jurisdiction over the liquidation of the branch. Thus, home-country deposit insurance would work in tandem with home-country bankruptcy jurisdiction and avoid the drawbacks of the separate entity approach to bankruptcy. Whether, and if so to what extent, acceptance of the principle of the unity of the bankruptcy would require harmonisation among nations on priorities of creditors is beyond the scope of this chapter. Within the European Community, the Commission has proposed a 'winding up' directive that would give home-country authorities exclusive responsibility for winding up branches of EC banks; this approach would work effectively with home-country deposit protection if that were to be proposed.

For deposit insurance, the Banking Matrix envisions a second-best solution: the application of host-country rules with special requirements for branches of foreign banks and agreement that, in the event of bankruptcy, the host country would have jurisdiction over the disposition of the assets of branches of foreign banks. Although this approach is theoretically inferior to the use of harmonised and home-country rules for deposit insurance and bankruptcy, we do not believe the alternative is realistically achievable in the foreseeable future. We would be happy to be proved wrong.

3.3 SUBSIDIARIES

Unlike branches, subsidiaries are separately incorporated under the laws of host countries and are therefore similar to domestically owned banks. Subsidiaries of foreign banks have their own capital, which is within the regulatory and supervisory jurisdiction of host-country authorities. Because such subsidiaries are part of a multinational organisation, however, a host country might still be concerned with the condition of a parent bank and the extent to which it might serve as a source of strength by standing ready to inject capital into its host-country subsidiary.

3.3.1 Entry

As with branches, the relevant policy goals for entry of subsidiaries are competition, and safety and soundness.

Competitive markets. Promoting competitive markets requires that foreign ownership of domestic banks should not be prohibited. But two major competitive issues do arise with respect to the establishment of subsidiaries. The first is whether non-banking firms can establish banking subsidiaries in the host country. Some countries that limit the non-banking powers of banks also limit the ownership of banks by nonbanking firms. The prohibition against non-bank ownership of banks has been justified on the grounds of either safety and soundness or competition. The arguments are that non-banking parents cannot serve as a source of strength for their subsidiaries as well as banking parents can, and that the prohibition of ownership by non-banks prevents concentrations of power and conflicts of interest. The issue of ownership of banks, like the question of non-discriminatory restrictions on branch entry, might best be addressed through international harmonisation of rules.

The second competitive issue regarding entry for subsidiaries is whether foreign banks can establish subsidiaries at multiple locations within the host country when domestic banks are not free to do so. Such geographic restrictions, even if applied to foreign banks on a non-discriminatory basis, could be viewed as anticompetitive. This problem, like that which arises for branch entry, could be solved by international harmonisation of intranational rules, for example, by prohibiting geographic restrictions.

When a country has a federal structure other difficulties appear. If it permits subnational governments, such as states or provinces, to define the scope of interstate banking, as the United States does for subsidiaries, certain problems may arise in dealing with foreign banks. Foreign banks may, for example, need to be 'domesticated' by being assigned to a home state or region for the purpose of the application of host-country rules. A more serious problem arises if subnational governments discriminate between foreign and domestic banks, for example, by permitting only domestic banking organisations to acquire banks within their jurisdiction. Such policies violate the principle of non-discriminatory treatment, and host countries with federal systems may have to resort to federal statutory or constitutional changes to resolve such problems.

Our approach to promoting competitive markets for the establishment of subsidiaries calls for host-country rules and harmonised rules, as indicated in the Banking Matrix. Harmonisation may be necessary with respect to rules relating to ownership and geographic location. In other respects, application of non-discriminatory host-country rules to the establishment of subsidiaries – in contrast to the establishment of branches – does not seem to compromise competition. Moreover, unlike the establishment of branches, the creation of host-country subsidiaries requires compliance with the corporate laws of the host country.

Safety and soundness. The goal of safety and soundness provides a justification for the host country to impose certain conditions on entry, such as capital requirements equivalent to those applied to domestic banks. If the source-of-strength doctrine is accepted, the host country's interest in the safety and soundness of the subsidiary's foreign parent is similar to its interest when the host-country entity is a branch. As a result, the host country may have an interest not only in the capitalisation of the subsidiary but also in the capital adequacy of the parent banking institution. For example, the Federal Reserve Board requires foreign banks seeking to establish or acquire banking operations in the United States to meet 'the same general standards of strength, experience and reputation' as are required of domestic banking organisations and to serve on a continuing basis as a source of strength to their banking operations in the United States.[1] Application of the source-of-strength doctrine would be facilitated by more widespread international harmonisation of capital standards.

The Basle accord, in conformity with the earlier BIS agreement on consolidated supervision, envisions that for supervisory purposes home countries will apply bank capital requirements on a consolidated basis. Such consolidation would complement, but not replace, the capital requirements applied to a subsidiary by the host country. The purpose of applying home-country capital requirements on a consolidated basis is to ensure that the group as a whole has adequate capital to support all of its activities; and these requirements may affect the activities of subsidiaries. But a host country would nonetheless want to ensure that the subsidiary itself had adequate capital to support its activities. This is consistent with the host country's interest in the safety and soundness of its own banks.

The Banking Matrix, therefore, reflects our view that, to ensure safety and soundness, host-country rules should apply to the establishment of subsidiaries. But because we have recommended international harmonisation of capital standards for branch entry, most countries would already be adhering to the same standards.

3.3.2 Operation

Both goals relevant to the entry of subsidiaries – promoting competitive markets and ensuring safety and soundness – are, of course, also relevant to their operation. In general, the same considerations and rules apply.

Competitive markets. One additional issue arises with respect to permissible activities of subsidiaries. Competition in a host country would be promoted by permitting subsidiaries to engage in at least the same activities as domestic banks; but it would be even further enhanced by permitting subsidiaries to conduct the same activities they are permitted at home. As in the case of branches, basic rules for permissible activities would need to be harmonised to avoid competitive inequalities. These considerations suggest that the entry in the matrix could be the same as that for branches, that is, home-country rules and harmonisation.

But even the European Community is using host-country rules – that is, a policy of national treatment – for subsidiaries. However, the national treatment policy for subsidiaries is somewhat misleading. The Community relies on home-country rules – subject to the constraint of an agreed list of activities – to determine the permissible activities for branches and banks providing cross-border services. This serves as a tool for regulatory convergence. The almost inevitable harmonisation of rules for permissible activities that will result from this process will also affect subsidiaries. Similarly, beyond the Community, if home-country and harmonised rules were used for branches, there would effectively be harmonised rules for subsidiaries.

The Banking Matrix reflects our choice of host-country and harmonised rules for operations of subsidiaries. We view harmonisation as the critical element of this entry whether it occurs through *de facto* market pressures, through convergence resulting from negotiated harmonisation only for branch activities, or through explicitly negotiated harmonisation about the permissible activities of subsidiaries. We have entered host-country rather than home-country rules where harmonisation has not occurred primarily on practical grounds because subsidiaries, unlike branches, are separately incorporated host-country entities.

Other policy goals. Because subsidiaries are separately incorporated in the host country, the remaining policy goals – avoiding systemic risk and consumer protection – can be furthered by treating the subsidiaries under host-country rules exactly like domestically owned banks. Measures to deal with systemic risk as well as consumer protection measures can be applied without regard to the ownership of a bank.

4. Overview of the matrix

Our analysis, whose conclusions are set out in the Banking Matrix, relates the choice of rules governing international trade in banking services both to the means by which such services are provided and to the policy goals countries seek to achieve. The most obvious conclusion is that no single rule can be applied to all the combinations of methods and goals. Moreover, with the exception of disclosure requirements, no single rule can support a particular policy goal for every method by which the banking service is provided. The analysis also demonstrates that of all the goals, promoting competitive markets and ensuring the safety and soundness of banks depend most heavily on harmonisation.

With some important exceptions, our analysis suggests that home-country rules should be applied to cross-border services, host-country rules to subsidiaries, and harmonised rules or special host-country rules to branches. For cross-border services, in general, host-country regulation – that is, national treatment – is not appropriate. Those services should be governed by home-country rules: they enhance competition, the systemic risk is small, and only the home country can provide deposit insurance. However, even for cross-border services, home-country rules do not adequately address safety and soundness and the disclosure aspect of consumer protection. If foreign banks solicited retail deposits from host-country residents, the host country would have a concern with safety and soundness that could be addressed through international harmonisation of prudential standards. However, if the home country provided, through its own deposit insurance system, protection to such depositors that the host country considered adequate, the host-country's concern with the prudential standards applied to the foreign bank would be lessened. This consideration serves to highlight a more general point about the analysis: the choice of rules for one combination of goals and methods may affect the choice for another.

In contrast to the rules for cross-border services, host-country rules are generally appropriate for subsidiaries. The reason is that subsidiaries can, for the most part, be regulated just as their domestic counterparts are without raising any special concerns about safety and soundness, systemic risk or consumer protection. Application of the source-of-strength doctrine would be facilitated, however, by more widespread international harmonisation of capital standards. In any event, as the matrix indicates, international harmonisation of rules may be necessary to promote competitive markets with respect to both entry and operation of subsidiaries. Harmonisation seems the most useful solution to the competitive problems raised by host-country restrictions on the ownership of subsidiaries conducting a banking business, on the geographic locations at which they can be initially established or subsequently operated, and on the services that they can provide. But harmonisation would not be easy to accomplish: for example, it could require the United States to remove its restrictions on interstate banking, and it could require Japan and the United States to permit banks to offer securities services.

The treatment of foreign branches raises the most complicated questions. These arise because branches, though located and doing business in a host country, are an integral part of banks located in the home country. Thus, by their very nature, branches are subject to conflicting regulatory regimes that can be reconciled for the most part only through harmonised rules.

Our analysis suggests that ensuring safety and soundness and competitive markets when services are provided by branches of foreign banks requires harmonised rules, home-country rules where harmonisation is not deemed necessary, and home-country enforcement. This is the EC approach under the Second Banking Directive. Competition, particularly with regard to geographic location and permissible activities, would be enhanced by this approach. The goal of safety and soundness requires harmonisation of prudential regulations, but such regulations ultimately must be enforced by the home country. Harmonisation of prudential rules is also important because it permits greater use of home-country rules to promote competitive markets.

Once the goal of safety and soundness is assured, the main rationale for discriminatory restrictions on competition is removed. This is another example of the interdependence among the rules selected for the various combinations of methods and goals.

Our analysis further suggests that host countries might justifiably apply different rules to branches of foreign banks than to domestic banks for purposes of avoiding systemic risk and protecting depositors. Arguably, such policies might not be truly 'discriminatory' because domestic banks and the branches of foreign banks might not be in 'like situations', at least for these purposes. In any event, special treatment may be necessary to avoid the potential risk arising from participation by branches in host-country payment systems. Requiring branches to pledge or maintain marketable assets might also be justified to cover potential losses of host-country depositors or insurers. But such rules would be ineffective without host-country jurisdiction over the disposition of branch assets in the event of bank bankruptcies. Application of special host-country rules to protect host-country depositors could be avoided through harmonisation of deposit insurance schemes and application of the home-country scheme to deposits in host-country branches; in that event, home-country rules should also be used for bankruptcy. Although this alternative is theoretically preferable, we did not adopt it in the matrix because of the considerable practical difficulties in achieving harmonisation of deposit insurance schemes and in reaching an agreement providing for exclusive home-country jurisdiction over bank bankruptcies.

We can also analyse the way in which international banking services are provided from the perspective of each of the policy goals. For example, for systemic risk and deposit insurance, the matrix shows that quite different rules may be required for different forms of operation. Systemic risk is of minimal concern for cross-border services. For subsidiaries, systemic risk can be handled by the rules applicable to domestic banks because the subsidiaries are regulated for safety and soundness by the host country. In the case of branches, the host country must apply special rules.

With respect to deposit insurance, for cross-border services, home-country rules must govern because the foreign bank has no presence in the host country. Although the host country can require that domestic deposits at branches of foreign banks be insured, it then has an interest in ensuring that the branch has sufficient assets to cover potential payouts to depositors. As discussed above, these interests could be addressed by an agreement on host-country jurisdiction over branches in the event of bankruptcy. For separately incorporated subsidiaries, host-country rules for deposit insurance can readily be applied.

Harmonisation of rules is important with regard to the policy goals of safety and soundness and competitive markets. Harmonised prudential rules help protect depositors or insurers against bank failures. The Basle accord indicates that this approach is feasible, but harmonised capital requirements are only a first step. Other aspects of prudential supervision, such as examination and reporting requirements, are also important. Harmonised rules with respect to the powers of banks and the geographic locations at which they can operate would clearly promote competitive markets. This is true for both subsidiaries and branches of foreign banks. In theory, one could allow subsidiaries to be governed by host-country rules; but as a practical matter, harmonising rules that govern competition for branches will necessarily result in the same rules for subsidiaries if competitive equality between domestic banks and branches of foreign banks is to be maintained.

In stressing the need for harmonised rules for competition, we do not mean to prejudge the content of such rules. In other words, we are not using harmonisation as a code word for deregulation. With regard to entry, however, harmonisation for competitive purposes should involve removal of restrictive measures that limit market access. With regard to branch operations, efforts to harmonise competition rules might result in agreement to permit the same powers to banks as now specified by the EC's Second Banking Directive. If so, the result would be liberalisation of existing rules in the United States and Japan. Although broadening powers would generally enhance competition if safety and soundness concerns were addressed, it might not always be possible politically. Nevertheless, without convergence of rules for powers of banks, problems in this area may continue to arise, with the risk of retaliatory actions that could curtail competition.[12] In the case of safety and soundness, harmonisation could involve re-regulation, such as strengthening capital requirements.

5. The appropriate forum

Our analysis suggests that an international framework for the provision of international banking services would require agreement both on basic principles – that is, whether host, home, or harmonised rules should apply in particular situations – and on the specifics of harmonised rules when that is the accepted principle. Achievement of such a framework, which goes considerably beyond the effort currently under way in the Uruguay Round, would, of course, require an international forum. In this section, we consider the ideal characteristics of such a forum and the extent to which existing international fora – the General Agreement on Tariffs and Trade, the Organisation for Economic Cooperation and Development, and the Bank for International Settlements – meet these criteria.

5.1 CHARACTERISTICS OF A FORUM

An appropriate forum might (1) include only countries whose levels of development were sufficiently alike that they had similar interests in the liberalisation of banking services; (2) include the relevant financial service regulators and finance ministry officials from such countries; and (3) have authority to formulate proposals, monitor their implementation and resolve disputes. These characteristics flow directly from our previous analysis.

The appropriate group of countries. As our analysis shows, competition and safety and soundness considerations are important in establishing a conceptual framework for international banking. Thus, at the outset, the forum should perhaps consist primarily of developed countries that have a common interest in the extent to which their home-country banks can operate in each other's markets. It may be extremely difficult to get more than a few developing countries to accept the same competitive principles as developed countries, particularly with respect to the entry of foreign banks. Many of these countries are quite concerned with foreign domination, and they see little to gain from liberalisation of the terms of entry of their banks into developed countries. Moreover, developed countries may be particularly concerned with safety and soundness problems that could arise from entry by banks from developing countries.

The forum should nevertheless have sufficient flexibility to accommodate a growing number of countries. For example, if a host country conditions entry for foreign banks on home-country acceptance and observance of certain internationally agreed supervisory standards, banks from countries not in the initial group but subsequently meeting such standards might be given the same rights of entry as those in the initial group.

Officials participating in the forum. The officials from the countries involved in devising an international framework would ideally include regulators of banking and other financial services (including central bankers) and finance ministry officials. Because of their expertise and previous experience in devising harmonisation measures, such as those developed by the BIS Committee on Banking Regulations and Supervisory Practices, banking regulators are clearly essential to the development of the more extensive harmonisation envisioned in our analysis. Moreover, with regard to the goal of safety and soundness, banking regulators are the officials who would implement any agreed-upon rules.

An important part of an effort to develop the international framework we envision would involve a determination of the powers that foreign banks may exercise in host countries. As we have indicated, this determination turns upon questions of competition as well as those of safety and soundness. If banks are to be permitted to offer a broad range of financial services, the expertise of non-banking regulators, such as securities and insurance regulators, will also be important in formulating international rules.

Moreover, in most countries, government officials other than regulators, such as those in finance ministries, deal with the formulation of policies regarding the basic structure of the financial system. To become effective, these policies often require legislative changes, and finance officials often take the lead in such a process. Although regulators clearly have an important role, their policy choices are frequently circumscribed by the broader legal framework for which the other government officials are responsible. Some of the harmonisation issues that we have discussed, such as additional powers for banking organisations, would require legislative changes and would be highly political. These issues have the potential to affect the political and economic interests of the participating countries and thus require the involvement of finance ministry officials as well as financial service regulators.

Authority of the forum. Ideally, the forum would be more than a meeting place. It would be an international institution with delegated authority from participating countries that enabled it to reach decisions binding on participants and that permitted it to monitor implementation of its rules and resolve significant disputes about them. The supranational character of the European Community, as discussed above, has been important to the ability of the EC countries to harmonise certain features of their banking laws as part of the internal market programme. Though the supranational structure of the Community goes far beyond what would be required for an international regulatory forum, any forum undertaking international harmonisation would be strengthened to the extent it possessed some supranational authority.

As our analysis demonstrates, the forum would inevitably confront issues that go beyond banking, at least as narrowly conceived. It would have to deal with whether banks should have the power to offer securities and insurance services, and with the appropriate structure for regulating banks offering such services. These issues would necessarily overlap with other issues regarding such services – for example, disclosure requirements for cross-border securities offerings or capital requirements for non-bank securities firms. There would also be overlap with the macroeconomic measures required to realise the full benefits from developing an international framework for banking services – for example, liberalisation of rules relating to capital movements.

The ideal international forum would have authority to deal with all issues involving financial services, but in practice it would be difficult to find one forum with such broad authority. Even on a national level, many countries have found it difficult to integrate different types of financial service regulation. A second-best, but more realistic alternative would be to have several fora whose efforts would be coordinated by a broader forum.

5.2 THE CHOICE AMONG EXISTING FORA

The creation of a new forum for developing an international framework for banking services along the lines we have suggested merits consideration. In the absence of a new institutional framework, the most likely fora for undertaking the effort are the GATT, the OECD and the BIS. How well do these fora meet the ideal criteria?

The GATT. The GATT falls short of the ideal forum in several ways. One problem is that it comprises a large number of economically diverse countries, many of whom have little interest in liberalising rules for financial services. In particular, few of the developing countries in the GATT are likely to agree to be bound by the same principles as developed countries. However, in accordance with an approach that has been suggested in the GATT negotiations on financial services, the developed countries and some of the more industrialised developing countries could try to reach agreement among themselves before trying to resolve their differences with other developing countries. Moreover, principles agreed to by a primary group of countries, in the GATT or elsewhere, might subsequently be applied to other countries whose banks are seeking to enter markets of countries in the original group. This broadening of application has already occurred in some instances with respect to the Basle accord.

Another problem with the GATT as a forum is that, for the most part, the participating officials are experts in trade in goods rather than in banking or other financial services. This emphasis was natural because, before the Uruguay Round, the GATT dealt solely with trade in goods. As this paper has suggested, liberalisation of international trade in banking services raises complicated issues that are best handled by specialists. If the somewhat autonomous GATT Financial Services Body being discussed in the Uruguay Round negotiations were to be established, it could conceivably play a role in the development of an international framework for banking services of the sort suggested here.

The BIS. Though it is closer to the ideal forum for international trade in banking services than the GATT is, the BIS also has some drawbacks. The G-10 countries that are represented on the BIS Committee on Banking Regulations and Supervisory Practices have a common level of development; but the group may be too narrow because it excludes a number of developed countries with similar interests in international banking services. On the other hand, the BIS Committee includes banking regulators with substantial expertise and experience in harmonising banking rules on an informal and non-binding basis; they have negotiated the risk-based capital accord, the Concordats, and the minimum standards for interbank netting schemes. However, the BIS does not formally include other financial service regulators or finance ministry officials, whose participation would be necessary to reach government-to-government agreements as opposed to understandings among bank regulators.

The BIS could play an extremely useful role in the international regulatory framework we have described as a specialised forum for issues involving safety and soundness and systemic risk. Other countries could be brought into the discussions of these issues after the BIS had formulated preliminary proposals. The proposals of the expanded group of banking officials could then feed into a broader forum that included government officials more attuned to competition and consumer protection considerations. Similar input to the broader forum could also be made by other financial service regulators.

The OECD. The OECD has some advantages as a forum for the purposes discussed in this paper. Currently, it comprises twenty-four countries at relatively similar levels of development.[13] Also, most of the relevant government officials from the finance ministries, central banks and supervisory authorities regularly attend meetings of its committees or the working groups established under its committees.

The OECD also has some experience with non-binding harmonisation of national laws. In the 1970s, the Committee on Financial Markets issued recommendations that came close to harmonisation of rules in the area of operation of unit trusts (mutual funds) and disclosures applicable to publicly offered securities. In addition, the Committee on Fiscal Affairs has developed a model tax convention to avoid double taxation. For the most part, however, the OECD has sought to establish the principle of non-discriminatory application of host-country rules rather than dismantle non-discriminatory barriers that could involve changes in the regulatory framework of a host country. Some of the latter work could be carried on by specialised fora such as the BIS. The OECD could thus be the broad forum that coordinated the efforts of other groups.

One problem with the OECD is that its members, unlike those in the European Community, have not surrendered any sovereignty to it. Decision making, as in the GATT, must be unanimous. Moreover, although its rules are legally binding, the OECD lacks a strong mechanism for settling disputes. If it were to play the role of the broad forum, its ability to resolve disputes would have to be greatly strengthened, a move that would involve a major change of style for the organisation. The OECD would also need to find ways of including non-member countries that meet certain criteria based, for example, on regulatory and supervisory standards as well as liberalisation of access.

6. Conclusions

This paper sets forth a conceptual framework for analysing international trade in banking services and uses it to suggest rules applicable to various forms of such trade. Determining the appropriate rules requires systematic examination of the policy goals involved in the regulation of banks, as well as of the methods by which international banking services are provided. Our framework – with the principles of host-country, home-country or harmonised rules – enables one to go beyond conventional verbal formulations, such as national treatment or effective market access, that often avoid or paper over underlying concerns and the complexities of the issues. Although reasonable people may differ over the details of our analysis and the solutions we propose for each combination of policy goals and methods of providing services, the systematic approach embodied in the matrix that relates the choice of rules to both the goals and the methods remains useful. Indeed, a similar approach could be used for other financial services, such as securities and insurance.

From the perspective of this chapter, the establishment of an appropriate international regulatory framework for trade in banking services is an ongoing, long-term effort. The current efforts of the Uruguay Round could be viewed as an important beginning. Our analysis suggests that consideration should be given to continuing this work in the OECD or the GATT, either of which could serve as the forum for agreement on the appropriate principles and could participate in or coordinate the efforts of other specialised fora in arriving at harmonised rules where they are deemed necessary.

Notes

1.   See Sydney J. Key (1990), 'Is national treatment still viable? US policy in theory and practice'. *Journal of International Banking Law*, 5 (9) (Winter), 365–81. An earlier version of this paper was presented at a Conference on World Banking and Securities Markets after 1992, International Center for Monetary and Banking Studies, Geneva, February 1990.

2.   See Sydney J. Key (1989), 'Mutual recognition: integration of the financial sector in the European Community', *Federal Reserve Bulletin*, 75, September: 591–609.

3.   Robin Leigh-Pemberton (1987), 'Ownership and control of UK banks', *Bank of England Quarterly Bulletin*, 27, November: 526.

4.   The Group of Ten, or G-10, actually consists of twelve countries: Belgium, Canada, France, Germany, Italy, Japan, Luxembourg, the Netherlands, Sweden, Switzerland, the United Kingdom and the United States.

5.   The original 1975 Concordat is reproduced in International Monetary Fund (1981), 'International capital markets: recent developments and short-term prospects', Occasional Paper No. 7, August, pp. 29–32. The 1983 revised Concordat is reproduced in 22 I.L.M. 901 (1983).

6.   See Hal S. Scott (1990), 'A payment system role for a European system of central banks', in Committee for the Monetary Union of Europe, *For a Common Currency*, pp. 77–106. A modified version of this paper was published in *Payment Systems Worldwide*, 1 (3), Autumn: 3–15.

7.   The standards were part of the 'Lamfalussy Report'; see Bank for International Settlements, *Report of the Committee on Interbank Netting Schemes of the Central Banks of the Group of Ten Countries*, November 1990.

8.   Another example of loss-limitation measures is the limitation on the amount a consumer may have to pay in charges on a lost bank card.

9.   The Group of Seven, or G-7, consists of Canada, France, Germany, Italy, Japan, the United Kingdom and the United States.

10.   Second Council Directive of 15 December 1989 on the coordination of laws, regulations and administrative provisions relating to the taking up and pursuit of the business of credit institutions and amending Directive 77/780/EEC (89/646/EEC), 32 *O.J. Eur. Comm.* (No. L 386) 1 (1989).

11.   See Board of Governors of the Federal Reserve System, 'Supervision and regulation of foreign-based bank holding companies', Policy Statement, 23 February 1979, F.R.R.S. 4-835. See also Regulation Y, 12 C.F.R. §225.4(a)(1) and Board of Governors of the Federal Reserve System, 'Unsound banking practices – failure to act as source of strength to subsidiary banks', Policy Statement, 24 April, 1987, F.R.R.S. 4-878.

12.   See Hal S. Scott (1989), 'La notion de réciprocité dans la proposition de deuxième directive de coordination bancaire', *Revue du Marché Commun*, 323, January: 45–56.

13.   Australia, Austria, Belgium, Canada, Denmark, Finland, France, Germany, Greece, Iceland, Ireland, Italy, Japan, Luxembourg, the Netherlands, New Zealand, Norway, Portugal, Spain, Sweden, Switzerland, Turkey, the United Kingdom and the United States.

PART FOUR

BANKING AND FINANCE IN EASTERN EUROPE

The role of finance in the restructuring of resource allocation in Eastern Europe[*]

T.M. Rybczynski

1. Introduction

An illuminating and helpful way of examining the role finance should and ultimately must pay in the transformation of Central and Eastern countries from command economies into democratically based market economies moving along the path of self-sustained and non-inflationary growth is first to restate briefly the basic functions the financial system performs in the West; secondly, to outline briefly how the financial arrangements have worked in the East; thirdly, to indicate how they must be altered to help the process of non-inflationary economic advance; fourthly, to point the way this can be achieved in the light of the development of Western economies and the evolution of their financial system; and, finally, to comment briefly on the wider policy implications the outlined proposals carry.

It is perhaps worth stressing that, while it has been accepted for some time that the transformation of command economies into market economies requires the re-establishment of property rights, liberalisation of prices and competition, little attention has been paid to the fundamental restructuring of the financial system. What is now becoming clear is that the former three conditions – property rights, liberalisation of prices and competition – are by themselves necessary but not sufficient conditions for the process of transformation and that the additional and indispensable requirement is the establishment of an open, flexible, competitive and efficient financial system.

2. Basic functions of the financial system in the West

Why this is so can be seen by examining first the basic functions of the financial system

*This contribution was also published in San Paulo Ecu Newsletter, Central and Eastern European Supplement, 3, January, 1991.

in Western economies. In short, the financial system performs three basic functions.

The first is to collect voluntarily generated new savings and allocate them to uses where they are expected to yield the highest rate of return consistent with the proclivity of savers to assume risk which is involved in every single decision to invest.

The second basic function, is to monitor the use made of past savings embodied in the physical, financial and human assets and to discipline the managers and/or owners of such past savings if the results they obtain are considered inadequate. The disciplining process may involve a change of management, winding up of a business, or change in ownership (involving also a change in management and often also of strategy) by way of mergers, takeovers and amalgamations.

The third fundamental function of the financial system is to create and manage the payments, clearing and settlement system the purpose of which is to economise on financial, human and real resources and to assist the division of labour which is the propelling force of economic advance.

Looked at from the dynamic point of view, the process of economic development does *not* involve any change in the basic functions as outlined above. It merely involves changes in the way these functions are carried out and in the type and character of organisations which perform them.

3. Main segments of the financial system in the West

At the risk of oversimplification one can say that the Western financial system is made up of three segments. They are first banks and other depository institutions, secondly, other savings collecting organisations and finally, capital markets. Banks and other depository institutions run the payments, clearing and settlement mechanism; they collect and allocate voluntarily generated new savings and they also monitor and discipline the use of old savings. Other savings collecting institutions collect and allocate new savings, and reallocate past savings. Capital markets merely facilitate the transfer of newly generated savings to ultimate users, facilitate the transfer of old savings from one use to another, and monitor and discipline the managers and owners of old savings through the mechanism of the market for corporate control.

4. The evolution of the financial system in the West

The relative importance of these three segments changes as economy grows and expands. In the early stage of industrialisation when per capita income and wealth are relatively low the bulk of new savings is mostly collected and allocated by banks and, to a certain degree, by other depository institutions. Also during this stage a large proportion of savings generated by successful industrial and commercial enterprises, is retained and reinvested by them. As mentioned above during this stage – described as a bank orientated financial system – other savings collecting institutions, such as life assurance companies and investment and unit trusts, play a very modest role in collecting and allocating new savings and likewise capital markets play only a very limited role in channelling newly generated savings and in monitoring and disciplining the use of old savings.

The next stage of economic development is characterised by non-financial enterprises raising a growing proportion of external funds through the capital markets which are also used by non-bank savings collecting institutions for allocating new savings and reallocating past savings. The financial system during this stage is described as market oriented – the actual degree of market orientation depending also on a regulatory framework and customs.

Finally, as industrialised economies begin to change into service economies, the relative share of manufacturing in total output begins to decline, but per capita income and wealth is high and growing. The relative importance of capital markets and markets for corporate control rises, as does the reliance of non-financial and also financial enterprises on external funds raised through capital markets from ultimate savers and from non-bank savings collecting institutions. This phase is described as one of securitisation.

In short, the first stage when per capita income and wealth are beginning to increase is characterised by an increasing degree of financial intermediation by banks. During this stage increased wealth is placed in the first instance in business (owned by savers), in property (owned by savers) and in very liquid assets in cash and deposits held with banks.

In the second phase the pace of financial intermediation slows down. The slowing down of the pace of financial intermediation tends to reflect the fact that further increases in income and wealth are increasingly held by their owners in the form of financial assets other than cash and deposits and tend to be placed mainly with long-term savings collecting institutions and also to a certain degree directly in various stocks and bonds.

The third stage is characterised by disintermediation, i.e., by a decline in the relative importance of banks as new savings collecting institutions. During this stage the bulk of additions to already high per capita wealth is placed directly or indirectly through the medium of capital markets (through non-bank savings collecting institutions) in financial assets with a smaller degree of liquidity and higher risk, i.e., various securities. During this stage the significance of the market for corporate control, functioning through the capital markets, also rises rapidly.

I mentioned this aspect of the evolution of the financial system of market economies because it is relevant to the restructuring of the financial system in command economies.

5. Financial systems in planned economies

In the classical or Stalinist type of the planned economy the financial system performs *none* of these three basic functions. It *does not* collect *voluntarily* generated *new* savings – please note the emphasis on voluntary – and *does not* allocate them to uses regarded as likely to yield the highest return consistent with the risk-taking proclivity of savers. Such new savings are determined in advance by planners, extracted compulsorily in a coercive way and directed, i.e., allocated, to uses by planners – who operate in physical quantities – who have no regard for the relative risk nor the benefits in relation to opportunity costs. Neither does this type of financial system monitor the use of old savings by reference to the benefits they generate as compared with cost; it does not discipline the owners/users of past savings using the objective cost/benefits criteria, nor does it re-allocate them by using such criteria. Again, these decisions are taken by the planners, operating in the terms of quantities of various products without regard to the demand side and real resource cost.

Finally, the financial system of this type does not establish and manage the payments, clearing and settlement system with the view to economising and reducing the use of money, credit and real resources. It merely acts as a mechanism designed to ensure that the physical production and distribution targets are achieved.

In such a system money is assigned the function of a unit of account and the financial system is made up only of a limited number of specialised banks. These comprise a central bank, which issues money (see below) and provides short-term (commercial) credits to finance working capital, an investment bank, which channels funds for investment purposes in the form of grants or low-interest non-repayable loans, a savings bank and a foreign trade bank.

There are two distinct circuits of commodity and its associated monetary flows. The first covers personal sector which uses cash. All employees are paid in cash and such savings as they generate they hold in cash or place them in savings accounts with the savings bank. Such *new* savings tend to reflect above all shortages of goods and account for no more than around 5 per cent of all savings estimated at between 25 per cent and 30 per cent of net material product or for between 17 per cent and 20 per cent of gross domestic product using Western estimates.

The second circuit is between the enterprises, cooperatives and other public bodies. This uses no cash at all except for payment of wages to the household sector. All payments among enterprises and cooperatives are by means of debit and credit entries with commercial banks. Banks make such transfers only against the documents covering the movement of relevant goods. No commercial credits are allowed.

The prices charged are decided independently by planners who also decide the size of wages – each enterprise and cooperative and other public body has a 'wages fund' – and the profit margins on individual products and turnover taxes. The latter (i.e., profits and taxes) together with depreciation are passed by way of bank transfers to the state budget which in turn makes transfers to investment bank(s) to finance investment projects decided by the planners by way of grants or low interest non-repayable loans.

Foreign trade and other foreign receipts and payments are also planned and channelled through foreign trade banks and linked to domestic prices by various multipliers, the exchange rate being based on the 'gold content' of the non-convertible currency.

Money supply is designed to reflect the transactions of the household sector and is planned accordingly in an entirely passive way. Money supply is in the hands of the Central Bank which, as mentioned before, also acts as the commercial bank supervising and channelling the flow of funds linked to working capital.

There are no financial markets, i.e., money, credit, capital and foreign exchange markets. There is an insurance fund which passes on its centrally planned receipts to the budget, the relevant outflows being again provided for by the budget, in effect working on a pay-as-you-earn basis.

The basic role of the financial system in this type of economy is to act as an instrument of control to ensure the fulfilment of the economic plan formulated in quantitative terms but containing also as its important elements, the budgetary (i.e., financial) plan and monetary cash and credit plans.

That an economy so arranged has failed to engender sustainable non-inflationary growth has been proved conclusively by the events of the last forty years, and the task ahead is how to reconstruct it and what priority to give to various specific areas and problems.

What now seems clear against the background of this highly compressed outline is that the financial area together with that of industry, should obtain an overriding priority. Without according a leading place on the reform agenda to the restructuring of the finance sector, the whole process of reform will lose momentum with profoundly detrimental social and political effects.

6. The transformation of the financial system of command economies

The restructuring of the financial system of command economies requires first of all the separation of the central banking function undertaking by the Central Bank from the 'commercial banking' activities involving the channelling of new savings as directed by the planners and the control of working capital of enterprises. This process is referred to as the replacement of a 'mono-bank' by a two-tier banking system. Secondly, it requires the conversion of all commercial banks into joint stock companies. This process necessitates the creation of an appropriate capital structure for each entreprise consisting of debt and equity capital, as well as the restructuring of banks' other liabilities, i.e., loans for investment and working capital. Thirdly, it demands that banks learn to compete for newly generated savings and use them in a way which yields the highest rate of return consistent with risk-taking proclivity of their depositors. Fourthly, banks in channelling the newly generated savings must use appropriate risk-evaluating techniques. Finally, banks must manage their liabilities and assets with full regard to prudential considerations.

However, the restructuring of banking assets requires also the simultaneous restructuring of the liabilities and assets of the industrial and commercial units which have been 'financed' by commercial and investment banks. This is so because banks' assets represent the liabilities of enterprises. Such enterprises must, likewise, first be converted into limited companies and endowed with a proper capital structure. Secondly, their liabilities and assets must be so readjusted that the assets they have produce sufficient income to service capital employed by generating adequate rate of return which covers opportunity cost of capital employed, including risk premium.

While there are probably enterprises where the adjustment of assets may not require changes in their total size or composition and no reduction in the labour force, there are also probably a number of enterprises which could be viable only if either the number of assets is reduced or their composition altered or the labour force reduced, or both.

A contraction of the labour force without a reduction in assets does not cause problems of financing on the micro level although it does give rise to the problem of how to maintain employment on a macro level. A reduction in assets, however, whether or not associated with a decline in labour force, requires also a contraction in liabilities, i.e., in the loans obtained from commercial and investment banks.

The contraction and restructuring of assets of industrial units – prior to privatisation – needs a special agency capable not only of creating viable units but also of taking over full responsibility for the liabilities in the form of loans and possibly equity capital. This means that the loans enterprises owed to the banks will be replaced on banks' books by obligations issued by a special agency.

A special agency in turn will ask the government to guarantee such obligations and pay a modest positive real rate of interest and finance such liabilities by funds obtained from government. Alternatively, the agency can act merely as an intermediary, the Minister of Finance issuing directly such securities to banks and financing them from the budget by taxation or borrowing. In either case such securities issued to banks must be looked at as 'dead-weight' debt in Western countries covering war expenditure and similar spending. In such a case it is the tax payer who must carry the burden of past misallocation of resources.

At the same time banks, investment and commercial, having likewise been converted into joint stock companies with various classes of capital and deposits will have government securities or securities issued by a special agency. These securities can either be immobilised by requiring each bank to hold a certain proportion of its assets in such securities or indeed requiring the State, if holding part of the new loan or equity capital, to offset these two items against each other. In such a case the burden falling on the tax payer will be negligible.

If the process of replacing the non-viable liabilities of industry by government securities given to the banks can be and is financed by proceeds from privatisation of industrial and financial enterprises, the cost to tax payers will be lower. This in turn raises the question of the size of the non-viable debt in relation to the possibilities of obtaining adequate receipts from the sale of capital of the remaining viable enterprises.

The restructuring of banks on the lines suggested, would enable the new financial system to perform the basic function in the same way as the financial systems work in the West (i.e., collecting and allocating new savings to uses which yield highest rate of return consistent with risk, monitor and discipline the owners/managers of past savings so that they produce highest risk adjusted rate of return, and operating efficiently the payments, clearing and settlements system).

In view of the fact that per capita wealth and income in Central and Eastern European countries is relatively low it would appear desirable, in the light of historical experience in the West, that the restructured financial system should be initially centred on the banks and probably to a small extent on other depository institutions, and that capital markets, at least in the years immediately ahead, would play a relatively modest role. This view bears on the 'design' of the financial system policy-makers in these countries and in the West should be contemplating.

7. Present position in Czechoslovakia, Hungary and Poland

At present all Central and Eastern European countries have accepted the need for the creation of a 'two-tier' banking system. Three countries, Czechoslovakia, Hungary and Poland, with which this section is concerned, have converted their banks into joint stock companies. They have also accepted the need to create money, credit and capital markets and have taken steps in this direction involving the creation of new, marketable and transferable government obligations, the establishment of a stock exchange in Hungary and there are firm plans to the same effect in Poland. They have already set up, or are in the course of doing so, or are contemplating the establishment of independent long-savings collection institutions, such as life assurance companies. They all recognise the need for and are about to set up supervisory bodies designed to give protection to depositors and investors; and finally Hungary and Poland have already embarked on privatisation of non-financial enterprises, the former country successfully involving foreign capital in joint ventures.

In more specific terms, Poland has now accomplished the separation of the central banking function from commercial banking and the provincial offices of the central bank have been taken over by one of nine separate commercial banks even though the bulk of business is concentrated in three of them. All banks are permitted to handle business throughout the country and to compete for deposits and use funds wherever they wish. Despite the establishment of one new private bank and the presence of some foreign banks by way of representative offices, the degree of competition is very limited and the assumption of the functions performed by Western banks has hardly started. This is so mainly because no significant progress has been made in the restructuring of industry and commerce and the very slow process of privatisation, notwithstanding the fact that the statutory basis for this has been put in place. There is a plan to establish a modern stock exchange to be modelled on the French example to replace the existing very primitive and *ad hoc* arrangements. There are also plans to establish a modern type of life and non-life insurance industry. In short, the basic foundation stones have either already been put in place or are being created but the process of making the new structure work together with the restructuring of industry has as yet to begin in earnest.

Hungary is in a similar position to that of Poland. Although there are some ten banks, the bulk of business is in the hands of three. The progress of privatisation has been faster than in Poland and, as mentioned already, has involved participation of foreign capital both by way of joint ventures and investment in newly listed Hungarian companies. However, looked at in a longer prospective the progress achieved so far, though satisfactory, is still modest. There is a stock exchange now covering government securities and also debt and equity in a small number of privatised companies. It is true to say that the significance of the capital market is very limited. The banks collect and allocate new savings but in performing the latter function (allocation) the degree of freedom they have is still limited in that they still have to fund old clients. In sum the new financial system in Hungary has now a sound basis from which to operate but is still constrained because of a limited advance made in the restructuring of industry and commerce.

In Czechoslovakia the legal basis for privatisation is now in place, the existing banks have been converted into limited companies but advances in the restructuring of industry and the reorientation of finance have been negligible. Privatisation and restructuring of industry has not yet started. There is no stock exchange. The banking system is still made up of two commercial banks, two investment banks, the savings bank and the foreign trade bank. The whole process of changing the way the financial system functions has yet to start.

8. Some wider implications

This examination of the role of the financial system in what used to be and to some extent still are planned economies tends to suggest that the process of structural reform of the financial system and of industry must proceed, to the extent that this is possible, or be carried our simultaneously with the broad macroeconomic programme. This implies that the sequencing of various measures should place this element on the top of the economic agenda rather than lower down and that unless this is done the cost of transition, in terms of loss of output, unemployment and inflation is likely to be higher than necessary.

The second point arising from our examination is that the main burden of establishing the basic functions the financial system must perform must inevitably fall on the banking system, simply because at the present stage of economic development other segments of the financial system are not suited to this role, be it with regard to the collection and allocation of new savings and the monitoring and disciplining of managers and/or owners of past savings. While non-bank financial institutions and capital markets are needed, their role for some time to come will be relatively modest.

This view implies that the efforts of policy-makers should be concentrated in the immediate future above all on the restructuring of the banking system and of industry both by changing the framework within which they operate and also by developing necessary managerial skills including that of risk assessment.

The third point bears on monetary policy and the process of monetary privatisation. Such evidence as exists about the ability of private sector to buy newly restructured industrial and financial companies tends to indicate that this is very limited. Furthermore, as shown by the British experience of privatisation, the bulk of risk and debt capital so purchased is likely to be sold only to the buyers capable and willing to acquire and hold them and that such buyers in Eastern Europe must be banks.

This has important implications for monetary policy if the prices of newly issued shares are not to collapse, and poses some important questions. Although the ability of individuals to buy newly issued obligations can be increased by offering them to employees on favourable terms, or making arrangements for individuals to pay for them by instalments, or making bank credit available for this purpose, the basic problem of how to handle this from the monetary policy point of view remains.

9. Conclusions

This chapter has tried to see what should be the proper role of the financial system in Central and Eastern European countries as they pass through a transitional period from authoritarian, command economies into democratically based market economies. To do so we have first tried to show in a highly compressed way what functions the financial system has performed and performs in the developed countries of the West. How the relative importance of the various functions has changed and how the financial system has evolved as they progressed from poor agricultural economies to rich industrial and service economies.

Secondly, we have endeavoured to outline in a summary manner the functions of the financial system in command economies and to show how they have performed and how they differ from those in the West.

Thirdly, against this background we have attempted to indicate what needs to be done to transform the financial system in the East so that it can assume and efficiently discharge the functions performed by the financial system in the West and also to indicate what type of financial system, at the present stage of economic development, can be expected to suit them best and enable them to move to the path of self-sustaining and non-inflationary growth.

Our conclusions were that the restructuring of the financial system must be undertaken simultaneously with the restructuring of non-financial enterprises, that this process requires a contraction of the liabilities of non-viable and not properly structured non-financial firms, and that there must be a corresponding contraction of the assets of commercial and credit banks. Such an operation can be best undertaken by a special agency (as has been done in Eastern Germany) which can take the burden of non-viable industrial enterprise liabilities and replace it with its own obligations. Such operations can be financed either from the budget or later result in removing the newly created liabilities of a special agency with receipts from privatisation.

Of course, a similar approach must be adopted towards banks which would work on the basis of a two-tier system and which should be placed within the regulatory framework of universal banking.

The important conclusion arrived at was that this element of transition should be placed on top of the sequencing of various measures and unless this is done the cost of transition may be higher than necessary with detrimental effects in the social and political areas.

Bibliography

Davies, A.A. (1958), *The Development of the Soviet Budgetary System*, Cambridge University Press. Cambridge.

Finansi i socialisczni struitel (in Russian), Moscow: Gozfinanzdat, 1959

Meznerics, I. (1986), *Banking Business in Socialist Countries*, Leyden: A.W. Sijhoff.

Rybczynski, T.M. (1985), 'Banking in the USSR', in H.L. Auborn (ed.), *Comparative Banking*, London: Waterlow.

Rybczynski, T.M. (1985), 'Shifting financial frontiers: implications for financial institutions', in D.E. Fair, *Shifting Frontiers in Finance*, Dordrecht: Martinus Nijhoff.

Rybczynski, T.M. (1986), 'The internationalisation of the financial system and the developing countries', *World Bank Staff Working Paper*, 188, World Bank, Washington DC.

Rybczynski, T.M. (1987), 'The anatomy of financial crises, a comment', in R. Portes and A. Swoboda (eds.), *Threats to International Financial Stability*, International Centre for Monetary and Banking Studies and CEPR.

Rybczynski, T.M. (1988), 'Financial system and industrial restructuring', *National Westminster Bank Quarterly Review*, November.

Usokin, M.M. (1957), *Organizacja i planowanie kratkosrocza kredita* (in Russian), Gozfinanzdat.

CHAPTER FIFTEEN

The role of multilateral lenders in the reform process of Eastern European countries

Jacques Girard

1. Introduction

The intention of this chapter is to present a few observations on the analytics of adjustment programmes in the Eastern European economies and to illustrate some particularly important issues. The role of multilateral organisations is in effect to support the historic transformation sweeping across these countries, with unprecedented challenges to their governments and the international community. These challenges have been rendered even more difficult by severe external economic disturbances, namely the collapse of the COMECON economic and trade system and the shift to hard currency accounting and payments, the growing uncertainty concerning the supply of fuels from the Soviet Union and the impact of the Gulf crisis. To what extent these shocks could undermine the process of structural reform is a crucial issue, which affects the scope and design of multilateral organisations' interventions.

Given the number and complexity of problems involved, and their close interrelationships, there is no simple solution for solving the puzzle which, furthermore, changes its composition and its form as a result of the dynamics of the transition process. The following presentation is thus more like the enumeration of question marks with some elements to answer them, rather than an integrated approach.

2. The roots of the economic crisis

In reviewing the issues regarding adjustment, one must be aware that Eastern European economies constitute a diverse group at different stages of development, of greatly varying size and with different histories, traditions and factor endowments. During the past decades, they have been introducing relatively comprehensive economic and institutional reforms that have modified them, to varying degrees, from typical Soviet-type centrally planned economies to ones in which market forces have been allowed to play an increasing, but still limited, role. Nevertheless, up to very recently these countries have continued to retain fundamental common features, namely: pervasive administrative intervention and control pursued in order to achieve economic and social objectives, social ownership of most means of production and the secondary and subordinate role of the private sector.

Growing macroeconomic imbalances and heavy debt burdens have grabbed centre stage in the current discussions on the priorities, making a case for shock tactics as opposed to a more gradual approach. This is a new situation, in the sense that during the 1980s the performance of the traditional centrally planned economies did not appear to be such that the situation could be characterised as one of imminent economic crisis. For these economies there was no economic disaster threatening that would have urged sudden radical change. Indeed, the situation was one of stagnation, with a decline of productivity increase to zero, highlighting long-run problems rather than the threat of crisis (Sachs and Lipton, 1990a). Now one should not forget that a difference in dynamism with Western European countries (East versus West Germany, Czechoslovakia versus Austria . . .) was thus increasing with the resurgence of European performance in the mid-1980s. But, still, that failure of the centrally planned economies certainly did not look the same as imminent economic crisis even if there was already some concern about their growing external debt. In other words, some years ago the central problem of transition management seemed to be one of structural reforms, macroeconomic stabilisation being hardly mentioned at all in debates. Actually, what happened is that the reform process initiated by the forerunners, Poland and Yugoslavia, has coincided with a substantial acceleration in the inflation rate. Why was it so?

Such imbalance could not have developed without lax monetary policies. The important point is that monetary policy has been overly expansionary to cover deficits not in the fiscal budget but in the enterprise and banking sector, which have accumulated heavy losses, becoming apparent only in the late 1980s. Thanks to lax credits, investment accumulated in capital goods that was not consistent with the countries' comparative advantages and their products could not sell at a profit in the international markets or in an unprotected domestic market. Therefore, those investments were a source of loss from the very beginning and resulted in an excess of expenditure over income for the country as a whole. Such losses were masked with protection and could be sustained without a decline in the standard of living through large external borrowing. When finally the inflow of money decelerated and when heavy payments started to fall due, those countries which had relied most on external financing were faced with a deep foreign debt crisis. The authorities responded to the threatening crisis by partial reforms, which simply accentuated financial imbalances (Kornai, 1990).

In their attempts to decentralise the economy, the authorities gave more freedom to enterprises, which were nevertheless still not constrained by normal competition rules. Production remained highly monopolised, protected from international competition, and last but not least had the wrong incentives (Hare, 1990). Workers pushed for higher wages, either because they controlled management or because the managers had no reason to resist, as they borrowed funds whenever they could, either from the banking system or from each other (interenterprise credits). The authorities pumped money into the economy at increasing rates, partly to satisfy the enterprises' ambitious requests for investment funds, partly to avoid closing down loss-making firms and partly to subsidise consumer goods. By this route, the fall into a remarkable combination of accelerated inflation, massive shortages and an external liquidity crisis was in effect unavoidable. Looking to the future, the crucial issue is thus that stabilisation and systematic reform are both needed simultaneously: everything on the reform agenda is urgent (Sachs and Lipton, 1990a).

3.   The sequencing of a stabilisation and systematic reform programme

How quickly, and with what combination and sequence of measures can reforms be implemented that will allow a market-based supply response of enterprises to macro-economic stabilisation? This single question actually raises a number of complex features (Solimano, 1990).

Looking back at the 1980s and the failure of the piecemeal approach to reform attempted by Communist regimes in Hungary, Poland, Yugoslavia and the Soviet Union, gives a clearer view of the mechanisms involved. In the initial stages of reform, price liberalisation tends to lead to price increases as the pent up demand for all kinds of goods brings suppressed inflation into the open. Both inflation and inefficiency, however, have been fed by soft constraints on enterprises, and especially through unrestrained access to credit, allowing for wage increases which further fuel inflation without concern for efficiency. With highly rigid economic structures, namely monopolistic state firms and limited mobility of both labour and capital, the impact of a tight macroeconomic policy could be excessively high social costs. With interlocking supply and production ties among enterprises, demand and liquidity constraints would lead to a chain effect of enterprise failures, independently of their economic and financial soundness.

The challenge is then how to rapidly implement policy reform packages which encourage efficient responses and limit output decline. Unfortunately, most components of such reforms require institutional and behavioural changes, which by nature are slow. In other terms, it seems highly unlikely that it will be possible to avoid a huge decrease in production during stabilisation, putting at risk even the efficient sectors of the economy. In these socialist economies, there is no way of identifying which firms should go bankrupt and which should be allowed to stay in operation, because the price system is so highly distorted. If it were not so, some interim solution could be thought of, for example financing selected enterprises' deficits through the government budget rather than through the banking system, with a view to phasing out aid over time. The approach could be designed so as to limit strains on the budget at a time when fiscal discipline is important. Nevertheless, as long as the right set of prices is unknown, nobody knows how to select enterprises economically eligible for assistance.

This suggests that macroeconomic stabilisation measures must be implemented in conjunction with the liberalisation of prices, so that accurate signals are sent to the policy-makers. But here the question of monopolistic pricing arises, with the bias of cost-plus practices having proven the impossibility of determining a rational set of prices. In turn, a demonopolisation preceding macroeconomic adjustment presents another dead end, as the kind of enterprise restructuring that is necessary can only be learned in the context of actual market performance. Furthermore, market competition requires the private sector to have a prominent share of the economy, which implies the privatisation of state enterprises. The latter cannot be properly achieved unless a reliable price structure allows a reliable valuation of firms. How then to get out of this dilemma?

The crucial step introduced under the auspices of the International Monetary Fund was to recognise that international trade was the most effective means to instil competition in the economy. Allowing foreign firms to import freely into these countries (and domestic firms to export freely to the convertible currency area) would immediately put domestic state enterprises under intense competition, at least for traded goods, and create a realistic structure of prices. This opening requires two major decisions: *the convertibility of the currency*, on the current account, and *the elimination of all trade barriers*, including import quotas and excessive tariffs (Giluran, 1990). A second major element introduced was to accelerate the liberalisation of the economy, in parallel with macroeconomic stabilisation. Thus, restrictions on the private sector had to be done away with as soon as possible and specific sectors demonopolised by dividing large multiplant enterprises into several independent units. Small-scale privatisation was urged, but large-scale privatisation of major enterprises, given the colossal scale of the reform, had to follow the initial stage of stabilisation and liberalisation.

The reform agenda of course extends well beyond these issues of stabilisation and transition management (CIA, 1990). For all of the countries of Eastern Europe, the task is not merely to dismantle the command system: it is the long-term task of building from scratch the architecture and the core components of modern market economies. From this perspective, four broad areas of reform and systematic change are critical (Kenen, 1990): reform of the enterprise system and modernisation of the obsolete means of production, modernisation of infrastructure, establishment of institutions supportive of a market-oriented economy, restructuring of the energy sector and rehabilitation of the environment. This radical set of reforms calls for a great deal of investment in the private and public sectors. Just to give an idea, a recent rough estimate has given a figure of 2000 billion ecu, or 500 per cent of the EEC's yearly gross fixed investment, the capital needed to bring Central and Eastern economies up to the level of the average West European economy. Needless to say, even split over the next twenty years, domestic capital cannot afford this. External capital is obviously essential, and the role of multilateral development agencies crucial in providing both resources and assistance to help select priorities, design efficient investments and ensure improved access of Eastern countries to external financing.

4. New external constraints and sectorial priorities

As they reach a particularly difficult stage in the process of structural reform, Eastern countries are faced with severe external economic disturbances: the impact of the COMECON price reform on 1 January 1991, the consequences of the Gulf crisis, notably the increase in oil prices, and the growing uncertainty concerning the supply of oil and gas from the Soviet Union, with respect to both deliveries and price.

Since the beginning of 1991, trade among CMEA countries is settled in convertible currencies. At the same time, trade prices are gradually adjusted to reflect world market prices. These changes are clearly in line with the domestic price reforms in these economies, and should play an essential role in this regard. The size of the adjustment is nevertheless considerable as concerns the terms of trade and external payments. Of course, there are many conceptual problems associated with a quantification of the likely impact of the COMECON price reform, and uncertainties prevail on how world market prices can be established. Nevertheless, a number of estimates, using a sectorial breakdown of trade, have concluded that the result will be a substantial terms of trade loss for Eastern European countries. There is a broad consensus that the reform will combine a decline in the export price of these countries to the Soviet Union, with a dramatic increase in the prices of oil and raw material exports from the Soviet Union to its COMECON partners. Individual losses will of course vary according to the share of their trade and their oil dependency.

These external shocks simply cannot be absorbed, given the level of external debt already achieved, without a major adjustment, either forced (as currently in Bulgaria) or through a similar process as the one experienced in the OECD area following the two oil shocks in 1974 and 1979. Nevertheless, from a macroeconomic point of view, in the short term a further decline in output and demand and an accelerated inflation are forecasted. Given the already unstable economic situation of most of these countries, and the fact that structural adjustment has barely started, the most vulnerable countries cannot rely on private international capital markets for bridging the external gap. The additional financing needs will have to be met from international institutions and bilateral official sources, reinforcing the pressure for accelerating the path of structural reforms, which should additionally incorporate urgent and specific measures dealing with the problems of the energy sector.

Drastic structural changes in the energy sector are needed, country by country, and from a global point of view (CEC, 1990). The Eastern countries have energy intensities on average three times those of the Western market economies. This situation results primarily from a system of pricing totally delinked from true resource costs and associated generalised wastes at all stages, from production to final consumption. A second important feature of the energy sector is that Eastern countries rely heavily (90 per cent) on imports of fuels, oil and gas, and, to a lesser extent, on electricity from the Soviet Union. Already, the USSR has unilaterally reduced exports to CMEA countries in 1990, and has announced further cuts in supply next year. Clearly a diversification of energy imports and improved interconnections are needed. Both issues mentioned should be approached on a broad regional basis. Furthermore there is a strong political case for integrating help towards Eastern Europe with the Western Soviet Union plan in preparation, thereby enhancing, from a Community perspective, the notion of a pan-European scheme.

The interrelated issue of environmental damage should also be mentioned. Intensive use of energy, with highly inadequate pollution abatement techniques, has been underway for decades. The resulting impact on the environment has had dramatic results on the health of the regional population, has affected economic activity with highly adverse costs, has contributed to acid rain regionally and in other countries, and has added to the pollution of the seas and of the earth's atmosphere. Additionally, some of the countries possess nuclear power stations which may not meet currently accepted safety standards.

The nexus of the issues outlined above, in the context of the dramatic macroeconomic and political changes currently sweeping Eastern countries, constitutes a unique and unprecedented development management challenge. The structural macroeconomic transition cannot avoid placing a major emphasis on energy production and consumption. The complexity of policy, institutional and physical adjustment in this sector, and the need for massive investment for greater efficiency and relaxed import costs, call for a large increase in technical assistance and expertise from Western countries. Energy (or electricity) plus Soviets was the key for transition to socialism, Lenin used to say. Energy, even not along the same line, is also the key for transition to the market.

5. Cooperation among multilateral organisations

To address simultaneously such complex and interrelated issues, multilateral organisations had, at the outset, clearly to divide the tasks, to agree on priorities and to coordinate closely. Given the special emphasis on the need to stabilise the economy and restore basic internal and external equilibria, the International Monetary Fund took the lead, in cooperation with other institutions and governments. Hence an agreement with the IMF on a stabilisation programme was made a *sine qua non* condition for interventions by the G-24 countries, the European Commission and the World Bank. Such a condition avoided external assistance to these countries being diverted from its original goal. The Hungarian situation in late 1989 is a good example, when the former communist regime, still in power, was negotiating simultaneously with the IMF and the European Commission, the latter being asked for a balance of payments loan. Clearly, that facility could have offered the government more freedom to resist the austerity measures that the IMF had long claimed necessary, but that were delayed in view of the forthcoming elections.

The IMF conditionality ensured that general finance for short- to medium-term objectives, not related to specific investment projects, could be optimally scaled and included in a consistent macroeconomic policy framework (Tith, 1990). Balance of payments loans, contributions to Reserve funds (as in Poland, and soon likely in Czechoslovakia) and, to a large extent, structural adjustment loans by the World Bank, thus all depend on the establishment of the IMF programme and the recognition of its objectives for actual successive disbursements. This coherent approach should also be considered, taking into account the collapse of the framework for trade in Eastern Europe. A shift to trade at world prices, including recent energy price increases, will lead to major trade-balance changes. Whatever the size and timing of the problem, Eastern Europe will need help from Western institutions in a coordinated way. The philosophy supporting the European Commission initiative is to coordinate G-24 specific financial action, conditional on IMF intervention. An interesting related issue for these countries in their move from bilateral trade to current-account convertibility is the pertinence of the European Payment Union model prevailing between Western European countries from 1950 to 1958. Here again, whatever the solution adopted (it has been argued that an EPU solution would slow the process of adjustment to international competition), it is clear that a Western coordinated assistance scheme, subject to IMF conditionality, is the most rational and efficient.

As argued above, experience so far indicates the absolute necessity to pay early attention to the supply aspects of the transition, which should ideally be dealt with at the same time and with the same rigour as demand management, instead of being left to lag behind. In this context, World Bank initiatives have appeared crucial in Poland and in Hungary to initiate structural changes and systematic transformation. Structural adjustment loans (SALs) in Poland and Hungary have established the broad guidelines for enterprise restructuring and privatisation, and financial sector reform. More traditional World Bank operations in the productive sectors, including energy and infrastructure, have strengthened and deepened the impact of reforms at the subsector and enterprise level. Because of their impressive amounts (total World Bank commitments in the financial year 1990 in Eastern European countries were 1.9 billion dollars or 12 per cent of total World Bank lending, and are projected at about 2.5 billion dollars in financial year 1991), their careful sectorial preparation, their technical assistance components and studies, and their policy action, World Bank interventions tended to give a framework for interventions by other institutions in these sectors at an early stage. Another interesting scheme, through which World Bank interventions are expanded, is its Expanded Cofinancing Operations (ECO) programme, under which partial guarantee is given to a country's international borrowing for financing designated projects; this scheme was used in July 1990 to help Hungary access international capital markets. This prominence of World Bank operations tends to become more balanced, as the size of external interventions needed is such as to imply the involvement of all other international institutions, bilateral institutions and commercial banks.

Project financing in Eastern countries, during this phase of transition, almost systematically raises issues at a sectorial level, or even at a regional level. In energy and environment, for instance, institutional and policy reforms, accompanying a clear development plan, are essential for any investment project to succeed. As the size of investments required clearly exceeds the available resources of any single institution, and as the dimension of the problems involved is much larger in scope than the local/national level, international cooperation is essential to ensure rationality and mobilisation of resources. Hence, sectorial programmes at a regional level have been, or are on the point of being, established: the Baltic Sea Environmental Programme, the Energy Regional Programme, the Regional Transport Projects (TEM, TER). It is interesting to note that never before have such a range of problems been addressed by all multilateral organisations in such close cooperation on such a scale.

References

Central Intelligence Agency (1990), 'Eastern Europe: long road ahead to economic well being', Paper presented to the Joint Economic Committee, 16 May.

Commission of the European Community (1990), 'Energy for a new century. Energy outlook of the USSR and Eastern Europe', Working Document W:13, Directorate General for Energy, May.

Giluran, M.G. (1990), 'Heading for currency convertibility', *Finance and Development*, September.

Hare, P.G. (1990), 'From central planning to market economy: some micro economic issues'. *The Economic Journal*, 100, June.

Kenen, P.B. (1990), 'Transitional arrangements for trade and payments among the CMEA countries', IMF Working Paper, unpublished manuscript, September.

Kornai, J. (1990), 'The affinity between ownership forms and coordination mechanisms: the common experience of reform in socialist countries', *Journal of Economic Perspective*, 4 (3), Summer.

Lamb G. (1987), 'Managing economic policy change', Institutional Dimensions. World Bank Discussion Paper No. 14.

Sachs, J. and Lipton, D. (1990a), 'Poland's economic reform', *Foreign Affairs*, Summer.

Sachs, J. and Lipton, D. (1990b) 'Creating a market economy in Eastern Europe: the case of Poland', *Brookings Papers on Economic Activity* I.

Solimano, A. (1990), 'Macro-economic adjustment, stabilisation and growth in reforming socialist economies', World Bank Working Paper, April.

Tith, N. (1990), *Reform and Adjustment in Centrally Planned Economies: Current Issues*, IMF Institute, July.

CHAPTER SIXTEEN

Outlook for finance and banking in Central and Eastern Europe: strategic imperatives and foreign capital

James T. Larkin

1. Introduction

Over the past year we have witnessed a confluence of geo-political events that are truly epoch in proportion:

- The disintegration of communism in Central and Eastern Europe and the introduction of democracy, liberalisation and market economies.
- The unification of Germany.
- Major steps toward the economic integration of Western Europe.
- The dismantling of the Warsaw Pact.
- The Charter of Paris for a new Europe agreed among thirty-four North American and European states ending as much as seventy years of confrontation and division for some.

The Charter of Paris celebrates Europhorically the climax of all of these events and adopts a blueprint for unity, democracy and prosperity among the members of the Atlantic Alliance and the East.

But the grandiose terms of that charter do not address the question of economic aid and financial assistance requisite to the successful political and economic transformation of the East; nor do they address how one balances achieving the goals of the European Community's internal market on a timely basis with achieving the goals of a permanent liberalised, democratic, market-oriented Eastern Europe – both of which are equally urgent as guarantors of peace and security.

President Mitterand has sounded a call to action when he says that: 'We Europeans have 10 years in which to win our race against history.'

While I agree with the urgency of his message, I don't think we have ten years. And it is not simply a European race against history, but a race of the Atlantic Alliance against history.

I consider the next five years to be the most perilous time in history – for the Atlantic Alliance, for the European Community and for Central and Eastern Europe.

In order to transform Central and Eastern Europe into market economies urgent steps must be taken now to:

- develop viable local capital markets by restructuring Eastern European banks;

- infuse capital in the form of governmental aid to finance regional projects rather than local country projects;
- provide education and technical expertise on how to operate within market economies.

The great peril is that this is either not happening or not happening fast enough. And if these steps are not taken urgently there exists the very real possibility that the recent ideological divide in Europe will be supplanted by a social and economic divide that will threaten the very democratic goals that have been achieved. And that portends a threat to the security, peace and prosperity of the Atlantic Alliance, the European Community and the East.

Let's examine why Westerners have not developed a cohesive strategy for dealing with Central and Eastern Europe. There are several reasons:

- Insufficient understanding of the general economic and financial conditions of the East.
- Lack of understanding of the diversity of the East.
- The focus on and the cost of German unification.
- Priorities attendant to completion of the European Community's internal market.
- The crisis among Western banks.

2. Insufficient understanding of the general economic and financial conditions of the East

Transition to democracy and a free market system means jettisoning much, if not all, of the system of centralised resource allocation including monopolistic production structures, autarkic trade policies, non-convertible currencies and a pervasive system of subsidised prices.

It is difficult for most Westerners to obtain firm and detailed information in a rapidly changing situation in which there are no reliable statistics and most laws and customs have been developed from unfamiliar Marxist–Leninist principles.

Westerners are confronted with the legacy of planned economies. There is no true commercial infrastructure; the legal system was not designed to cope with standalone shareholder owned companies; property rights are non-existent; and banks have no experience in making credit judgements. In effect, there is no experience of competition which was shunned in favour of inherently inefficient, subsidised monopolies. And, of course, investment decisions were highly political resulting in increased debt rather than productivity.

One must understand that the Leninist–Stalinist tradition imposed a remarkable homogeneity on the economic systems of countries which had previously attained very different degrees of economic development – a homogeneity characterised by the systemic distortions intrinsic to centralised planned economies and the macrostabilisation problems which are the consequence of excess demand created by the system.

3. Lack of understanding of the diversity in the East

However, in generalising about the East one has to keep in mind the diversity. Eastern Europe is no longer a 'Bloc – there is the re-emergence of the Hanseatic League States in the Baltic, the re-emergence of Central Europe and the threatening re-Balkanization of South Eastern Europe. And economic character and experience of the countries is different.'

3.1 POLAND

After a decade of piecemeal reforms, Poland was no closer in mid-1989 to a market economy. The latest Polish 'model' adopted in 1990 has introduced a radical economic stabilisation programme but is threatened by a failure to introduce structural reforms alongside. Poland and probably several other Eastern European countries need to create a capital market if they are to stimulate a lasting economic revival which is self-sustaining.

3.2 HUNGARY

If the economic problems of Poland have received the most publicity over the past decade, those of Hungary are no less fundamental. Economic reform began in the 1960s but its objectives were not real reform but rather to demonstrate how market socialism was superior to market capitalism. So for years a mixed system obtained, where on the one hand full employment was the priority at the expense of inefficiency and low labour productivity, and on the other decentralising reforms were introduced which put Hungary far ahead of other Comecon members. The right of individuals to engage in private activities and the role of entrepreneurship were recognised. But despite these radical changes Hungary is still far from being a market economy.

Hungary is now encountering both domestic and international problems as a result of the systematic failure of its earlier 'dual dependency' which subjected managers to apparent market disciplines while still being subject to overriding political and social constraints. This situation was further complicated by unreliability of such market signals as were available, given the serious distortions in prices, interest rates and exchange rates. The recent social unrest and the government's retreat over petrol price increases emphasises the challenges of adjustment domestically.

Externally Hungary faces a serious debt service bill which in proportion to its GDP is higher than that of Poland.

If it were not for an IMF programme, as well as the considerable efforts of the EC on behalf of the international community generally, Hungary would be unable to meet its obligations.

3.3 CZECHOSLOVAKIA

Superficially Czechoslovakia looks healthier than either Poland or Hungary due to its very low level of international debt. However, this very lack of foreign capital means that technological innovation remained slow and the industrial structure and machinery is even more outdated than elsewhere in North Eastern Europe.

Now, thanks to its low debt burden, Czechoslovakia should be able to attract some of the best terms in the international market. However, lenders will want to see full convertibility and/or investment protection guarantees. Full convertibility will require a unified exchange rate and the more fundamental market-orientated reform of the domestic economy.

In order to make convertibility a worthwhile policy objective, therefore, an effective system of price formation must be set in place, linking domestic prices to world market forces.

4. The focus on and cost of German unification

Clearly one of the major sources of private bank funding and government aid to Eastern and Central Europe might have been Germany.

But the cost of German unity is worrisome for both West Germans and their neighbours. Earlier assessments of the cost were substantially overoptimistic. As a result, for German unification alone, Germany will become an active borrower on international capital markets despite its current-account surplus which is weakening.

This will keep international interest rates high and be another inhibitor to aiding the Eastern and Central European region.

And the transfer of payments to East Germany – estimated by the Bundesbank to exceed DM100 billion in 1991 alone – could and probably will complicate negotiations for the EMU.

5. Priorities for completion of the EC's internal market

For those of you who may have forgotten, Franz Josef Strauss after his years as West Germany's Defence Minister, published in 1965 a remarkable book, *The Grand Design*. It was remarkable for its honesty and political realism.

It was even more remarkable because Franz Josef Strauss was prescient – he foretold of future events and recommended solutions to events that would transpire twenty-five years later – now – in 1990 – and one of those events was the positive influence of a unified Western Europe on the East.

He said:

> a massive drive to achieve, step by step, a European political federation
> . . . would provide a powerful attraction to these Eastern European
> countries now under communist domination.

Strauss *was* prescient. Only in 1985 did the engine of European unity, at least in the economic sense, get restarted under the Delors Plan for 1992.

And clearly the economic integration of Western Europe *has* provided a powerful attraction to the Eastern European countries. And while the political and economic systems of those countries have been disintegrating for years, the ultimate moves towards democracy and liberalisation of the last year have received a large impetus from events in Western Europe – not the least of which is *Europe 1992*.

But events of 1990 raise questions.

- Should some of the currently dedicated financial resources being invested by members of the Community in completing the internal market be allocated to the East where they would provide much needed capital to support democratisation and economic change?
- Should the Eastern countries be integrated into the common market now?
- And would the integration of Eastern countries into the European Community delay, postpone or defeat the objectives of 1992?

As an interested observer, my answer to the first two is no. And my answer to the third question is yes.

Just as the government of Germany is recognising that they will have to look on East and West Germany as two different economic areas for several years, I am impressed with the suggestion of some German economists that we look on the

European Community and Eastern Europe as two separate, integrated markets of two different market velocities equalising over time.

One would suggest that nothing should be allowed to interfere with the economic integration of Western Europe by 1992. Why? Because an integrated Western Europe – unified either economically or politically – is a guarantee of a peaceful Europe both West and East. Political federation is not the real objective. Economic integration is not the real objective. These are only a means to a greater end. And that end is a peaceful Europe – a peaceful Europe for your children and my children.

But giving this priority to completion of the internal market is once again an inhibitor to providing aid to the East.

6. The crisis among Western banks

Private commercial banks historically have been a major source of lending to developing countries. But at this critical time it can be said quite authoritatively that the Western private banks in the aggregate have no meaningful strategy for Central and Eastern Europe.

With a few notable exceptions, the banks around the world are no longer in a position to provide unlimited investment in, or funding for, major international activities.

The unprecedented strong growth of banks around the world over the last two decades has ended as they count the cost of overzealous lending and unsustainable international expansion.

The new capital standards introduced last year by the Bank for International Settlements in Basle have added to banks' operating costs by forcing them to raise billions of dollars in new equity.

7. The consequences of not doing enough

There are several reasons why Westerners have not yet developed a cohesive strategy for dealing with Central and Eastern Europe.

But let us reflect for a moment on the consequences of not doing enough.

● Unfulfilled expectations and economic problems can adversely impact the development of democracy.

- Economic reform can be defeated by disintegration of the Soviet Union by what President Gorbachev has referred to as 'Unbridled nationalism and mindless separatism'.
- Ethnic divisions will re-emerge all over Eastern Europe. It was just a year ago that John Paul II warned that we must be careful that the rapid political changes in the East don't unleash nationalistic feelings and ethnic conflicts.

But already we have the problem of minorities and nationalities arising again in Hungary, Romania, Bulgaria and Czechoslovakia – problems that have already pushed Yugoslavia to civil war.

- The split of Europe into a wealthy Europe and a poor Europe.
- The specter of a flood of migrants from the East to a more promising future in Western Europe – the United Nations estimates it could be as many as 25 million people.

It is eminently clear that economic failure in the East will result in uncontrolled migration to the West.

And all of this can result in an economic and political instability that will threaten democracy and economic reform in the East, prosperity and peace in the West. We could all be back where we were in 1914 with problems emerging in Europe with greater intensity than in the past.

For this reason, Atlantic Alliance governments should urgently develop a common strategy for helping democratise and economically develop the Central and Eastern European region.

8. Three necessary steps to transform Central and Eastern Europe into market economies

8.1 DEVELOP VIABLE LOCAL CAPITAL MARKETS BY RESTRUCTURING EASTERN EUROPEAN BANKS

Eastern European countries need to create a capital market from within if they are to stimulate revival which is self-sustaining.

In his American Express Bank award winning essay, Dr Larry Brainand of Bankers Trust Company points out that:

> The reason why such efforts have so far failed is that they have not yet addressed the balance sheet losses that lie at the heart of the problem.

He suggests that:

The only effective way to implement financial discipline is . . . to clean up the balance sheets of enterprises and banks.

Since restructuring of enterprise balance sheets will assist in eliminating bank losses from ongoing credit activities, he suggests that 'restructuring of enterprises and banks should, therefore, proceed together'.

However, banks should be treated differently than enterprises given their 'pivotal role in the financial system'.

The banks should be restructured and:

The best way to do this is to recapitalise the banks by first lifting the bad loans out of their portfolio and then providing a mechanism for injecting new capital. One approach used in Chile in the mid-1980s and now being implemented in Yugoslavia is for the government to 'purchase' the banks' bad loans (identified by means of a special portfolio audit) with long-term bonds paying a positive net income flow from the government bonds. Given improved accounting practices and effective prudential supervision, the banks could be transformed into profitable institutions to form the core of an emergent capital market structure.

The government would have to absorb the losses on the bad loans and transfer new resources to the banks via interest payments on the bonds. These actions could prove costly to the fiscal budget, but removing such losses in a one-step operation with fiscal costs spread over the life of the bonds is likely to be less costly than doing nothing. This action is essential to eliminate the mis-allocation of resources by the banks and to facilitate the creation of a capital market. It should also discourage the disintermediation of credit flows outside the banking system, thus improving the central bank's ability to control monetary conditions.

8.2 INFUSE CAPITAL IN THE FORM OF GOVERNMENTAL AID TO FINANCE REGIONAL PROJECTS RATHER THAN LOCAL COUNTRY PROJECTS

Major efforts have been mounted to provide aid to Central and Eastern Europe:

- The European Bank for Reconstruction and Development with an initial capital of $13 billion.
- The European Community has committed over $30 billion.
- The IMF and the World Bank have committed close to $20 billion.
- And a commitment of some $370 million by the US Congress for 1991.

But these sums are paltry when confronted with the immensity of the task. Moreover the funds tend to be given to individual governments and to individual local projects rather than to the region as a whole. And that can be a major error and a formula for failure as the United States learned in the 1970s.

The current situation in Eastern Europe is not unlike the economic prostration in Western Europe in the late 1940s. The answer then was not targeted sums to individual governments, but a Marshall Plan for the economic recovery of all of Western Europe.

Would it not make sense now for the European Community, Canada and the United States, working together, to mount an Atlantic Plan for the recovery of Eastern Europe and wouldn't this address the question of economic aid and financial assistance left out of the Charter of Paris?

In an Atlantic Plan there could be a role for the private banks to assist in financing recovery. But this would probably involve some form of guarantees by the governments participating in the plan.

8.3 PROVIDE EDUCATION AND TECHNICAL EXPERTISE ON HOW TO OPERATE WITHIN MARKET ECONOMIES

Otherwise the Western banks have taken a very cautious approach to Eastern Europe. No major role is anticipated in the short run in the domestic markets and the main emphasis seems to be on servicing Western customers as they are expanding their presence in the region.

Much of the cautious attitude of bankers towards Eastern Europe can be explained by the current crisis they are experiencing and the repercussions of the LDC debt crisis of the 1980s. After a huge expansion of the loans to Third World countries in the 1970s, many banks found themselves having to write off large amounts of uncollectable debt.

And it is doubtful that there will be any meaningful transfer of foreign capital into commercial banking in the Eastern economies until financial market restructuring takes place.

On the other hand there is a major role that Western banks can play in education and training. While the investment would be relatively small, the yield would be enormous.

Let me give an example of what I mean. I believe that the Western banks should perform the following roles:

- Lend executive talent to the financial institutions of the Eastern countries with the objective of training people in how banks operate in market economies.
- And at the same time finance the education of promising Eastern European bankers at Western business, economic and banking schools.

Consider that if the top 100 Atlantic Alliance banks were to finance the education of one Eastern banker each for one year at Western schools over a ten year period, a thousand market oriented bankers would be infused into the East over the same period.

9. Conclusions

By restructuring the Eastern European banks, infusing capital in the form of aid by a member supported Atlantic Plan directed at regional recovery and by providing technical expertise and education on market economies, these are most likely the preconditions which will attract foreign capital from both the private banking and industrial sectors. The steps need to be taken now.

Jan Urban, an editorial writer for the Prague daily, *Lidove Noviny*, sums up the urgency of our challenge succinctly:

> Democracy in Eastern Europe can lose unless it can prove economically and politically more profitable than dictatorship.
>
> Central and Eastern Europe have arrived at an extremely difficult and risky moment – a period when much depends upon the political wisdom of Western democratic countries.
>
> Central and Eastern Europe poses nearly all the basic conditions for economic growth and prosperity: raw materials, short distances for transportation, energy, arable land and a relatively skilled and educated pool of manpower.
>
> What it needs is capital for revitalization, general technical know-how and a comprehensive blueprint.

CHAPTER SEVENTEEN

Dresdner Bank's strategy in the former German Democratic Republic

Hartmut Amberger

1. Introduction

Of all strategic business areas in recent years, Dresdner Bank's strategy in the former GDR was undoubtedly the most ambitious, the most complicated and the most speedily realised task to which the bank has addressed itself. But at the same time it was the least typical – and for that very reason the most fascinating. This is because, in the case of the GDR, history was written more quickly than any of us could imagine. The swiftness of the first peaceful revolution in Germany took even optimists by surprise. Nobody was prepared. While strategies normally anticipate future developments, all that remained here was to react. The strategic assignment was to conceive a swift response to the completely altered situation.

I will briefly recall the major events spanning almost exactly one year. On 7 October 1989, national celebrations still took place on a grand scale to commemorate the 40th anniversary of the GDR under Erich Honnecker; 9 November 1989, the Berlin Wall fell; on 1 April 1990, the decision was taken to introduce a new banking system; 1 July 1990 the DM was introduced into the former GDR and Western banks were allowed to engage in active business; 3 October 1990, formal reunification.

A year and a half later, we are represented in East Germany by 128 offices online, roughly 4700 employees, approximately 570,000 new customers and 950,000 new accounts. Each day we solicit some 2000 new clients.

How did we, as Dresdner Bank, proceed? For the sake of clarity I would like to break down our strategic deliberations into various working steps. Basically, these stages reflect the order in which we went ahead, although in some cases they did run parallel to each other and interdependently.

2. A sequential strategy

In the *first phase* we had to take the *basic strategic decision* whether the former GDR was of any interest at all to us as a banking market. If so, whether we should operate in selective business areas or across the board and whether we should move slowly or quickly. At this early stage (around December 1989) it was still totally uncertain how, what was then still the GDR, would develop in political, economic and social terms. Would the GDR remain an independent country? Would Western banks be permitted to operate there and if so, on what legal basis? To what extent did our competitors intend committing themselves there? Would two different currency areas – DM West and Mark East – remain? In view of this uncertainty and the absence of practically any information of relevance to a decision, finding the right answer required almost visionary capabilities.

Our bank's decision to commit itself fully and swiftly, even without precise information on the market, was based on four precepts:

1. A bank operating on a major European scale cannot pass up the opportunities offered by a completely new market of 16 million people.
2. East Germany, with its close relations to, and experience of, all East European countries, could assume a key strategic role in East–West trade in the course of time.
3. Economic development in the GDR itself was assessed very positively at medium and long range – although admittedly at this stage with a fair share of optimism.

Besides these three objective reasons, a fourth subjective and almost emotional aspect played a significant role.

This was our bank's own history and name. In 1872 Dresden had been our birth place and the seat of our head office. Before the Second World War our activities had concentrated on East Germany. In view of the dramatic events there, we felt a moral obligation to offer the people support and solidarity in their striving towards freedom and an economic system governed by free market principles and worth living in. We wanted to give them hope and help them cope with their enormous economic problems.

On 2 January 1990, we became the first Western bank to make its debut in East Germany, by opening an office in Dresden. Today we know that this swift penetration strategy was absolutely right. We received much valuable information on the state of the economy, and the way in which people there think, and made initial contacts with companies, authorities and associations. For the staff of this first office twelve-hour working days were not long enough. People were prepared to wait for hours in order to obtain information on bank and non-bank-related matters. There were many questions which we could not yet answer. Too much still remained to be settled, political decisions had not yet been taken and uniform legal regulations were not in sight.

In the *second phase*, the timely, *systematic market preparation* shortly after the collapse of the Wall was decisive for the success of our present offices and for the fact that we are by far the best known of all Western banks in the former GDR. We began preparing the ground at a time when there was still no question of conducting active banking business. Our objective was to familiarise ourselves with problems on the spot, to obtain more precise information on the people's attitudes and behaviour and to establish initial contacts with companies and strategically important persons in banking, trade and industry.

Examples of the information, counselling and training programmes were widespread telephone campaigns in West Germany on GDR-related subjects, announced in full page press advertisements; series of articles in East German newspapers on subjects referring to the free market system and banking; specific, direct mailings to companies; attendance at tradeshows in the GDR; individual visits by West German counsellors to combined works and state-owned companies in the GDR, aimed at establishing contacts; establishment of a business contact office for the computer-aided arrangement of partners and cooperation agreements and the initiation of business; round-table events in our Western offices at which representatives of both Germanies could come together; establishment of our own management consultant company, 'Ost-West-Consult', enabling us to offer firms advice on business management; setting up of special GDR desks in West German cities to answer and coordinate customer inquiries, requests for financing and the arrangement of cooperation; the provision of management seminars for executive staff in the East, special seminars for particular professions and general marketing seminars in collaboration with university professors from East and West (the term 'marketing' was as familiar to the East Germans as the term 'glasnost' five years ago in the West), together with the establishment of marketing clubs; information events for people starting up in business, which were attended by some 10,000 participants.

It was not until the *third phase* had been reached that the *systematic collation* of precise statistical, *structural demographic information* on the former GDR began. Virtually no information existed on market potentials and their structures, on exactly how the East German banking system was organised or on the various banking groups' products and target sectors, to say nothing of the structures of customer demand or the acceptance of Western banks and their products.

The *fourth phase* of our strategy was a *precise stocktaking*. This presented a sorry picture, pointing to the inadvisability of any active commitment in the GDR in the short term. The economic prowess of the ex-GDR corresponded approximately to that of the small state of Hesse; productivity was only about one-third of the West German figure; the infrastructure was completely outdated and inefficient (road and rail network, telecommunications, power supplies, etc.); environmental damage was catastrophic; residential property was in a desolate state; technical equipment in the enterprises, particularly in the field of electronic data processing, in no way satisfied modern requirements; in the corporate customer sector there were neither balance sheets in key with the market situation, presenting a current valuation of assets and liabilities, nor cost accounts or profit and loss statements of any practical use; know-how on marketing and customer orientation, sales strategies, advertising and sales promotion was non-existent.

But these depressing factors contrasted with positive expectations for the future which were, however, unquantifiable and hence impossible to assess precisely: the mentality, language and way of thinking are basically identical, even though forty years of socialist national economy have left surprisingly deep traces; the introduction of a common currency and with it the strength and stability of the DM would only be a matter of time; the high-powered West German money and capital market would guarantee adequate financing funds; the people are willing to work, technically capable and prepared to learn; the introduction of a free market economy should release forces similar to those in the reconstruction phase of the old Federal Republic after the Second World War; the willingness to invest and transfer know-how on the part of the Western world – in particular the Federal Republic – can be considered high; in the long term the role which East Germany could play as the 'gateway to Eastern Europe', both in terms of its experience and geographical location, will presumably be of strategic significance; the opportunities for development of the former GDR are considered higher than those of other Eastern bloc countries, thanks in no small measure to the economic strength of West Germany and its stable political environment.

The fifth phase: strategic alternatives for the establishment of a distribution structure. Fundamentally, we had the choice of three strategic alternatives. Either to establish a branch network of our own, try and participate in the reorganisation of the old banking system by purchasing or acquiring an interest in an existing bank, or both. Our acquisition plans centred on the Deutsche Kreditbank AG, which had succeeded the state-owned Staatsbank and controlled practically the entire corporate banking sector in the GDR. But to concentrate exclusively on this strategy would have been risky. The bank was encumbered with the image and staff of the old Socialist Unity Party. What would happen to this bank's portfolio of old corporate loans worth many billions, in view of the uncertainty as to whether a large part of its corporate customers would be able to survive? How complicated and long would the joint venture negotiations be, and what were their prospects of success?

In the face of this scenario, Dresdner Bank decided to adopt a dual strategy with the aim of completely covering the entire area of the GDR. That is to say, we opted for the more laborious but safer policy of building up our own branches with the parallel option of perhaps taking over parts of the Deutsche Kreditbank's branch network. In the meantime a joint venture has been realised with the Deutsche Kreditbank under the name 'Dresdner Bank Kreditbank AG'. We have taken over roughly one-third of the total branch network without assuming any of the bank's old commitments. We shall shortly be increasing our present 85 per cent stake to 100 per cent, followed by a merger with our bank. We are now represented by fifty-six branches of our own and seventy-two joint venture offices, that is to say 128 branches altogether. In the second development stage up to the end of 1991 we intend boosting our presence to over 150 branches.

Phase six: determining a target group strategy. In West Germany we are familiar with clearly defined target groups in our business with private and corporate customers. Our positioning here is towards high net worth individuals in the personal market and the middle corporate segment on the wholesale banking side. Such a specific target group policy is at present not possible in the former GDR. The socialist system has levelled incomes and financial circumstances for the most part. Private customers with exceptionally high incomes or assets are rare. The only professional grouping with marked preferences so far has been the comparatively small circle of self-employed, craftsmen and small businessmen.

Phase Seven: product strategy. Any product strategy must be closely guided by its relevant target groups and their structures of demand. But in East Germany it is precisely this aspect which is lacking in clarity and contour at present. As long as the corporate structure is still in such a state of upheaval and no notable income and asset distinctions exist in personal banking, the products cannot be appropriately geared to target groups.

In *retail banking business* within East Germany, common Western products such as the various types of deposit and investment account, time deposits or consumer and building loans were previously unheard of. We must bear in mind that the people in what used to be the GDR were only familiar with a standard savings account bearing statutory interest and that loans were 'allocated' only in very restricted cases to certain target groups and for set purposes. Accordingly the need for information and explanation is very great.

In the meantime, we have collected some market data on East Germany's future intentions and attitudes towards saving, consumption and investment, as well as to the complex living accommodation and residential construction.

Market surveys indicate reliable information on the following preferences:

- a financial reserve as a 'nest egg';
- demand for semi-luxuries and durable consumer goods; and
- desire to own property.

The attitude towards financial precaution in particular indicates a degree of 'economic sense' which many of us here in the West had not expected. A lot of people had anticipated a real orgy of consumption.

Medium- and long-term property financing will be of particular significance. An enormous amount of pent-up demand has accumulated here due to the poor state of building repair and the extremely low ownership ratio of 11 per cent.

As a rule, on the corporate side, too, demand concentrates on bare survival and not yet on highly sophisticated tailor-made products, such as financial engineering or intelligent cash-management systems. Since practically all the companies in the ex-GDR were government or public property, the entire industrial portfolio has been handed over to the newly established GDR Public Trust with instructions to sell the firms worldwide wherever possible, to revamp them or to wind them up where they offer no hope of survival.

Under these circumstances it is naturally extremely difficult for banks to grant loans at their own risk. With regard to lending possibilities we distinguish between various segments:

- 'Old companies' confronted with the situation just described.
- 'New businessmen', i.e., people setting up in business without the burden of old loans but with new ideas, marketable products, fresh employees and organisational structures. Here the banks can offer their assistance and financing in most cases.
- The so-called '1972 firms' which were dispossessed by the East German government at that time and can now take their company over again.
- The relatively small but important group of businesses and craftsmen which were never nationalised, managed to survive under the old regime, were virtually unrivalled in their market niches and earned comparatively well.

I would now like to turn to some practical problems which we had to deal with *in phase eight* when *implanting the Dresdner Bank strategy*. Whether this operationalisation can actually still be defined as 'strategy' is a matter for debate. The borderline between strategy and improvisation is blurred here.

A few concrete examples will serve to illustrate the practical problems we had to cope with. The search for suitable office premises regularly proved fruitless. There were none which, after justifiable investment, would have satisfied the demands made of a modern bank branch. In consequence, most of the newly established Dresdner Bank offices were imported from the West in container form. Technical equipment of Western standard was neither installed nor available on the market, from EDP hardware and networks through cash terminals, cash dispensers and self-service machines to such simple things as modern sanitary facilities. The entire equipment had to be imported from West Germany. But some of the biggest problems arose through the catastrophic shortcomings in telephone network capacities. Hour-long waiting and booking periods were the rule. Despite energetic attempts to expand the telephone network rapidly, demand is increasing faster than the technical facilities. Communication was, and still is, a real bottleneck. This also applies to the long mailing times. Courier services via the East German highways – even though these are meanwhile congested with cars from the West – in most cases are still far quicker than postal delivery. Our entire logistics have thus become a first-rate strategic problem. Many things have been changed in the meantime by heavy investments in advanced communication systems. All our offices have now gone online. For this we also use satellite links. By the end of 1991 all the branches are to be equipped with cash dispensers and statement printers. Up to now approximately 3500 terminals have been installed, and we shall have another 1000 by the end of this year.

These are some of the intensive efforts which Dresdner Bank has made to develop a leading position on the East German banking marketplace. The market shares we have carved for ourselves in most business areas are considerably higher – where we are already in a position to measure them – than in the old Federal Republic.

Of course the starting up costs were high. Our commitment is quite clearly an investment in the future. A return on this investment cannot be achieved in the short term. If things go well we can expect to break even in around two to three years.

3. The broader view

Many people abroad are following reunification with goodwill and approval, but on the other hand they are concerned that Germany will turn its back more and more on the West. I do not subscribe to this opinion. On the contrary, what is taking place at present is the transplantation of our Western interpretation of democracy, a free market economy and modern technologies to the East. But it is true that the integration of East Germany – and to an increasing extent of all Eastern Europe – will require solutions to a large number of problems calling for complete commitment on the part of all countries in Western Europe to prevent the economic and social collapse of the East in their own interests too. In the medium term this will certainly tie up energies more intensively in the East which we have so far concentrated exclusively on the West. This is particularly true of a country like Germany, being located at the intersection of East and West. In the long term the integration of Eastern Europe into the Western community of values holds out great opportunities for us all, as the dismantling of borders and systems releases enormous economic potential.

Dr Röller, the Chairman of our Board of Managing Directors, made the following statement at the bank's last Annual General Meeting:

> The whole of Europe is on the agenda – for Dresdner Bank, too. Our business policy, as one of the leading European banks, is geared to the Single European Market and to Eastern Europe. We are already present in Prague and Warsaw and will be making our debut in Budapest shortly. We have maintained a representative office in Moscow since 1973. In other words, our strategic objective is the whole of Europe.

Entirely in this spirit, there can be absolutely no question of the Federal Republic reducing its efforts to create a united Europe. One thing only has changed, namely that there are now 16 million more Germans wishing to be integrated into this united Europe.

List of Contributors

Michel Aglietta is Professor at the University of Paris-X Nanterre and the *Centre d'Etudes Prospectives et d'Informations Internationales* (CEPII), Paris

Hartmut Amberger is Domestic Manager of Dresdner Bank, Frankfurt

Claude Belhomme, Claude Dupuy, Nada Matta and **Raoul Salomon** are at the Research Department of Caisse des Dépôts et Consignations, Paris

Angen Berges and **Francisco J. Valero** are Lecturers at the Universidad Autónoma de Madrid and members of *Analistas Financieros Internacionales*, Madrid

Richard Dale is Coopers-Deloitte Professor of International Banking and Financial Institutions at Southampton University

Jacques Girard is Head of Division in the Financial Research Department of the European Investment Bank

Christian Huveneers is Lecturer in Economics at the University of Louvain-la-Neuve, Belgium

Sydney J. Key is an economist with the Board of Governors of the Federal Reserve System, Washington

James T. Larkin is Vice-Chairman of American Express Europe

Giovanni Majnoni, Salvatore Rebecchini and **Carlo Santini** are at the Research Department of the Bank of Italy

Jørgen Mortensen is Senior Research Fellow at the Centre for European Policy Studies (CEPS), Brussels

Ugur Muldur is Administrator at the Commission of the European Communities. He was formerly employed in the research department of *Caisse des Dépôts et Consignations*, Paris

Geoffrey Nicholson is a Vice-President and Director of the Boston Consulting Group, specialising in insurance and banking

Jack Revell is a Consultant Director of the Institute of European Finance at the University of Bangor, Wales

Tad M. Rybczynski is a Visiting Professor at the City University, London

Hal S. Scott is the Nomura Professor of International Financial Systems at Harvard Law School

Alfred Steinherr is Director of the Financial Research Department at the European Investment Bank in Luxembourg

Patrick Van Cayseele is Lecturer in Economics at the University of Leuven, Belgium and Senior Research Fellow at the Maastricht Economic Research Institute on Innovation and Technology

José Viñals is at the Committee of Governors of the Central Banks of the EC. The paper was written when the author was at the Research Department of the *Banco de España.*

Index